With Pleasure

With Pleasure

*Thoughts
on the Nature
of Human Sexuality*

REVISED EDITION

Paul R. Abramson
Steven D. Pinkerton

OXFORD
UNIVERSITY PRESS
2002

OXFORD
UNIVERSITY PRESS

Oxford   New York
Auckland   Bangkok   Buenos Aires   Cape Town   Chennai
Dar es Salaam   Delhi   Hong Kong   Istanbul   Karachi   Kolkata
Kuala Lumpur   Madrid   Melbourne   Mexico City   Mumbai   Nairobi
São Paulo   Shanghai   Singapore   Taipei   Tokyo   Toronto

and an associated company in Berlin

Published by Oxford University Press, Inc.,
198 Madison Avenue, New York, New York 10016

Oxford is a registered trademark of Oxford University Press

Abramson, Paul R., 1949–
With pleasure : thoughts on the nature of human sexuality /
Paul R. Abramson and Steven D. Pinkerton.—Rev. ed.
p.   cm.
Includes bibliographical references and index.
ISBN 0-19-514609-3 (pbk.)
1. Sex.   2. Sexual excitement.   3. Pleasure.
I. Pinkerton, Steven D.   II. Title.
HQ23.A25   2001
306.7—dc21   2001021922

1   3   5   7   9   8   6   4   2

Printed in the United States of America
on acid-free paper

*To pleasures
everlasting and ephemeral
derived from my daughters,
Annaka and Sienna
(P.R.A.)*

*To my lovely wife, Heidi,
with dreams of Kauai
(S.D.P.)*

Preface to the
Revised Edition

You hold in your hands a revised edition of *With Pleasure: Thoughts on the Nature of Human Sexuality*. You may be wondering, "Why a revised edition? What could possibly need revision? Isn't sex the same as it was seven years ago, when the first edition of this book came out?" Yes and no. Now, as then, the most obvious fact about sex is that it feels good—*extraordinarily good*. *With Pleasure,* which was first published in 1995, explains *why* sex feels so good and examines the far-reaching implications of the pleasurability of sex in all its guises. In this book we argue that pleasure is the premier evolutionary motivator and, therefore, that the pursuit of sexual pleasure is as natural as a bear seeking honey. But sex is risky, for individuals (who might contract a sexually transmitted disease) and society alike, hence the repressive influence of religion on sexual expression, and the similarly repressive effect of the current AIDS epidemic.

What has changed since *With Pleasure* was first published? AIDS, for one, has exploded into a worldwide pandemic. Countries that had little previous experience with AIDS, like Russia, have witnessed exponential growth in the number of people infected with the human immunodeficiency virus (HIV), which causes AIDS. And countries like the United States have seen a transformation in the *meaning* of HIV infection—from an incurable and presumably fatal disease to a still incurable but medically manageable condition. Thus, in some regions of the world, HIV/AIDS is now more threatening than ever, whereas in others, it is less threatening than when *With Pleasure* first appeared. It seemed to us that these new developments in HIV/AIDS epidemiology merited a revision of our chapter on how the pursuit of pleasure confronts our fears about acquiring this noxious disease.

The Internet is another area in which rapid alterations of the sexual landscape have occurred. Since the initial publication of this book, the Internet has evolved into the more picturesque and popular World Wide Web. The web offers myriad sexual options and opportunities—from simple chat exchanges to streaming video and live sex shows. Advancements in web-based technologies, satellite video transmission, and pay-per-view promise to fundamentally change the way in which unisex (aka masturbation) is experienced. Consequently, these changes reinvigorate the long-standing debate over the evils of solitary sex and the threat that unisex poses to the traditional monogamous couple and family. What if sublime sexual release were available without any interpersonal commitments and entanglements? Would *you* go for it?

The Clinton-Lewinsky scandal also has called into question our ideas about what, exactly, constitutes sex. President Bill Clinton testified that he had not had "sexual relations with that woman" when, in fact, he had received oral sex from "that woman" numerous times. (Monica Lewinsky once described her position as "Special Assistant to the President for Blow Jobs.") In other words, according to the highest elected official in the land, fellatio is not a sexual act. Apparently, many people agree with him. When we asked undergraduates what they considered "sex," the majority said that receiving oral sex did not count, and neither did giving it (Bogart et al., 2000).

All of this raised a fundamental question about the malleability of our sexual perceptions and behaviors. Sex, obviously, can change. So can books. Although the basic facts and theories in this revised edition of *With Pleasure* are the same as the original, we have updated the HIV/AIDS chapter and the chapter that focuses on the future of sex. We hope that the reader will appreciate these updates and will embrace this volume *with pleasure*.

Los Angeles, California   Paul R. Abramson
Milwaukee, Wisconsin   Steven D. Pinkerton
January 2001

Acknowledgments

As Cicero noted in 54 B.C., "Gratitude is not only the greatest of virtues, but the parent of all the others." Lest we be accused of being without virtue (and to give praise where praise is due), we therefore wish to extend our thanks to the many people who provided guidance and inspiration in the long road from incipient theory to published book.

First and foremost we want to thank our friends and colleagues who sacrificed their scant leisure time to provide feedback and insightful comments on various drafts of the manuscript. The list of reviewers includes Joe Allen, Allan Brandt, Gil Herdt, Heino Meyer-Bahlburg, Angela Pattatucci, Paul Robinson, Jim Slater, Don Symons, and Don Tuzin. We also wish to thank our students from the UCLA "Last Stand" Personality Seminar (Jeff Blum, Monique Cloud, Mario Heilmann, Paul Okami, Alan Shafer, and Jeff Wachsmuth) for contributing their thoughts on an early draft.

Thanks are also due to Sydel Silverman and the Wenner-Gren Foundation for Anthropological Research for their support and funding of a landmark interdisciplinary conference (Theorizing Sexuality: Evolution, Culture and Development, March 19–27, 1993, Cascais, Portugal), which provided a forum in which to discuss and debate both nascent and established theories of human sexuality. The conference was organized by Paul Abramson and Gilbert Herdt. Participants included Robert Bailey, Richard Berk, Lawrence Cohen, Franz de Waal, Michel Feher, John Fout, David Greenberg, Thomas Gregor, Gert Hekma, Edward Kaplan, Igor Kon, Lenore Manderson, Heino Meyer-Bahlburg, Paul Okami, Angela Pattatucci, Mary Pavelka, Alice Schlegel, Donald Symons, Donald Tuzin, Carole Vance, Kim Wallen,

Jeffrey Weeks, and Jean Wilson. (The research presented at this conference is summarized in Abramson and Pinkerton, eds., *Sexual Nature/Sexual Culture*, University of Chicago Press, 1995.)

We also wish to extend our heartfelt thanks to our editors at Oxford University Press, Joan Bossert and Catharine Carlin, who believed in this project from the start and nurtured it to the finish. Thanks are also due to the entire Oxford staff (editing, marketing, promotion, and sales) for making the publication experience a delightful one.

Our acknowledgments would, of course, be sadly incomplete without our profound thanks to our spouses and families for tolerating the usual sorts of inconveniences a project such as this invariably entails and for providing needed encouragement and a willing ear.

Contents

With Pleasure

1.
Introduction

Oscar Wilde, the master of paradox, once intoned, "I adore the simple pleasures, they are the last refuge of the complex."[1] Unfortunately, *sexual* pleasure, as Wilde discovered, is seldom simple. In many ways, Wilde is emblematic of the vagaries of sexual politics, having been disgraced and jailed for his homosexuality. What started as a simple (but brazen) libel trial—initiated by Wilde against the Marquess of Queensbury for claiming that Wilde was "posing as a sodomite" and thereby adversely influencing his son, Lord Alfred Douglas—ultimately backfired against Wilde when evidence obtained from previous lovers irrefutably demonstrated that he was, in fact, a "sodomite."[2]

This is a book about sex, and about sexual pleasure in particular. In it we assert the obvious—that sex is pleasurable—and examine the myriad implications of this seemingly innocuous assertion for evolutionary, cultural, and psychological theories of human sexual expression.

Our point of takeoff is the duality of human sexuality. Sex is pleasurable, true, but it is also necessary for the survival of the human species. The long-standing tension between the procreative and the pleasurable aspects of sex has befuddled theoreticians ranging from Aristotle to Freud. The failure to adequately resolve this conflict has resulted in the conceptual muddle of the present day, in which sexual enjoyment is sometimes pathologized as an obsessive/compulsive disorder, rather than celebrated as an evolutionary adaptation extraordinaire.

The notion that sex is pleasurable appears, at first glance, almost too obvious to merit additional comment. However, the pleasurability of specific sexual acts is not always so obvious. One may question, for example, whether sadomasochism is pleasurable. The influential French philosopher Michel Foucault answered in the affirmative:

> The practice of S/M is a creation of pleasure . . . and that's why S/M is really a subculture. It's a process of invention. S/M is the *use* of a strategic relationship as a source of pleasure (physical pleasure). . . . [This] possibility of using our bodies as a possible source of very numerous pleasures is something that is very important.[3]

One may similarly question the pleasurability of anal intercourse. Although many gay men enjoy anal sex, not all do. Nor do all enjoy both roles, insertive and receptive, equally. Nevertheless, anal sex can be pleasurable for both parties. It is therefore strange that female pleasure in anal intercourse is so often overlooked. In heterosexual activities it is presumed that anal sex is instigated and enjoyed solely by the male (insertive) partner, never the female (receptive) partner. Yet, there is clearly no anatomical basis for this gender disparity—an anus is an anus. As Eve Sedgwick observes, "although there is no reason to suppose that women experience, in some imaginary quantitative sense, 'less' anal eroticism than men do . . . [no] one even pretends to name or describe (never mind value) the anus as a site of *women's* active desire."[4] Lesbians, we hasten to add, also practice various forms of anal eroticism.

In general, however, the inherent pleasures of sex are widely appreciated. This being the case, why is pleasure so often overlooked in theoretical discussions of human sexual behavior? And why do cultural, historical, and religious treatises so often fail to emphasize this readily apparent characteristic of human sexuality? These are among the many topics to be examined in this book.

Reproduction and Pleasure

From the pristine vantage point of religious, political, and evolutionary doctrine, it is sometimes argued that the sole function of human sexuality is reproduction. As a consequence, nonreproductive expressions of sexuality are deemed illicit, immoral, or illogical. However, we believe the primacy of reproduction to be vastly overemphasized, and the insistence on procreation as the end-all of human sexuality to be inherently misguided. Although, according to some, dogs, pigs, and sheep copulate exclusively to reproduce, this clearly is *not* the case for more advanced species such as the higher primates, especially humans.

Indeed, we shall argue that, at least in humans, sexuality has undergone a functional bifurcation, so that human sexuality now serves pleasure no less than procreation. As we shall show, this duality of purpose is evident physiologically, psychologically, and culturally. In other words, contrary to beliefs fostered by the prevailing Western/Judeo-Christian tradition, people were *meant* to enjoy sex!

Of course, according to the theory of evolution via natural selection, the *ultimate* function of sex is genetic reproduction; in other words, the purpose of sex is to propagate parental genes, and thereby to reproduce the species. The evolutionary function of *sexual pleasure,* in contrast, is to motivate people to engage in precisely those conjugal activities (i.e., penile-vaginal intercourse) likely to result in conception. In the language of *evolutionary psychology,*[5] sexual pleasure is an *adaptation* that solves the problem of sexual motivation in humans and the higher primates. (An adaptation as an evolved solution to a problem that is relevant to either survival or reproduction.[6])

Pleasure is thus the motive force behind procreation. But the impetus it provides is not specific to reproductive sex—the sexual drive can be satisfied by any of a number of diverse, nonreproductive behaviors. This loophole in the evolutionary scheme permits sexual pleasure to be co-opted to other purposes, such as the facilitation of bonding and the reduction of personal and interpersonal tensions. With regard to the evolution of human sexuality, it therefore appears that pleasure is no less central than procreation. Sex isn't just for reproduction anymore—it's also for pleasure. The intense pleasure that accompanies sex may serve to motivate copulation and thereby facilitate reproduction, but this is no longer its sole function. Instead, human sexuality has bifurcated: reproduction taking one route; unadulterated pleasure another. In other words, humans experience pleasure for pleasure's sake, not necessarily for reproduction's sake.

Of course, it's exceedingly difficult to disentangle the pleasurable aspects of human sexuality from the reproductive. The two conceptions are inextricably linked in the human psyche, via the simultaneous identifications of sex with reproduction (S = R), and sex with pleasure (S = P); a simple contraction then yields the false identification of pleasure with reproduction (P = R). The persuasiveness of this logic is beautifully exemplified by the medieval European belief that the only fecund sexual encounters are those that yield mutual enjoyment to the partners

*Throughout, an asterisk preceding a note number indicates a substantive note.

involved. Thus, it was believed that female as well as male orgasm was required to ensure conception, for without orgasm, "the fair sex [would] neither desire nuptial embraces nor have pleasure in them, nor conceive by them."[7] As recently as the turn of the century, the *Reference Handbook of Medical Sciences* advised that "conception is probably more likely to occur when full venereal excitement is experienced."[8] Nevertheless, there is in fact no *necessary* link between the pleasurability of sex and its reproductive function. The imperative to copulate could just as well be driven by hormones, for example.

Perhaps the following thought experiment will help to clarify this point: Imagine a man with Herculean control over his reproductive system, who, when sexually aroused, can *decide* to have an orgasm without ejaculating, ejaculate without orgasm, or ejaculate with orgasm. Such a man would have no need of contraceptive devices because he could freely enjoy heterosexual intercourse without the possibility of impregnating a female partner. If, on the other hand, he and his partner desired offspring, their attempts to conceive could be conducted—on his part at least—with businesslike aplomb, unencumbered by the threat of the loss of self-control that often accompanies orgasm. For this man, then, the reproductive and pleasurable aspects of sex would be entirely distinct (provided that we focus exclusively on orgasmic pleasure and neglect the precedent pleasure that accompanies the sexual act itself).

Though fictional, perhaps this example is not too far-fetched. To most people, male orgasm and ejaculation are nearly synonymous, in that orgasm is viewed as the psychological concomitant of the physical act of expelling sperm.[9] The prevalence of this view notwithstanding, male orgasm and ejaculation are in fact separate phenomena.[10] For instance, some men ejaculate without orgasm, as a result of damage to the central nervous system. On the other hand, experiments in which the brain has been artificially stimulated demonstrate that men can experience orgasmic pleasures without ejaculation. Young, still infertile boys are also capable of orgasm, as are postmenopausal women. Physiologically then, reproductive sex need not be pleasurable, and, as is well-known, pleasurable sex need not be reproductive.

Furthermore, reproductive sex—that is, penile-vaginal intercourse between fertile individuals—constitutes but a miniscule fraction of the range of human sexual expression. Alternative sexual practices, such as masturbation, oral and anal sex, petting, and so on, are widespread. Even penile-vaginal intercourse is practiced far more often than necessary to ensure the continuation of the species. Therefore, while procreation is indisputably the ultimate function of sex, this reproductive aspect alone cannot account for the variety of meanings and practices encompassed by human sexuality. Such an understanding requires consideration of the ancillary concept of *sexual pleasure*. The notion of pleasure provides a unifying framework in which to consider the various meanings and subsidiary functions of human sexuality.

Not only are nonreproductive sexual behaviors common, the motivation for most sexual encounters is also nonreproductive. Although the pursuit of pleasure is undoubtedly the most prevalent rationale for engaging is sex, it is by no means the only function, or meaning, of sex. Sex satisfies many needs beside procreation and pleasure. Sex may be used, for example, to express feelings of intimacy and love for a partner, as a means of reducing intra- or interpersonal tensions ("the best part of fighting is making up"), or to strengthen an existing emotional bond. These functions are largely *by-products* of the pleasurability of sex, in that their successful expression depends on sex being enjoyable. Sex fosters intimacy, for example, by providing a means for the giving and sharing of pleasure. In this way, sexual pleasure forms the basis for the myriad meanings of human sexuality prevalent in contemporary Western society.

The rise and legitimization in Western societies of the pursuit of sexual pleasure can be traced to the sexual revolution that marked the decline of Victorianism at the turn of the twentieth century. In Victorian America, many medical and moral authorities advised that sexual intercourse be limited solely to the purpose of procreation, even in marriage.[11] Pleasure, when mentioned at all, was linked to lustful, bestial, and uncivilized behavior. More commonly, it was simply not discussed: "For most nineteenth-century Americans, to speak of sex was to speak of procreation."[12] By the end of the century, however, a sea change was evident in popular attitudes regarding sex, as more Americans came to view intercourse as an undeniable source of visceral pleasure rather than as merely an instrument of reproduction. In the words of historian Estelle Freedman:

> Over the course of the nineteenth century, as white American women bore fewer and fewer children, the reproductive function of sexuality became less central. Although some middle class Victorians may have heeded advice to limit sexual intercourse, others experienced sexuality as a nonprocreative act. The evidence of contraceptive use, abortion, and homosexuality, of a tension over eroticism within American sexual ideology, and of the political defense of a sexuality limited to reproduction all suggest that Americans struggled to come to terms with the potential of an erotic, nonprocreative sexuality.[13]

Furthermore, as we argue later, the expansion of pleasure over procreation as the dominant meaning of human sexuality in the twentieth century is adaptive for the species as a whole.*[14] A focus on pleasure rather than reproduction encourages alternative forms of sexual expression, both in the practices selected (e.g., oral sex and mutual masturbation), and in the choice of partners, either of the same or the opposite sex. Nonprocreative encounters permit sexual desires to be satisfied without the risk of increasing the population of our already overburdened planet. Some of these activities are also associated with beneficial health outcomes, such as decreased transmission of sexually transmitted diseases, including the human immunodeficiency virus that causes AIDS.

The ideas outlined here will be expanded upon in the chapters that follow. At this point, however, it might be instructive to consider in greater detail just what we mean by "sexual pleasure."

Sexual Pleasure—What a Concept!

What is *sexual pleasure*? Unfortunately, the concept denoted here by "sexual pleasure" is a rather slippery creature, weighted down by considerable pop psychological baggage, and subject to cross-cultural and cross-historical variation. Nevertheless, it is desirable to have some definition of this concept, however inexact, to provide an anchor for subsequent discussions. With this in mind, we offer the following very simple (and regrettably vague) definition: Sexual pleasure consists of those positively valued feelings induced by sexual stimuli. Notice that this conceptualization encompasses a broad range of sexual pleasures, from the soothing sensations of sensual massage, to the explosion of feeling that accompanies orgasm.

Although the positive sensations we are calling sexual pleasure can be evoked, to some extent, by erotic thoughts, fantasies, and direct neural stimulation, we assume here for the sake of simplicity that stimulation of the genitals, breasts, or other relevant body parts (i.e., the erogenous zones) is necessary to initiate these feelings. According to this simplified model, the experience of sexual pleasure begins when the skin receptors in one or more erogenous zones are stimulated, and ends with a positive evaluation within the brain that the sensations experienced are indeed both pleasurable *and* sexual in nature.

The interpretive function of the brain in the experience of sexual pleasure cannot be overemphasized. The sensory signals arriving at the brain following stimulation of an erogenous zone are not inherently pleasurable, or even inherently sexual. Instead, interpretation of these signals by the brain is required for the impinging sensations to be recognized as sexually pleasurable. It is this interpretive stage that admits the profound influences of culture and context in the experience of sexual pleasure. With regard to context, it is often claimed that sex isn't really sex for a prostitute plying her trade; sex with a lover, however, is an entirely different matter. A rather extreme example of the pervasive influence of culture is provided by the Manus, a pre-World War II society in Papua New Guinea. Among the sex-negative Manus:

> Intercourse between husband and wife was considered to be sinful or degrading, and was undertaken only in strict secrecy. Women considered coitus to be an abomination which they had to endure, even painfully, until they produced a child.[15]

Unfortunately, the definition of sexual pleasure provided here neglects several of its more salient aspects, including the pleasure of giving pleasure. For example, in the butch/femme lesbian culture of the 1940s and 1950s, the butch partner often derived her greatest erotic satisfaction from pleasuring her femme counterpart, "if I could give her satisfaction to the highest, that's what gave me satisfaction"[16]; in such stereotyped role playing it was neither expected nor desired that the femme should reciprocate. This does not mean, however, that the butch's pleasure necessarily lacked a physical component. According to Elizabeth Lapovsky Kennedy and Madeline Davis:

> Many butches were and remain spontaneously orgasmic. Their excitement level peaks to orgasm when they make love orally or digitally to a woman. The nature of this orgasm is unclear. Some describe it as physical, while others think it is mental.[17]

The popular 1993 film, *The Crying Game*,[18] can be used to illustrate one of the main aspects of our conception of sexual pleasure—namely, the interpretive role of the mind. Politics and mayhem notwithstanding, this Academy Award-winning film's plot follows the basic modern love story, up to a point. Thus, boy meets girl, boy falls in love with girl, boy and girl decide to have sex. But then, in the pivotal sex scene, the boy discovers—much to his dismay—that the girl is really a guy, penis and all. The boy responds by vomiting uncontrollably.

Why? Wasn't the boy in love (or at least in lust)? And wasn't he also highly aroused sexually? So what triggered his disgust? Presumably, his reaction sprang from his brain rather than his heart. Despite his intense attraction and physiological arousal, this encounter was no longer interpreted as *heterosex,* but was instead *homosex.* Even with love and lust, the circumstances were no longer acceptable, and, therefore, no longer arousing to him.

As conceptualized here, sexual pleasure encompasses a loosely defined collection of physiological and psychological responses. Physiologically, it appears that the capacity for sexual pleasure is "hardwired" in the sense that it constitutes an innate and universal aspect of human sexual anatomy. However, like any intrinsic characteristic, sexual pleasure is moderated by and unfolds within a particular physical and cultural milieu. It is therefore subject to the cultural vagaries of permissibility and restriction that influence both the overt expression and subjective experience of sexual pleasure.

Even if the capacity for sexual pleasure is innate, and in some sense "basic" for the human species, one might argue that pleasure is secondary to procreation (or reproduction). This is certainly true for the "lower" species of mammals, which, if they experience pleasure at all, are nonetheless restricted sexually to the reproductively fertile estrus periods of the female. For these animals, sexual pleasure (if it exists) is clearly subservient to reproduction. With the primates, however, one begins to see a bifurcation in the functional meaning of sex. Although the reproductive cycle of many nonhuman primates remains at least partially bound to hormones, sexuality is no longer entirely restricted by the female cycle.

In humans the divergence of the reproductive and the nonreproductive is even more striking. Essentially free of the hormonal regulation of sexual desire, women can—and do—engage in sex at any time in their cycle, irrespective of fertility status. For men and women, pleasure is not dependent on fecundity. Sexual desire is evident in postmenopausal women and in prepubescent children of both sexes. Furthermore, human sexual anatomy is specialized for pleasure no less than procreation. The sole function of the clitoris, for example, is the generation of pleasure. Pleasure, not reproduction, also provides the most parsimonious explanation of the presence of numerous nonobvious erogenous zones, such as ears, toes, and the backs of kneecaps. Similarly, the wide variation in sexual practices observed across cultures, and even within cultures, is largely inexplicable within a reproductively oriented explanatory framework. Psychologically, pleasure drives the human desire for sex, and also provides the foundation for ancillary sexual functions, such as emotional bonding. In sum, the evidence suggests that the pleasurable and procreative aspects of human sexuality are conceptually, anatomically, and psychologically distinct.

Standing on the Shoulders of Giants

Naturally, we are not the first authors to examine the concept of pleasure. Philosophers ranging from Aristotle and Plato to Michel Foucault have also had much to say on this topic, as have psychologists including Havelock Ellis[19] and Sigmund Freud, anthropologists such as Margaret Mead,[20] Bronislaw Malinowski,[21] and Lionel Tiger,[22] and of course, the modern sexologists[23] Alfred Kinsey,[24] and William Masters and Virginia Johnson.[25] Hence, it seems appropriate at this point to briefly comment upon some previous conceptualizations of sexual pleasure.

Not surprisingly, interest in the concept of pleasure, both sexual and otherwise, has a long history. For Aristotle, and to a lesser extent Plato,[26] the central concern was whether pleasure was always good, always bad, or contingent upon the motives and restraint exercised by the actor. In the *Nicomachean Ethics,* Aristotle summarizes the various arguments for the position that pleasure is bad, including the notion that "pleasures are an obstacle to good sense: the greater the joy one feels (e.g., in sexual intercourse), the greater the obstacle; for no one is capable of rational insight while enjoying sexual relations."[27] Ultimately, however, Aristotle rejects this argument, noting that "it is the pursuit of excess, but not the pursuit of necessary pleasures, that makes a man bad."[28]

Sigmund Freud made elaborate use of the concept of pleasure, most notably in his famous *pleasure principle.*[29] The pleasure principle is the desire for immediate gratification and tension reduction. It is presumed to be the modus operandi of the id, which is defined in turn as the dynamic chaos of forces that strive for discharge above all else.[30] Tension is perceived as pain; discharge as pleasure. Eating, drinking, and sex each subdue a particular tension, in accordance with the pleasure principle.*[31]

More generally, in psychoanalytic theory (particularly as developed in Freud's *Three Contributions to the Theory of Sexuality*), "sexuality is divorced from its too close connection with the genitals and is regarded as a more comprehensive bodily function, having pleasure as its goal and only secondarily coming to serve the ends of reproduction."[32] However, Freud and his followers considered most nonreproductive sexuality to be "perverse": "We term sexual activity perverse when it has renounced the aim of reproduction and follows the pursuit of pleasure as an independent goal."[33] Similarly, Richard von Krafft-Ebing, who has been called "the most influential sexual psychologist of the last quarter of the nineteenth century,"[34] counted among the perversions "any expression of the sexual impulse which fails to correspond to the purposes of nature, i.e., of procreation."[35]

The famous (and occasionally inscrutable) French philosopher Michel Foucault also devotes considerable attention to the concept of pleasure.[36] Of particular relevance to this book is his exegesis of the multiple discourses of sexual pleasure and their frequent assimilation into a disproportionately moralistic framework. Regarding the sexual mores of the late-nineteenth century, Foucault asks:

> Was this transformation of sex into discourse not governed by the endeavor to expel from reality the forms of sexuality that were not amenable to the strict economy of reproduction: to say no to unproductive activities, to banish casual pleasures, to reduce or exclude practices whose object was not procreation?[37]

Even in the relatively permissive classical Greek culture, sex was unduly scrutinized by philosophers, doctors, and dream interpreters. And so it continues down to the present. Sex is dissected and debated throughout our culture, from the barroom to the Supreme Court. Indeed, it sometimes seems that there is more talk about sex than there is sex itself. As Edward Abbey observes in *Down the River with Henry Thoreau*:

> Modern men and women are obsessed with the sexual; it is the only realm of primordial adventure still left to most of us. Like apes in a zoo, we spend our energies on the one field of play remaining; human lives otherwise are pretty well caged in by the walls, bars, chains, and locked gates of our industrial culture.[38]

Is such a preoccupation with sex natural? Healthy? Or possibly disturbed and perverted? We believe that the emphasis—some would say, *over*emphasis—attached to everything sexual is an obvious consequence of the evolutionary significance of sex. People are obsessed with sex, quite simply, because it's in their genes. All other factors being equal, evolution favors those with a strong libido, provided that the pursuit of sex does not otherwise interfere with the struggle for survival. In nonhuman animals the libido is bound by hormones, whereas it is nearly synonymous with the desire for pleasure in humans. Evolutionarily then, a pronounced desire for sexual pleasure is adaptive rather than pathological, leading, as it should, to increased reproductive opportunities. Unbridled passions, however, are inimical to civilization, hence the institution of laws and regulations to control the overt expression of sexuality and, by misguided extension, the attempt to restrict the production and distribution of "obscene" materials thought capable of exciting sexual lusts. Although the pursuit of pleasure is natural, its regulation, to some degree, is nevertheless inevitable.

The Varieties of Sexual Experience

As a concept, sexual pleasure has numerous discernable connotations. It can denote enjoyment, gratification, sensual delight, satisfaction, and so on. It is also multiply determined, reflecting the interacting influences of nature and culture,[39] as well as the vagaries of the particular historical epoch in which it unfolds. Whatever the potential of sexual pleasure may be, it is ultimately interpreted and evaluated according to the prevailing social contexts and interpersonal themes of the times. This variety in sexual expression arises because the *experience* of sexual pleasure is infinitely malleable. When conceived of as sin, sex is experienced with distress and turmoil; when conceptualized as a joyous revelation, it is embraced with both subtle and expansive pleasure.

This emphasis on the plasticity of sexual pleasure challenges conventional notions of sexuality in several ways. For example, nonnormative behaviors are often deemed nonsexual because they are inconsistent with conceptions of "normal" sexuality. At various times, Western culture has vilified behaviors such as oral-genital and penile-anal contact as perversions of the "natural" sexual instinct. These "pathological" forms of behavior were not acknowledged as belonging to human sexuality because (according to this point of view) sexuality has but a single function—to perpetuate the species.

In other cultures, however, oral-genital sex is considered neither perverse nor unnatural, and in some cases is even recruited for important ritual functions. For example, the Sambia, a warrior culture that inhabits the isolated southeastern highlands of Papua New Guinea, believe that ingested semen is critical to strength and masculinization. Young boys are therefore expected to perform ritualized fellatio on older boys as an integral component of normal male psychosocial development.[40]

Sambia males pass through three distinct sexual stages. First they are fellators, seeking manhood through the semen of others. Then, after they have "accumulated" an adequate reserve of semen, they become fellatees. Later, in the final stage of development, all homosexual activity ceases and they are socially recognized as men, with wives, children, and all the accouterments of heterosexuality.

Ritualized homosexual activity is not unique to this group. More than fifty comparable cultures in Melanesia are known to have similar ritual complexes to ensure proper gender development.[41] But, at what point does ritual end and sexual enjoyment begin? Robert Stoller and Gilbert Herdt suggest that no clear demarcation exists for the Sambia:

> Social anthropologists might argue that Sambia homoerotism is only a facade, a performance with a precise set of rules, clearly defined as not truly erotic and openly recognized as an essential step to heterosexuality . . . but our Sambia friends would not recognize such a description of their experience. . . . *They do not just accept fellatio; they want it.* Almost all the boys indulge with fine erotic enthusiasm.[42]

The plasticity of sexual pleasure—and ultimately of sex itself—is also evident in the historical record. In ancient Greece the propriety of a sexual behavior was determined by the roles (i.e., dominant/submissive) assumed by participants and by the impact of the behavior, not by the participants' genders or the specific type of behavior.[43] Sexual proscriptions were oriented toward individual responsibilities (e.g., not being carried away by pleasure; striving for a state of tranquility; moderation in sexual appetite) instead of instituting universal codes of conduct.[44] Homosexual relationships between men and boys were thus tolerated, and even encouraged, provided that certain cultural norms were respected.

Various forms of prostitution, both male and female, were also prevalent in ancient Greece. Female prostitutes ranged from the lower class brothel "whores" (*pornoi*), with whom sex could be had for mere pennies, to the highly educated, talented courtesans known as *hetairai*.[45] The hetairai occupied a unique position in Greek society. Unlike other women of their time, the hetairai were permitted entree into men's society and the world of political affairs, and often served as advisors and confidantes.[46] Of intermediate status were the streetwalkers, who frequented the taverns and thoroughfares of Athens:

> In Attica there is a girl. Europa is her name.
> She has a warm clean lodging, she lives a life of shame.
> And anyone can know her, though his purse is far from full.
> Dear Zeus, why did you trouble to change into a bull?[47]

Female concubines and male slaves were also available for the pleasure of the Greek citizen, as were, to a much lesser extent, the charms of free women. The devaluation of virginity (for lovers rather than wives, of course) is evident in the following poem from the *Palatine Anthology*:

> You cherish your maidenhead
>   Why should you care?

When you go down to Hades
    No lovers are there.
Love's pleasures are kept for the
    living alone.
In Acheron we are but
    Ashes and bone.[48]

The sexual outlets available to male citizens were thus quite varied. Similar though less conspicuous opportunities also existed for Greek women. Male prostitutes could be procured for a price, and sexual adventures with male slaves were not unheard of. Women might also enjoy the embraces of other women, no less in the city-states of Athens and Sparta than on the infamous island of Lesbos. Indeed, "at Sparta love was held in such honor that even the most respectable women became infatuated with girls."[49] And, as always, self-satisfaction provided yet another option for both men and women (the Aegean port of Miletus was an ancient manufacturing and exporting center of the "dildo" trade[50]).

The overall picture of sexual life in ancient Greece is thus one of unfettered freedom (or licentiousness, according to one's tastes). As the late-nineteenth-century commentator Dr. William Sanger described the scene:

> Into the arts practiced by the graduates of the Corinthian academies it is hardly possible to enter, at least in a modern tongue. Even the Greeks were obliged to invent verbs to designate the monstrosities practiced by the Lesbian and Phoenician women. . . . One may form an idea of the shocking depravity of the reigning taste from the sneers which were lavished upon Phryne and Bacchis, who steadily adhered to natural pleasures.[*51]

Just Say No

The sexual moralizing and sexual restrictions adopted by the Christian world during the early Middle Ages stand in stark contrast to the Greek sexual ethic. Although ostensibly based on the gospels themselves, official Church doctrine was significantly influenced by the teachings of St. Augustine.[52] According to Augustian precepts, as a result of Adam and Eve's fall from grace, all manner of sexual activities were sinful, *including* penile-vaginal intercourse between a husband and his wife. Historian Vern Bullough summarizes St. Augustine's views as follows: "Though coitus must be regarded as a good since it came from

God, every concrete act of intercourse was evil, with the result that every child, literally, could be said to have been conceived in the sin of its parents."*53

Marital intercourse, though sinful, was justified provided that it was undertaken to increase the size of the Christian flock. But even then, *enjoying* the procreative act was viewed as a sin by many theologians—the Christian sexual ideal being one of pleasureless reproductive intercourse. Although some later theologians acknowledged that a modicum of pleasure could be enjoyed without shame as long as the couple did nothing to impede the natural function of procreation, it remained a sin to engage in intercourse solely for pleasure. As historian Jean-Louis Flandrin explains:

> There is a moment when the simple animal enjoyment, which is the pleasure of sex, drowns all other feelings; or so said the theologians. And many, including Pope Gregory the Great in the sixth century, believed that it was almost impossible to be pure after marital copulation. But what was certainly a mortal sin was to embrace one's spouse solely for pleasure.[54]

However, the nature of this sin—whether mortal or merely venial—underwent a transformation sometime around the end of the sixteenth century. Thus, when

> intercourse was undertaken for the satisfaction of concupiscence . . . it was thought to be a safeguard to marital faith which involved venial sin only. As a venial sin, the pleasure involved ranks with minor daily transgressions . . . and like other sins of its type, it was taken care of in the daily recitation of the Paternoster.[55]

The ideal of restraint in marital relations is further reflected in the belief of St. Jerome that it is scandalous for a husband to treat his wife the way he treats his mistress.[56]

The Canon Law is also very clear regarding the ultimate purpose of marriage: "The primary end of marriage is the procreation and education of children; its secondary end is mutual help and the allaying of concupiscence."[57] Thus, procreation secures the foundation for the institution of marriage itself, as well as providing the only licit justification for engaging in marital intercourse. Despite this ultimate emphasis on procreation, the Canon Law is not silent on the matter of pleasure. Indeed, the allaying of "concupiscence"—the lustful desire for pleasure—is cited as a secondary function of the marital sacrament. That is, marriage is provided, in part, so that men and women can exorcize their sexual lusts in a licit, morally sanctioned manner, via marital intercourse. Extramarital affairs were nevertheless common among medieval nobility.[*58]

The Catholic Church's prohibitions on prostitution, homosexuality, and masturbation are well-known, as perhaps is their scriptural basis:

> Know ye not that the unrighteous shall not inherit the kingdom of God? Be not deceived: neither fornicators, nor idolators, nor adulterers, nor effeminate, nor abusers of themselves with mankind.[59]

These prohibitions can be further understood in the context of a procreative bias. They may, in fact, be quite simply and concisely summarized by the admonition that "*all* nonprocreative sex is sinful."

Lessons from the Past

Given the enormous disparity in how sexual behaviors have been conceptualized and practiced, it seems reasonable to propose that such behavioral forms are neither inherently sexual nor normative, but that they are instead abstractions (or permutations) of what we call "human sexuality." This, of course, is not meant to minimize the critical significance of penile-vaginal intercourse for the survival of the species (or more precisely, for the furtherance of individual genes). Instead, it challenges the assumption that sexual behaviors must be functionally relevant to genetic replication—that is, that reproduction is the exclusive "natural" function of human sexuality.

Sex, evidentially, is what we make it. If there is a single common denominator underlying human sexual expression, it's pleasure, we would argue, not reproduction. In the modern era, in any case, sex is much more likely to be pleasurable than procreative. Nonprocreative sex is seemingly everywhere and everything. So much so that it is easier to define by negation: "nonprocreative sex" encompasses those sexual activities that cannot result in conception. Nonprocreative sex therefore runs the gamut from infantile and prepubescent sexual explorations to postmenopausal and infertile geriatric sex. Sex at the wrong time of the month, or with a partner rendered permanently infertile, is also nonprocreative, as is sex that employs effective methods of contraception, including condoms, diaphragms, and "the pill." Homosexual sex is clearly nonprocreative, but so are many of the activities in which heterosexuals engage, including masturbation, oral sex, anal intercourse, and yes, even passionate kissing. If it isn't penile-vaginal intercourse, sans contraceptives, between two fertile individuals at the right time of the month, then it isn't procreative sex. Clearly, then, very little sex is of the procreative variety. And given the current population explosion, perhaps this is a good thing.

Preview of Coming Attractions

This book is divided into six broadly themed chapters, plus an epilogue, in addition to this brief introduction.

Chapter 2 (Sex as Procreation: Is That All There Is?) draws from a wealth of sources, including evolutionary theory, ethology, primatology, and the cross-cultural and historical records to argue that, despite years of repression and counterprogramming, it is time to acknowledge the simple truth that sex and reproduction are conceptually distinct. Sexual pleasure, not reproduction, provides the foundation for "sex" as it is commonly experienced. Reproduction, in fact, can reasonably be viewed as a by-product of pleasure. In this chapter we also show how sexual pleasure evolved as a means to ensure that people procreate, and consider the implications of humanity's too great success in this area. We then examine from a philosophical perspective the seemingly inane question of why pleasure feels good, and the limits of how good sexual intercourse can feel.

Given the extreme power of sexual pleasure, it is not surprising that people have attempted to regulate it and harness it for profit. In Chapter 3 (The Regulation and Marketing of Sexual Pleasure) we examine the manner in which sexual pleasure has historically been restricted and marketed. This chapter explicates the commoditization of sexual pleasure—as distinct from the regulation and privatization of reproductive rights and kinship—and proposes a novel explanation for the genesis of the sexual marketplace. We also reconsider Freud's views on the necessity of sexual regulation as a means of ensuring social stability, and suggest how prostitution and pornography might have arisen from related social compromises. Adam Smith, Friedrich Engels, and the ancient Sumerian epic, *Gilgamesh,* are all discussed.

In Chapter 4 (The Biology of Sexual Pleasure) and Chapter 5 (The Psychology of Sexual Pleasure) we investigate the nature of the "beast" that is sexual pleasure. In the first of these related chapters, contemporary research on genetics, hormones, and the brain are examined in relation to the broader issues raised in Chapters 2 and 3. Among the topics discussed are the nature of orgasm, evolutionary theories of female orgasm and homosexuality, the evidence for "pleasure centers" in the brain, and putative genetic and hormonal influences on sexual orientation. The conceptual foundations of "homosexuality"—as a theoreti-

cal construct—are also considered in cross-cultural perspective to determine what, if any, implications they have with respect to the ongoing
search for a biological basis of sexual orientation.

Chapter 5 continues the discussion begun in the preceding chapter
by considering how personality, cultural, and familial factors interact to
determine a person's sexual beliefs and practices. Differences between
individuals, genders, and cultures are examined in light of the physiological influences identified in Chapter 4. For example, given that the basic
sexual anatomy is similar across cultures, how can female orgasm be
viewed as a birthright in one culture and be completely unknown in
another? Cultural relativity is also evident in how gender is conceptualized, as demonstrated by cultures in which a "third gender," neither
male nor female, is socially recognized. The psychological bases for the
myriad influences of culture on sexuality are discussed in depth. The
discussion then turns to the phenomenology of memory, with particular
attention paid to people's surprising inability to remember even relatively recent sexual experiences. Fetishes and Freud round out this chapter, which concludes with a discussion of sexual addiction and the implications of this conceptualization for sexual behavior in the age of AIDS.

The AIDS epidemic is surveyed from the conceptual vantage point
of sexual pleasure in Chapter 6 (AIDS: The End of Pleasure?). We argue
that AIDS discourse has been medicalized and sterilized for mass consumption and that the importance of sexual pleasure has been lost in the
debate. Many people worldwide are willing, quite literally, to risk their
lives for sex. As we show, this risk-taking, though seemingly irrational,
can be justified within a cost/benefit framework that recognizes sexual
pleasure as a valued commodity. A model for quantifying risk is presented in Appendix B, and model-based recommendations for decreasing the spread of AIDS are proposed. These models subtly reemphasize
the central premise of this chapter: that the power of pleasure as a
motivator for sexual risk-taking must be acknowledged, and must in-
form the interventions that we, as a society, undertake to combat the
spread of AIDS.

In Chapter 7 (Porn: Tempest on a Soapbox) we examine the legal
and historical foundations of the concept of obscenity, and the extent to
which these foundations rely upon the identification of sexuality with
reproduction. The chapter begins with an examination of the extensive
links between the "anti–vice" crusades of the eighteenth and nineteenth
centuries and then contemporary fears of masturbation and contraception. As we explain, similar fears of homosexuality have also found
shelter under the antiobscenity banner. More recently, a small group of

radical feminists has allied itself with demagogues from the far right in the fight against pornography. Their arguments, and a brief rebuttal, are provided. We then suggest that the assumption that all depictions of nonreproductive sexuality are either pornographic or obscene conflicts with the intent of the First Amendment by discouraging open discourse, particularly in the form of challenges to conventional views of morality.

Finally, in a brief epilogue we consider, somewhat whimsically, the future of sex. Will sex be necessary for reproduction in the "brave new world?" And will it continue to be interpersonal, or will "virtual sex" replace the face-to-face encounters people currently cherish? If science fiction and the current proliferation of high-powered, CD-ROM–based computer systems and sexually themed software are any indication, sex could become an increasingly solitary activity in the future. But is virtual reality the ultimate form of safe sex, or the last refuge of the socially inept? Only time, and the epilogue, will tell.

2.
Sex as Procreation: Is That All There Is?

The ancient Romans liked the idea of nature. In fact, they liked it so much that they codified it as a principle, known as *natural law*. This principle distinguished the laws enacted by mere humans from the laws inherent in glorious nature. And just what did natural law encompass? The third century A.D. jurist, Ulpian, explained:

> Natural law is what nature has taught all animals. This law is not unique to the human race but common to all animals born on land or sea and to birds as well. From it comes the union of male and female which we call marriage, as well as the procreation of children and their proper education [*educatio*]. We see in fact that all other animals, even wild beasts, are regulated by an understanding of this law.[1]

The notion that nonprocreative sex was "unnatural" or a "crime against nature" was quickly co-opted by the still coalescing Christian Church,[2] and by the middle of the thirteenth century was explicitly incorporated into orthodox Christian doctrine. Thus, Saint Thomas Aquinas argued that nature designed semen and ejaculation to create children and thereby perpetuate the species. To expend semen for any purpose other than reproduction was "contrary to nature"[3] and was therefore sinful. Saint Thomas identified four activities as particularly abhorrent: masturbation, bestiality, homosexual copulation, and heterosexual coitus in other than the Church-mandated "missionary" position.[4]

Though it now sounds quite archaic, one of the most heinous sins of all (even within the sacred bounds of the marital union) was engaging in sex for the sake of pleasure. According to the Church, intercourse was to be performed with as little emotion as possible.[*5] However, since it was recognized that some enjoyment of the physical accompaniments of the "sexual act" was unavoidable, St. Paul counselled abstinence for followers wishing to remain pure. And for those unable to control their animal lusts, there was always marriage:

> It is good for a man not to touch a woman. Nevertheless, to avoid fornication, let every man have his own wife, and let every woman have her own husband. . . . I say therefore to the unmarried and widows, It is good for them if they abide even as I. But if they cannot contain, let them marry: for it is better to marry than to burn.[6]

It was not until the late sixteenth century that the Church legitimized sexual pleasure for husbands and wives—provided, of course, that procreation remained the aim of the sexual union, and that no contraceptive methods were employed.[7] Nonprocreative sex, however, remained taboo.

Roman and Christian writers were not the only ones to advocate a primarily procreative role for sexuality.[*8] Plato's *Laws,* for example, suggested that sex should be limited to spouses, and engaged in solely for the purpose of reproduction. Plato also distinguished the pleasures of same-sex intercourse from those of procreative sex between a man and a woman, the former of which he considered "unnatural."[*9]

On the other hand, despite lofty proclamations extolling the "naturalness" of procreative sex, there is ample evidence of the prevalence of nonprocreative sex in the ancient world.[10] The practice of depicting the pleasures of sex—either explicitly (in word) or implicitly (in artistic form)—is nearly as old as the written and pictorial record. *Gilgamesh* and other stories from the ancient world proclaim and extol the ecstasy of nonprocreative sex. In Western culture this form of erotic expression reached its zenith in the classical Greek aesthetic. In addition to the musings of Plato and Aristotle, a wide variety of Greek authors and artists addressed themselves to the theme of sexual pleasure. Included in the gamut of Greek texts and art-forms are gynecological treatises,[11] vase paintings and poetry,[12] plates, sculpture, mosaics,[13] and drama (e.g., Aristophanes' *Lysistrata*).

Sexual themes are also represented in abundance in the poetry and art of ancient Rome. The Latin epigrammatic poet Martial, for instance, catalogs a variety of heterosexual pleasures thusly:

> *Last night the soft charms of an exquisite whore*
> *Fulfilled every whim of my mind,*

Till, with fucking grown weary, I begged something more,
  One bliss that still lingered behind.
My prayer was accepted; the rose in the rear
  Was opened to me in a minute;
One rose still remained, which I asked of my dear,—
  'Twas her mouth and the tongue that lay in it .[14]

Yet, despite the tales told by ancient art and artifacts, and by contemporary (i.e., twentieth century) tomes heralding the widespread prevalence of nonprocreative sex (e.g., the Kinsey volumes), reproductive sex still reigns supreme in the public and private consciousness as the nonpareil, "natural" function of human sexuality. Evidence of its sovereignty is readily apparent in the continued legislation against "sodomy" in the United States and elsewhere, in the popular idealization of woman as mother, in the existence of restrictions on contractual marriage, in prevailing theological doctrines, and so on. Even today, procreation is still assumed to be the premier biological function—and the ideal expression—of human sexuality.

However, in this chapter we would like to suggest that, despite popular ideology and declarations to the contrary, procreation is neither the sole, nor even the principal, function of human sexuality. In support of this blasphemy we provide a different interpretation of the biological and social record—one that is shaped by such diverse influences as Latin poetry, ancient Greek art, and observations of nonhuman primates.

Thus, although the evolutionary function of sex is certainly the continuation of the human species (or at least the genes of particular individuals), procreation is hardly the only, or even the dominant, meaning of sexuality in contemporary Western society. This is not to deny that in some cases men and women have sex to conceive children. Rather, we wish to emphasize the obvious fact that reproduction is not the only—or even the most popular—reason for engaging in sex. In particular, we deny the implication, arising from the view of procreation as the only legitimate rationale for sex, that forms of sexual expression other than penile-vaginal intercourse are somehow immature, unnatural, or evolutionarily maladaptive.

Just How Natural Is Nonprocreative Sex?

We begin by considering data from the animal world: in particular, nonhuman primates. It is often presumed (quite erroneously) that humans are the only intelligent, social, or conscious inhabitants of this planet. Nonhuman animals are viewed as glorified robots, governed solely by biological urges and surges (i.e., genes, reflexes, and hormones). In contrast, the exalted human brain ponders, evaluates, and makes decisions before acting. But is there really any good reason to believe that humans are unique in their capacity to reason? Although we can never know *subjectively* what it's like to be a bat (i.e., we can never feel what it feels), we can nonetheless extrapolate from externally observable behaviors to its putative mental life.[15] This exercise is fraught with dangers, of course. Many researchers would even deny that the bat has any mental life to extrapolate to.

However, there is generally greater consensus where sexual behavior is concerned. Despite the anthropomorphizing of dog and cat owners (who, for example, may refuse to have their tomcat neutered for fear of derailing his feline sex life), the prevailing view among biologists is that most animals, governed by "nature" (essentially, hormones), have sex for the purpose of furthering their genes, without any conscious recognition of the significance of this natural urge or the pleasure that might accompany its satisfaction.*[16]

A closer examination of nonhuman sexuality, however, reveals far greater complexity than the simplistic "animal as automaton" view implies. Not all sex among animals has reproductive aims.[17] Nor is all such behavior clearly lacking in emotional significance for the participants. Indeed, the speciousness of this view was even recognized in early Christian documents.[18] As anyone who has spent any time around animals can attest, homosexual and other nonprocreative behaviors are readily apparent in the lower species. Primates are particularly notorious for their displays of nonreproductive sexuality (the title of Kurt Vonnegut's *Welcome to the Monkey House* is an oblique reference to such displays). Homosexual and masturbatory behaviors are commonly observed among male dolphins as well, as are beak-genital and flipper-genital contact between males and females.[19] In fact, virtually every eutherian (placental) mammalian species displays some form of nonreproductive sexuality.[20]

However, next to humans, the most sexually diverse member of the animal kingdom is probably the little known *bonobo,* or "pygmy chimp." At first glance the bonobo looks much like an ordinary chimpanzee (the "pygmy" label being largely a misnomer). Indeed, bonobos (*Pan paniscus*) are very closely related to the common chimpanzee (*Pan troglodytes*), their respective branches of the evolutionary tree having diverged "only" 3 million years ago.[21] (The bonobo and the chimpanzee are believed to be the closest extant relatives of *Homo sapiens,* with whom they shared a common ancestor a mere 10 million years ago.[22]) Bonobos may be distinguished from their chimpanzee cousins by their more graceful builds, paler lips, and their turn-of-the-century coiffures. As bonobo expert Franz de Waal observes: "[Bonobos have] long, fine, black hair so neatly parted in the middle that you would swear each individual spends an hour a day in front of the mirror."[23] Bonobos display a rich social life, in which they employ verbal, facial, and gestural forms of communication. They also appear to be somewhat less aggressive than common chimps.

The relevance of these primates to the current discussion is this: like their human relatives, bonobos enjoy a diverse sexual repertoire, including oral-genital sex, masturbation, intergenerational (adult-juvenile) sex, and so on. In the words of de Waal, "bonobos behave as if they read the *Kama Sutra*, performing every position and variation imaginable."[*4] One species-characteristic behavior that merits additional comment is the genital contact known as "G-G rubbing" observed between pairs of females.[*25] In G-G rubbing, female bonobos rub their vulvas together with approximately the same rhythm as that of a male thrusting during intercourse. (In the male analog of this isosexual behavior, "mutual penis rubbing," one male lies on his back while another thrusts against him.[26])

Sexuality serves a variety of purposes among bonobos, ranging from conflict avoidance and resolution, to providing empathy and support, in addition to the obvious function of procreation. Furthermore, unlike chimpanzees, gorillas, and other nonhuman primates, bonobos often mate face-to-face, "missionary style."[27]

In summary, if "natural" is defined as "present in or produced by nature," as it is in our dictionary,[28] then given humankind's primate heritage, nonprocreative sexuality cannot properly be considered unnatural.

Sex: It's Not Just for Procreation Anymore!

One might argue (and many have) that nonprocreative sex—including, but not limited to, masturbation, oral sex, and sex between persons of the same gender—is evolutionarily maladaptive because it does nothing to further the lineage of the individuals involved and, in many cases, "wastes" energy and precious resources such as sperm. Men, for example, have been admonished against "spilling their seed" by authorities ranging from the Christian Church to such vocal individuals as singer/reactionary/orange-juice-peddler Anita Bryant. (In ancient Persia, a punishment of 800 lashes awaited any man who "involuntarily" emitted his seed.[29])

Incidentally, the widely cited biblical reference to the spilling of seed

(Genesis 38:9) does not refer to masturbation, but instead to the practice of *coitus interruptus*. The verse in question reads:

> And Onan knew that the seed should not be his; and it came to pass, when he went unto his brother's wife, that he spilled it on the ground, lest that he should give seed to his brother.

In this verse, Onan breaks the Hebrew law of the levirate by intentionally spilling his seed rather than impregnating the wife of his deceased brother.[30] However, the fact that this is but an unfortunate misreading of Genesis has done nothing to stop the onslaught of admonitions against masturbation, or "onanism" as it is sometimes called.*[31] Nor has it prevented the introduction of singularly bizarre remedies for preventing autoerotic stimulation (to be discussed further in Chapter 7). In 1870, for example, the prestigious British medical journal *The Lancet* advised "guarding the penis for a time against improper manipulation" by "keeping up slight soreness of the body of the organ . . . sufficient to render erection painful." Presumably, this was necessary to avoid the insanity inevitably produced by excessive "manipulation" of this popular body part.

Masturbation was also believed to diminish the sexual incentive for men (and women) to marry; the desire for marital sex presumably being lost "when by this means they appease their lustful appetites."[32] Moreover, the pleasure that accompanies the ejection of semen was itself considered an abomination:

> The intrinsic malice of pollution [meaning self-induced orgasm of any kind] consists most probably in the intense sexual enjoyment and satiation of pleasure, occurring outside the legitimate bond of matrimony, which the effusion of seed produces—and not only nor principally in the voluntary frustration of the seed itself. Reason requires its prohibition, for if this pleasure, which nature only permits to entice men into matrimony, were to be lawful outside of it, men would avoid the married state . . . and the natural and legitimate propagation of the species would be defeated. [However,] the effusion of semen would be legitimate for medical purposes if only it could be achieved without causing pleasure.[33]

One of the most persistent rationales for the condemnation of masturbation is a misguided belief in the omnipotence of sperm, for "sturdy manhood . . . loses its energy and bends under too frequent expenditure of this important secretion."[34] An especially novel means of conserving "this important secretion" was practiced by male members of the

Oneidan sect, a utopian community founded in New York in the middle of the nineteenth century. Oneidan men were taught that orgasm drained them of vital fluid, enervating the body and the spirit. They were therefore instructed to practice a peculiar form of male continence in which ejaculation, but not intercourse, was avoided.[35]

In Western cultures sperm-depletion anxieties can be traced back as far as Hippocrates and the fifth century B.C.[36] However, such beliefs are not restricted to the Western world. For example, men on the island of Yap in the South Pacific believe that too frequent ejaculation causes physical weakness and increases susceptibility to certain diseases.[37] Similarly, in the Taoist tradition of ancient China, the expenditure of semen was believed to entail a corresponding loss of masculine yang essence.[38] (We shall return to this topic in Chapter 7 when we consider masturbation and its relationship to pornography in greater detail.)

But is sperm really a resource in need of strict conservation? While the typical male expels billions of spermatozoa with each ejaculation, the reservoir is quickly refilled, with a return to full potency in about two days. Furthermore, men produce sperm continually throughout their postpubertal lifetimes, usually ceasing only in extreme old age (or at the time of death). It is therefore hard to see how the spilling of limited quantities of the male seed could threaten the survival of the human race. In contrast, the ovum is, in many ways, a limited, nonrenewable resource, the capacity for egg production being essentially fixed at birth. Few women, however, endeavor to ensure that no egg falls unfertilized; nor have the moral practitioners advanced this neglected cause.

Of course, if *all* of a man's sperm are "spent" in nonprocreative activities, then his genes will not be passed on—at least not directly—a situation that might be considered individually maladaptive in that it violates the evolutionary imperative to propagate one's genes. Exclusive homosexuality, and the lack of offspring it nominally implies (ignoring modern biomedical marvels such as artificial insemination), could be considered maladaptive in this restricted sense (however, see Chapter 4). Yet for the majority of people who engage in nonprocreative sex (and the majority of people *do* engage in nonprocreative sex), these activities in no way diminish the capacity to reproduce themselves and their genes should they desire to do so. Although the total number of sexual experiences in a person's lifetime is clearly bounded, it is also very large; furthermore, only a very small proportion of these experiences need result in pregnancy for the human race to reproduce itself.

Moreover, the fact that some sexual activities cannot lead to conception should not be held against them, so to speak. No woman has ever become pregnant from playing basketball, attending the opera, or dancing, yet seldom are these activities proscribed for that reason alone, at least in modern times. (Throughout its history the Christian Church has periodically attempted to ban *all* pleasurable activities, including dancing and attending the theater.[39] Perhaps in doing so the Church merely sought to err on the side of caution by eliminating all activities that could reasonably precede sex. Taken too literally, this often prompted some rather absurd prohibitions—on baths, wine, and so forth.)

Why, then, is nonprocreative sex held to a different standard than other "reproductively safe" activities, such as skiing, movie going, or swimming in public? We have already dismissed the argument that views nonreproductive sex as wasting a limited natural resource. Provided that pregnancy is a possible outcome of at least *some* sexual encounters (and even with modern contraceptive methods, many such opportunities continue to exist), procreation will occasionally occur. We have also argued, based on evidence garnered from observations of one of humankind's closest relatives on the evolutionary tree, that nonprocreative sex cannot properly be considered "unnatural" if "natural" is accorded its customary meaning (if a "dumb animal" like the bonobo can engage in oral-genital sex, how unnatural can it be?*[40]). Of course, according to Church teachings, people should be able to rise above such bestial instincts in pursuit of loftier spiritual ideals.

Perhaps nonprocreative sex is taboo because the behaviors themselves are "perversions" of the "natural" function of the sexual apparatus (which, of course, is implicitly construed as reproduction). This view was succinctly expressed by Dr. Lyttleton (a headmaster at Eton, a prestigious English boys school), who said: "All exercise of a bodily faculty for the sake of pleasure and except for the purpose for which the faculty was given is wrong."[41] Notice that the fault here lies not with the pleasure one feels, but with the reason one feels it. It is all right to enjoy coitus (sans contraceptives, of course), but only if one's purpose is to create another young lad to bolster Eton's rolls, or a lass to rule the Commonwealth. Similar application of this principle to other bodily functions would condemn kissing (which is a perversion of the natural gustatory function of the oral cavity) and simple caressing (since this pleasure is certainly a violation of the "proper" function of the touch receptors of the skin, whatever that function might be). The absurdity of this position should be clear. Furthermore, if as claimed here, the elicitation of pleasure is a main function of human sexuality, then the preceding argument is effectively disarmed. That is, perhaps pleasure is itself "[a] purpose for which the faculty was given."

If our views are correct, then it follows that nonprocreative sex should be conceptually divorced from issues of reproduction. This very thing may, in fact, be occurring on an evolutionary time scale. As one moves up the phylogenic ladder, beginning with the most primitive of unicellular animals, reproduction bifurcates into asexual and sexual forms. Indeed, Ina Jane Wundram suggests that the distinction between reproduction and sexuality can be traced back as far as the protozoa, which exhibit a "sexual-like behavior that is not followed by reproduction."[42]

Presumably, sexual reproduction is beneficial to the more advanced species because genetic mixing provides diversity, and therefore greater adaptability to changing environments, as well as a mechanism for avoiding harmful mutations.[43] In asexual schemes (e.g., cloning), if something goes wrong, and this error continues to get duplicated, reproductive havoc will prevail. Sex, that many splendored thing, prevents this unfortunate scenario by constantly creating new genetic types.

To take this model a step further, we suggest that sexual reproduction itself has bifurcated in the higher primates (such as bonobos and humans). In these species, sex and reproduction are no longer synonymous, but instead are differentiated in both form and function. "Reproduction" now consists of male-female vaginal intercourse between fertile individuals, at the right time of the month (ovulation), and without the interference of contraception. "Sex," on the other hand, encompasses everything else. Since sex is now divorced from reproduction, it is free to serve other beneficial functions among the higher primates, including facilitating bonding, enhancing group cohesion, promoting conflict resolution, and so on. In many ways, nonprocreative sex is now closer in meaning to hugging and kissing than to baby-making intercourse. Nevertheless, society insists on viewing all sexual activity through the foggy filter of reproduction and the "survival value" of these behaviors. Need this be so?

By way of contrast, consider, for example, eating. It, too, is crucial for the survival of the species, but the customs and food preferences of different cultures seldom address the "survival value" of eating. All preferred diets are ultimately imperfect, and instead reflect cultural tastes and available resources. Many Americans who eat a traditional high-fat, high-protein diet are horrified by the sparse diet of the Japanese, not to mention the witchety grub-loving cuisine of Australian Aborigines. Yet, whether cooked or raw, feral or cultivated, the actual choice (or preparation) of food has little relevance to survival; instead, it is the nutritional balance underlying those choices that matters. Similarly, the actual manner in which various people express their sexuality merely reflects current fashion or custom, and has little relevance to the survival of the species.

Furthermore, since human beings are extraordinarily fertile, and since the biggest problem facing us is over- not underpopulation, we have enormous freedom and flexibility, *as a species,* to express all kinds of behaviors that are functionally related to sexual pleasure, because even without an express intent to reproduce, people *will* be fruitful and multiply, if only by chance. This conclusion follows from several considerations, including the extreme pleasure people derive from sexual intercourse, the long duration of female fertility and male potency, and the not insignificant failure rates of even the best modern contraceptive devices. As long as large numbers of people continue to enjoy heterosexual intercourse—and we see no reason to suggest that this will cease to be the case any time soon—babies will continue to be born, and humanity's status as "lord and master over the dominions of Earth" will remain secure.

Finally, we would like to suggest that nonreproductive sex may actually be *advantageous* for the species as a whole. The argument, which follows, is based on the simple observation that *too much* reproductive sex is as great a threat to the survival of the species as is *too little.* At this juncture humankind can ill afford to continue increasing the population and depleting the natural resources of Earth. Because nonreproductive sex offers alternative avenues of sexual expression that, by definition, cannot increase the number of human inhabitants of this planet, such activities may help mitigate the threat of extinction from overpopulation.

Oral Sex as a Form of Birth Control

In 1798, the English economist and clergyman Thomas Malthus published (anonymously) his first version of "An Essay on the Principle of Population." Over the next twenty-eight years he completed four subsequent editions, and in 1830 he provided a synopsis of his thesis titled "A Summary View of the Principle of Population."[44]

Malthus' theory of population dynamics is quite simple. It presumes a discrepancy between the rate of population growth and the resources necessary for subsistence. According to Malthus, whereas population increases geometrically (e.g., 1, 2, 4, 8, 16, . . .), food and other relevant resources only increase arithmetically (e.g., 1, 2, 3, 4, 5, . . .), producing an ever-widening gap. Some mechanism is therefore necessary to keep population growth consonant with the resources essential for subsistence.

This essay has had an extraordinary impact upon the progression of science. From the time of its inception to the present, it has provoked continuous debate and scrutiny. Perhaps most important, Malthus' essay also proved instrumental to one of the most momentous theories in the history of science—natural selection. Charles Darwin recalls:

> One day something brought to my recollection Malthus' *Principle of Population*. . . . I thought of his clear exposition of "the positive checks" to increase . . . which keep down the population. . . . It then occurred to me that these causes or their equivalents are continually acting in the case of animals also; and, as animals usually breed much more rapidly than does mankind, the destructions every year from these causes must be enormous in order to keep down the numbers of each species, since they evidently do not increase regularly from year to year, as otherwise the world would long ago have become densely crowded with those that breed most quickly. . . . Why do some die and some live? And the answer was clearly, that on the whole the best fitted live. From the effects of disease the most healthy escaped; from enemies the strongest, the swiftest, or the most cunning; from famine, the best hunters or those with the best digestion; and so on. Then it flashed upon me that this self-acting process would necessarily improve the race, because in every generation the inferior would inevitably be killed off and the superior would remain—that is, the fittest would survive. Then at once I seemed to see the whole effect of this. . . . The more I thought over it the more I became convinced that I had at length found [as a consequence of reading Malthus] the long-sought-for law of nature that solved the problem of the origin of species."[45]

The fortuitous impact of Malthus' work on Darwin is all the more extraordinary when one realizes that it had the identical—though independent—impact upon the co-founder of the theory of natural selection, Alfred R. Wallace. Wallace also notes:

> The most interesting coincidence in the matter [i.e., the simultaneous discovery of natural selection], I think, is, that I, as well as Darwin, was led to the theory itself through Malthus—in my case it was his elaborate account of the action of "preventive checks" in keeping down the population of savage races to a tolerably fixed but scanty number. This had strongly impressed me, and it suddenly flashed upon me that all animals are necessarily thus kept

down—"the struggle for existence"—while variations, on which I was always thinking, must necessarily often be beneficial, and would then cause those varieties to increase while the injurious variations diminished.[46]

Although Malthus was by no means the first author to emphasize the exponential power of population growth, his essays codified the extraordinary implications of human fertility. These implications include the extent to which "misery" (e.g., war, pestilence, famine, etc.) functions to keep this power in check, as well as the very real possibility that the human population could exceed the resources required for subsistence. As the world becomes more and more overburdened with a rapidly expanding human population, it certainly seems reasonable to examine whether nonprocreative sex constitutes an essential (or "natural") extension of the Malthusian "preventative checks" on population growth.[*47]

The explosive nature of human population growth is strikingly illustrated in the following quotation by Paul and Anne Ehrlich. They observe that:

> Our own species, *Homo sapiens,* evolved a few hundred thousand years ago. Some 10,000 years ago, when agriculture was invented, probably no more than 5 million people inhabited Earth—fewer than now live in the San Francisco Bay Area. Even at the time of Christ, 2,000 years ago, the entire human population was roughly the size of the population of the United States today; by 1650 there were only 500 million people, and in 1850 only a little over a billion. Since there are now well past 5 billion people, the vast majority of the population explosion has taken place in less than *a tenth of one percent* of the history of *Homo sapiens.*[48]

The deleterious effects of the world's current population explosion are readily apparent: rapid deforestation and desertification, widespread famine, global warming, and so on. Moreover, the myriad adverse consequences of overpopulation are intricately intertwined. The increased utilization of scarce energy resources required by the growing population results in more and more pollution, which facilitates global warming. Global warming, in turn, creates crop failures, coastal flooding, desertification, water shortages, general stress on the ecosystem, and so on, all of which stimulate conditions favorable to the occurrence of widespread famine.[49]

One further implication of the ever-growing global population (which is expected to double by 2050[50]) is that people are engaging in all too much reproductive sex. That is, whether by design, accident, or some combination thereof, there is more than enough reproductive intercourse to ensure the continuation of the species. This should not be surprising. All that is required for humankind to reproduce itself is for each individual, on average, to raise to childbearing age one or more reproductively viable offspring. In other words, if only a handful of a man's billions of sperm successfully fertilize eggs, they will have more than fulfilled their collective purpose—to propagate their host's genes.[*51] Similarly, only one-half of one percent of each woman's eggs would need to be successfully fertilized to ensure the continued expansion of the human race (ignoring abortions, miscarriages, and other complications).[*52]

The inescapable conclusion arising from these considerations is that reproductive sex now actually *threatens* the survival of the human race via the destruction of the planet wrought by excessive overpopulation.[*53] Returning to Malthus' thesis, perhaps nonprocreative sex could (and does) act as a "check" on population levels by diverting sexual energies away from activities that would otherwise increase the number of human inhabitants of Earth. In this somewhat limited sense, oral sex (for example) can truly be considered a contraceptive activity.

These ideas are neither new, nor necessarily restricted to humans. Aristotle's *Politics,* for example, suggests that during severe food shortages in ancient Crete, men were encouraged to have "intercourse with males" to reduce the threat of further overpopulation.[*54] In a nonhuman analogy, the incidence of male-male sexual behavior in caged rats has been observed to increase with overcrowding, suggesting a possible substitution of the nonprocreative for the procreative.[*55]

Of course, if too much energy were diverted into nonreproductive sexual activities—so that procreative sex became a rarity—then alternate forms of sexual expression would cease to be advantageous for the human race. However, such a scenario seems extraordinarily unlikely given how extraordinarily pleasurable sexual intercourse[*56] and orgasm are (and as a consequence, how often they are repeated), how long the human female is typically fertile (approximately thirty-seven years), and the tremendous number of sperm each human male is capable of producing. Indeed, if the current exponential rate of population growth is any guide, humans are a bit *too* fertile.

Thus, in a nutshell, our argument is that nonprocreative sex is advantageous for the species as a whole, provided that it remains an adjunct to penile-vaginal sex and does not entirely supersede it. In a somewhat analogous vein, although Sigmund Freud considered nonreproductive sexual activities such as oral-genital and anal-genital stimulation to be "perversions" (a term arising, no doubt, from a view of nonprocreative sex as a perversion of the "natural instinct" to reproduce), he further held that such activities were pathological only if "instead of appearing *alongside* the normal sexual aim and object . . . it ousts them completely and takes their places in *all* circumstances."[57] The "perversions" thus become pathological only when practiced to the exclusion of "normal" sexual activities (i.e., heterosexual coitus). In much the same way, nonprocreative sex is advantageous to the species as a whole only so long as it remains a complement to—rather than a replacement for— reproductive sex.[*58]

An additional consideration bearing on the primacy of reproduction in human sexual relations is the percentage of human sexual behavior devoted exclusively to procreation. Naturally, this percentage varies by cultural group and historical period. Certainly, in a liberal atmosphere, with contemporary life spans and modern methods of contraception, procreation represents a small fraction of sexual expression—especially when viewed from earliest infantile masturbation to geriatric sexuality. It therefore seems rather odd that a behavior that is so limited in practice should be considered the sole natural function of human sexuality.

Although reproductive sexual intercourse is the instrument whereby the survival of the species is ensured, it constitutes but a small portion of modern human sexual experience. On the other hand, it seems readily apparent that the primary basis for human sexual expression and intimacy is sexual pleasure, whether the desire is ultimately expressed as hetero- or homosexual intercourse, mutual masturbation, or some other form of intimacy. Reproduction may therefore be viewed as a by-product of sexual pleasure, since pleasure provides the incentive for engaging in reproductive sex and its nonprocreative counterparts. Penile-vaginal intercourse is thus no more "natural" or "unnatural" than any other sexual activity.

While the ultimate (i.e., evolutionary) function of sex is clearly reproduction and the furtherance of the genes, the preceding arguments suggest that sexual pleasure is, in some sense, primary, in that it provides the incentive for sexual expression, and hence drives evolution. Pleasure is the motivator that gets people to "do it"—both reproductively and nonreproductively. Rather than being *the* function of sexual pleasure, perhaps the continuation of the species is instead merely a by-product of the pleasurability of sex.

It remains, however, to specify more precisely the manner in which sexual pleasure ensures reproduction, and to explain how this superlative mechanism came into being. To do so will first require a brief digression through evolutionary theory and its relation to sexual pleasure.

The Evolution of Sexual Pleasure, Part I

Current evolutionary thought suggests that any heritable trait that increases the reproductive success of those who possess it will tend to increase in proportion within the gene pool. It is easy to see how this would work. As an example, suppose that *extraversion,* considered as a character trait, is strongly associated with reproductive success. Therefore, extraverted people will have more children who grow to maturity and themselves reproduce than will less outgoing individuals. Furthermore, suppose that extraversion is heritable (i.e., that the children of extraverted people will tend likewise to be extraverts). An extraverted couple would then have extraverted kids, and lots of them, who in turn would produce numerous extraverted grandchildren, and so on. Provided that less extraverted people have fewer children, and that there is no difference in survival between introverts and extraverts, the proportion of extraverts in the population would steadily grow with each generation.

Clearly, then, nearly any trait that increases the frequency of reproductive sexual intercourse between a man and a woman will increase in prevalence, provided that it is heritable, because such a trait increases reproductive fitness (i.e., number of viable offspring) almost by definition. (Examples of pathological traits that simultaneously increase copulatory behavior *and* decrease reproductive fitness can, of course, be devised.[59])

One promising candidate for such a fitness-enhancing trait is the capacity for intense sexual enjoyment. It stands to reason that in our evolutionary past individuals who experienced greater pleasure in sex were more likely to seek it out, and were therefore likely to have more offspring than did people who did not enjoy sex as much. Then, provided that a differential capacity for sexual pleasure is heritable (which seems a reasonable assumption since this capacity is largely a function of human physiology), the proportion of the population that found sex *very* pleasurable would have steadily increased with each generation. The pleasurability of sex is thus an evolved adaptation that facilitates reproduction. In other words, sex is pleasurable so that people will have sex.

Even granting that sex should be better than a poke in the eye with a sharp stick, does this really explain why sex feels *so* good? That is, does it actually need to feel *that* good for people to repeat it? Wouldn't they continue to engage in sex if it only felt "pretty good"? Most people enjoy repeating behaviors, such as drinking an ice-cold beer, that feel "pretty good." Not great, like sex, but clearly pretty good (especially after a long, hot day working around the house). The question is, given a high fertility rate and a penchant for repeating "pretty good" behaviors, why isn't "pretty good" good enough?

The reason, we believe, is that there are many disincentives that work against reproductive sexual behaviors. For one thing, intercourse is a dangerous activity; not so much now, but in the evolutionary past—tens of millions of years ago—when the mechanism of sexual pleasure probably first evolved. These dangers ranged from the violence that might be necessary to procure and retain a mate,[*60] to the increased vulnerability to attack experienced during intercourse itself. Sexually transmitted diseases and various infections posed additional threats to those engaging in sexual intercourse. The danger was even greater for women, who faced the possibility of pregnancy and attendant complications, including maternal death, infertility, and miscarriages. All of these perils made intercourse a precarious proposition for our distant ancestors.

However, we need not invoke such horrendous possible consequences as maternal death during childbirth to understand the monumental power of sexual pleasure. Perhaps observing or experiencing menstruation or natural childbirth was a sufficient disincentive for the less pleasurably inclined. If the prevalence of menstrual taboos is any indication, men (and perhaps women, too) often have adverse reactions to normal genital functions.[61] In the Judeo-Christian tradition, for example, menstruation is viewed as a "curse"—God's punishment on all women for Eve's transgression in the Garden of Eden. In Victorian America, menstruation fears were manifested in the belief of physicians that menstruation made women weak, diseased, and dependent, and even caused temporary insanity in more emotional women.[62] The contaminating effects of menstrual blood are also feared by Sambia men in New Guinea.[63] Heterosexual intercourse is nevertheless highly valued: "While most [Sambia] men regard coitus with some trepidation, and the act itself is laden with shame . . . [they] generally regard it as intensely exciting and pleasurable (and no less so *because* it is dangerous)."[64]

Furthermore, despite the joys of conception and maternal bonding, childbirth is a painful and messy process that is not for the faint of heart. The experience of childbirth is, at least in theory, yet another disincentive to penile-vaginal sex. Again, what might offset this disincentive? The answer, of course, is an extraordinarily powerful drive for sexual pleasure. As Freud observed, "women who conceive without pleasure show later little willingness to endure frequent childbirths, accompanied as they are by pain."[65]

Pleasure also provided an incentive for our ancestors to seek sexual partners even when distance, competition, and other hardships prevailed. The capacity for intense sexual pleasure ensured their participation in sex, despite a plethora of disincentives.

Obviously, however, there is (and was) a limit to how good sex can feel, or more precisely, to how much energy can be expended in the pursuit and enjoyment of sex. Deleterious consequences may result if too much time and effort are expended in the pursuit of sex because reproduction, after all, is only one of several evolutionarily significant activities. Resources must also be allocated to procure food by hunting or foraging; to ensure the safety of oneself and one's family or other social unit; to find adequate shelter; and so on. A delicate balance is required between reproduction on the one hand, and survival (including the survival of offspring) on the other. Millions of years of evolution have arrived at just such a balance. Like the baby bear's porridge in the tale of Goldilocks, the pleasure that modern *Homo sapiens* feel is neither too hot nor too cold—it is, instead, just right.

The Evolution of Sexual Pleasure, Part II

To summarize: The evolutionary function of sexual pleasure is to encourage humans to engage in penile-vaginal intercourse, and thereby to propagate their genes. People have sex because it feels good, not necessarily because they consciously desire offspring. The mechanism of pleasure is an evolutionary adaptation that solves the motivational problem of ensuring that sex takes place despite its myriad drawbacks. Sex, after all, is time consuming, messy, and dangerous. And these costs must have been magnified many times over for our ancient protohuman ancestors. Pleasure, though, made sex worthwhile. It provided the benefit needed to offset the sizable costs associated with intercourse, such as time and energy expenditures, vulnerability to attack, the dangers of pregnancy and childbirth, and so on. Natural selection therefore favored those who experienced greater pleasure in sex because they tended to invest more of their energies into the pursuit of sex, and hence begat more offspring, many of whom inherited copies of the enhanced pleasure-seeking genes.

For animals other than primates, sexual pleasure seems relatively less important. Although the question of whether or not dogs and cats truly enjoy sex can never be answered definitively, the point is really rather moot. Regardless, pleasure is not the primary reason that dogs and cats have sex. Instead, the sex lives of canines and felines are controlled by hormones and pheromones, and are restricted to temporally limited periods of female fertility and sexual receptivity.

Unlike other species, human females don't have specially delineated periods of sexual receptivity (estrus), and males don't respond mechanically to scents emitted by copulable females. People are not ruled by hormones, but instead by lust—that is, by the pursuit of pleasure. Why? What advantage does the mechanism of pleasure (viewed as a motive force) confer upon the individual, in comparison with the seemingly obsolete hormonal solution?

The principal advantage of the pleasure mechanism is *freedom*. Freedom from a fixed hormonal schedule. As a motivational system, hormones are quite rigid. When a male dog,[*66] for example, encounters the scent of an estrous female, his mating behavior "program" takes over and nothing, including fences, doors, and busy highways, will keep him from locating and copulating with his paramour.[*67] The costs may be high, but he has no real choice; with hormones it is either now or never. Nor can the female control her costs: She can become pregnant only when in estrus, but she cannot choose the timing of these periods of fertility.

For men and women the reproductive imperative is restrained by logic and reason. Sexual pleasure may be sublime, but it is hardly worth dying for. For the most part (though significant exceptions occur), logic and reason dictate whether and when sexual encounters will take place.[68] In this "rational" model (explored further in Chapter 6), the decision to engage in sex is undertaken after a careful (though largely unconscious) analysis of the costs and benefits ("utility") of sex, versus the utility of abstaining.[69] Pleasure is reduced to a single factor in a complicated cost-benefit analysis. In theory, this decision procedure allows the costs of sex to be minimized while the benefits are retained. Clearly, a large cerebral cortex is required for such complex decision making.[*70]

The preceding rational model is idealized, of course. Not all sexual decisions are rational from a purely utilitarian standpoint, and many of the costs and benefits are largely intangible, or at the very least, unquantifiable. Nevertheless, the point we wish to make is that the mechanism of pleasure affords humans (and perhaps other apes as well) an unprecedented degree of control over their sexuality. This freedom, in turn, provides a superior solution to the problem of maximizing sexual benefits while simultaneously minimizing attendant costs.

More generally, pleasure—not just sexual pleasure, but any of various visceral pleasures—provides the basis for learning via reinforcement. Pleasure reinforces behaviors that are worth repeating. Many forms of pleasure reward behaviors that enhance the survivability of the individual (such as eating ripe rather than immature or spoiled fruit), whereas sexual pleasure enhances the survivability of the species at the expense of individual survivability. In other words, pleasure, like natural selection, rewards adaptive behaviors. However, the two mechanisms differ greatly in temporal scale: Whereas pleasure provides nearly immediate gratification, evolutionary "rewards" are affected over tens, hundreds, and thousands of generations.

Pleasure also provides a primitive categorization mechanism, and a concomitant, evolutionarily advantageous, compression of information. Thus, people need not be biologically "programmed" separately to enjoy the taste of ripe bananas, oranges, apricots, and so on. Instead, they are programmed to like sweet things. The simple rule is "eat things that taste good (i.e., provide gustatory pleasure), and don't eat things that don't." A laundry list of the edible versus the inedible is unnecessary; edibles, by and large, taste good, so a simple rule to eat whatever tastes good suffices. With regard to sex, the rule apparently is, "if it feels good, do it." Hence, if there is a category, it must include all sex, not just procreative sex.

Finally, and highly speculatively, pleasure and its close relative, pain, combine to form a natural system of morality. Although we agree with Kant that notions of "right" and "wrong" are not inherently sensible,*[71] pleasure and pain nevertheless provide a moral code that is sympathetic to evolutionary concerns. By this we mean only that if the pleasurable and the painful define behavioral categories to be sought and avoided, respectively, then those animals that let pleasure and pain guide their behavior should have an evolutionary advantage over those that do not. Evolution, in this sense, rewards the moral.

The Two Types of Pleasure

In order to consider the evolution of sexual pleasure further, it will be helpful to distinguish between two types of pleasure: First, the pleasurable erotic feelings elicited by stimulation of the genitals or other erogenous zones (especially during intercourse), and second, the intense pleasure of orgasm. These two types of pleasure will be referred to here as *fore-pleasure* and *orgasmic pleasure* (the term "fore-pleasure" is originally due to Freud and clearly reflects the central importance of orgasm in his theory of sexuality—all other pleasures are merely anticipatory). These two pleasures are obviously distinct, and if, as suggested earlier, sexual pleasure is evolutionarily adaptive, one might wonder which of the two types shoulders the greater motivational burden. In the extreme form one might even ask, "Is orgasmic pleasure necessary?"

This question is motivated by the observation that the genital stimulation that accompanies penile-vaginal intercourse is exquisitely pleasurable for most people; so much so that orgasm is often delayed as long as possible to maximize fore-pleasure.[*72] Indeed, the relatively long time required for human males to ejaculate (compared with other primates) could be an adaptation meant to maximize fore-pleasure.[73] Of course, the longer sex takes, the greater the costs to the participants (in terms of vulnerability, time, and energy expenditures). Shorter sex should therefore be favored by natural selection. Perhaps the greater pleasure enjoyed during prolonged intercourse is sufficient to counteract this negative pressure. That is, in our evolutionary past, maybe those who took longer experienced greater pleasure, hence engaged in intercourse more frequently and had more children. It might seem, therefore, that fore-pleasure alone would be sufficient to ensure that sexual behaviors get repeated.

This being the case, it is not immediately clear what function (if any) is served by orgasm. (Only male orgasm is considered here; the female counterpart is discussed in Chapter 5.) As noted in the introduction, orgasm and ejaculation are conceptually, anatomically, and physiologically distinct phenomena, despite their usual temporal coincidence. Theoretically, there is no obvious reason why orgasm—particularly its pleasurable aspects—should accompany the ejaculation of sperm. Indeed, if the genital stimulation of intercourse is pleasurable enough, and if such stimulation eventually induces ejaculation—which it usually does—then the necessity for pleasurable orgasm is undermined.

This theory is fine, as far as it goes, but it neglects the second half of the observation with which this discussion began—namely, that male orgasm is often delayed to maximize fore-pleasure. One of the most efficient ways for men to stave off orgasm is simply to stop having sex for a time, and resume only after a near return to physiological normality. This technique could, in theory, be repeated indefinitely, with the result that ejaculation need never occur. Fortunately for the species, however, ejaculation is usually accompanied by the ecstasies of orgasmic pleasure. The intense pleasure of orgasm provides the necessary reward for a job well done (the fact that orgasmic pleasure is infinitely more intense than the preceding fore-pleasure is also consistent with this explanation). Orgasmic pleasure, hence ejaculation, is thus a goal to strive for, rather than a pleasure-dampening nuisance. For this reason, it is a necessary component of the male sexual response. Of course, ejaculation is not automatic; fore-pleasure is required to ensure continued stimulation until orgasm. Thus, both orgasmic pleasure and fore-pleasure contribute to the ultimate goal of ejaculation.

But penile-vaginal intercourse isn't the only form of sexual expression that's pleasurable—nonprocreative sexual activities are enjoyable too. How, then, can sexual pleasure *ensure* that people reproduce? In other words, if people can experience all the gains of sex without any of the disincentives, why should they run the risk of possible complications arising from intercourse? (This question is especially relevant to women, for whom the risks are much greater.) Many people, for example, engage in masturbation as a form of self-pleasuring. Because masturbation has none of the possible adverse consequences (e.g., acquiring a sexually transmitted disease) associated with more social activities such as oral, anal, or vaginal intercourse, one might wonder why more adults haven't adopted it as their sole source of sexual pleasure.

Why indeed? First, despite a paucity of data on the subject, it seems safe to suggest that for most people masturbation is not as physically or emotionally satisfying as other sexual options.*[74] So, there may be a trade-off associated with interpersonal sex: greater threat of complications in exchange for increased pleasure and emotional satisfaction. But why penile-vaginal intercourse, with its attendant pregnancy-related risks, rather than oral or anal sex? Again, it is possible that differences in the pleasurability of these activities, or simply the desire for variety, explains why most individuals do not eliminate coitus from their sexual repertoires. Penile-vaginal intercourse is also the most egalitarian, and, in the missionary position, the most intimate of commonly practiced heterosexual activities. Intercourse might therefore serve to strengthen the emotional bond between sexual partners, as discussed further in the following section.

All this may be true, but perhaps an even more parsimonious explanation exists. A simple solution to the conundrum of why people (and other animals) continue to engage in penile-vaginal sex, despite the risks, is to assume that masturbation, oral, and anal sex are just unanticipated concomitants of the evolution of sexual pleasure, that, because they do not interfere too greatly with reproductive behaviors, have not been eliminated through the callous machinations of natural selection. Our theory, in its entirety, is then as follows. Sex is pleasurable to ensure that people engage in reproductive behaviors despite the sometimes substantial risks that these behaviors entail. But the pleasurability of sex, relying as it does on both physiological and psychological processes, cannot be restricted to purely reproductive behaviors, and for this reason a wide range of sexual activities can be enjoyed. This enjoyment is fine as long as it does not interfere with the propagation of genes, hence the regeneration of the species.

We have thus come full circle, returning to the arguments with which this chapter began. Because sexual intercourse is so pleasurable, and humans are so fertile, conception is bound to occur at a rate sufficient to ensure the continuation of the human race, even if other activities are enjoyed as well.

The Multiple Functions of Sexual Pleasure

Before concluding this evolutionary discussion, however, we should mention an alternative theory of the utility of sexual pleasure. In his influential (though greatly criticized) book, *The Naked Ape,* British naturalist Desmond Morris suggests a different, though somewhat complementary, purpose for the pleasurability of sex. Morris proposes that the primary function of sex is to facilitate the bonding of males and females in pairs, rather than to ensure procreation. In this scheme sexual pleasure is relegated to encouraging pair-bonding in much the way that it supports procreation in the theory outlined earlier. Morris observes that "the vast majority of copulation in our species is obviously concerned, not with producing offspring, but with cementing the pair-bond *by providing mutual rewards for the sexual partners.*"[75] The mutual rewards being, presumably, the pleasurable sensations that accompany sex.

While we agree that reproduction is no longer the principal rationale for "the vast majority of copulation in our species," we also consider the experience of sexual pleasure to be a goal unto itself. Although there can be little doubt that such pleasuring yields as a secondary gain the strengthening of the emotional bond between mated couples, we wish to emphasize that neither reproduction nor sexual pleasure *demand* such a bond in order to operate. Strictly speaking, pair-bonding cannot be the *primary* function of sexuality; in fact, in many instances evolution would favor promiscuity, at least for males.[76] To paraphrase a slogan currently in vogue, "he who dies with the most offspring wins." It is immaterial whether or not those offspring were conceived within the bounds of a monogamous relationship, their existence is all that matters. (Additional doubts about Morris' pair-bonding hypothesis are raised in Chapter 4.)

In the same vein as the previous quote from *The Naked Ape* is the following from Kinsey et al.: "No appreciable part of the coitus, *either in or out of marriage,* is consciously undertaken as a means of effecting reproduction."[77] Regardless of the source, the message is clear: Sex isn't just for procreation anymore. Moreover, given the prevalence of extramarital or "extramonogamal" sexual activity in modern society, it seems unlikely that the primary function of sex is simply to facilitate bonding. This is not to deny the evolutionary significance of interpersonal sex, and particularly sexual pleasure, in the formation of stable male-female pair-bonds, but rather to suggest that this function is of secondary importance, at best.

Besides reproduction and bonding, what other functions does sex serve? Among bonobos, sex is used to prevent hostility and ease social tensions, in addition to providing pleasurable satisfaction and ensuring reproduction.[78] (The bonobos credo being, apparently, "make love, not war.") This, in part, explains why bonobo sexual interactions occur between every possible age and gender combination (old with young, female with female, etc.). In support of this theory, de Waal observed marked increases in sexual behaviors around feeding time, when tensions regarding food distribution are particularly acute. In one such episode, a female bonobo literally snatched the food out of her male partner's hands in the midst of intercourse![79] Sex is also employed as a reconciliatory gesture following aggressive behaviors among male bonobos. In all, de Waal estimates that less than a third of all the sexual encounters he observed were reproductively motivated.[80]

Although bonobo sexuality certainly strengthens the ties between individuals, it does so without requiring the institution of monogamous relationships.[81] It is perhaps suggestive in this regard that male ejaculation did not occur in any of the sexual encounters de Waal observed, with the possible exception of male-female copulation.[82] Given the human propensity to view orgasm as the ultimate goal of sex (at least for males), this lack of climactic activity is rather surprising. However, remember that the majority of bonobo sexual encounters take place during tension-filled social situations. If ejaculation had occurred, then the male's ability to resolve or avoid additional conflicts via sexual overtures would have been severely diminished during the subsequent refractory period. In other words, orgasmic sex (if orgasm can be identified with ejaculation in the bonobo) would be a liability in this situation, at least for males.

Sexual play among spinner dolphins has also been observed to increase as the feeding grounds—where the animals engage in social competition for food—are approached.[83] One interpretation holds that this behavior is primarily aggressive muscle-flexing whose goal is to maintain dominance-subordinate relationships.[84] Although in many animals dominance relationships are expressed through sexual behaviors (especially isosexual contacts between males), the bonobo example suggests that the increased sexuality of spinner dolphins (as they prepare for the social interactions that accompany feeding) might in fact be a means of preventing—rather than a symptom of—aggression. The observation that spinner dolphins, like humans and bonobos, display nominally sexual behaviors in diverse social situations is also consistent with this explanation. Spinner experts Randall Wells and Kenneth Norris suggest that, "homosexually oriented behavior, such as beak-to-genital propulsion between females or copulation between males . . . can be viewed as the co-option of a sexual pattern into social concourse between dolphins."[85]

Do humans use sex to avoid conflict? At the personal level, the answer is an unequivocal *yes*. Many a lover's quarrel is settled, not by resolving the issues under debate, but by "crawling into the sack." This use of sex may also extend to larger social groupings. Anecdotal evidence suggests that female initiates of the Hell's Angels motorcycle "club" are (or were) required to have sex with each male member of the club in order to gain admittance. This could be interpreted as an attempt to forestall sexual access conflicts within the social unit. Likewise, women are exchanged in many tribal societies (e.g., in the highlands of New Guinea) as an integral component of peacekeeping negotiations.[86]

Based on the evidence summarized here, one might suspect that in the distant past sex played an important role in maintaining the cohesion of the social group by reducing tensions. Indeed, some evolutionary theorists (e.g., Morris) believe that it did, but not in the direct fashion of the bonobo, among whom potential adversaries enjoy a brief sexual exchange rather than escalating aggression. Instead, in humans the influence of sexual pleasure is hypothesized to have acted by way of enhancing the pair-bond. In brief, this theory holds that sex cements the bond, providing each male his own mate, thereby reducing sexual competition among males (cf. St. Paul's advice: "Nevertheless to avoid fornication, let every man have his own wife").[*87] Regardless of the merits of this theory, we note that in it, once again, the pleasures of sex are reserved for the monogamously bound.

Returning from our evolutionary past, sexual pleasure serves a wide variety of functions in contemporary society beside facilitating reproduction, pair-bonding, and the expression of feelings of intimacy. Sexuality is an integral part of many people's self-image and perception of worth; some people even *define* themselves in terms of their sexuality. Western culture's insistence on dichotomizing sexual object choice has even manufactured identity categories based on sexual orientation.*[88] In America, *gay* means much more than simply male sexual preference for men as opposed to women—it is indicative of enhanced freedom, self-esteem, and acceptance. Peer acceptance is also critical to adolescents' assessments of self-worth. Teenagers everywhere use sex to advertise their status as mature individuals, and thereby their independence from parents. Finally, for many people the emotional and physical release experienced during orgasm decreases tension and irritability. Of course, the pleasurability of sex further enhances, and very likely underlies, these additional functions, which are thus secondary benefits of the evolution of sexual pleasure.

The Qualia of Life

Unfortunately, the evolutionary focus of the previous sections omits a critical, perhaps even the most important, aspect of what pleasure really *is*. Pleasure is a feeling, a sensation, a subjectively experienced phenomenon. And this fact, it turns out, engages some rather intractable philosophical questions.

As an introduction to the dilemma posed by the inherently subjective nature of pleasure, consider the dubious proposition that animals (other than humans) are incapable of feeling pleasure. According to this view, although a dog may actively seek out his master and beg to be petted, and may roll his eyes and act as though in heaven while having his belly rubbed, he feels no pleasure; he only behaves *as though* he did.

Is such a situation plausible? On the one hand, we are tempted to respond without hesitation with a resounding *no!* Anyone who has spent any significant amount of time around animals, from mice to elephants, cannot seriously entertain the notion that they have no feelings. On the other hand, there is no *proof* that such is the case, and there never can be, given the subjective nature of the experiences in question. At best, we can analogize, and attribute pleasure, pain, and consciousness to other species*[89] according to how similar they are to humans.[90] That other great apes are conscious is indubitable; that dogs and cats feel pleasure and pain is also fairly certain; and so on down to insects, to which people typically, though unscientifically, deny consciousness.

In *The Expression of Emotions in Man and Animals,* Charles Darwin reports the following observations:

> With the lower animals we see the same principle of pleasure derived from contact in association with love. Dogs and cats mani-

festly take pleasure in rubbing against their masters and mistresses, and in being rubbed or petted by them. Many kinds of monkeys, as I am assured by the keepers in the Zoological Gardens, delight in fondling and being fondled by each other, and by persons to whom they are attached.[91]

And, of course, many primates also experience pleasures that are specifically *sexual*.[92]

Although most readers are probably inclined to grant consciousness to dogs, cats, sheep, and apes, it nevertheless remains conceivable that these animals lack a subjective inner life. Perhaps a simple thought experiment will help make this clear. Imagine a humanlike robot—a perfect simulation in every respect—that behaves in every situation and in every way like a human, but that nevertheless feels neither pleasure nor pain (nor anything else, for that matter). It does *react* as though it felt these sensations—for example, when it accidentally burns its hand, it quickly pulls it away from the source of heat, possibly shaking it and cursing wildly while doing so—and, like a human, it tends, all things being equal, to seek experiences known to be associated with pleasure and to avoid those connected with pain. In other words, its behavior, vis-à-vis pleasure and pain, is entirely indistinguishable from that of a human being, but it doesn't really *feel* the pain or *enjoy* the pleasure.

Clearly, the plausibility of such a robot depends on whether or not the functional mechanisms of pleasure and pain are truly separable from the subjective feelings that accompany them. (To introduce a bit of philosophic jargon, the subjective feelings and sensations associated with pleasure and pain shall hereafter be referred to as *qualia*.) Although it is clear from their behavior that dogs experience the functional manifestations of pleasure and pain, we can never know whether they also experience the associated qualia.

The question posed earlier, asking whether the qualia of pleasure and pain can be separated from their functional role, their "syndrome[s] of most typical causes and effects,"[93] is hardly novel. Related questions of the nature of the relationship of mind to body have troubled philosophers dating back at least to Aristotle. The most famous "resolution" of this problem, of course, is Descartes' suggestion that all substances belong to one of two basic classes: the physical or the mental. Descartes maintained that the mind and the brain are fundamentally different types of entities: the mind is *mental substance,* characterized by thinking, believing, and so on, whereas the brain is *physical substance,* the defining quality of which is that it occupies space. According to Descartes, despite being radically different kinds of substances, the mental and the physical nevertheless interact with each other, as when a belief that it's hot (a mental event) causes someone to open a window (a physical event).

Many people intuitively believe, like Descartes, in some form of *dualism,* in which the physical and the mental, though fundamentally different, interact through as yet undiscovered mechanisms. The nature of the posited interaction is problematic, however. As Princess Elizabeth inquired in 1643: "How can the [mind] of man, being only a thinking substance, determine his bodily spirits to perform voluntary actions?"[94] This and similar difficulties have led most modern scientists to reject dualism in favor of *materialism,* which posits the existence of only a single (physical) substance.[95] According to materialism, mental states are simply brain states, although the form that this equivalence assumes is the subject of continuing debate (for example, is pain always a *particular* brain state, or just *some* brain state?). Thus, in this view the mind arises from the functioning of the physical brain. However, the existence of qualia—for example, the way pain feels, as distinct from its functional role—presents a special challenge to materialism.

In dualistic terms, the functional basis of pleasure and pain is unarguably physical, being composed of skin and pain receptors, nerves, neurons, brain centers, and so on. The associated qualia, on the other hand, are intrinsically mental. This is not to say that qualia are necessarily divorced from the physical realm. The opposite is almost certainly true—qualia, it seems, arise from physical processes; pleasure and pain may very well be the subjective correlates of the firing of certain neurons in the brain. Though not entirely uncontroversial, this much is relatively unproblematic. However, difficulties arise when one attempts to explain how mental phenomena, such as qualia, can have physical effects, such as causing a particular behavior. A basic tenet of materialism, and one with which most scientists would heartily agree, is that the cause of a physical effect must itself be physical. It follows from this that qualia cannot have physical effects (such as influencing behavior) unless they are themselves physical entities. For this reason, various flavors of materialism attempt either to abolish, ignore, or reduce qualia to the physical events from which they arise.

The most common materialistic detour around the problem of qualia is simply to deny the causal efficacy of qualia. In this view, qualia are held to be merely epiphenomenal. That is, qualia are assumed to be mere by-products of physical events in the brain, and to possess no causal powers distinct from the brain events themselves. The counterintuitive nature of this claim is readily apparent. Most people believe that when they touch a hot stove, it is the feeling of pain that causes them to withdraw their hand. The pain seems to play an integral, causative role in the behavioral sequence. Nevertheless, according to many materialistic theories, the pain cannot be causally efficacious. Instead, the pain arises as a by-product of some brain event, such as the one that initiates the behavioral act of withdrawing the hand from the hot stove.

However, the existence of qualia is, we believe, both self-evident and evolutionarily significant. The preceding sections presented a simplified account of the evolution of sexual pleasure, viewed as a *mechanism*. To reiterate: Pleasure is adaptive because it provides a nonrigid motivational system for ensuring evolutionarily advantageous behaviors. People have sex because it feels good. The question is *why* it feels good. To return to the canine and robot examples, couldn't people respond appropriately *without* feeling pleasure? Intuitively, the answer is *no*.[*96] But we can do better than this.

It is commonly assumed that consciousness (including pleasure and pain) is an adaptation, shaped over the millennia by the forces of natural selection.[97] Suppose this is true. Suppose, in particular, that qualia have an evolutionary history of their own. What, then, is the adaptive significance of qualia?

To examine this issue, assume that a "qualialess" robot of the sort described earlier has been constructed. In fact, assume that a whole society of these superrobots has been produced, the first two—one "male" and one "female"—by humans, and the remainder by an unspecified form of artificial sexual reproduction that, like human reproduction, is subject to the forces of natural selection. Or, if you like, imagine a race of creatures identical to humans in every way but one: They do not experience the qualia of pleasure and pain. Now leave these two races—ours and the qualialess one—and return after 10 million years of evolution by natural selection. Has one race won out over the other?

If there truly were an evolutionary advantage to qualia, one might expect the human race to have dominated, perhaps even obliterated, the qualialess race. But is this really a reasonable expectation? Remember that both races react *identically* to pleasurable and painful stimuli and situations; their behavior is in all instances and details identical. However well adapted one race is to its environment, the other should be equally so. Whatever qualities one might capitalize on to increase its fitness, so might the other one. Thus, ignoring random effects, there should be no difference in survival or reproduction, hence neither race should predominate over the other in this mock evolutionary competition.

The ineluctable conclusion is that *if* qualia are truly evolutionarily adaptive, they must be more than merely epiphenomenal, they must be causally efficacious in motivating behavior.[98] That is, pleasure and pain necessarily have behavioral consequences. This really is not surprising. A trait must have *some* causal efficacy to be evolutionarily advantageous.[*99] Furthermore, this result confirms the intuition that the way pleasure and pain *feel* plays an important role in determining behavior. Pleasure and pain derive their status as motive forces from the feelings that accompany them. A sensationless pain is not a pain. There would be no reason to avoid it; hence, it would have no behavioral consequences. The functional roles of pleasure and pain *demand* that they be felt.

Unfortunately, because qualia are inherently subjective, *how* pleasure and pain feel cannot be captured in any physical description. As Thomas Nagel explains in his seminal essay, "What is it Like to be a Bat?":

> The subjective character of experience . . . is not captured by any of the familiar, recently devised reductive analyses of the mental, for all of them are logically compatible with its absence. It is not analyzable in terms of any explanatory system of functional states, or intentional states, since these could be ascribed to robots or automata that behaved like people though they experienced nothing. It is not analyzable in the causal role of experiences in relation to typical human behavior—for similar reasons.[100]

Even if the physiology of pleasure were to turn out to be no more complicated than the firing of a few neurons in the limbic lobe of the brain, a complete description of the phenomena of pleasure—as people experience it—would remain elusive.

To summarize the argument once again: If the qualia of pleasure and pain are evolutionary adaptations, then they must be causally effective. In humans, at least, the capacity to experience the sensations associated with pleasure and pain is a necessary prerequisite for exhibiting the appropriate behaviors (including pleasure seeking and pain avoidance); that is, the qualia play a *causal* role in eliciting appropriate behaviors.[*101] Thus, according to this argument (and assuming its premises) mental phenomena such as qualia *must* be able to influence physical behavior, as suggested by Descartes but refuted by most right-thinking modern scientists.

Naturally, there are a number of ways to avoid this somewhat unsavory conclusion. One could, for example, insist that the qualia themselves did not evolve, but simply *are,* and always have been. However, given the intricate connection between qualia and the behavioral mechanisms of pleasure and pain (which most surely *did* evolve), this seems a rather untenable position. A more promising approach is to argue that qualia are the intrinsically mental constituents of a physical property. According to this theory, any robot that exactly mimics human responses to pleasure and pain must *necessarily* experience the associated qualia, so that the behavioral/functional roles occupied by pleasure and pain are inseparable from the qualia. A robot that displayed the appropriate behaviors but lacked the associated qualia would be an impossibility, much as heat (a property) is a necessary concomitant of molecular motion (a behavior). Although this view seems plausible enough, it is somehow unsatisfying, and seems to beg the question at hand: Why should pleasure be associated with evolutionarily adaptive behaviors?

Perhaps, as Nagel suggests, there are facts beyond the reach of human concepts.[102] If so, it is likely that the nature of mind-body interactions is one such fact.

Childhood, Leisure, and Sexual Pleasure

If sexual pleasure is an evolved adaptation in humans, that is, if people are hardwired for pleasure, one may ask when the associated behaviors manifest themselves. The answer is, in infancy and early childhood, as amused (or aghast) parents can attest. Like smiling and laughter, interest in genital stimulation begins early, and for most people, never entirely fades. We believe, consistent with Freud's theory of human sexuality, that childhood sexual feelings, interests, and motivations are naturally heterogeneous, or "polymorphously perverse" (meaning that all sexual possibilities are open), because childhood is a time for exploring the world, including the proximal world of the flesh.[103] As puberty unfolds, however, the drive for sexual pleasure is intensified and, according to Freud, the aim of the "sexual instinct" (or *libido*) shifts from self-pleasuring to the consummation of reproductive activities. (This shift is especially noticeable in postpubertal males as an increasing emphasis on orgasm and ejaculation.)

If heterogeneous sexual pleasure is overtly manifested in childhood because of the freedom of exploration and the absence of procreative pressures and constraints, what happens to polymorphous perversity as childhood melts into adulthood with its attendant responsibilities? The answer, we believe, is evident in the circumstances that characterize childhood: exploration, leisure, and the absence of adult responsibilities. We propose, somewhat in defiance of Freud, that when these conditions extend into adulthood, so does sexual heterogeneity. Historically, as societies developed and citizens' lives became both safer and comparatively less arduous, heterogeneous (e.g., oral, anal, genital) sexual pleasure was incorporated into adulthood to a much greater degree than it previously had been. In many cases, favorable circumstances prevailed for only a subclass of society, as would be predicted by the differential opportunities for leisure. In late eighteenth/early-nineteenth century Hawaii (before the arrival of the Christian missionaries), for example:

> The sexual conduct of the hereditary aristocrats, who lived in or close to the political centers, was noticeably different from that of the commoners who, as agriculturists, fishermen and artists, resided and labored apart from the chiefly courts. By our standards the entirety of Hawaiian society was sexually very permissive, but at the courts erotic pastimes figured prominently in the lives of the leisured nobles. Sexual liaisons, both heterosexual and homosexual, were freely formed and just as freely broken off.[104]

A somewhat analogous situation existed in ancient Greece, where numerous outlets for heterogeneous sexual pleasure existed for male citizens (though not entirely absent, fewer such outlets existed for women).[105] For men, both heterosexual (female) and homosexual (male) prostitutes were available as sexual partners, as were slaves of both genders. We presume that these particular options were viable, in part, because male citizens in ancient Greek society had ample *leisure* time. And what is the best model of idyllic leisure? Childhood, of course.

Because childhood is a natural time for heterogeneous sexual pleasuring, it seems reasonable that ancient Greeks citizens would co-opt aspects of childhood (i.e., heterogeneous) sexuality into their conception of leisure. In many respects, this suggestion mirrors Thornstein Veblen's notion of leisure.[106] For example, because of the prevalence of slaves and noncitizens for "demeaning work," plus the subjugation of women to perform these duties, male citizens in ancient Greece could remain conspicuously exempt from all useful employment. They therefore had plenty of time for nonproductive activities and could emphasize intellectual or aesthetic pursuits as "serviceable evidence of an unproductive expenditure of time."[107] Perhaps heterogeneous sexual pursuits were utilized as tangible evidence of the nonproductive consumption of time.

This is not to suggest that ancient Greek citizens were the first consumers of heterogeneous sexual pleasure, nor particularly prone to these pursuits.[108] Indeed, we propose that heterogeneous sexual pleasure has been pursued in varying degrees by humans of all geologic ages, as suggested by the sexual behavior of our primate relatives. However, the burdens of adulthood usually relegate such pleasuring to childhood. Only when cultures minimize the burdens of adulthood—as, for example, in ancient Greece—can leisure be created, thereby permitting (though not guaranteeing) some form of heterogeneous sexual pleasuring.

The particular form (or the absence) of heterogeneous sexual pleasure is largely determined by the existing cultural milieu—meaning that leisure is not *invariably* associated with polymorphous sexual pleasure, although leisure provides the opportunity for it. (In any case, such pleasuring is always an extension of "natural" childhood sexuality.) One of the reasons that leisure does not invariably produce childlike, heterogeneous sexuality in adulthood is the presence of cultural rules and regulations that seek to restrain sexual expression.

As human beings form groups, regulations are needed to foster cooperation, settle disputes, maximize resources, provide safety, and so on. Unfortunately, sexual pleasure is ripe for regulation because it is critical to kinship, marriage, childrearing, and related concerns, and because it profoundly affects the manner in which adults spend their time.

Historically, if one group or another wants to control how adults spend their time (leisure or otherwise), or to maximize their numbers, a first step is to implement sexual restrictions in service of these goals. Under such a system two conditions typically prevail. First, work, societal duties, and so on take priority in adulthood; second, sexual intercourse within marriage is strictly enforced, and concomitantly, alternative expressions of sexual pleasure are tabooed. Because sexual pleasure is so inherently appealing (or frighteningly intoxicating, depending on one's viewpoint), these rules and restrictions are necessarily punitive and repressive, so as to offset the magnificent power of sexual pleasure.

3.

The Regulation and
Marketing of Sexual Pleasure

In William Blake's famous poem *The Marriage of Heaven and Hell,* he challenges the sanctimony of libidinous restraint—particularly as evidenced in Milton's *Paradise Lost.* Blake warns:

> Those who restrain desire, do so because theirs is weak enough to be restrained; and the restrainer or reason usurps its place & governs the unwilling.[1]

This poem provides a particularly fitting introduction to the regulation of sexual pleasure and the questions it evokes. Such as the most basic query: Why do we restrict and encumber this many splendored thing? And why do we consider ourselves so noble when we do? Blake's poem reaffirms the vitality of passion and desire, and the creative acts they inspire. Desire provides a counterpoint to oppression, the virus of regulation and restraint.

Is restraint invariably viral? Obviously not. Even where the pursuit of sexual pleasure is concerned, the necessity for restraining and regulating violent and nonvolitional acts (e.g., rape and other forms of sexual abuse) is nearly universally endorsed. Thus, it becomes important to understand how, and why, restraint is implemented en masse, as well as how it is internalized by individuals, as both a decision-making process and an emotional reaction. Such is its importance that Freud made sexual restraint (and the tension, neuroses, and anxiety they engender) the cornerstone of his theory of the human psyche. Ultimately, this tension appears as the psychosexual equivalent to Newton's third law of motion—namely, it is the "motion" (e.g., havoc, turmoil, passion, etc.) that results from the interplay (or collision) of the momentum of sexual pleasure with the forces of sexual restraint.

But what makes sexual pleasure so momentous? Obviously, sex feels extraordinarily good; it therefore elicits frequent repetition, even if we must pander our dignity (e.g., lie, cheat, hoard, steal) to procure continued sexual opportunities.[*2] Furthermore, sexual pleasure bears witness to other critical behaviors (e.g., bonding, reconciliation, conflict avoidance) and social systems (e.g., marriage, kinship, power, status). The importance of sexual pleasure thus extends beyond the individual, to the social relationships and institutions that pervade the human condition.

The central question is whether sexual pleasure *requires* containment. And if so, what is the down side to such restraint? Paradoxically, in times of extreme sexual repression the prevalence of sexual crimes and "perversions" often increases. In reference to medieval sexual behavior, G. Rattray Taylor, author of *Sex in History,* argues that:

> It is an important psychological, as it is also a physical fact, that every action breeds an equal and opposite reaction. While the Church claims that repressive measures were required because of the immorality of the times, it seems more probable that, in reality, the immorality of the times was a result of the pressures applied.[3]

Furthermore, limits on freedom invariably mean limits on sanity. A pessimistic Taylor observes that, "the Church never succeeded in obtaining universal acceptance of its sexual regulations, but in time it became able to enforce sexual abstinence on a scale sufficient to produce a rich crop of mental disease."[4]

Nevertheless, some measure of sexual regulation is obviously necessary to discourage violent and coercive acts, and to control how the valuable "commodity" known as sex is "marketed." Regulation is also important because sex has the potential to produce enormous secondary gains, such as prestige, offspring, family connections, and so on.

Regulating sex is a no-win situation. It is neither easy nor virtuous, nor likely to win one friends. The interplay between social regulation (whether religious, male dominance, statutory, etc.) and the correlates of sexual pleasure (such as friendship, marriage, and so on) engenders a complex web of meanings that binds contemporary human sexuality. As is increasingly apparent, sexual behavior is often governed less by the desire to share sexual pleasure than by the social regulations that dictate the age, gender, behavior, and relationship characteristics that must (or should) accompany sexual expression. Throw into this already murky soup such complications as the existence of gender-based power differentials, the dynamic complexity of interpersonal relations, and the wiles of human emotion, and the improbability of achieving true social stability through the regulation of sexual behaviors becomes clear. In *Sex and Reason,* Richard Posner observes that:

> An optimal system of regulation is a function not only of the social costs of the practices one seeks to regulate but also of the cost of effective regulation (ineffective regulation can be bought cheaply). History and current practice appear to teach that laws regulating sex are inefficacious because most sex crimes are either de jure or de facto, victimless.[5]

However, because sexual pleasuring has the potential to create offspring (and hence, heirs), some form of imposed order is necessary to protect families, recognize kinship, and so on. Similarly, the potential of sex to create constituents (e.g., more religious members, more friends, more enemies), and thereby multiply power, provides a strong incentive to those who would seize this power through the regulation of pleasure. Moreover, if sexual pleasure can be stolen, forced, or manipulated to support a variety of hostile functions, then regulation may be required to maintain social harmony and, ultimately, some semblance of social stability. One of Freud's many insights into the individual sexual psyche and its relationship to society is the observation that such harmony often entails sexual sacrifice on the part of those whom it is intended to protect.

Freud, Repression, and Regulation

Freud observed that modern civilization requires that each person relinquish some part of his or her sexual freedom for the "good of society."[6] This benefits society both because the imposition of rules and regulations lessens social disorganization, and because it increases the economic and creative productivity of its members through the psychical mechanism known as *sublimation*. Many late-nineteenth-century writers went so far as to suggest that the construction of the edifice known as civilization is a more-or-less direct result of people rechanneling their sex drives into alternate pursuits, such as art, business, and intellectual activities.[7] For, as Krafft-Ebing noted over 100 years ago, "love unbridled is a volcano that burns down and lays waste all around it; it is an abyss that devours all—honour, substance and health."[8] But repression of the sexual instinct is not without costs to the individual who sublimates his or her drive.

Freud, like many other turn-of-the-century commentators, drew a causal connection between the quickening pace of "civilized" American and European life and the seemingly concomitant epidemic of neuroses he observed. The rise of the city and the economic changes fostered by the industrial revolution meant, for many people, an abandonment of the more tranquil rural way of life that dominated past centuries. But, whereas many of his contemporaries placed the onus of blame for modern humanity's neuroses on these environmental factors, Freud recognized the pivotal role played by society itself—and not just its accouterments— in the genesis of nervous disorders.

In addition to the stresses and strains imposed by industrialism, there were also socially sanctioned rules of sexual conduct with which to contend. According to historian Mark Connelly, in the latter half of the nineteenth century, middle-class American life was subject to a particularly repressive code of personal behavior:

> At the core of the code were two related propositions. There was, first, a belief in a unified and responsible self that, through the exercise of will and conscience, could (and must) control and repress the unruly and base sexual instincts. Its corollary was that "civilization" and "progress," as well as personal economic and social advancement, depended on this control of the potentially dangerous sexual drive. These beliefs supported a sexual code that strictly prohibited premarital sexual relations, proclaimed monogamous marriage to be the only permissible context for sexual intercourse, and declared that even within marriage the only purpose of sexual relations was reproduction.[9]

The repressiveness of these Victorian norms, especially regarding the sexual lives of women, and its effect on the psychological well-being of turn-of-the-century men and women should not be underestimated. On society's role in the etiology of nervous disorders, Freud is quite clear:

> If one passes over the less definite forms of "nervousness" and considers the actual forms of nervous disease, the injurious influence of culture reduces itself in all essentials to the undue suppression of the sexual life in civilized peoples (or classes) as a result of the "civilized" sexual morality which prevails among them.[10]

Because of this,

> We have found it impossible to give our support to conventional sexual morality or to approve highly of the means by which society

attempts to arrange the practical problems of sexuality in life. We can demonstrate with ease that what the world calls its code of morals demands more sacrifices than it is worth.[11]

Freud held that a modicum of repression, particularly of the tendency toward polymorphous perversity, was an essential part of sexual maturation. In particular, he believed that the childhood infatuation with early "erotogenic zones," such as the mouth and anus, must necessarily give way to the primacy of the "genital zone" in mature sexuality.[12] However, he was also convinced that excessive repression of the sexual instinct could be detrimental to the psychological well-being of the individual.[13] Although Freud's conception of "normal" sexual development is never clearly enunciated, it appears from his 1908 treatise *"Civilized" Sexual Morality and Modern Nervousness* that he distinguished between self-repression of the "perverse" childhood instincts and externally imposed societal restraints. According to Freud, Victorian prudery (including the ideal of the passive wife who neither desires nor enjoys sexual intercourse) was a social disease, and a principal cause of neurosis and other common psychopathologies of the time (e.g., hysteria).

Although we agree with Freud that sexual repression is an important source of psychological disturbances, we believe that the repression required to transform infantile sexual preoccupations into "normal" adult sexuality may in itself be too extreme. Both external and internal regulation of the primordial, undifferentiated sex drive (or libido) are capable of producing toxic psychological tensions. Hence, if people are naturally polymorphous perverse, as Freud suggested, then perhaps it is best to leave them that way. Sexual socialization should extend only so far as needed to ensure successful social assimilation; when the demands thereby imposed become too great, society itself should change. In other words, perhaps we should instruct our society to accept homosexual and other noninjurious childhood sexual explorations, rather than teaching our children to eschew them.

The Societal Regulation of Sexual Pleasure

By what process is sexual pleasuring regulated at the societal level? One answer is that regulation is the product of collective needs that foster stability (in the ideal sense) or personal gains (in the more typical sense) in a particular (evolving) social-geographic-historical environment. For example, one simple way of conceptualizing the Catholic Church's regulation of sexual pleasure through the ages is to understand the Church's need to accumulate power. By effectively restricting all forms of sexual pleasure to a single act (penile-vaginal intercourse without contraception), in a single context (marriage), the Church sought to increase its constituency (hence its wealth, power, and so on) by funneling sexual energies exclusively into reproductive activities. (The restriction of sexuality to Church-sanctioned marriage, it should be noted, permitted the Church a say in the selection of partners.) This strategy—a form of institutionalized organizational reproduction—relies for its success on the tendency of children to adopt their parents' religion, as Pope Pius XI makes quite explicit:

> Christian parents should, besides, realize that they are not only called upon to propagate and sustain the human race on earth, they are not just intended to produce worshippers of the true God, but to give their sons to the Church to join the fellowship of the saints and the servants of God so that *the number of those who worship God and our Saviour should increase daily.*[14]

This strategy is not foolproof, however. In the Protestant Shaker sect in the nineteenth century, celibacy was held up as a sexual ideal for both men and (especially) women—an ideal that obviously discouraged the reproduction of the congregation.[15] As a result, it was necessary for the Shaker Church to actively recruit new members from outside the sect to maintain its size. There was also, of course, regeneration from within, as not all Shakers followed the arduous path to celibacy. Some, unable to remain "virgin celebates," married instead. But even in marriage sexual expression was limited to procreative intents. Sexual pleasure—principally male pleasure, for "Shakers saw woman as a victim, who was used by irresponsible men for their selfish pleasure"[16]—was strictly verboten. The proscription on pleasure was necessary, they believed, to protect women from the immeasurable selfishness of men, rather than to curtail lust, per se, as in Catholic theology.

The secondary implications of the Catholic Church's insistence that the only good sex is reproductive marital sex include discouraging homosexuality and contraception (both of which interfere with the production of heirs and additional constituents), illegitimatizing pornography (which promotes illicit interest in sexual pleasure), and relegating women to a primary role as providers of children (a.k.a. heirs and constituents).

Paradoxically, although the power of the Church to regulate sexual behavior has eroded greatly in recent years—at least in terms of the availability of both contraception and pornography, and in the changing status of women—prohibitions against homosexuality persist with vehemence and force. Why should homosexuality be any different from contraception? Both limit procreation, hence the production of heirs and constituents. Yet, despite the Church's admonishments, contraception has been embraced by a significant minority, if not a majority, of Catholics in the United States. Why is contraception (and pornography, for that matter) a lesser evil than homosexuality? And furthermore, now that abortion has been normalized (at least to some degree), why is it championed as a basic right, but homosexuality is not?

Homosexuality: What's the Message?

The lack of guaranteed rights for all Americans—regardless of sexual orientation—constitutes one of the final vestiges of our racist, sexist past. Look at it this way. A woman has a legal (and we believe, moral) right to terminate a pregnancy within the first trimester, as decreed by the Supreme Court of the United States. But, in many states, this same woman does not have a legal right to let another woman stimulate her genitals (or, for that matter, to marry her). Why is it okay to terminate a fetus, but not okay to let a same-sex partner touch one's genitals? The underlying logic is ludicrous, and unnecessarily pernicious to countless homosexual and bisexual men and women.

Presumably, the intransigence of laws regulating homosexual behavior mainly reflects political (hence economic) realities and perceptions. With a power base of only 1 to 10 percent of the U.S. population (estimates vary widely), gay and lesbian political organizations lack the persuasive political power of conservative and fundamentalist religious groups. As long as more moderate and liberal Americans likewise disparage freedom of sexual choice (or fail to make their prochoice voices heard), homosexual rights will continue to fall prey to predatory political expediencies.

In contrast, abortion—being potentially relevant to all women (and a number of men)—has a much broader political base. In addition to the obvious coalition of liberated women and men, many otherwise conservative or moderate voters disingenuously favor abortion rights as a means of population control for the disadvantaged and disenfranchised (i.e., as a mechanism for trimming the welfare rolls), the insidious implication being that otherwise, nonaborted (lower-class) fetuses would reek economic havoc among the taxpaying public. (Even Margaret Sanger, founder of the American birth control movement, defined the purpose of birth control as, "more children from the fit, less from the unfit."[17])

That such opportunistic beliefs could be embraced across ideological boundaries simply reemphasizes the fact that such questions are ultimately decided by political packaging and the strength of advertising campaigns.

Nowhere is the power of packaging more evident than in the history of contraceptive promotion.*[18] Contraceptives have existed in various forms for hundreds of years. (Primitive contraceptives include condoms and diaphragms made from the intestinal membranes of sheep, and spermicides derived from animal dung.[19]) However, it was not until the early to middle part of the twentieth century—when condoms were promoted as a means of facilitating familial stability rather than as disease prophylaxis—that they gained broad public support.[20] Like abortion, contraceptives provided the nuclear family with a mechanism for limiting family size, with all the social and economic implications this entailed (such as population control of the welfare class, and an increased standard of living for the family unit).

In the 1960s, however, the popularity of the condom as a contraceptive device faded significantly, due to the wide availability of "the pill." Marketing of this venerable device has therefore come full circle—the condom is once again being advertised as a disease preventive, and has become an integral part of what most people regard as "safe sex." In the current climate of fear surrounding the AIDS epidemic, the prevailing message is "if you're going to have sex, use a condom." (The topics of AIDS, safe sex, and the role of condoms in preventing the spread of sexually transmitted diseases are considered in detail in Chapter 6.)

As these examples illustrate, to twist Marshall McLuhan's famous maxim, *the message is the miracle.* Or, as Madison Avenue has known for years, packaging is everything. Homosexuality, unlike abortion or contraception, has yet to find the right message—one that can, in turn, be effectively packaged.

But how can homosexuality be packaged? This complex question admits no easy answers. Many justifications (both reasonable and asinine) have been advanced for destigmatizing homosexual behaviors and granting acceptance to those who practice them, including the right to privacy, the prevalence of artistic genius (from Michelangelo to Mapplethorpe), the necessity of nonprocreating aunts and uncles whose lack of offspring frees them to tend to their nieces and nephews, the observation that many other animals display homosexual behaviors, because homosexuals "can't help it, it's their biological nature," or simply because it's the right thing to do. Unfortunately, none of these reasons, excuses, or theories has managed to place homosexuality on an equal footing with heterosexuality.

And what of the future? Despite recent (limited) advances toward the goal of securing equal rights for all Americans, there is little cause for celebration. Many Americans oppose the establishment of guarantees protecting gay rights at either the state or national level. It sometimes seems as though the American ideal of equality and justice for all is being held hostage in a dark backroom, somewhere in Washington, D.C. Perhaps what is necessary—the ransom as it were—is a message or a package with a novel and compelling economic incentive. The more homosexuality, the fewer welfare kids, or some such nonsense.

The Marketing of Sexual Pleasure

Sexual pleasure is a tradeable and marketable commodity. This conclusion is neither startling nor novel, nor even limited to humans (bonobos, for example, often use sex as a form of barter[21]). However, the implications of the marketability of sexual pleasure are seldom considered.[22] For instance, what is a "fair price" for sex? And how does the marketability of sex affect the complex negotiations of courtship and marriage? Is sex bartered equally by men and women, or is there some kind of trade-off? If unequal, who does the trade in sexual pleasure benefit more?

The sale of sexual pleasure and the exchange of sex for instrumental gain are evident in both explicit and implicit forms, as exemplified by prostitution and marriage, respectively.[*23] In prostitution (both male and female), a contractual arrangement is negotiated whereby sex is exchanged for financial or other considerations. In marriage, the exchange is obviously more subtle, and in most cases is entirely free of sexual exchange (such as marriages entered into freely by individuals of equal social standing). That other forms of marriage are less free is perhaps an incidental component of the manner in which primates (humans included) form social groups and relationships.

More generally, marriage has been conceptualized as a socially sanctioned, private, relationship wherein men gain exclusive rights to impregnate women, and women gain economic stability and familial status.[24] These characteristics of marriage are necessary, in part, to ensure social continuity through the smooth transition of property ownership between generations. Marriage creates legitimate heirs both literally (via sex) and figuratively (by providing a criterion upon which the concept of "legitimacy" can be based). That is, marriage provides a mechanism to ensure paternity, hence legitimacy (maternity is obvious, as reflected in the old saw, "mother's baby, father's maybe"). And what better way to ensure paternity than to insist on sexual exclusivity (monogamy) as an integral component of the marital arrangement?*[25] Thus, the conditions of marriage—viewed as a regulator of sexuality—are generally responsive to naturally occurring problems within the social and physical environment, many of which concern reproductive issues.

However, we wish to extend this observation and argue further that sexual pleasure per se is and always has been highly valued, independent of its role in encouraging penile-vaginal intercourse (which ipso facto, often results in conception), and its facilitation of social stability through marriage. In fact, its value may very well have been appreciated *prior* to the recognition of the relationship between sexual intercourse and conception, and almost certainly before the creation of contractual systems for marriage and kinship. That is, sexual pleasure was coveted and protected because it had enormous value in its own right. It is the corporeal "love which moves the sun and the other stars."[26] If this is indeed the case, this argument is easily extended to include the possibility that marriage and kinship systems arose primarily in *response* to a perceived need by men to protect their sexual "ownership" of women.

It seems reasonable to suggest that sexual pleasure was initially prized for the intense feelings it engendered. Later, the realization that sexual intercourse also had the potential to produce additional human beings transformed it into an extraordinarily powerful, and perhaps even sacred, commodity. Consequently, additional sexual regulations concerning marriage, kinship, and so on, became necessary to establish proprietary rights over, and rules for the sale and exchange of, sexual pleasure. The cross-cultural record provides ample evidence of the commerce in sexual rights. Anthropologist William Davenport observes that:

> Custodial rights over sex and reproduction in women in some societies may be regarded as forms of capital assets which can be traded and accumulated. This is notably the case in some Australian Aborigine societies . . . Wealthy men are those who, in return for services performed, have received these rights from other men. Put simply, custodial rights over sex in women, in effect, means the power to grant women in marriage, and in those societies which have very few forms of valuable capital, such rights constitute a source of power and influence. Furthermore, sexual rights in females not yet born are also recognized, and these, too, can be

traded, accumulated and inherited. Thus there is such a thing as sexual futures in these societies.[27]

When the link between sex and conception is comprehended, virginity and fertile females (daughters, sisters, wives, etc.) become obvious targets for expropriation by males. In many cultures, proof of virginity is required prior to the payment of bridewealth. Such proof is often provided in the form of a bloodied sheet, displayed shortly after the couple consummates their marriage.[28] (Evidence that virginity per se has existed as a separate commodity in Western society may be gleaned from the existence in nineteenth-century England of a two-tiered pricing system for prostitutes—one price for virgins and a much lower one for experienced women and girls.[*29])

Of course, not all cultures place a high value on premarital virginity. Anthropologist Alice Schlegel suggests that female virginity is valued in those societies in which young men can realize instrumental gain (in the form of a large dowry or inheritance, or advanced social position) through the seduction and impregnation of a nubile young woman.[30] Sexual access—virginity—is therefore commoditized, and premarital sexuality is denied to adolescent females, and by extension, to adolescent males as well.[31] This restriction of sexuality to marriage creates libidinous incentives for young men to achieve the social status and financial standing required to procure a wife (a situation that recalls, once again, Freud's suggestion that sexual sublimation drives economic advancement). (It also provides yet another rationale for the prohibition on adolescent masturbation. If sexual pleasure is a primary incentive for marriage, then masturbation—the act of self-pleasuring—can be expected to exist outside the realm of social sanctions.)

More generally, once "privatized," women become male "property," thereby creating explicit boundaries for sexual pleasure, especially as it relates to procreation. These boundaries may be considered a precursor to private property, since they establish rules for enclosure (who controls sexual resources) and exclusion (who has access to them). Such proprietary rights are invariably discriminatory, because, while men make the rules, women conceive and bear the children.

Because expropriated fertile females are often exchanged (as when daughters are sold as brides) or produce additional assets (children), a system of commercial regulations becomes necessary. In this view, the codification of marriage and kinship relationships is ultimately a consequence of the establishment of proprietary rights over sexual pleasure.

Economic theorists such as Friedrich Engels,[32] and the somewhat eccentric Charles Fourier before him,[33] also examined the relationship between private property and marriage. However, the theory expounded here differs from theirs in a number of significant ways. Engels argued that private property developed from the domestication of cattle and the commodities (including slaves) that resulted from the trading of these livestock. He also suggested that cattle and surplus commodities belonging to men were the progenitors of gender inequality. That is, prior to the privatization of property, men and women were equals, albeit within separate spheres of influence. Men ruled hunting; women ruled home. In contrast, once men became shepherds and ranchers (hence, property owners), their arrogance and avarice compelled them to assume absolute supremacy both within and outside the home. As Engels noted, "the 'savage' warrior and hunter had been content to take second place in the house, after the woman; the 'gentler' shepherd, in the arrogance of his wealth, pushed himself forward into first place and the woman down into second."[34] Thereafter, male dominance resulted in the establishment of father-rights, marriage, and monogamy, in turn producing a single family that subsequently became the basic economic unit of society.

We consider Engels' assumption of the absence of gender inequality in "primitive" peoples to be naïve, or at the very least, an extension of what Marianna Torgovnick has called the *primitive discourse* (i.e., making primitives the polar opposite of Europeans and Americans).[*35] In either case, this assumption fails to appreciate the importance of innate gender differences in power, strength, and reproductive constraints (such as pregnancy, childbirth, and so on). Because sexual pleasure is highly coveted, these inherent gender differences in power produce differential capacities for imposing sexual regulations or accumulating sexual pleasure, which in turn create further inequities.

In contrast, we presume that the hoarding and exchange of sexual pleasure (or procreative rights) *preceded* the domestication of cattle, and that gender inequality originated from innate differences in power that allowed men to regulate *all* highly valued "commodities," and thereby subjugate women. Thus, we disagree with suggestions that "sexually proprietary male psychologies are evolved solutions to the adaptive problems of male reproductive competition and potential misdirection of paternal investments in species with mistaken paternity."[36] Overall, men are bigger, stronger, and more aggressive than women. We believe that this simple observation leads to a more parsimonious hypothesis of why men are prone to, and better able to, establish proprietary rights over valued entities.

Economics 101: Sex and Economic Theory

Engels is not the only theorist whose views are relevant to the marketing and social control of human sexuality. The economic ruminations of Adam Smith, Thorstein Veblen, and Karl Marx are also pertinent to the present discussion.

We presume that the initiation of sexual regulations resulted from a complex blend of desires to protect procreative rights[37] and access to pleasure, as well as socially cooperative needs to prevent or attenuate conflicts arising from the pursuit of sexual pleasure.[38] Thus, sexual rules and traditions are institutionalized both to protect (primarily male) individual rights and to promote group harmony. However, in human societies these rules and traditions also regulate "property" (e.g., wives), "labor" (e.g., offspring), and "capital" (e.g., dowries), and are therefore extraordinarily resistant to change. Property owners clearly have a vested interest in preserving the regulations that protect their holdings, whether sexual or otherwise. These regulations generally concern the exclusive right to possess, utilize, and dispose of property, as well as to enjoy the benefits and prerogatives inherent in that right. Although we have been conditioned to regard property as a tangible entity, we are herein extending the interpretation of property (at least in a historical sense) to include a valuable experience—sexual pleasure—that is relevant to a host of other proprietary claims (e.g., inheritance).

The rationale underlying the protection of procreative rights is largely consistent with Adam Smith's belief that labor (in this case, offspring), as opposed to natural resources, is the true source of all wealth.[39] Referred to as his second great law, the Law of Population, Smith bluntly noted that "the demand for men, like that for any other commodity, necessarily regulates the production of men."[40] In this regard, sexual pleasure may be viewed as a commodity "consumed" by nearly all members of society, and its regulation viewed as an attempt to standardize the "production" and establish the "market value" of this resource. However, although we envision some resemblance between the regulation of sexual pleasure and Smith's economic perspective, we do not believe that the sexual market is driven in the same manner as the wealth of nations (i.e., individual self-interest matched in an environment of comparably motivated individuals, and so forth). On the other hand, using another Smithian metaphor, it does seem that powerful monopolies, such as the Roman Catholic Church, tribal leaders, and so on, have conspired to enforce "prices" through the imposition of restrictions on free sexual trade (e.g., rules for marriage) and to banish sexual innovation and experimentation. This conspiracy, in turn, makes it impossible for a Smithian sexual marketplace to prevail. The hypothetical Smithian marketplace would permit a more open flow of sexual pleasure, and would perhaps be propelled by mechanisms like competition, unfettered accumulation, and so forth.

There are also a number of obvious parallels between our perspective and Thorstein Veblen's theoretical framework.[41] Veblen argued that the institution of ownership began with the "ownership" of women. He suggests that women were the first object of proprietary rights because (1) men have a natural propensity toward dominance and coercion; (2) owning women provided objective evidence of the prowess of men; and (3) men had specific interests in utilizing the services of women (e.g., producing children, labor, etc.). These conclusions bear a striking resemblance to much of what has already been argued in this chapter. Where we differ from Veblen is that we believe that the desire to accumulate sexual pleasure was the original impetus to "own" women, and thereby the progenitor of the entire market system.

Finally, although we have introduced a variety of essentially capitalistic assumptions, our perspective is also consistent with selected Marxian conclusions. The reduction of sexual pleasure to a commodity, and the marketing of sexual pleasure, are both consistent with the Marxian premise of an economic basis for society. The selling of sexual pleasure might also be deemed a precursor to the selling of labor. Both represent the selling of human capabilities, and both are easily corrupted and debased. Thus, we believe that the incipient market system of sexual commodities, which includes pleasure, marriage, and kinship, is relevant to other market systems, and their consequent interpretations.[42]

Sex among the Sumerians

The long history of sex in the marketplace is well documented in ancient texts. The Sumerian epic *Gilgamesh* (circa 3000 B.C.), in particular, contains several explicit references to the exchange of sexual pleasure for financial and other forms of remuneration.[43] For example, Tablet 1, columns 2 to 6, describes a strategy, initiated by the Stalker, to bring Gilgamesh's counterpart, Enkidu, to civilization. The primary component of the Stalker's strategy is to use a temple prostitute (or love-priestess) to seduce Enkidu and entice him into the city:

> Here he is, courtesan; get ready to embrace him. Open your legs,
> show him your beauty. Do not hold back, take his wind away.

Seeing you, he will come near. Strip off your clothes so he can mount you.[44]

While the prostitute is unnamed—being identified only by her cultic role, *samhatu* and *harimtu*—it is clear that she is a priestess in the service of Ishtar, the Babylonian goddess of pleasure,[45] and the instrument through which Enkidu gains consciousness, language and identity. Evidently, sexual allure is a divine attribute, as further indicated by the remarks of the god Enki (who praises his own penis) and the goddess Ishtar (who discusses her sexual powers).[46] Clearly, if sexual pleasure is divine, then it is also valuable and likely to be highly coveted.

Another episode of interest is contained in Tablet 2, columns 1 to 3. Gilgamesh is about to enter the "bride house," apparently to insist upon his right to "deflower" the brides of his city. However, Enkidu blocks his way. They fight the "great fight," which paradoxically results in their great friendship.[*47] Entering the bride house to deflower virgins can be interpreted as having considerable meaning for our theory. Gilgamesh's "right" has obvious relevance to the value and accumulation of sexual pleasure, as well as the commoditization and ownership of sexual pleasure. In several ancient (and some more or less contemporary) societies, it is *le droit de seignor* (the right of the master) to deflower female virgins just prior to, or as a part of, the marriage ceremony or puberty rites. For example, in ancient Rome, the father-in-law of a newly married woman was accorded the right to initial intercourse with his son's wife. Similarly, among the Banaro of Papua New Guinea this perquisite is bestowed upon the father-in-law's ritual brother.[48] Since Gilgamesh was ultimately prohibited from exercising this right, perhaps Enkidu's actions symbolize an important cultural change—the assignment of sexual "ownership" rights to individual husbands, as opposed to the accumulation of such rights by clan rulers or powerful chieftains.

The story of *Gilgamesh* is not the only example of Sumerian literature with relevance to the current discussion.[*49] Ancient Sumerian marriage, which has been ingloriously characterized as "a practical arrangement in which the carefully weighed shekel counted more than love's hot desire,"[50] is described thusly in a Sumerian love song addressed to King Shu-sin by his bride:

Bridegroom, you have taken your pleasure of us, Tell our mother, she will give you delicacies, My father, he will give you gifts.[51]

We believe that the gender-based inequality in access to sexual pleasure evident in the ancient texts reflects the differential abilities (and possibly proclivities) of men and women to impose regulations and restrictions on the enjoyment of sex, and, in Marxian terms, the reproduction of the labor force.

The Sexual Barter System

Clearly, the regulation of all types of sexual pleasure is decidedly more advantageous for men than it is for women. It follows that this system originated primarily to protect male investments in the accumulation of pleasure and the protection of reproductive rights. However, it must also have had at least marginal benefits for women, because such benefits would be required to make the system work. But what did women gain from this arrangement? How did it protect *their* interests?

It is our belief that both genders are hardwired for sexual pleasure and that pleasure is an evolved mechanism that motivates people to engage in penile-vaginal intercourse, which thereby ensures the survival of the species. However, traditions, rules, and regulations now encumber sexual pleasure with myriad additional meanings that can dictate— and even overwhelm—thought and action. To strip away this confusion of meanings it might be instructive to consider sexual pleasure, for both men and women, in our distant evolutionary past. This thought experiment, it is hoped, will provide a foundation for hypothesizing sexually dimorphic "base rates" in sexual pleasure, as well as for understanding the subsequent ontogeny of sexual regulations. Ideally, this exercise would also allow us to isolate the basic properties of sexual pleasure in original man and woman from the confounding effects of culture and history.

We presume that "in the beginning" (metaphorically speaking, of course) men and women found sex pleasurable and therefore sought to consume and accumulate this commodity. However, the "Garden of Eden" was short-lived, not because of forbidden fruits, but because of different gender strategies for sexual gain. Women, because of their smaller size and limited strength, expressed their interest in sexual pleasure primarily through signs and gestures. Men, on the other hand, because of their physical advantage, often resorted to force, or more often, the threat of force. And it was this use of force, we propose, that ruined the utopian "garden." This is not to suggest that all men utilized force to gain sexual access to women. Force obviously produces resistance and noncompliance, which can diminish sexual pleasure and physically endanger the aggressor. Presumably therefore, many men also expressed their interest in sex through physical signs or gestures. (Evidence of this strategy, as well as various methods of reconciliation, is readily apparent in other primates.[52] Among chimpanzees the most prominent reconciliation behaviors are kissing and embracing, whereas genital stimulation is featured in bonobo reconciliations.)

Nevertheless, there were—and always will be—men who used force against women in the pursuit of sexual pleasure. Sexual pleasure is very satisfying, and the associated desire can seem overwhelming. Thus, we may presume that there have always been men who utilized any available means to obtain it.[*53] As a consequence, women have always had to contend with the prospect of force—and hence domination[54]—in the arena of sexual relations. (This observation is also consistent with the primate evidence.[55] Forced copulation has been reported in both the orangutan and the chimpanzee, as well, of course, as in humans.)

It is our contention that women long ago "traded" their "interests" in sexual pleasure and accepted a male-biased system for the marketing of sexual pleasure, in exchange for protection from sexually predatory males. Women were (and still are) at a number of disadvantages compared to men in their ability to protect themselves. In addition to the obvious gender disparity in physical prowess, women were also disadvantaged by their assumed role as primary caregivers to their offspring. In the past, even more so than today, the bulk of a woman's lifetime was spent either pregnant, nursing, or otherwise caring for small children. At these times women were especially vulnerable to attack by men or (other) animals. This vulnerability to assault may have motivated women to concede to any system that offered at least partial protection from sexual domination and other physical harms. Presumably, women who were protected, even if only to a limited degree, were more likely to lead a full reproductive life than were their more vulnerable contemporaries. Protection thus enhanced their survival, and the survival of their offspring.

Although marriage reduced the threat of sexual force, it by no means eliminated it. Instead, it merely constrained the class of potential perpetrators to members of two groups: husbands and "outlaws." (Curiously, the concept of marital rape—i.e., the rape of a wife by her husband—has only recently gained legal currency in Western societies.[56]) Establishing affiliations with husbands reduced the threat of violence, and thereby allowed sexual pleasure within a protected, though limited, context. Repeated sexually pleasurable experiences between wives and husbands might then have fostered a strong social bond. Furthermore, husbands—and the rest of the male society—had a vested interest in protecting their valued commodity against threats from outsiders, or from those who felt above the rules (i.e., outlaws). Hence, sexual regulations (and rituals) served common social and economic interests.[57]

As one example, we believe that social regulations regarding nudity and modesty are a direct result of the expropriation of fertile females. The "privatization" of fertile women engendered strong incentives to disguise their availability and to conceal their fertility. Clothing of the sort considered here (i.e., excluding deliberately sensual attire) deaccentuates sexual attractiveness, and also serves a variety of other functions, acting as an inhibitor, an obstacle that must be removed, a symbol of rank and status, and so forth. In small, close-knit societies merely covering the "fertile" genitals often provides a sufficient boundary or deterrent (and even this may be unnecessary when, as with the Aborigines of Australia, social sanctions forbid looking at another's genitals[58]). However, as societies grew larger and became more "modern"—thereby producing more extensive and uncertain consumer markets for fertile females—more clothing, and increasingly elaborate systems of regulations regarding female modesty, were deemed necessary.

These speculations are generally consistent with the early written record, particularly ancient Greek literature,[59] where dominance is a central theme in the portrayal of sex, especially as it relates to violence against women.[60] Rape as a means of sexual access, as well as a form of subjugation and even punishment, is evident in the literature of both ancient Greece and Rome.[61] This should come as no surprise. Women are still sexually victimized, and, according to some authorities,[62] the desire to harm and humiliate is often a precursor to male sexual arousal, particularly in the "perversions." And, in some cultures, violence *is* the norm. Among the Gusii of Kenya, for example:

> Sexual arousal occurs only in combination with hostility and antagonism. From girlhood, females are taught to encourage, and at the same time to frustrate, men, while boys are schooled to demand, and forcefully gain, sexual satisfaction. Normal intercourse has to take the form of ritualized rape if it is to provide mutual gratification.[63]

To summarize, we believe that the labyrinth of rules and regulations surrounding sexual pleasure originated in the male's desire to protect his own access to fertile females while limiting the access of competing males. This is clearly an adaptive strategy, at least as far as the males themselves are concerned. But what of females? Male stewardship, or "ownership" if you will, provided protection from harm and interloping males, and helped ensure access to water, food, shelter, and so on, for the protected woman and her offspring, thereby increasing survival rates. This strategy may thus have been adaptive for females as well.

The problem with this system, as is readily apparent today, is that although women ostensively traded their sexual rights for protection, the reality is that women were often—and still remain—essentially unprotected. Despite marriage and modesty rules, rape and sexual abuse of women are still endemic (even within marriage itself). Furthermore, in most societies the legal system for protecting women is weak and arcane. Until women obtain full and equal *political* power, their relationships—sexual and otherwise—will remain unbalanced.

This conclusion contrasts sharply with Engels' suggestion that group marriage, as allegedly practiced in several cultures, provides a means of circumventing the pernicious influences on gender equality of marriage, monogamy, and private property.[64] Group marriage—which is distinct from polygamy or loosely paired marriages—extends sexual access for both the husband and wife to the husband's brothers or wife's sisters, as well as to the husbands and wives of the brothers and sisters. Such an arrangement obviously provides greater sexual diversity and opportunities for both men and women, thereby reducing gender equalities with regard to access to sexual pleasure. However, the demands of pregnancy, childbirth, and childrearing still have the potential to produce differences along gender lines. Thus, in contrast to Engels, we do not consider group marriage a gender equalizer. We believe, instead, that increased economic and political power for women is the only way to balance (or reconcile) the proprietary power of men. This increased strength would serve as a "balance of power" to facilitate more equitable compromises between the sexes, thereby permitting women freedom of choice, aspiration, and opportunity.

Although we have emphasized the problems the current system entails for women, this is not meant to imply that it is entirely beneficial for men. Men have accepted a variety of compromises (e.g., monogamy, sexual restrictions, etc.) to facilitate this arrangement. Problems associated with the frequency of sexual relations among married couples (and the endless complaints therein) are an all-too-familiar consequence of such compromises. Two distinct accommodations to these problems have been adopted in response to male disgruntlement arising from the imposition of monogamy and other sexual restrictions: pornography and prostitution. Both offer sexual variety (vicariously in the case of pornography), and thereby permit men to reclaim a portion of that which was sacrificed—a strategy known as having one's cake and eating it too.

The Pleasures of Pornography

There are literally thousands of publications marketed in the United State whose raison d'être is to provide sexual stimulation and serve as masturbatory aids to men. Few, if any, such magazines currently exist for women. Even *Playgirl,* once envisioned as the female counterpart to the immensely successful men's magazine, *Playboy,* no longer features extensive male nudity; rather, it now targets a more diffuse audience, including both heterosexual women and gay men, by emphasizing fantasy rather than anatomy.*[65] Indeed, the most sexually exciting material consumed by most women is the so-called romance novel. As feminist writer Ann Barr Snitow observes:

> How different is the pornography for women, in which sex is bathed in romance, diffused, always implied rather than enacted at all. This pornography is the Harlequin romance.*[66]

Although these novels fulfill a fantasy function much like men's magazines, they are nonetheless marketed as basically innocent—the sex being clearly secondary to, and necessarily accompanied by, love. And unlike the pornographic books bought by men, these novels are not intended to provoke, or accompany, female masturbation. In stark contrast, there can be little doubt as to the subject matter—or function—of a publication titled *Screw, Big Brown Jugs,* or *Stud.* We believe that this discrepancy in the availability and marketing of sexual materials reflects underlying gender inequities arising from the manner in which sexual pleasure is both regulated and experienced by men and women. Thus, disparate factors such as the historically limited social acceptability of pornography for women, as well as men's greater sexual responsiveness to visual stimuli, must ultimately be taken into account.

This issue is, of course, more complicated than it initially appears. While it is easy to castigate the pornography industry for exhibiting a callous disregard for women, the economic implications of this charge are often overlooked. Pornography is produced and marketed in a particular way because it serves a particular clientele, and satisfies a particular need. Pornography is intended primarily for men as an adjunct to masturbation. To rail against the sexism in the marketing of pornography is akin to railing against the sexism in the marketing of tampons. They, too, are designed for a particular purpose, with a particular gender in mind.

The pornography industry, like all industries, is in the business of making money. Pornography makes a lot of money—from *Playboy* magazine to XXX videos. This industry would obviously produce, and capitalize upon, pornography *for* women as well, if a demand existed. Although some heterosexual couples rent X-rated videos to watch together as a prelude to sex, the eroticism depicted therein primarily targets the male libido; unlike men, women seldom rent pornographic videos for solo viewing. (Several companies now market "softcore" videos designed to appeal to women. The sex in these videos is more romantic and discrete [no genital close-ups, for example], and the plot and fantasy elements are better elaborated than they are in male-oriented pornography. Nevertheless, it is clear that these videos are intended to be watched by couples, rather than viewed solo.)

According to Lillian Faderman, author of *Odd Girls and Twilight Lovers: A History of Lesbian Life in Twentieth Century America,* several lesbian film companies emerged in the 1980s, indicating curiosity at the very least, if not actual demand.[67] However, the emphasis of these films was often sexual empowerment as much as sex itself:

> Sheer sleaze was less an express value in lesbian porno films than promoting lesbian sexual freedom to explore. . . . Generally the lesbian film companies emphasized the erotic rather than the pornographic. Lavender Blue Productions, for example, produced *Where There's Smoke* in 1986, in which the sex is even politically correct: two women drink tea and have gentle conversation before they make love orally, with soft guitar music in the background.[68]

Faderman suggests that interest in lesbian porn faded quickly because it "could not escape from the influence of interpersonal values that have been considered characteristically feminine."[69] In her opinion, the lesbian pornography of the 1970s and 1980s was basically an experiment by "sexual radicals" to remold themselves in the image of men.[*70]

Overall, then, it would appear that there simply isn't the interest, need, or motivation among *most* women to consume pornographic material.[*71] And, in the absence of demand, there is no supply. The industry has certainly tried, but past efforts (including *Playgirl* magazine) have failed to make a significant impact.[72] Hence, the industry continues to target the market it has (men), in a manner that appeals to its audience (explicit sex).

Furthermore, although the pornography industry was initially dominated by men, women are no longer an invisible entity, whether behind the camera, or behind a desk in an executive office. On the other hand, the women who appear in pornography are nearly uniformly maligned as completely lacking in morals, sexual and otherwise. Or, if not maligned, they are presumed to be the hapless victims of male svengalis who have robbed them of their free will and forced them into a life of "degradation."[73]

The prevalence of pornography is readily explicable within the theoretical framework proposed here. As suggested throughout this chapter, sexual pleasure is regulated for a variety of reasons—from the protection of property and assets, to the enhancement of power and status. Many of these regulations involve limiting sexual access, and in such situations people will desire alternative outlets for sexual expression. For a variety of reasons, both biological and cultural, men and women generally seek different kinds of outlets. Men, according to the written (and pictorial) record, favor sexual outlets that involve overt visual cues and direct genital stimulation, culminating in orgasm. If volitional sexual partners are unavailable (for whatever reason), men select contractual sexual partners (e.g., prostitutes) or employ fantasy-evoking sexual stimuli (such as pornography) to accompany and facilitate masturbation.

The primary function of pornography is to provide a graphic prompt to the sexual fantasies that initiate or accompany male masturbation. Because men often fantasize about women they don't know personally,[74] pornographic fantasies permit the viewer to have sex with a variety of sexual partners, if only vicariously. If it is true, as some have suggested, that sexual variety is a biological imperative for men,[*75] then pornography renders a vital service to the institution of monogamy by permitting men to engage in numerous fantasy affairs without actually committing adultery. Pornography has also been employed as a therapeutic aid to improve the sex lives of married (and other long-term) couples through the introduction of a fantasy element. Furthermore, it should be remembered that masturbation remains a valid and valued sexual outlet for many people. Incidentally, it is also safe sex (more on this in Chapter 6).

Society derives a number of indirect benefits from pornography as well. For one, pornographic narratives and images constitute an archival record of the forms and functions of human sexuality in past and contemporary societies. Nearly everything known about the history of human sexuality—which ultimately provides the foundation for sexual knowledge in general—arises from the study of surviving pictorial or written pornography, dating back to the ancient Greeks and Sumerians.

Pornography also serves a didactic purpose: It teaches sexual anatomy and functioning to sexually maturing members of a species (*Homo sapiens*) that has repressively privatized the genitals and all forms of sexual expression. Clothed, or groping through the night, people have little opportunity to learn about sex through direct observation. This is due, in part, to the placement and structure of the female genitals, which make them difficult to observe casually, by either sex, in either sexual or nonsexual situations.[*76]

The circumstances under which people become educated about human sexuality stand in sharp contrast to the manner in which they typically learn about other important human characteristics and behaviors. Generally, children (and to a lesser extent, adults) learn by observation and imitation. However, where the mechanics of sex are concerned, this usually is not an option. Thus, drawings, paintings, pictures, and movies that detail sexual anatomy and sexual functioning are an important component of the inductive process whereby people, especially boys and men, learn about sex.[*77] Even the most ludicrous X-rated story line (and accompanying acrobatic action) has some instructional value.[*78] Whatever amusement (or disdain) is evoked provides an opportunity, and a framework, for examining personal attitudes toward the expressions of sexuality depicted on the screen.

Lastly, some pornography has significant aesthetic value. But, because of pornography's explicit power and novelty, it is often difficult to evaluate its aesthetic worth, or even to distinguish the pornographic from the nonpornographic. Our mistakes, however, can be quite illuminating. We need only recall that James Joyce's *Ulysses* was deemed obscene in this country to appreciate the vagaries of defining what is pornographic. Likewise, Henry Miller (*Tropic of Capricorn*), D. H. Lawrence (*Lady Chatterley's Lover*), and Vladimir Nabokov (*Lolita*) have all been subjected to censorship by the United States' archaic obscenity laws. That such literary lions as these have suffered the slings and arrows of literary censorship highlights the temporal situatedness of obscenity determinations and suggests caution in applying the noxious epithet "obscenity" to contemporary works of art and literature. (This issue is addressed in considerable detail in Chapter 7.)

On the other hand, we certainly do not mean to imply that every type or example of pornography is worthwhile—especially if it contains elements that obviate or obfuscate its sexual value. Violence in pornography (the real kind, as opposed to benign bondage fantasies) and criminally punishable activities (such as adult-child sex) debase the sexual relevance of the material, as well as the actors and actresses themselves. Like art, the value or worthlessness of pornography is ultimately a function of its purpose, design, and execution; it is not inherent in the genre itself. In the immoderate words of Camille Paglia:

> Is pornography art? Yes . . . Pornography is human imagination in
> tense theatrical action . . . [it] makes many wellmeaning people
> uncomfortable because it isolates the voyeuristic element present in
> all art, and especially cinema.[79]

It appears that pornography, like beauty, resides in the eye of the beholder. However, the protection of pornography as a form of free speech
is another matter entirely (see Chapter 7).

The same is true, in many ways, of prostitution. While the sale of
sex may occasionally involve coercion, humiliation, and other forms of
physical and emotional violence that degrade and harm the prostitute,[*80]
there is nothing *inherently* damaging in the practice of prostitution. Indeed, given the ubiquity of prostitution across cultures and historical
epochs, it is even possible that the good outweighs the bad where the
sale of sex is concerned.

The Pleasures of Prostitution

Social acceptance of prostitution has varied widely throughout history, between cultures, and within societies. The *hetairai* (courtesans) of
ancient Greece were an integral and highly respected component of the
female triumvirate that provided for the every need, desire, and whim of
the male citizenry:

> We have hetairai for our pleasure, concubines for our daily needs,
> and wives to give us legitimate children and look after the house-
> keeping.[*81]

And if courtesans, concubines, and even wives, proved insufficient to
satisfy his lusts, a Greek citizen could visit a local brothel or solicit the
attentions of a streetwalking prostitute. The ubiquity of saleable sex is
reflected in the following Greek epigram:

> *Rose-girl, rose of a girl, tell me:*
> *What will you sell me?*
> *Yourself?*
>   *Your roses?*
>   *Or both?*[82]

Coupled with the availability of young boys, men in ancient Greek
enjoyed a veritable smorgasbord of sexual options—something for every taste and every pocketbook.

Modern American society represents the other end of the continuum, with the sale of sex banned in forty-nine of the fifty states, and heavily regulated in the fiftieth (Nevada). Despite its illegality, however, prostitution continues to flourish throughout the United States. Perhaps this should not be surprising. At one level or another prostitution has always been a significant, even if largely underground and widely denigrated, factor in American society.

During the nineteenth century, prostitution was implicitly tolerated because it protected "decent women," including wives and daughters, from unwanted sexual advances, and promoted familial stability by decreasing the impetus for men to "cheat" on their wives with unpaid, romantically available sexual partners.[83] The notion that prostitution provides a channel for sexual energies that would otherwise be directed against chaste women did not originate in the United States. Similar sentiments were expressed by theologians in medieval Europe and are cited in the pre-Christian era writings of Horace, who recommended brothels thusly: "Young men, when their veins are full of gross lust, should drop in there, rather than grind some husband's private mill."[84] Even the reverend St. Augustine acknowledged the social benefit rendered by prostitutes:

> What can be called more sordid, more void of modesty, more full of shame than prostitutes, brothels, and every evil of this kind? Yet remove prostitutes from human affairs, and you will pollute all things with lust; set them among honest matrons, and you will dishonour all things with disgrace and turpitude.[85]

The nineteenth-century philosopher, Arthur Schopenhauer, offered the complementary observation that "there are 80,000 prostitutes in London alone: and what are they if not sacrifices on the alter of monogamy?"[86] If prostitution is the world's oldest profession, then this, it would appear, is the world's oldest justification.

By the end of the nineteenth century, prostitution had become so prevalent in the United States that even Little Rock, Arkansas reportedly had nineteen brothels, and Lancaster, Pennsylvania no fewer than twenty-seven.[87] Furthermore, as historians John D'Emilio and Estelle Freedman note, the brothels served a varied clientele:

> Prostitutes were available to serve the sexual needs of men of every class and ethnic background. Fifty-cent "crib houses" catered to casual laborers who sat on wooden benches waiting for a turn so quick that they barely took down their pants. One- and two-dollar joints might attract young clerks and other white-collar workers.

Fancy parlor houses with ornate decor, racy music, and expensive liquor won the loyalty of the more economically privileged.[88]

At that time, prostitution was officially restricted to segregated "red-light" districts with names like The Tenderloin (New York), Storyville (New Orleans), and the Barbary Coast (San Francisco).[89] Over 50 percent of the men in New York City were said to frequent prostitutes, averaging three visits each per week.[90] Progressive feminists of the era maintained that prostitution was the natural outcome of artificial restraints on women's social and economic activity.[91] "Low wages and poor working conditions," they argued, "practically forced women into prostitution."[92]

Whereas some feminists opposed increased regulation of prostitution because it interfered with the prostitute's ability to pursue a livelihood, others favored its complete abolition. The so-called social purity movement emerged in the latter half of the nineteenth century when women's groups, former abolitionists, temperance workers, and ministers joined forces in opposition to prostitution, public immorality, and especially the double standard that held women to an ideal of purity, even as men enjoyed considerable freedom to satisfy their "animal lusts," principally with prostitutes.[93] In addition, growing concern about the detrimental effects of venereal diseases such as syphilis and gonorrhea led many members of the medical profession to campaign vocally for the prohibition of prostitution under the banner of "social hygiene,"[94] with the result that by World War I prostitution had been declared illegal in most U.S. jurisdictions.[95] However, the net effect of this legislation was largely to decentralize prostitution and to drive it underground, facilitating a linkage to organized crime. As John Burnham summarizes, after the turn of the century:

> In city after city so-called "vice commissions" . . . investigated and recommended that the universal system of toleration give way to repression. The spontaneity with which the segregated [red-light] districts disappeared in the years around 1910 is truly remarkable. Beyond the roles of municipal reform, feminist agitation, the purity crusade, and the white slavery scare, social hygiene propaganda was the vital factor in the demise of the old order.[96]

Although both the American antiprostitution campaign and its contemporary English counterpart were more successful in displacing than eliminating prostitution, the sexually repressive environments they reflected and sustained were evident in increased legislation against pornography and nonprocreative sexuality, as discussed further in Chapter 7. In a review of this tumultuous period, feminist writer Judith Walkowitz observes:

> These then are the historical links between feminism and repressive crusades against prostitution, pornography, and homosexuality. Begun as a libertarian struggle against the state sanction of male vice, the repeal campaign helped to spawn a hydra-headed assault against sexual deviation of all kinds.[97]

In England, for example, concerns over an alleged "white slave trade" in young women impelled passage of the Criminal Law Amendment of 1885, which raised the age of consent for girls from thirteen to sixteen, but also outlawed consensual sex between adult men, thereby providing a legal foundation for subsequent antihomosexual prosecutions.[98]

Given the ubiquity and perseverance of prostitution in the face of periodically strenuous efforts by law enforcement officials to eradicate it, it is natural to wonder if it wouldn't be better to simply end the hypocrisy and decriminalize sexual commerce. Why should it matter if cold hard cash (or warm soft plastic) exchanges hands? Doesn't "dinner and a movie" amount to essentially the same thing? As former madam Polly Adler wryly observes in *A House Is Not a Home*:

> The women who take husbands not out of love but out of greed, to get their bills paid, to get a fine house and clothes and jewels; the women who marry to get out of a tiresome job, or to get away from disagreeable relatives, or to avoid being called an old maid— these are whores in everything but name. The only difference between them and my girls is that my girls give a man his money's worth.[99]

Among the most original arguments for the legalization or decriminalization of prostitution[*100] is the "maximin" analysis advanced by legal scholar David Richards.[101] The philosophical (i.e., ethical) foundation of Richards' argument for the decriminalization of prostitution is the belief that the basic principles of justice should be established by the "maximin strategy," which seeks to "maximize the minimum condition, so that if a person were born into the worst possible situation of life allowed by the adopted moral principles, he would still be better off than he would be in the worst situation allowed by other principles."[102]

When applied to the question of prostitution, the maximin argument assumes the following form. Because economic incentives are clearly the primary impetus that drives women (and to a lesser extent, men) to become prostitutes, and since people have no control over the economic circumstances into which they are born, anyone—through no fault of their own—could find themselves so economically disadvantaged that prostitution appeared the most attractive of the limited economic options available to them.[*103] It follows that society has an ethical obligation to treat prostitutes no worse than any one of us would expect to be treated under similar circumstances. According to Richards, this obligation includes, at the very least, decriminalization.[*104]

Men seek prostitutes (both male and female) for a number of reasons. The main reasons, no doubt, are availability and convenience. Prostitutes provide a coveted service in exchange for an easily quantified and readily obtained commodity: money. Economically, it may be less expensive for a man to pay for sex than to expend the time, energy—and yes, money—required to obtain it "for free." (It may also be less risky for men who are married or otherwise attached to visit a prostitute than to have an affair.) Perhaps prostitution provides a close enough approximation to the pleasures of freely given sex, in some cases. Of course, the closeness of the approximation depends on the individual's valuation of such elements as desire, exclusiveness, and intimacy. For many men, the contractual and nonexclusive nature of the prostitute-customer relationship minimizes the appeal of this type of sexual encounter. For others, these issues are less important, or are conceptualized or compartmentalized differently—indeed, the illicitness and anonymity of the encounter can even be a turn-on. In any case, the principal intent of prostitution is to approximate the characteristics of (or offer alternatives to) volitional sexual encounters. Obviously, the market value of prostitution is enhanced in proportion to its ability to serve as a reasonable substitute for an unavailable commodity in the sexual marketplace. If oral-genital sex, for example, is unavailable or highly restricted in the "free" sexual market (including marriage), then the unsatisfied demand will inflate the worth of this practice in the commercial sex marketplace. Indeed, this appeared to be the case for fellatio, circa 1970: "Every married guy who comes in here wants to stick it in my mouth because their wives won't let them."[105] Thus, in some sense, prostitution provides a natural counterweight to society's repression of sex. Where religious strictures or other forms of repression dominate, prostitution can be expected to flourish.

It sometimes seems that prostitution concerns power nearly as much as it does sex. The power to decide who has sex, and what kind, and under what circumstances, is no less a prerogative of the prostitute than it is of the Church. Female prostitution serves both as an emblem of the economic and status differentials that exist between the genders, and as a subtle mechanism for ever so slightly evening the scales. As sexual iconoclast Camille Paglia suggests:

> Prostitution is not just a service industry, mopping up the overflow of male demand, which always exceeds female supply. Prostitution testifies to the amoral power struggle of sex, which religion has never been able to stop.[106]

That religion is incapable of restraining the powerful forces of sexual pleasure should come as no surprise. Sexual pleasure, in and of itself, is an extremely valuable commodity, and is marketed accordingly. It is used and abused, traded, bought, and sold. It lies at the center of procreative rights, inheritance, and the modern family. In short, it is one of most cataclysmically compelling forces in nature. It is no wonder, then, that efforts to restrict sexual pleasure are continually renewed, but invariably fail.

But *why* is sexual pleasure such a powerful impetus? So powerful that men and women alike will brave otherwise daunting restrictions and obstacles (including sexually transmitted diseases, such as AIDS) in order to obtain it? Is the pursuit of sexual pleasure in our blood? Our brains? Our very nature? In the next chapter we consider such questions, as we examine in detail the biology of sexual pleasure.

4.

The Biology of Sexual Pleasure

Ultimately, the foundations of human sexual pleasure *must be* biological, regardless of the triviality or momentousness of cultural influences. To give just one example, penile erection is evident in the male fetus by the thirty-eighth week in utero, long before cultural conditioning could have a significant effect. Even more suggestive is the existence of the clitoris, an organ whose sole function is to provide pleasure. Like the penis, the clitoris makes its anatomical debut well before birth.

Physiological specialization for pleasure is especially evident in orgasm. One might argue that male orgasm is subservient to ejaculation, and thereby satisfies a reproductive purpose. But why then do women orgasm as well? Women can certainly ovulate and conceive without it. Moreover, women seem to achieve orgasm more readily during clitoral masturbation and oral-genital sex than during vaginal penetration. This implies that female orgasm is relatively *less* common during reproductive sexual activities. So, if not pleasure, what is its purpose? Finally, there is "phantom orgasm," a phenomenon experienced by some men with spinal cord injuries. Does phantom orgasm merely signal a remembrance of things past,[*1] or is it an evocation of a hardwired neural process?

Although physiology lays the biological foundation for sexual functioning, learning, culture, and other environmental influences determine the manner in which humans ultimately experience and express their sexuality. There is enormous variability in the experience of pleasure, much of which arises from disparate cultural norms and expectations, particularly in regard to gender differences in human sexual behavior.

Superficially, men seem to enjoy sex more than women, or at the very least, they appear to want it more often. Is this due to neural wiring, or to cultural withering? (Or perhaps what *counts* as sex is itself gender dependent.) The enormous cultural variability in erotic stimuli (e.g., breasts, buttocks, nylon stockings), and preferred pleasurable outlets (e.g., penile-vaginal intercourse, oral-genital and anal sex) also testify to the importance of the environment in shaping human sexuality.

The cross-cultural record is replete with examples that challenge the strong version of physiological determinism (i.e., the claim that biology is destiny). For instance, if homosexuality is hardwired, and thus physiologically determined, it should be a relatively stable personality characteristic. This, however, is not always the case.*2 One might argue that although social sanctions against homosexuality might cause what *appear* to be instabilities or reversals in sexual orientation, one's "true" orientation remains fixed in a physiologically determined mold. But even then, how does one explain ritualized homosexuality in Melanesia, wherein *all* males, as a cultural norm, go through a homosexual initiation period? Or, for that matter, how is same-sex erotic play among heterosexual adolescents in Western cultures explained? Immaturity? A walk on the wild side? Finally, how does one explain bisexuality? Is it a reinstatement of the polymorphous perversity of childhood? Confused homosexuality? Or what?*3

As a first step in considering such issues, we shall examine the biological basis of sexual pleasure and its relevance to procreation. It is important to notice at the outset that pleasure and reproduction are distinct even at the physiological level. Infertile males and females do not experience diminished physiological sensations of sexual pleasure solely as a function of their infertility. In fact, following vasectomy, many men experience increased sexual pleasure and a greater desire for sexual intercourse.4 Even castrated men on effective androgen replacement therapy usually have normal sexual interests, despite their inability to reproduce.*5 The same is true of people with 46,XY-syndrome, a rare chromosomal abnormality that results in an insensitivity to masculinizing hormones, which renders these genetic males developmentally female. As a final example, prepubescent children are capable of orgasm (hence, pleasure) but not reproduction. Thus, it is readily apparent that sexual desire and pleasure persist in the absence of reproductive capacity.

But what is the basis for this experience of pleasure? The genitals obviously play a central role, as does the brain. For many people, the breasts, anus, mouth, lips, ears, thighs, fingers, and toes—among other body parts—also function as erogenous zones, and are thereby implicated in sexual pleasure. As men and women approach orgasm, the muscles of the arms, legs, back, feet, face, and hands—in short, the entire body—tighten to the point of cramping, the toes curl, and the face distorts in a wild expression of animality. It is virtually impossible to separate those parts of the body that participate in sexual pleasure from those that don't. The whole of the body and the mind are involved, particularly in orgasm.

A Body Made for Sin

If people are asked what physical aspect of sex they enjoy most, their responses fall into two broad classes. For some, climax provides the ultimate pleasure, while for others the extended buildup of excitation brought about by rubbing, fondling, and romancing is the most enjoyable part. Clearly, these two aspects, fore-pleasure and orgasmic pleasure, are not inseparable. Many women never achieve orgasm. Furthermore, it is certainly possible to voluntarily forego the climax to an extended session of sustained fore-pleasure, although folk mythology (and many experts) suggest that orgasmic denial increases irritability and frustration. Indeed, it was not until 1917 that the American Medical Association passed an official resolution declaring that sexual abstinence was *not* detrimental to health.[6] In contrast, Tantric monks believed that sexual excitement and fore-pleasure signaled the presence of the divine, and therefore denied themselves release, prolonging the precedent pleasures for as long as possible.[7]

But what really *is* orgasm? Is it physiological, psychological, or some combination thereof? Given the importance of fantasy in eliciting orgasm in some men and women, and of direct genital stimulation for others, the most parsimonious explanation follows the path of least resistance: orgasm, it appears, is a complex melding of physiological and psychological components into what is commonly experienced as a unified whole. Less ethereally, at the physiological level orgasm is an "explosive discharge of accumulated neuromuscular tensions."[8] Psychologically, orgasm may be experienced as a loss of self or denial of the ego, and is often described in terms usually reserved for altered states of consciousness; thus, at orgasm, "time stands still," "all thought ceases," "the universe is one," and so on.

With regard to the physiology of the male orgasm, Krafft-Ebing said it best over 100 years ago:

The sexual act is accompanied by a pleasurable feeling, which, in the male, is evoked by the passage of semen through the ejaculation ducts to the urethra, in consequence of the sensory stimulation of the genitals. This pleasurable sensation occurs earlier in the male than in the female, grows rapidly in intensity up to the moment of commencing ejaculation, reaches its acme in the instant of free emission, and disappears quickly after the ejaculation. In the female the pleasurable feeling occurs later and comes on more slowly, and generally outlasts the act of ejaculation.[9]

Though somewhat dated, this description is essentially correct in its particulars, although what he meant by "outlasts the act of ejaculation" is anybody's guess.

The extreme tension that builds up in men and women prior to orgasm has psychological as well as neuromuscular components, and may also have additional physiological correlates. The psychological aspects of preorgasmic sexual tension are no doubt familiar to anyone who is, or was at one time, a teenager. Psychosexual tension is readily transformed into frustration. According to Freud, mounting sexual tension "soon passes over into the most obvious unpleasure if it cannot be met with a further accession of pleasure."[10] To Freud, psychosexual tension is an ever-escalating force that, like a runaway train, is either derailed, causing extreme discomfort and frustration, or quickly reaches its ultimate destination, orgasm. Freud even proposed a hormonal explanation for the buildup of sexual tension as an alternative to the "widespread hypothesis that the accumulation of the sexual substances creates and maintains sexual tension."[11]

One such hypothesis holds that the build-up of seminal fluids in the prostate is the source of the tension that men feel prior to the release provided by ejaculation. As a corollary, some have even proposed that the intensity of orgasm varies in proportion to the quantity of ejaculate. For example, Masters and Johnson suggest that:

A larger ejaculate volume may account in part for the male's relatively greater pleasure in an initial ejaculatory episode after a significant period of continence than in a repeated orgasmic experience at the termination of his first refractory period.[12]

A more direct explanation, and one equally in keeping with subjective experience, is that intensity varies with tension itself: the greater the psychological tension, the better the orgasm. One implication of this theory, if true, is that condoms—which are nearly universally denigrated as reducing fore-pleasure (see Chapter 6)—might also heighten orgasmic pleasure for both partners, to the extent that they prolong sex and thereby increase psychosexual tensions.

Whatever Freud's insights into male sexual psychophysiology, his theories of female sexuality fall wide of the mark in a number of respects. Perhaps his most egregious error was insisting that the clitoral focus of the sexual activities of young girls must accede to vaginal (read "reproductive") dominance in maturity:

> The clitoris in the girl, moreover, is in every way equivalent during childhood to the penis; it is a region of especial excitability in which auto-erotic satisfaction is achieved. The transition to womanhood very much depends upon the early and complete relegation of this sensitivity from the clitoris over to the vaginal orifice. In those women who are sexually anesthetic, as it is called, it is because the clitoris has stubbornly retained this sensitivity.[13]

Thus, in Freud's view, women are expected to gain primary pleasure from vaginal intercourse rather that clitoral stimulation. Those who are unable to reach vaginal orgasm are considered "anesthetic," while women who continue to enjoy clitoral stimulation are "fixated" at a childhood stage of sexual development, although, according to Freud, even in mature women the clitoris "still retains a function: the task, namely, of transmitting the excitation to the adjacent female sexual parts, just as—to use a simile—pine shavings can be kindled to set a log of harder wood on fire."[14]

Once again, the pernicious effects of a procreative bias are readily apparent. As Freud was well aware, evolution is badly served by a sexual anatomy that ordains the clitoris the center of female sexual pleasure; therefore, he hypothesized a transfer of sensitivity to the vagina. However, the truth of the matter is that Freud was simply wrong. As demonstrated by Kinsey and his associates, many if not most women are vaginally "anesthetic" and require stimulation of the clitoris or labia to reach orgasm.[15] Masters and Johnson subsequently suggested that all vaginal orgasms were in fact illusory, and that female orgasm during intercourse, when it occurred, resulted not from vaginal sensitivity, but from the indirect stimulation of the clitoris.[16] In the early 1980s, however, the debate over the status of the purely vaginal orgasm was rejoined when researchers reported the discovery, in some women, of a small region on the innermost third of the vaginal wall—the G-spot—the stimulation of which allegedly brought these women to immediate climax.[*17]

Of course, not all women are orgasmic. But does this mean that some women are incapable of orgasm, or simply that they have yet to find the right circumstances, stimuli, or partners? The evidence is far from conclusive, but our guess is the capacity for orgasm is a human (and possibly primate) universal. Reportedly, in certain Polynesian societies (such as the Mangaia—see Chapter 5), *all* women are orgasmic, apparently because their male partners are knowledgeable, skilled, and patient.[18] In America, the repression of female sexuality, especially nonprocreative sexuality, has resulted in widespread inhibition and guilt, and a concomitant inability to reach orgasm.[*19] G-spot or no, penile-vaginal intercourse is usually a far less effective means of bringing about orgasm than is direct clitoral stimulation, whether manual or oral. Many women who are unable to reach orgasm during intercourse regularly climax from clitoral masturbation.

From an evolutionary standpoint, the existence of female orgasm presents a bit of a puzzle. Although clitoral (and to a lesser extent, vaginal) pleasure provides an incentive for women to engage in intercourse, and is thus clearly adaptive, the function of female orgasm is not nearly so obvious. (In men, orgasm is a correlate of ejaculation; it provides the ultimate reward for successful emission—see Chapter 2.) Naturally, a number of theories have been advanced to explain the existence of female orgasm. One of the most popular, the "pair-bonding hypothesis," has already been mentioned in Chapter 2. According to this theory, orgasm serves to strengthen the bond between mates. In the words of Beatrix Hamburg, a developmental psychiatrist:

> The ability of the human female to experience orgasm comparable to the male enhances the reward value for both. It maximizes the utility of sexual behavior as a potent form of interpersonal bonding.[20]

As mentioned in Chapter 2, it is highly doubtful that orgasm exists solely to promote monogamous relations; indeed, monogamy itself may be an evolutionarily recent phenomenon. Furthermore, the evidence suggests that in nonhuman primate females orgasm is unlikely to be induced by intercourse with a single male. Far from reinforcing monogamy, female orgasm may instead have evolved to entice females into mating with multiple partners in rapid succession.[21] (The utility of this "promiscuous" behavior will be discussed shortly.)

It has also been suggested that both the intrauterine contractions that accompany female orgasm and the prolonged time spent in a horizontal period during recovery from orgasm may enhance the motility of sperm toward the egg.[22] However, the evidence for these hypotheses is scant.

Finally, it is entirely plausible that, rather than being an adaptation, female orgasm is simply an accidental by-product of the existence of male orgasm.[23] According to this proposal, the clitoris is the female homologue of the male penis, and female orgasm is the analog of the male experience. (The obvious comparison is to the presence of nonfunctional nipples on men.) Evolutionary psychologist Donald Symons even goes so far as to suggest that "the ability of females to experience multiple orgasms may be an incidental effect of their inability to ejaculate,"[24] and compares multiple orgasmic capacity in women to the ability of prepubescent boys to achieve repeated orgasms (but not ejaculations).

As Symons' suggestion highlights, it is important to distinguish male orgasm from ejaculation. Although the two are often nearly coincident in time, they are nevertheless independent phenomena. Prepubescent boys, for example, are fully capable of erection and orgasm, but not the ejaculation of semen, which requires a functionally mature prostate gland. In men, spinal cord injuries, with concomitant loss of genital sensation, may abolish ejaculatory competence while sparing the capacity for orgasmic response.[25] Conversely, although erection and ejaculation can persist on a spinal reflex basis in men whose higher cord pathways have been severed, the absence of consciously felt penile sensation may preclude orgasm.[26]

Ultimately, the brain is critical to orgasm, and to sexual pleasure in general, for both men and women. The subjective experience of pleasure is dependent upon a complex interaction of mood, feelings about one's partner (and one's self), the erotic potential of the particular activity, time since last orgasm, and so forth. In other words, pleasure depends on the contents of the brain. But it also depends on the anatomy of the brain, especially the existence of specialized "pleasure centers" that register sexual enjoyment.

What's the Brain Got to Do with It?

How do humans and other animals experience sexual pleasure? Are there distinct pleasure centers in the brain?*[27] And if so, do they manifest sexual pleasure per se, or just undifferentiated, amorphous pleasure? These are among the questions about to be addressed.

Although our principal concern is human pleasure, mucking around in live human brains is a difficult task: clinically, experimentally, and ethically. We shall therefore consider, as a first step, the evidence for pleasure in other animals, particularly rodents and monkeys. Before getting started, however, several cautionary reminders are warranted.

First, we need to emphasize that the brain is a heterogeneous structure composed of many distinct functional regions. The different parts do different things, and in distinct species certain parts may be missing or, if present, may perform disparate functions, or operate in completely dissimilar ways, making cross-species comparisons difficult. One source of this variation is evolution, which has led to increasing specialization in the brains of the higher primates, especially humans. There may thus be adaptations of certain brain functions—with concomitant enlargement or reorganization of the relevant brain parts—that are apparent in one species but are not shared by others. In this way, brain size and morphology are related to evolutionarily significant information processing, storage and retrieval needs; this produces, at some level, different brains for different animals, including humans.[28] These issues should be kept in mind as we cross species boundaries from rodents, to nonhuman primates, to human beings. (A glossary of some of the more technical terms appearing in this chapter is provided in Appendix A.)

Pleasure Centers in the Brain

In the 1950s, James Olds and his colleagues set out to discover where pleasure dwells. Armed with a very fine needle electrode and some captive rats, they performed a series of experiments in which they surgically implanted an electrode into a rat's brain, and then (once the wound had healed) followed the rat as it moved about freely.[29] The placement of the electrode permitted direct stimulation of a region of the brain known as the hypothalamus and certain other midbrain nuclei, so that Olds, his colleagues, or the rat itself could electrically stimulate these parts of the brain at will. These regions were selected for this experiment because they were presumed to contain, among other things, the center for sexual processes.

Olds discovered that for the rat electrical stimulation of these neural centers was more rewarding than food. So rewarding, in fact, that a starving rat would ignore food in favor of the "pleasure of stimulating itself electrically." (Some rats stimulated their brains "more than 2,000 times per hour for twenty-four consecutive hours!"[30]) Although it's impossible for us to know what the qualitative sensations experienced by a rat or other animal (or indeed, even another human!) feel like, it certainly seems reasonable to equate the reward of electrical stimulation with pleasure, as Olds himself often did. (We should note that electrical stimulation is not *inherently* pleasurable; Olds' results pertain only to the rat's hypothalamus and related structures. Excitation of other brain regions elicits extreme pain in both rats and humans.)

But was this pleasure *sexual* pleasure? Subsequent studies provide more direct evidence of a sexual connection.[31] These studies found that electrical stimulation of a male rat's hypothalamus induced discharge of seminal fluids from the penis. Interestingly, erection did not occur, although masturbation was more likely following electrical stimulation. In contrast, copulation was no more likely, even with an estrous female.[32] This raises the important question of whether the "wiring" for sexual pleasure is different from the "wiring" for procreation (or copulation).

A similar observation pertains to male pygmy goats. Goats with lesions in a certain circumscribed region of the hypothalamus[*33] lose the ability to ejaculate but retain other noncourtship (and decidedly nondebonair) sexual behaviors, such as penis licking, scent-urination (the partially erect penis directs urine into the face, beard, and front legs), and flehmen (lip curling, following scent-urination into the mouth and nose). These three behaviors are usually prominent when goats are sexually aroused, which suggests that when copulatory behavior is blocked, sexual energy is displaced and other activities (such as penis licking) are potentiated.[34]

In summary, electrical stimulation of the hypothalamus and related structures induces seminal discharge or ejaculation, at least in the rat.[35] In contrast, *lesions* of these regions of the brain cause copulatory behavior (in rats, cats, dogs, goats, and rhesus monkeys) to disappear.[36] Not all types of sexual behavior are affected, however, suggesting that different mechanisms or locales exist for copulatory and noncopulatory sexual behavior. This is an important point: neuroanatomically, not all sexual behavior is directly concerned with reproduction.

Similar results obtain for various primate species. In squirrel monkeys, for example, electrical stimulation of certain regions of the thalamus and related brain structures elicits discharge of seminal fluid from the penis.[*37] Stimulation of a different brain region (this time in the hypothalamus) evokes penile erection and ejaculation in the macaque.[*38] According to the authors of this study, the electrically produced erections did not differ from normal monkey erections, either in the studied individual or his peers. (Paradoxically, when the electrical stimulation was brief and infrequent, it was pleasurable; however, when it was prolonged, the stimulation was aversive, and the monkey would try to escape from his constraints.)

So much for rats and monkeys. What of the comparable data for humans? Although ethical constraints prevent duplicating the often barbaric animal experiments just described, there are at least two cases in which human beings were subjected to similar treatment.[39] In one instance the subject was a male psychiatric patient, and in the other, a female epileptic. Both had electrodes inserted into their brains for "therapeutic" purposes. Although the therapeutic value of this procedure may be questioned, it did produce one interesting result: When the septal region or the amygdala (both parts of the limbic system) were electrically stimulated, these individuals reported that they experienced sexual arousal and pleasure. So much pleasure that the male patient reportedly stimulated himself as often as 1,500 times per hour. Not surprisingly, he also begged for a few more jolts just before the apparatus was put away.

Thus, the existence of neural pleasure centers in mammals ranging from rodents to humans seems fairly well established. A number of important questions remain, however. First and foremost, what is it, precisely, that activates these pleasure centers in a behaving animal (or human)? Few of us have access to a lever we can pull to gain instant gratification, so how do *we* excite these "pleasure cells"? In particular, do these cells "light up" during sex?

Unfortunately, the relevant experiments have never been performed. This leaves us facing a bit of conundrum. The problem is as follows. Sexual behavior in lower mammals, such as rats, appears to be completely governed by hormones. This is less true of primates, of course, and hormonal control is nearly absent in humans. As we've argued in preceding chapters, pleasure—not hormones—is the primary impetus for sex in humans. If pleasure has replaced hormones as the motivator for sex, so much the better. But if hormones themselves are sufficient to ensure procreative sex in lower mammals, what function is served by sexual pleasure in these animals?

One solution to this puzzle is simply to deny that rodents actually experience pleasure. The experimental evidence in animals indicates only that direct stimulation of certain brain regions elicits behavior *interpretable* as pleasure seeking. But is it *really* pleasure? And if so, is it sexual pleasure? Maybe the rewards of electrical stimulation are experienced nonsexually, despite the proximity of the pleasure centers to brain areas controlling other aspects of sexual behavior. Or perhaps these regions are never stimulated in the natural environment with the intensity of the experimental situation, so that the observed behavior is merely an artifact of the laboratory. The available evidence is much too scanty to allow us to untangle these issues, at least with regard to the animal data. In humans it certainly appears possible to elicit sexual feelings by stimulating the brain electrically. But again, this doesn't necessarily mean that these cells also respond when a person has sex, or if they do, that this constitutes pleasure. Is sexual pleasure synonymous with the firing of particular neurons? We simply don't know.

92 / With Pleasure

This brief summary essentially exhausts the available data on sex and the living human brain. Fortunately, another rich source of information exists in the form of human cadavers and the brains they contain. The problem here is obvious: Dead people can't talk. Hence, as with the animal data, the subjective aspect so crucial to understanding pleasure is lost. Nevertheless, nonliving brains do have something to tell us.

Tales Brains Tell

One of the most interesting research projects to investigate the biological bases of human sexuality is Simon LeVay's examination of a particular neuroanatomical difference between homosexual and heterosexual men.[40] This study builds upon a body of research that has demonstrated that male and female humans (and other animals) have slightly different brains. For example, male rats have fewer synapses interconnecting the neurons within the hypothalamus than do female rats. In addition, the region of the hypothalamus known as the sexually dimorphic nucleus (SDN) is five times larger in male rats than in female rats. Since the anterior hypothalamus, in conjunction with hormones, appears to govern sexual behavior in rats, the discovery that this region is sexually dimorphic (differs by sex) comes as no great surprise.

Analogous findings for humans have also been reported. Various hypothalamic nuclei have been suggested as functional homologues to the SDN in the rat, especially the four interstitial nuclei of the anterior hypothalamus, which are labeled INAH1 through INAH4. Each of INAH1, INAH2, and INAH3 has been reported to be larger in men than in women.*[41] Of course, this does not necessarily have any relevance to human *sexual* behavior. It suggests only that *gender* differences are apparent in these nuclei. Nevertheless, because related brain regions are believed relevant to sexual behavior in other species, and because these nuclei display pronounced gender differences in humans, they seem like an obvious place to expect neural disparities between gay and heterosexual men. The underlying assumption, presumably, is that the convergence in sexual object choice demonstrated by gay men and heterosexual women is due to anatomical similarities in the hypothalamus.

Based on postmortem analyses of tissue from three groups of subjects: six (presumably) heterosexual women, sixteen heterosexual men, and nineteen gay men, LeVay determined that the third interstitial nucleus of the anterior hypothalamus (INAH3) differed significantly between heterosexual men and women on the one hand, and between gay and heterosexual men on the other (no difference in size was observed for the other three nuclei). On average, INAH3 was twice as large in heterosexual men as in either homosexual men or heterosexual women. In contrast, this nucleus did not differ significantly in size between heterosexual women and gay men. From this evidence, LeVay concluded that the basis for the sexual dimorphism of INAH3 was not biological sex, as such, but sexual orientation, and therefore that "sexual orientation has a biological substrate,"[42] at least in men.

This still leaves the arrow of causality undetermined, however. Does the difference in brain structure identified by LeVay *cause* homosexuality, or is homosexual behavior in some way responsible for the size disparity in INAH3? LeVay (like many other researchers who come down firmly on the side of nature in the nature/nurture debate) suggests it's the former, that is, anatomy and physiology determine sexual orientation.

Given the controversial nature of these claims, it is probably not surprising that this study has taken a beating within the scientific community.[43] Some of the criticisms have been just, but others are unfair. It is significant, however, that LeVay's results have yet to be replicated. Neuroanatomical studies of this type are notoriously sensitive to experimental methodology, making replication all the more critical.[44]

Another important question concerns the generalizability of these results, both because of the small sample size employed, and because many of the brains—including those of all the gay men—came from men with AIDS (none of the women had AIDS). Perhaps AIDS itself was responsible for the smaller INAH3 sizes observed in the gay men (a possibility LeVay discounts because the sizes of the other three interstitial nuclei were comparable in the heterosexual and homosexual men),*[45] or maybe the mere fact that these were men who contracted AIDS distinguishes them in some critical aspect from the "average" gay man (for example, they might have been more sexually adventurous).

Although the methodological limitations of this study suggest circumspection with regard to the results obtained, it seems more productive to question how these findings—especially LeVay's contention that sexual orientation has a biological basis—fit with the other data in this area. At one level LeVay's claim is vacuous: everything we are and everything we do has a biological basis.[46] As LeVay himself acknowledges in the preface to his book, *The Sexual Brain*:

> As the last sentence of the summary of the paper, I wrote: "This finding . . . suggests that sexual orientation has a biological substrate." By that, I was implying that there are some aspects of mental life that do *not* have a biological substrate—an absurd idea.[47]

But the possible implications of this claim run deeper. The sexual dimorphisms observed by LeVay and others presumably arise quite early in life as a product of the interactions of hormones with the developing organism. Is sexual orientation, either completely or in part, also determined at this time? And is this preference for one sex over the other a permanent and intransigent aspect of one's personality? Finally, what role do cultural and environmental influences play in shaping sexual orientation? These are complex issues that go to the heart of the controversy over biological determinism.

For now, we'll leave the extreme positions in the nature/nurture debate to the more belligerently inclined. Adopting an interactionist stance, all forms of human sexual behavior, heterosexual and homosexual alike, are probably influenced by both biological and cultural factors, acting separately or in concert.[48] Attempts to separate the biological from the cultural are fraught with difficulties. Ultimately, all behavior rests on biology, even behaviors that reflect significant cultural biases and influences. And because the brain mediates sexual behaviors ranging from the simple to the intricate, it seems reasonable to expect that sexual orientation would at some level be encoded within the brain. The existence of brain regions that are dimorphic with respect to sexual orientation therefore says little about ultimate causes.

Is Homosexual a Noun?

The question that interests us is not whether biology or the environment is the greater contributor to sexual orientation, but how these influences interact in different people to produce the variability in sexual object "choice" evident throughout history, both within and across cultures. The cross-cultural study of sexuality clearly demonstrates that homosexuality is not a unitary phenomenon. However, biological approaches to sexual orientation often fail to appreciate the complexity of the concepts involved. The existence of categories labeled *heterosexuality* and *homosexuality* is seldom questioned. According to this view, people belong to one or the other of these categories (bisexuality is conveniently dismissed), and in many versions of the myth, "once a homosexual, always a homosexual."

Part of the problem is that there are no agreed upon definitions of such terms as *sexual orientation, heterosexual,* or *homosexual.* LeVay, for example, defines sexual orientation as "the direction of sexual feelings or behavior toward individuals of the opposite sex (heterosexuality), the same sex (homosexuality), or some combination of the two (bisexuality)."[49] Though an admirable effort to gain a handle on this most slippery of concepts, this definition confounds two separate issues, behavior (how one acts) and feelings (how one experiences his or her sexuality). These aspects are conceptually distinct, as suggested by the proverbial male sailor who has sex with another man after months at sea, but still maintains that he is "straight." Furthermore, as the teenager just discovering and adamantly denying that he is gay exemplifies, it is even possible to "feel" one way but perceive oneself in another. Thus, there are at least four distinct conceptualizations to consider: existentialism (homosexuality as a state of being), behaviorism (homosexual acts), self-identification (sexual identity), and sexual orientation (desire, fantasy, etc., as distinct from overt behavior). The question of the relationship among these various aspects is critical to understanding just what it is that should be explained by a biological theory of homosexuality.

To begin with, we need to decide whether *homosexual* is a concrete entity (noun), or merely a descriptor (adjective).[50] In other words, is homosexuality simply a behavior in which certain people occasionally (or consistently) engage, or does it constitute a fundamental characteristic of the self—that of *being* a homosexual? Would we even bother to recognize (or heatedly argue about) homosexuality if society did not pathologize it? In a different context, might it be merely curious, or perhaps even trivially commonplace? And if so, why do we consider it to be a unifying theme of identity? Imagine, that society had instead decided to classify people by the beer that they drink. Such a classification scheme would obviously be trivial because the resulting identities would be based upon an inessential characteristic that reveals little of substance.*[51] Similarly, perhaps homosexuality is a biological nonentity that arises as a descriptor merely because society has maligned nonprocreative sex too severely. That is, by making *homosexual behavior* taboo, society may have created *homosexuality* as a cultural entity.

Evidence that this is so may be found in the recent historical record. In the Middle Ages, homosexual acts were condemned by Christians and Jews alike as an "abomination" and a "sin against nature,"*[52] yet the performance of a homosexual act did not, in and of itself, brand the sinner as a distinct category of being. Having sex with a same-sex partner no more made one a "homosexual" than coveting a neighbor's wife made one a "coveter."[53] However, with the rise of science, and the psychiatric profession in particular, in the late eighteenth and early nineteenth centuries, homosexual behaviors became pathologized, and those who practiced them became deviants, degenerates, "inverts,"—in other words, "homosexuals."[54] As John De Cecco suggests:

It was nineteenth-century psychiatry that made homosexual behavior a mental "condition"—either love-sick or gender-sick or both—that enveloped the personality and became its core. The psychiatric name of this mythical state has endlessly changed as new variations arrived at the doctors' consulting room doors, from the original pederasty, contrary sexual feeling, psychic hermaphroditism, sexual inversion, and the lovely Italian *l'amore invertito,* to the less blatant but still pernicious sexual orientation disturbance and egodystonic homosexuality[55].

Indeed, it was not until 1869 that the German term *homosexualität* was coined for this "condition."[*56] In that year, Karl Maria Kertbeny described a "homosexual urge" that "creates in advance a direct horror of the opposite sex, and the victim of this passion finds it impossible to suppress the feeling which individuals of his own sex exercise upon him."[57] Even then, however, homosexuality was typically characterized as predominantly an inversion of gender (masculinity/femininity) rather than of sexual orientation or behavior.[58] This heightened interest in what had hitherto been a stigmatized and often criminalized behavior, but not a defining characteristic of an individual, dovetailed nicely (and certainly not coincidentally) with the nascent social purity movement, which sought to ban prostitution as a means of shoring up the family. In a review of this historical period, John Marshall observes, "the emphasis throughout (and the reason for the link between homosexuality and prostitution) is upon the regulation of male lust and the channeling of sexuality into an institutionalized pattern of 'normal' heterosexual monogamy."[59] The resultant scientific and social scrutiny to which homosexual behaviors and those who practiced them were subjected, in turn, may very well have created the modern homosexual.

All of this illustrates just how complex the issues surrounding homosexuality and sexual orientation really are. There are obviously wide variations in sexual expression, both between individuals and between cultures. Even within an individual there may be discordance between *preference,* which tends to exist as an enduring facet of one's personality (though not always), and *behavior,* which is often situationally determined. Many macho American boys, who grow into macho American men, engage in clandestine homosexual activities as adolescents. And many other men and women suddenly "discover" their "true" homosexual proclivities after years of being happily and heterosexually married:

Confessions of a false lesbian: I was married to a man when I first came out, and when I fell in love with a woman I searched my past hard and long for evidence that I had "really" "always" been a lesbian. Much more eager to prove to myself that I was a lesbian than to find evidence that I wasn't, I just couldn't say to myself, "I choose to be a lesbian." I was afraid I'd have to be straight unless I could prove I wasn't.[60]

Furthermore, the manner in which people express their sexuality is not necessarily discrete, but is instead embedded in a larger network of cultural meanings. American men who want to try something different rarely engage in same-sex relations, preferring instead to widen their heterosexual repertoires. In America, homosexual diversions are deemed inconsistent with both machismo and, in some interpretations, maleness itself.

As touched on earlier, the Sambia warriors of Papua New Guinea provide an especially striking example of the transience of "homosexuality."[61] Survival in the forbidding landscape of the New Guinea highlands necessitates that Sambia men be as strong and courageous as possible. To the Sambia, the essence of male masculinity and strength (*jerungdu*) is semen; the more semen, the more macho the man. However, because the "semen organ" is initially "solid and dry" (i.e., incapable of ejaculation), semen is thought to be absent in boys. To masculinize the boys requires some means of infusing them with semen. The Sambia solution is for young "bachelors" to act as donors, providing semen to the preadolescent boys through fellatio. In time, by swallowing adult semen, the boys become men.[*62] They can then act as donors themselves, becoming fellatees rather than fellators. Eventually, each Sambia youth finds a wife and begins raising a family (following marriage is a period of bisexual behavior that ends with the arrival of the couple's first child—all homosexual activities cease when a man becomes a father). Thus, *all* boys—who ultimately become husbands, fathers, and fierce warriors—go through a period of exclusive homosexual behavior as a necessary step on the road to manhood.

In stark contrast to the American mythology, the Sambia believe that adolescent homosexuality, and the ingestion of older men's semen, is essential to masculine development and toughness. Both boys (receptive) and men (insertive) participate in these homosexual activities, yet seldom does either have any trouble shifting to his eventual heterosexual role. The homosexual behavior of adolescence and bachelorhood is rarely continued into "adulthood" (i.e., after a man's first child is born). When it is, it typically takes the form of bisexuality, in that the sexual alliances with boys supplement heterosexual contacts with a wife and a full family life. Rarely does a man profess an exclusive preference for boys, for to do so is to invite the scorn of the entire community, and to admit weakness and a lack of *jerungdu,* making one a "rubbish man."[63]

Age-structured homosexuality also challenges a cherished American myth, that of the exclusive homosexual identity. According to this myth, a person either is or isn't a homosexual, and whatever one is, he or she is for life. In America, the alleged incongruence between having a heterosexual identity and participating in homosexual behaviors leads to the further assumption that *any* homosexual activity is, ipso facto, evidence of a homosexual identity. To Americans, it would appear, "you are *who* you do."

The Sambia are not unique in practicing ritualized homosexuality; additional examples can be found in Melanesia, Africa, and South America, as well as in the historical record.[64] Other interesting variations in culturally defined homosexual behavior include role-specialized homosexuality in which same-sex activity is permitted for people who occupy certain culturally defined roles, such as shaman or healer. In traditional North American Indian cultures, a *berdache* is a man who adopts a female gender role by acting, dressing, and assuming the social responsibilities of a woman, including, in many cases, taking a husband.[65] Though less common, some Native American women also cross gender boundaries, becoming, in effect, culturally constituted men.[66] In either case, gender-reversal is thought to be divinely inspired. According to legend, the berdache dreams of his or her eventual transformation (it is said that such dreams sometimes appear while the dreamer is still in the womb[67]). Berdache are therefore revered as powerful spiritual leaders, or shaman.

Analogous instances of gender-reversed homosexuality and identity transformations can be found on nearly every continent.[68] For, although traditional Western science usually conceptualizes gender as a simple dichotomy,[69] a distinct third gender—neither male nor female—is readily apparent in a number of cultures. The origin of the third gender is typically found in gender role reversals (as in the berdache), or in genital anomalies (such as pseudohermaphroditism). Members of the third gender represent a different gender category and are not merely gender "noise."[70] (See Chapter 5 for more on the third gender.) It should be noted, however, that because sexual behavior and assumed gender role are concordant in such cases, there is usually no homosexual stigma attached to same-sex behaviors.[71] In the case of berdache women, Evelyn Blackwood suggests that

Native Americans did not consider her sexual activity an imitation of heterosexual behavior. Her sexual behavior was recognized as lesbian—that is, as female homosexuality.[72]

Although "homosexual," this behavior remained unstigmatized because "North American ideology disassociated sexual behavior from concepts of male and female gender roles and was not concerned with the identity of the sexual partner."[73]

In some contemporary Western cultures men may take the insertive role in anal intercourse with other men without being branded a "homosexual." This is especially true in Latino (e.g., Mexico, Brazil) and Mediterranean (e.g., Greece, Turkey) cultures where masculinity and femininity are defined by specific actions and particular roles.[74] The erect, forceful inserter maintains an "active" masculine—hence heterosexual—identity, whereas the penetrated male is deemed "passive" and feminine, hence homosexual. Although Americans often view such distinctions with suspicion, "activo" and "passivo" are nonetheless significant categories in many cultures. In these cultures, inserters are often married and have children, whereas insertees are more consistently homosexual. This distinction finds further support in the historical record, particularly in ancient Greek culture, which praised "heterosexual" men who practiced insertive same-sex anal intercourse as an adjunct to their opposite-sex affairs, but condemned "homosexuals" who assumed the receptive role otherwise reserved for women.[75]

The question is, which of the many "homosexualities" are biologists trying to explain? It clearly isn't the situational homosexuality of the prisoner serving a life sentence. It might not even be the life-long homosexuality of the Freudian prototype, unable to disentangle himself from his mother's apron strings. In fact, the targets of biological explanations of sexual orientation—and especially homosexuality—are seldom specified. This uncertainty in the phenomenon being described, it seems to us, casts aspersions on the whole enterprise.

Furthermore, if homosexuality means so many different things (behavior, identity, feelings, passive/active),*[76] and if it is, at least in part, culturally constructed, then how can it also be physiologically determined (in a nontrivial way)? Perhaps there are many types of homosexuality, only a subset of which are strongly influenced by biological factors. Or maybe biology only biases the individual one way or another, with the path ultimately taken being shaped as much by cultural as by physiological influences. In either case, it is natural to expect the biological influences at work to have a genetic basis.

Designer Genes?

But what does it mean to say, for example, that homosexuality has a genetic basis? In many ways, the claim that a certain trait is genetic is vacuous. The ultimate basis for *every* trait, whether physical or behavioral, is genetics. But if the intent underlying the question, "Are there genes for trait *X*?" is not the vacuous ontological question, "Did genes play a role in the development of *X*?", then what *do* we mean when we claim that genes for a particular trait exist?

One interpretation holds that what we really mean to ask is the evolutionary question, "Was trait *X* designed by natural selection to serve some function—that is, is it an adaptation?"[77] However, this interpretation seems much too strict. When researchers report finding a "gene for Huntington's disease," for example, they certainly do not mean to imply that Huntington's disease is an adaptation ("designed," one would suppose, to debilitate people). Clearly, not every heritable condition enhances reproductive fitness. A particularly cogent example is the hereditary blood disease, sickle cell anemia. Sickle cell anemia is a homozygotic disease, meaning that a person is susceptible only if he or she inherits the same noxious form ("allele") of the gene from both parents. People who inherit only a single copy of the noxious allele (along with a copy of the "normal" allele) do not develop sickle cell anemia; such people are called *heterozygotes*.

Given the death and disease caused by the "sickle cell gene," it may seem surprising that natural selection has not eliminated it. However, this gene survives because it displays what is known as a heterozygotic advantage[78]; that is, it confers a selective advantage on heterozygotes relative to homozygotes (people who have two copies of the "normal" allele). In particular, people with one and only one copy of the noxious allele exhibit increased resistance to malaria. Thus, one copy of the sickle cell allele is better than none, but two copies can be deadly. Because of the advantage conferred upon heterozygotes, the debility caused to homozygotes is apparently tolerated by natural selection.

Although the gene responsible for sickle cell anemia susceptibility is adaptive for heterozygotes in areas where malaria is prevalent, sickle cell anemia itself is hardly adaptive. The answer to the adaptationist query, "Was trait *X* [sickle cell anemia] designed by selection to serve some function?" is therefore *no,* in contrast to the answer to the initial question, "Are there genes for trait *X* [sickle cell anemia]?" Thus, the adaptationist interpretation fails to fully capture the intended meaning.

So what do we mean when we ask whether there are genes for a trait

X? Simply this: Are there particular genes that significantly predispose one to express trait *X*? The trait in question need not be an adaptation; it could be a by-product or covariate of an adaptation, or a trait that selection pressures have yet to eliminate from the population. Questions of a possible genetic etiology for cancer, homosexuality, and so on, are usually of this nature. What we want to know is whether everybody is equally likely, from a genetic standpoint, to get cancer, or whether there are genes that predispose one to develop this disease.

In the realm of human sexuality, the most thoroughly researched genetic question concerns the etiology of homosexuality. From an evolutionary perspective, it seems unlikely that homosexuality *could* be genetically based. Because exclusive homosexuality doesn't contribute in any obvious way to the fitness of the individual and his or her genes, so the argument goes, natural selection should long ago have eliminated it as a behavioral category. This conclusion is a bit too simplistic, however, because it presumes that homosexuals *never* reproduce. In fact, in many cultures homosexuality is an age-structured behavior whose participants are expected later in life to marry and have children.[79] Even in Western societies homosexuality and reproduction are not mutually exclusive. One of history's most infamous homosexuals, Oscar Wilde, was married and had a family. Although one might suggest that he married and fathered children as a cover for his homosexuality, he was obviously *capable* of becoming sexually aroused by his wife, and thereby furthering his genes. Nevertheless, it seems reasonable to suppose that, overall, exclusively homosexual men and women would exhibit decreased fecundity. As an obvious consequence, relatively fewer children in each successive generation would carry the hypothesized homosexual-determining allele, so again, we would expect (genetically determined) homosexuality to eventually disappear.

A number of theories have been advanced to explain why homosexuality remains prevalent, despite the evolutionary obstacles. One such theory is based on the notion of heterozygotic advantage, as discussed earlier for sickle cell anemia.[80] This proposal posits the existence of two distinct alleles for the putative sexual preference gene, say allele *A* and allele *B*. A predisposition toward same-sex preferences would be expected only of *AA* homozygotes, for example, whereas heterosexuality would predominate among *BB* homozygotes and all heterozygotes (*AB*). Hence, if heterozygotes enjoyed a reproductive advantage over *BB* homozygotes, who lack the "homosexual" *A* allele, then this allele could be maintained in the population despite the limited reproductive success of (homosexual) *AA* homozygotes. One problem with this theory is that it is exceedingly doubtful that a human phenomenon as complex as sexual orientation could be determined by a single gene, or a simple combination thereof. Otherwise, this proposal appears plausible enough, although no one has yet suggested a reasonable candidate for the fitness advantage heterozygotes supposedly enjoy.

The evolutionary concept of "inclusive fitness" forms the corner-stone of another popular theory of the durability of homosexuality. The notion of inclusive fitness is predicated on two related observations.[81] The first is that the gene itself, rather than the individual as a whole, is the basic unit upon which natural selection operates.[82] Genes, in this view, are basically "selfish," and are interested only in ensuring that copies of themselves get passed along to the next generation. The second relevant observation is that siblings share roughly 50 percent of their genes with one another; that is, they have copies of about half of the same genes. Combining these observations, we see that, from the point of view of the individual gene, it hardly matters whether the copy in Person A or the one in his or her sibling gets perpetuated (assuming that the sibling shares the gene, a 50–50 proposition). In other words, it is to a person's advantage (meaning it is beneficial for his or her genes) to assist siblings to reproduce, because half of the genes that would be so propagated are shared by both individuals. It has therefore been sug-gested that homosexual aunts and uncles indirectly enhance the survival of their own genes by helping siblings raise their children.[83]

Of course, homosexuality would have to be a heritable trait in order for natural selection to influence its prevalence in the population. Several investigations of possible genetic contributions to homosexuality, includ-ing familial and twin studies, suggest that this is the case. Researchers have long noted the high concordance rates for homosexuality among identical (monozygotic) twins.[84] Statistically, the twin brother of a gay man is more likely to be gay than is the twin brother of a straight man, and similarly for lesbians and their twin sisters. The analogous results also obtain for nontwin siblings (who have half their genes in common); for instance, brothers of gay men are about four times more likely to be gay than are brothers of heterosexual men.[85] Of course, siblings—identical twins included—usually share the same familial environment, so these results cannot preclude environmental effects (and in many cases they actually support an environmental interpretation). Nevertheless, taken in aggregate these findings suggest that a tendency toward homo-sexuality is heritable, at least in part, under certain conditions.[86]

However, this type of research has a number of limitations, and there-fore caution is advised in interpreting these results. First, it is exceedingly difficult to tease apart the influences of genetic and environmental factors in the determination of complex behaviors. This task is further complicated by the existence of possible genetic-environmental interactions. One may also question whether twins, identical or otherwise, constitute a representative sample from which results can validly be extrapolated. Twins are, after all, rather rare, and are subjected to quite different environmental pressures (such as having one's individuality usurped) than are nontwin siblings. The twins who volunteer or are otherwise recruited for sexual orientation studies may not even be representative of twins taken as a whole. Finally, the most obvious shortcoming of existing studies that argue for a genetic explanation of homosexuality is the failure to locate the hypothesized "sexual orientation gene" (or genes).

X Marks the Spot

Evidence for the heritability of homosexuality does not end with the twin studies mentioned previously. Additional clues may be derived from genetic research involving that ignoble and pesty creature, the fruit fly (*Drosophila melanogaster,* to be precise). This particular species of fly enjoys an exalted status among geneticists due to its short lifespan and rapid rate of reproduction, which allow numerous generations (and the genetic transmission between them) to be studied within experimental time constraints.

In a notable series of studies, Dean Hamer, Angela Pattatucci, and their colleagues at the National Institutes of Health examined courtship patterns in *Drosophila*.[87] Courtship behavior in *Drosophila* is gender stereotypic: males do it one way, females do it another. But mature males will also court immature males. This "homosexual" courtship behavior continues until the immature males get old enough to discourage courtship attempts by producing antiaphrodisiac compounds and by actively rejecting the unsolicited advances of the older males.

Geneticists working with the fruit fly have discovered a variety of genes related to courtship behavior. More important, they have discovered a specific, genetically distinct strain of *Drosophila* that seems to prefer courtship the "homosexual" way.[88] This strain has been dubbed, somewhat tongue in cheek, the *fruitless* fly. Adult fruitless flies aggressively court other adult males, including other fruitless males, and naturally occurring, generic, "wild-type" males. (The fruitless phenotype is only expressed in males. Fruitless females behave just like their wild-type sisters.) Fruitless males will sometimes also court wild-type females, which suggests a bisexual, rather than exclusively homosexual, preference. Furthermore, the fact that fruitless males court adult males and are themselves courted by other fruitless males implies that their mating preferences cannot be attributed to sexual immaturity. These findings provide preliminary evidence for a genetic component in same-sex courtship behaviors, at least in the lowly fruit fly. And while there are monumental differences between fruit flies and people, this work provides a suggestive model for extrapolation.

Although there can never be an airtight argument "proving" that homosexuality (or heterosexuality, for that matter) is genetically determined in *humans,* the isolation of a gene (as in *Drosophila*) that is highly correlated with homosexuality would certainly strengthen existing arguments. As a first step toward isolating such a gene in humans, Hamer, Pattatucci, and colleagues performed a pedigree analysis on a group of self-identified gay men, searching for men with homosexual brothers.[89] This strategy was based on the assumption that a genetically influenced trait will tend to aggregate in families. Using this technique they identified a total of forty pairs of homosexual brothers. Next, they examined the prevalence of male homosexuality in the extended families of these forty pairs. Interestingly, they found more homosexual relatives on the *maternal* side of the family, such as maternal uncles and the sons of maternal aunts. To the trained geneticist this finding suggests the possibility that male homosexuality is a sex-linked or a recessive trait that is transmitted by the maternally contributed X chromosome.

The next task was to determine where on the X chromosome the genetic influence for sexual orientation might reside. Using sophisticated DNA mapping techniques, Hamer and colleagues were able to identify a region (designated Xq28) on the long arm of the X chromosome that was shared by thirty-three of the forty pairs of homosexual brothers. It is important to emphasize that this does not mean that the gene or genes responsible for male homosexuality have been found, if indeed they even exist.[*90] Only a region, and a candidate region at that, has been identified. Several hundred other genes also occupy this region. Hamer and his collaborators are therefore very cautious in interpreting this finding, suggesting only that they have uncovered evidence that a genetic influence may exist for a small subgroup of male homosexuals with brothers who also happen to be homosexual.

Further caution is warranted by the fact that seven pairs of homosexual brothers did *not* share the Xq28 region where the gene(s) presumably lies. Furthermore, only 13.5 percent of the original sample of homosexual men even had homosexual brothers. Although 13.5 percent is a higher rate of concordance than would be expected from chance alone (most reliable estimates place the incidence of male homosexuality at far less than the oft-cited 10 percent figure), and therefore indicates a familial influence of either genetic or environmental origin, this percentage still represents only a small minority of the sample population. Thus, even if homosexuality *is* genetically determined in the men under study, there may be millions of gay men and lesbians to whom these results do not apply. It may very well be that there are various types of homosexuality, some of which are genetic, some of which are environmental, and some of which involve a combination thereof.

Suppose for the moment that the Xq28 region of the X chromosome *is* linked to male homosexuality. Would this mean that all men possessing the identified region would necessarily be gay? Certainly not. For one thing, in the final analysis it isn't the *possession* but the *expression* of a gene that's important. Put another way, it's a long road from genotype to phenotype. Which genes get expressed, as opposed to which get inherited, can depend critically on the environment.

The importance of the environment is readily demonstrated by reptiles, such as the crocodile, in which biological sex is determined by environmental rather than chromosomal factors. In such temperature-dependent reptiles a potential for the animal to develop into either sex exists at embryogenesis, with the eventual sex determined by an as yet unknown temperature-dependent mechanism.[91] Even stranger, perhaps, are certain species of fish that maintain a bi-sexual potentiality throughout their lives, and are able to change from male to female (or vice versa) whenever the social environment favors such a transformation.[92]

These examples illustrate an important lesson about genetics: Genes unfold in particular environments that can either maximize or minimize the genetic influence. Even a trait that is predominantly determined by "nature" (genes) may require an intricate interaction with "nurture" (the environment) for its expression.[93] Furthermore, genes rarely act in isolation to influence a trait or characteristic. Most traits are oligogenically or polygenically determined, meaning that the expression of a cohesive group of genes is necessary for the trait to be realized. Even minor changes to the environment can affect large numbers of genes, and thereby have a major impact on the developing organism. Finally, genes, in and of themselves, are *never* the whole story. Genetically, humans and chimps are amazingly similar, sharing over 99 percent of the same genes. Yet, as Stephen Jay Gould notes, chimps will never be able to type, much less create, a work such as Homer's *Iliad,* something that we humans accomplished over 2,000 years ago.[94]

However, after all is said and done, a crucial question remains unanswered: If genes determine or otherwise influence human sexual orientation, how do they do so? Although, as yet, there is little firm evidence to support the claim of genetic determinism, most researchers who subscribe to a biological account of homosexuality believe that sexual orientation is determined quite early in life, through the organizational effects of perinatal hormones on the developing brain.[95]

The Hormones Made Me Do It

Genes influence human behavior indirectly, by specifying the molecular compounds called proteins and enzymes that compose and control the human body. Proteins, in turn, are assembled into tissue, which differentiates as muscle, organs, fat, and so forth. As a human fetus develops further in utero, certain of the already formed organs, such as the gonads (the testes in males and the ovaries in females), exert additional developmental influences by means of the steroidal sex hormones they produce. In this fashion, genes affect growth, maturation, and structure, the last of which, in concert with environmental constraints, ultimately determines behavior.

But how do sex hormones work? In two ways, at least. First, they exert an *organizational* or *structural* influence on the developing brain and body. Sex hormones play a critical role in the sexual differentiation of both the brain and the genitals. Evidence indicates, for example, that specific hormones regulate neuronal development and guide selective neuronal death in the fetal brain. Hormones are also instrumental in the development of the sex organs and external genitalia. These organizational influences are expressed only during brief critical periods of perinatal life. The structural effects themselves, however, are almost always permanent.

The organizational effects of sex hormones are most apparent in the role played by the masculinizing hormones known as *androgens*. In the absence of sufficient levels of prenatal androgens, the external genitalia automatically develop in a female direction, even in a genetic (XY) male.[*96] Hormones also influence the development of: (1) sexually dimorphic nuclei in the hypothalamus, (2) gender-specific patterns of synaptic connectivity in the brain, (3) gender-specific expression of genes, neurotransmitters, motor neurons (and their muscular targets), and so on. The influence of androgens extends well beyond the hypothalamus and related regions, as evidenced by the widespread distribution of androgen receptors throughout the prenatal brain.[97]

Hormones also work *activationally* in the developing and mature animal. Whereas organizational effects produce permanent structural alterations, hence exert a lasting influence on the animal even in the absence of the hormones that initiated them, activational effects require the continued presence of the hormone for full manifestation.[98] In humans, the activational effects of sex hormones include adjusting the functionality and performance of neural circuits, eliciting the changes that accompany puberty, and regulating women's menstrual cycles. In nonhuman animals, hormones also control female copulatory behavior. Activational and organizational hormonal effects are not always clearly differentiated. As a general rule, however, whereas structure is affected by organizational influences, function is affected by activational influences.*[99] A further distinction is that activational, unlike structural, influences are not limited to a critical phase of development, but are instead reversible and repeatable.

The bulk of existing scientific knowledge about the developmental and activational effects of sex hormones is due, once again, to our fine furry friend, the rat. In the basic experimental paradigm, prenatal and postnatal exposure to androgens is manipulated to study the developmental effects of these hormones. For example, castrating a male rat just after birth—so that the developmental influences of testosterone (one of several androgens) are blocked*[100]—causes various brain structures, such as the SDN, to become feminized. On the other hand, prenatal administration of androgens masculinizes genetically female rats. In either case, the adult sexual behavior of the experimentally altered rat is determined by the gender role imposed upon it by the experimental hormone manipulations rather than by its genetic sex. Thus, perinatally castrated males display the sexual behavior characteristic of females, and vice versa.

These experimental manipulations demonstrate the profound effects that sex hormones have on organizing the brain and activating sexual behavior. They are successful, in large part, because rats display gender stereotypic mating behavior. That is, following castration or the administration of sex hormones, it is relatively easy to classify the rat's sexual behavior as fitting either the male or female stereotype. Both male and female mating behaviors appear to be hormonally regulated via organizational and activational pathways. One such behavior is *lordosis* in the female rat. Lordosis is a reflexive curling of the back that exposes the female's genitals and thereby facilitates intromission by the male. Only female rats normally display lordosis, which is dependent on ovarian hormones. Without lordosis a male rat, quite literally, cannot enter a female regardless of how hard he tries. Thus, intromission is regulated by lordosis, which in turn is controlled by sex hormones. In other words, rat sex is hormonally dependent—so much so that a male rat castrated just after birth, and suffused with the predominantly female sex hormones estrogen and progesterone, will display lordosis as an adult.

But rats, fortunately, aren't people. The question is whether these findings have any particular relevance to human beings. There are obviously major differences between humans and other primates on the one hand, and lower mammals such as the rat on the other. First off, primates do not require a specific posture for sexual intercourse: hormonally controlled arched backs are not a prerequisite for primate sex. In fact, primates are often quite acrobatic in their sexual positions. There is also a wide variety of reasons humans (and to a lesser extent other primates) engage in sex: pleasure, love, conflict resolution, power, money, and so on. In light of such differences, it seems unlikely that humans should be slaves to their hormones. Nevertheless, as puberty and menopause demonstrate, humans are not entirely free of hormonal influences. So the question remains, to what extent is human sexual behavior hormonally determined?

We begin by considering the influence of hormones on sexual orientation. Until quite recently, many researchers, taking a cue from nature, believed the "cause" of homosexuality to be a simple imbalance in the relative quantities of male and female sex hormones circulating in the blood.[101] After all, a male rat that is castrated at birth and later infused with female hormones displays female stereotypical sexual patterns. Thus, in a sense, hormones make the rat "homosexual." Similarly, one might argue that the fact that some homosexual men are effeminate (by conventional standards) points to a hormonal imbalance as the "cause" of male homosexuality (similar comments apply to female homosexuality).

There are several problems with this line of reasoning. To begin with, what the castrated rat displays is female typical *mating* behavior, not an erotic emotional attraction to same-sex partners.[102] Gay men don't desire other men only for sex, but also for love, companionship, and so on. Although it is unclear what, precisely, human homosexuality really "is," it decidedly is *not* just a mating pattern. Furthermore, neither gonadectomies (removal of either the ovaries or testes) nor female menopause are reported to have any significant effect on sexual orientation. And, although some homosexuals exhibit behavioral gender nonconformity,[103] this is not necessarily indicative of crossed hormonal influences.[104] Finally, the most extensive review to date of the relevant scientific literature found no conclusive evidence linking hormone levels with sexual orientation in men*[105]; similar results have also been reported for women.[106]

The hormonal imbalance theory of homosexuality also has an unfortunate corollary. If too many female hormones or too few male hormones make a man homosexual, then it should be possible to "cure" him by repeated androgen infusions. This and similar "treatments" were tried on homosexuals in the 1940s and 1950s, with few "successes."[107] Although some homosexuals reportedly switched their sexual orientation (perhaps to avoid further hormone treatments), many later reverted to homosexuality. In any case, there was little evidence of persistent alterations in core sexual orientation.[*108]

Not only are adult hormone levels decidedly *not* the cause of homosexuality, we shall argue directly that it is this *freedom* from hormonal control that allows humans to express their sexuality in diverse ways, including homosexually. (The possibility remains that prenatal hormones exert an organizational effect that shapes adult sexual orientation through differential structuring of the brains of heterosexual and homosexual individuals. This is one avenue through which genetic influences might be expressed.[109])

Before discussing hormonal control in humans further, it might be instructive to consider our primate cousins. When studying hormonal influences in primates, it is especially important to distinguish sexual capabilities and motivation, from the act of copulation itself. Many female primates (including women) are considered to be "continuously copulable," meaning that copulation can take place anytime, not just at certain points in the estrus cycle. But this doesn't mean they are continuously *receptive* to copulatory advances. The pioneering sex researcher Frank Beach summarized the situation particularly well:

> No human female is constantly receptive . . . any man who entertains this illusion must be a very old man with a short memory or a very young man due for bitter disappointment.[110]

Although most primates, from monkeys to humans, are *capable* of copulation at almost any time, sexual interest, particularly on the female side, may be a different matter. In fact, Kim Wallen, a noted primatologist, suggests that it is *sexual motivation,* not the ability to copulate, that is under hormonal control in nonhuman primate females.[111] Unlike the female rat that can copulate only when lordosis is activated by ovarian hormones, the female primate is free to copulate anytime she pleases—the key phrase being *anytime she pleases.* Wallen argues that hormones control the female's motivation for sex, so that while she may be capable of copulation anytime, sex in practice usually occurs only during fertile periods of her estrus cycle. This, at least, appears to be the case for rhesus monkeys living in the wild, where sexual access can be restricted by limiting male proximity to females. In general, it is the female rhesus who decides when and with whom she will mate, and who initiates courtship.

But why control the desire to mate rather than mating itself? First, tying sexual interest to estrus increases the likelihood of conception. Enhancing female interest in sex obviously increases the probability of copulation because a sexually motivated female is very likely to find a mate. Moreover, if she is in estrus *and* sexually interested, both copulation and conception are rendered more likely.

The ability to copulate at will also allows sex to be co-opted for purposes other than reproduction. In many primate species sex is employed as a means of diffusing tensions and as a gesture of appeasement. This strategy is taken to the extreme, as noted before, by the bonobo and, of course, by the human being. Many primate females also mate quite "promiscuously," regardless of whether or not conception is possible at that time. This has the effect of further clouding the already murky question of paternity, should the female later bear offspring. Sarah Hrdy suggests that this strategy, known as *multimale mating,* and the doubtful paternity that ensues, is advantageous for the female and her offspring because males will bestow preferential treatment on infants that *could* be their own.[112] This preferential treatment, in turn, translates into greater survivability.

Another popular evolutionary explanation for the "loss of estrus" (i.e., the lack of strict hormonal regulation) in women proposes that freedom from restrictive cyclical sexual and reproductive patterns facilitated pair bonding by permitting year-round sexual congress, and reduced male aggressiveness and competition for females by increasing sexual availability, thereby promoting social harmony.[113]

None of this would be possible if copulation were restricted to brief intervals of female fertility, as it is in lower mammals, such as rodents. Indeed, even in the rhesus, nonfertile copulation occurs when the conditions are right, such as when a pair is isolated from the rest of the troop. As Wallen observes for captive monkeys:

> Under social circumstances where females must attract and court a sexual partner, female motivation can determine whether copulation occurs. In contrast, under circumstances where partners are provided and few behavioral alternatives exist, females may passively accommodate male initiation, or may even initiate sex even when not strongly motivated.[114]

Thus, the level of motivation required depends on the social situation, particularly the disincentives that must be overcome. In the wild, sexually interested female rhesus monkeys in search of mates experience intense aggression from other females in the group. Under most circumstances, this aggression is sufficient to prevent mating. Not so, however, for a hormonally driven female monkey that is motivated to find a mate and copulate.

Does all this sound familiar? Well it should. Wallen's hypothesis is entirely consistent with the theory proposed here: Sex and reproduction are separate and perhaps evolutionarily distinct entities. What *we* are calling sex—the pleasure, excitement, desire for sexual contact—is quite similar to Wallen's concept of sexual interest. It is the motivation for seeking sex. The drive for sex—pleasurable as it is—propels us to engage in a variety of sexual behaviors, some of them procreative (or copulatory), some of them not. Furthermore, as we have indicated in the previous chapters, we believe that one reason human sex is so extraordinarily pleasurable is to overcome the disincentives associated with reproduction (e.g., the pain and danger of childbirth, menstruation, etc.), as well as geographical and social obstacles to finding sexual partners.[*115] And, as suggested in a previous chapter, the desire to clarify paternity is an important rationale for restricting sexual access. The imposition of such restrictions can be viewed as an attempt by male-dominated societies to negate an evolutionarily successful female strategy (multimale mating) that grants women greater sexual control.

In any case, the precise nature of the relationship between hormones and sexual behavior in the human female is difficult to ascertain. The evidence for fluctuations in sexual interest with ovarian hormone levels is equivocal at best.[*116] It is clear, however, that the emancipation of sexual behavior from the tyranny of hormonal control reaches its zenith in humans. Neither the ability to copulate nor, it would appear, the desire to do so is strongly regulated in women, who are therefore free to pursue sexual pleasure when and with whom they choose, with little regard to the fecundity of the union.

Hormones also exert minimal control over male sexuality in humans. Testosterone may serve to potentiate the male sex drive (in that castration causes a decline in sexual desire in most men—an effect that is easily reversed with androgen replacement therapy[117]), but even low levels of testosterone appear sufficient to motivate sexual behaviors. If female primates are "continuously copulable," male primates are even more so, despite the possibility of small fluctuations in circulating hormone levels. On the other hand, there are many people with normal sex hormone levels who have little or no interest in sex.

This discussion suggests the further hypothesis that sexual pleasure is the human substitute for hormonal control of sexual interest in lower primates (see also Chapter 2). The clitoris, orgasm, and the positive sensations associated with genital stimulation diminish the need for hormonally regulated sexual interest in women. Women do not require the male displays of hormonally driven courtship behaviors observed in the lower primates because they have an inherent capacity to enjoy sex, and because there is such a broad range of sexually exciting stimuli (much of which is symbolic). This, of course, is true for men as well. In addition to being attracted to the nude form of the opposite sex, humans are quite capable of being aroused by written or pictorial depictions of sex.

It is not surprising that visual representations of sexual acts and the naked body are sexually arousing since they activate the same visual pathways as the "real thing." But why should *reading* erotic literature be sexually exciting as well? The answer, of course, lies in the amazing human ability to imagine situations and events, and to react as though these fantasies were tangible realities. The human psyche is thus responsible, in large part, for the almost infinitely generalizable human capacity for sexual pleasure.

Sex with the Lights Out

For reproductive sex, the sex of one's partner matters quite a bit. The appropriate partner for a woman is a man, and for a man is a woman. In fact, sex with a same-sex partner is tautologically nonreproductive. But for nonreproductive sex, the sex of one's partner really shouldn't matter. Genital stimulation is genital stimulation, regardless of the sex of the person doing the stimulating. In fact, from a purely physical standpoint, one would expect a same-sex pleasure-giver to be much more competent, since he or she has expert knowledge of what it takes to do it right. The congruence in sexes should, other things being equal, facilitate greater identification and empathy, hence greater sexual pleasure between partners. While some men may be able to intuit or learn what really pleases a woman (and vice versa), the advantage conferred by the similar anatomies of same-sex partners cannot help but increase the overall pleasurability of sexual encounters, at least in theory.

So why doesn't the devoutly heterosexual person enjoy same-sex stimulation in practice? (And likewise for homosexuals and opposite-sex stimulation?) At the neural level, it seems reasonable to suppose that all stimulation, regardless of the source, is routed to the same pleasure centers. Yet somehow the "pleasure neurons" are never activated, or if activated, the sensation of pleasure is shunted or extinguished before it reaches consciousness. If this is so, the cognitive influences that might intercede in this evaluation process become of paramount interest. Is it really possible to negate physical reality simply by closing one's eyes or turning out the lights? And if so, what does this imply about the physiological basis of sex? Does sexual fantasy provide a bridge whereby one can ignore the overt experience and merely enjoy the covert one? Or does it simply enhance the overt experience? Finally, is sexual fantasy—the desert isle and all—located in one of those tiny nuclei of the brain, or is it determined by something else?

Clearly, the ability to construct elaborate alternative realities is subject to great interpersonal variation. Some people fantasize all the time, while others seldom do. For some, fantastic images can supplant physical reality. For others, fantasy is but a poor substitute, a weak imitation of the real thing. Eyes open or eyes closed, the sex of one's partners matters greatly to the vast majority of heterosexuals and homosexuals. For most, this preference for a particular sex is a permanent and immutable aspect of their personalities.

In other instances, preferences—especially for the opposite sex—may be learned or otherwise culturally influenced. The role of learning in determining sexual preferences is a particularly important and underresearched area of inquiry. Orgasm and sexual pleasure are very powerful positive reinforcers. For instance, suppose a heterosexual woman "accidentally" has a same-sex sexual experience (or fantasy) that leads to orgasm. Would she then acknowledge a hitherto denied homosexual or bisexual interest? What if she repeated this scenario several times? Could she then "learn" homosexuality or bisexuality? What if this occurred in a society, unlike our own, that did not pathologize, stigmatize, and punish homosexuality? Might not sexual preferences be more fluid under such circumstances? (Given the "costs" of being homosexual in contemporary Western society, a powerful bias toward "learning" heterosexuality would be expected to exist, if such learning is possible.[*118])

These comments serve to reemphasize the fact that sexual pleasure is not strictly anatomically determined. The body parts certainly matter (a great deal in some cases), but sexual pleasure requires more than physical stimulation, it also requires cognitive and emotional elaboration of that stimulation. Personality, learning, and morals all affect how stimulation is interpreted: as pleasure or pain, good or bad, beautiful or disgusting. The manner in which the mind and society influence sexual pleasure is the topic of the following chapter.

5.

The Psychology of Sexual Pleasure

Shortly after the protagonist (Jimmy) of *The Crying Game* discovers that his "girlfriend" (Dil) is really a man, the following intimate exchange takes place:

Jimmy: "I should've known, shouldn't I?"
Dil: "Probably."
Jimmy: "I kinda wish I didn't."
Dil: "You can always pretend."

But can one really pretend? On a purely physiological level it would certainly seem possible. After all, genital stimulation, whether by a man or a woman, sends the same sensory signals to the brain. Yet somehow the sex, appearance, and identity of the person providing the stimulation are all critical determinants of whether or not the stimulation is perceived as pleasurable. Many people, heterosexual and homosexual alike, are strongly attracted to only one of the two sexes. And, all things being equal, most people would prefer an attractive partner to an unattractive one. Even then, whether or not pleasure is experienced is significantly influenced by *who* the attractive, appropriately sexed pleasure-giver is, not to mention the context in which the stimulation occurs. Certain partners, such as family members, are taboo. Others are considered undesirable, or even repulsive, for whatever reason.

But who decides which partners are appropriate and which are taboo? What determines sexual attractiveness? And, borrowing a line from Tina Turner, "what's love got to do with it?" Definitive answers to

114

these questions remain elusive, but the role of culture in shaping sexual attitudes is clear. Incest taboos forbidding marriage and intercourse between closely related family members are human universals, and incest avoidance is observed in a wide spectrum of animal species. Nevertheless, incestuous relations were common in the royal families of medieval Europe and, though usually illegal, are not unknown in modern society. Why is sex with a parent or child unthinkable to most people, but acceptable to others? The answer lies somewhere between our ears, in the pinkish mass known as the human brain.

Individual and cultural differences are likewise needed to explain, in retrospect, the ancient Hawaiian aristocrats' lust for extremely obese women,[1] and the Renaissance European male's desire for similarly "Rubenesque" figures. In contrast, current Western norms identify female attractiveness with slender, well-toned bodies and youthful facial features. Gone is the curviness of the pinup girl of the 1940s and 1950s. Why this fluctuation in ideal body shapes? And why do suntans keep fading in and out of fashion? Even more puzzling, why are female breasts such an attraction to American men, while women go topless in many tropical climes (and parts of Europe) without arousing undo excitement? Why is it, for example, that among the Bala, an agrarian society in central Africa, men greatly prefer women with large breasts, whereas the men of Mangaia, a Polynesian society notable for its lustful expression of sexuality, do not find female breasts at all arousing.[2]

The pervasive influence of culture is obvious in all these examples. What's attractive depends on the times, the culture, and the circumstances. However, not all aspects of attractiveness are subject to the vagaries of temporal and cultural influences. According to some evolutionary psychologists, what people find attractive are precisely those features of appearance that have been reliably correlated with reproductive success throughout human evolution. For example, Donald Symons argues that the appearance of youth and healthfulness is universally associated with female sexual attractiveness because these qualities act as de facto markers for reproductive fitness. Thus, Symons predicts, in all societies in which women attempt to alter their appearance (through the use of cosmetics, diets, exercise, and dress), the tendency will be toward the accentuation of youth and health. Men, for their part, are assumed to have inborn mechanisms for detecting these qualities in women.[3]

Cultural influences are also evident in the experience of love. For many people, sex without love is unthinkable. Despite the changes wrought by the tumultuous sexual revolution of the 1960s and 1970s, the cultural norm in most Western societies continues to emphasize an interdependent ideal of love and sex.[4] It is still the case, in other words, that love sanctions sexual pleasure.[5] In other cultures, love is immaterial, or is even considered a nuisance that complicates otherwise free and easy sexuality.[6] But what is love? Is it, as some have suggested, a hormonal imbalance, or is it a hypnotic state, as proposed by Freud?[7] Or, perhaps, as Shakespeare observes in *As You Like It*:

> Love is merely a madness, and, we tell you, deserves as well a dark house and a whip as madmen do; and the reason why they are not so punished and cured is, that the lunacy is so ordinary that the whippers are in love too.

More to the point, what is the connection between love and sexual desire? And why do people invariably desire the one(s) they love? Or is this backwards? Maybe, instead, people love the ones they desire.[*8] (Displaying an obvious heterosexist, pro-procreation bias, the great nineteenth-century sexologist Richard von Krafft-Ebing observed that "since love implies the presence of sexual desire it can only exist between persons of different sex capable of sexual intercourse."[9])

According to many historians, the notion that marriage should be based on love is a relatively recent, and predominantly Western, development.[10] In the past, marriage was essentially an economic and familial arrangement—love had nothing to do with it. Even now, marriage remains a predominantly economic arrangement in some cultures. Among the inhabitants of the Irish island of Innis Beag, for example, "courtship is almost nonexistent, and most marriages are arranged with little concern for the desires of the young people involved."[11] Even still, with the passage of time spouses would often grow to love one another. Perhaps they learned mutual respect, or maybe trust breeds emotional closeness. No doubt sex, too, played an important role in deepening the emotional bond (see the discussions of the pair-bonding hypothesis in Chapters 2 and 4). It is easy to imagine how the pleasures of sex could become associated with one's spouse through classical conditioning or some other learning mechanism. In this view, love is a by-product of marriage that arises from the psychological association of sexual pleasure with one's spouse.[*12]

In modern Western cultures, marriage and love are inextricably interwoven: "first comes love, then comes marriage . . ." But where does sex fit in? ". . . Then comes baby in the baby carriage." Marriage and love are thus prerequisites for sex—at least reproductive sex.[*13] It was not always so, however. In the Middle Ages the passionate expression of sexual love between spouses was heatedly discouraged by the Church, which saw a threat to religious authority in a man's ardent love for his wife and a wife's amorous love for her husband.[14] Thus, St. Jerome warned husbands long ago that "nothing is more foul than to love a wife as though she were an adulteress."[15]

Regardless of which comes first, sex or love, the symbiotic relationship between them is readily apparent. Love makes the sex better, and sex makes the love better.[16] The positive associational role of sexual pleasure in marriage should therefore not be underestimated. Sexual incompatibilities and dissatisfaction remain among the leading causes of divorce in America and elsewhere.

However, it is often hard to separate love from lust. Indeed, skeptics might insist they're inseparable, being one and the same thing. Whatever the case, it appears that the human mind determines whether people lust after their spouses, their lovers, or after inanimate objects such as lingerie or shoes. As Oscar Wilde observed in his immortal story, *The Picture of Dorian Gray*, "It is in the brain, and the brain only, that the great sins of the world take place."

But how does the brain influence the manner in which people experience pleasure, and with whom (or what) they find satisfaction? And what, in turn, influences the brain? Although we haven't all the answers to these complex questions, we nevertheless have some ideas, which we shall describe shortly.

Our examination of the role of the sexual mind and the society that shapes it begins with a consideration of how individuals differ in their sexual attitudes. Each individual manifests a unique sexual personality and tastes. Some like it hot. Some like it cold. Some like it in-between. Humans, it seems, are rarely homogeneous in their personal preferences, whether for ice cream, automobiles, or sexual stimuli. With regard to sex, there are important differences between individuals, and between groups. Men are different from women; homosexuals are different from heterosexuals; you are different from your neighbors; and we all are different from Sambia warriors. Why? What is the source of these differences? And how can they best be characterized?

You've Got Personality

What accounts for differences in sexual attitudes and behaviors? Presuming similarities in race, age, gender, and country of origin, why do people think and act so differently from each other when it comes to sex? Why does one woman chose to become a nun, and another a prostitute? These are obviously very different sexual lifestyles, yet they might be adopted by very similar women, even sisters. Why does one woman constrain her sexuality, while the other flaunts it?

Perhaps it has something to do with the manner in which we *think* about sexual pleasure, and how we categorize and process sexual stimuli. Perhaps it also has something to do with our *personalities*—the traits and characteristics that serve as our psychological rudders.

People vary enormously with respect to personality traits. Some people are shy, some are outgoing. Some are depressed, some happy-go-lucky. Some are ambitious, some are lazy. And so on. Not surprisingly, these characteristics translate into very different behaviors, having disparate consequences. Ambitious actions, for example, produce quite different consequences than do lazy actions: Ambitious people are likely to acquire greater prestige, more money, better skills, and so forth, than are their less ambitious counterparts. (They are also more likely to suffer from hypertension and ulcers, and are more vulnerable to heart attacks and strokes. The implications of personality psychology thus extend well beyond the mental to encompass physiological concerns as well.)

Not surprisingly, people also vary in their sexual personalities. Some are sexually repressed, while others are exuberant. Some feel guilty about sex, while others enjoy it without regret. And, like the characteristics cited earlier, different sexual personality traits engender different behaviors and resultant consequences. These differences are the focus of the psychological research of Donn Byrne and Don Mosher.

As a means of characterizing the sexual components of personality, Byrne and Mosher devised tests that, broadly speaking, distinguish the sexual moralist from the sexual philanderer.[17] Among the aspects of sexual personality measured by these tests are sexual guilt and repression, masturbation guilt, and erotophobia-erotophilia. The power of these tests is their ability to detect subtle differences in sexual personalities.

Although the results of these tests are usually fairly predictable, they can sometimes be quite dramatic. For example, as one might expect, sexually contrite individuals have less sexual interest and experience than their more libidinous counterparts. There is nothing surprising here: Sexual guilt should obviously influence sexual behavior. But the effects of guilt can be much more subtle, as exemplified by the fact that sexually guilty people—even very intelligent ones—have greater difficulty absorbing and retaining sexually relevant information than do their less guilty counterparts.[18] Guilt, it appears, acts as a filter, selectively blocking potentially embarrassing material, and repressing any that manages to sneak through. This finding has important real-world implications, since it suggests that contraceptive information and "safe sex" messages are less likely to be assimilated by those who suffer from excessive sexual guilt.

Along the same experimental lines, personality psychologists have developed a word association test that includes several sexual double-entendres (i.e., words such as "dick," "prick," and "ball" that have legitimate as well as slang meanings).[19] The sexually guilty are less likely to perceive the sexual meanings of these double-entendres, and when required to produce an associated word, they often stumble and fumble for a response. They do fine with words like "chair," "mother," and "rose," but "pussy" produces panic. In many cases, they become so distraught by the (unconsciously perceived) sexual meaning of the double-entendre that they are completely unable to respond.

Further studies have demonstrated that the sexually contrite are more likely to eschew contraception, avoid pornography, restrict the range of their sexual activities, and so forth.[20] Their psychological reactions to unwanted pregnancies, sexually transmitted diseases, and pornographic movies are also more severely adverse than those of less guilty individuals.[21] Furthermore, these sexual inhibitions are experienced physiologically as well as psychologically. For example, the sexually contrite experience significantly less arousal to erotic stimuli than do more libidinous people.

Why? One (not very likely) possibility is that the sexually contrite differ from the sexually libidinous on some critical, though as yet unspecified, physiological dimension, and therefore have a lower capacity for the enjoyment of sex. They are, so to speak, different by nature. One piece of evidence against this unlikely hypothesis is that psychotherapy is often successful in lowering the inhibitions and enhancing the sexual pleasure of the sexually disinterested. If a "talking cure" can produce such profound changes, then these differences are probably not direct consequences of genetic programming; rather, they presumably arise as products of parental rearing and socialization.

Of course, not every aspect of sexuality is quite so malleable. Gender identity and sexual orientation can be extraordinarily resistant to change. Nevertheless, there are enormous individual differences among homosexuals, just as there are among heterosexuals. Some are prudes, some enjoy monogamy, and some are philanderers. And while the percentages of prudishness and philandering may vary (often along culturally stereotypic lines), the appearance of such characteristics is not limited to any one category. Rather than being hardwired, the particular manifestations of such characteristics seem to depend on relevant experiences in the familial and cultural environments.

However, the greatest differences in sexual characteristics are obtained by comparing men with women, not by comparing heterosexuals with homosexuals, or the promiscuous with the contrite. That men and women differ sexually is not surprising, given the vast dissimilarities that exist in both sexual anatomy and reproductive responsibilities.[*22] For example, women can have multiple orgasms and they can also have children. What *is* surprising is that the differences that exist aren't even more pronounced.

More Similar Than Different

One area in which men and women differ significantly is in how they respond to erotica and pornography. As we've indicated in previous chapters, most of the explicit, commercially available pornography is targeted at a male audience, whether heterosexual or homosexual. One reason for this state of affairs is that the media typically utilized for erotic representations—including films, videos, and magazines—are well suited to graphic portrayals of nudes and people engaged in various sexual activities, which are precisely the types of visual stimuli that appeal to the average man.[23] Women, in contrast, tend to favor stimuli that incorporate more fantasy elements and that provide an emotional context for the erotica contained therein. Thus, in general, men prefer more explicit, "hardcore" representations, whereas women like their erotica a bit on the "softer," more imaginative side. Of course, erotica/pornography is largely an acquired taste, and the level of explicitness that men and women find appealing varies between individuals and sometimes increases with exposure.

Men and women also differ in their sexual fantasies. Men's fantasies, by and large, are truly *fantasies*. Men typically include things they have never done and never will. The male fantasy world is populated by beautiful women (famous actresses, models, and so on) who are always sexually available and willing to participate in all manners of outrageous sex, including threesomes, public sex, orgies, and bondage. However, if you ask a women to construct a fantasy, she will generally resurrect a previous sexual experience, or create a sexual fantasy about someone she knows in familiar, though romanticized, circumstances. In other words, women emphasize romance and intimacy in their fantasies, whereas men emphasize physicality and novelty.[24]

Other gender differences also exist. Men tend to initiate sexual encounters, to be more preoccupied with sex, and to place greater value on sexual variety.[25] Furthermore, whereas women typically emphasize intimacy in sexual relationships, men tend to focus on the sexual aspects of their intimate relationships. Men are also much more visually oriented, and are more likely than women to be aroused by the sight of a naked body, a nude pictorial representation, or a depiction of a couple making love.[26]

Of course, these differences are a matter of degree and are not necessarily evident in every culture. Although some researchers have argued that the relative consistency of such differences across cultures suggests biological (or evolutionary) determinism,[27] cultural influences are likely also to play a role. Societies that are organized along strict gender lines are especially likely to promulgate gender differences in the service of social organization and stability.[*28] If women were bigger and stronger, then perhaps the roles would be reversed.[*29]

But men and women are not really all that different in their sexual responses and proclivities. Unfortunately, it is often easier to establish that differences exist than to detect similarities because of the difficulty of separating cultural and social influences from purely psychological ones.[*30] The fact that men and women *do* respond differently to erotic stimuli is another confounding factor that acts to mask existing similarities.

Research into the supposedly greater sexual arousability of men amply illustrates these problems. The arousal question, it turns out, is a bit of a *non sequitur*. Studies suggest, in fact, that men and women are equally arousable, given the proper stimulus. Nevertheless, the presumption that men are more easily aroused than women is a long-standing myth, embraced by scientists and writers no less than by the lay public. This myth, unfortunately, has been put to many questionable purposes, not the least of which is to discourage and subjugate the sexual expression of women.

In America the myth of the passionless woman reached its modern zenith in the sexually repressed Victorian era of the mid- to late nineteenth century. As expressed by Dr. William Acton, a noted physician and acknowledged sexual authority, "the majority of women (happily for them) are not very much troubled with sexual feelings of any kind."[31] Such attitudes were codified via a "double standard" that at once elevated women to a position of exalted moral superiority over men while simultaneously denying their corporeal passions, even as it legitimized prostitution as an outlet for the supposed animal lusts of men. Marriage, motherhood, and family were hailed as the true calling of women, and the basis of a feminist ideology that was disdainful of sexual intercourse for any purpose other than procreation.[32]

The prevailing ideal of the passionless woman who received little enjoyment from intercourse may well have reflected male sexual incompetence as much as a lack of female desire.[33] Historian William Shade notes that "for women sexual intercourse in the nineteenth century was basically Hobbesian: nasty, brutish and short."[34] It is no wonder that female sexual passions were somewhat muted (in a vicious circle, a belief in the fundamental asexuality of women also provided men of that era with an excuse for their poor sexual performance and neglect of their partners' needs). Moreover, the fear of pregnancy, with its attendant dangers and the prospect of a painful parturition, must certainly have dampened female erotic fires. Indeed, the desire for greater control of reproduction may have been a significant factor in women's reluctance to engage in intercourse, since most believed that procreation, not pleasure, was the purpose of sex.[35] Thus, the available evidence suggests a severe neglect of female erotic potential rather than a fundamental absence of sexual desire. As a result of this neglect, some portion of the untapped sexual potential of Victorian women may have been diverted into masturbation and "sisterly" lesbianism.[36]

Modern research looking at gender differences in sexual arousal has employed two main tactics. The first is to note men's and women's responses to *Playboy* nudes or other male-oriented pornography. The second is to analyze the subjects' reported frequency of intercourse. Not surprisingly, these experiments invariably find that men are more arousable than women. However, the data generated by these experiments are unreliable for at least two reasons. The first centers on the obvious flaw of utilizing male-oriented stimuli to induce sexual arousal in both men and women. Should we really expect heterosexual women to be excited by photos designed to stimulate men?

The measures of sexual frequency employed in these studies are also problematic. Self-report behavioral inventories that ask a person, for example, how often he or she had intercourse in the previous week, are notoriously unreliable because people are often unable to accurately recall events from the past, even the immediate past.[37] People also have a tendency to lie, especially where sex is concerned.*[38] Furthermore, because heterosexual intercourse is a symmetric activity (one man, one woman), elaborate explanations of the male-female asymmetries in the frequency of intercourse reported by these studies are required to justify the validity of such measures.

Many studies of arousability are further compromised by the lack of a direct, genital measure of physiological arousal (such as penile enlargement) that is appropriate for both men and women. The use of gender-specific measures clearly limits the comparability of data obtained separately for women and men.

Fortunately, this need not always be the case. Several lines of research have demonstrated that if unbiased stimuli are utilized, such as erotic stories that appeal to *both* men and women, the purported differences in arousability disappear.[39] This result holds whether arousability is measured at the genital level, through measurements of pelvic blood flow,[*40] or at the cognitive level of self-reported arousal. Thus, it appears that men and women are equally arousable, although different stimuli may be required for optimal arousal.

What about gender differences in sexual pleasure? Don't men enjoy sex more than women?[*41] Perhaps, yes. Perhaps, no. Circumstantial evidence in favor of a "pleasure gap" is readily obtainable. As noted previously, males are the principal consumers of pornography, and prostitution flourishes today, as in years past, largely to satisfy the sexual appetites of men desiring the pleasures of nonprocreative sex. Masturbation is also more common and more frequent, on average, among men than women.[42] Thus, it appears that the sex drive—the drive for pleasure—may be greater in most men than it is in most women.[43] But this piece of information says nothing about the visceral and emotional *experience* of pleasure. The observed difference in drive may be partially due to socialization effects: In our culture women and girls are *taught* that men want sex more. On the other hand, perhaps there is a simple explanation related to differential orgasmic capacity. Men, with few exceptions, tend to be consistently orgasmic (meaning they reach orgasm most or all of the time given proper stimulation).[44] In contrast, some women are either completely unable to reach orgasm, or if able to, do so only rarely. Only about half to three-quarters of American women climax most or all of the time during sexual intercourse.[*45] Of course, many women are multiorgasmic, whereas men require a refractory period—a little rest as it were—between orgasms.

But are such differences rooted in physiology or in psychology? Unfortunately for men, the refractory period is a very real and inescapable fact of physiology. Worse yet, some men suffer from physiological dysfunctions that entirely preclude orgasm. On the other hand, it appears that, in Western countries at least, psychological inhibition and not psychological impairment is the most common cause of male sexual dysfunction.

For women the situation is equally complex, if not more so.[46] Unlike men, for whom an inability to reach orgasm is a statistical rarity, studies consistently indicate that as many as 10 percent of American women have never experienced orgasm.[47] It might be thought that the relatively high prevalence of anorgasmia (or, as it is known in the literature, "primary orgasmic dysfunction") demands a biological explanation. However, three related findings mitigate against this conclusion and instead suggest that psychocultural factors play a significant role in determining orgasmic potential. The first is that women who report having masturbated as young girls or adolescents tend to orgasm more readily during sexual relations with a partner.[48] This suggests that female orgasmic capacity, at least in part, may be learned. Indeed, many modern sex manuals provide detailed instruction on how best to induce an orgasm, from learning to relax, through direct and indirect clitoral stimulation, to locating the fabled "G-spot."[49] Furthermore, according to Kinsey, the decade in which a woman was born is strongly predictive of orgasmic potential: Women born in the 1920s were more consistently orgasmic than those born prior to 1900 (the *Sex in America* study uncovered a similar dependence of orgasmic capacity on generation of birth).[50] This trend, of course, nicely mirrors the increased concern about female sexual pleasure witnessed in post-Victorian American society. If failure to orgasm were purely organic in origin, one would not expect the prevalence of orgasmic dysfunction to exhibit such a trend, unless, of course, the etiological factors themselves had also abated during the period in question.

The existence of sexually libidinous cultures in which most if not all women regularly reach orgasm during heterosexual intercourse also provides evidence of strong social influences in female orgasmic capacity. The inhabitants of Mangaia, a small island in the South Pacific, provide a textbook example of such cultural influences.[51] In Mangaian society female orgasm is considered both a learned response and a male responsibility. All Mangaian women are reportedly orgasmic, with climax occurring after brief foreplay and prolonged intercourse. Male sexual performance, as measured by the pleasure he provides to his partner, is strongly emphasized by cultural norms; a "good" man is able to sustain intercourse for fifteen to thirty minutes or more, and ensures that his partner climaxes at least once before he reaches orgasm himself. The most important aspect of sexual intercourse for either a married or unmarried Mangaian man is "to give pleasure to his wife or woman or girl—the pleasure of orgasm; supposedly this is what gives the male partner his own pleasure and a special thrill that itself is set apart from his own orgasm."[52] Thus, as demonstrated by both Mangaian men (prolonged intercourse) and women (learned orgasmic capacity), physiology need not be a hindrance to ultimate pleasure. As Donald Marshall, who has made an extensive study of Mangaian culture, summarizes, "[the] Mangaian data indicate clearly that the female must learn to achieve sexual orgasm [and] that all Mangaian women do, in fact, learn to achieve this climax."[53]

Social pressures and taboos can also be adduced as explanations for gender-based differences in masturbation, sexual interest, and so on. More generally, the costs of sex are quite different for men and women, both physically and socially. Women can become pregnant, and pregnancy is a *big* difference. Furthermore, the pervasive and enduring double standard levies severe social costs upon women whose sexuality exceeds cultural expectations, while rewarding men who display qualitatively similar behaviors. Conceivably, as the arousability studies suggest, if the costs were the same for both men and women, no gender differences would emerge. Of course, one could argue that the costs *could* never be the same, being in some sense fixed by the different reproductive roles required of men and women. In any case, when the rules of the sexual game differ, with more at stake for women (e.g., pregnancy, loss of reputation, familial ostracism) than men, female interest and reported enjoyment may suffer accordingly.

As the Mangaian example indicates, the influence of culture on collective sexual attitudes and individual behavior can be significant. It might therefore be instructive to consider how culture interacts with the psychology of pleasure.[54] People are not the only ones who are sexually diverse—cultures also display pronounced differences in their sexual "personalities."

The Culture Club

Geothe, the great German philosopher and poet, noted long ago that "the best pleasures of this world are not quite pure." The obvious retort to this proclamation is: Pleasurable and pure by whose standards? Pleasure and purity vary enormously by culture. To the Sambia, male-male fellatio is both pleasurable and pure, as long as it is performed within highly circumscribed, ritual boundaries. Such is not the case for most Westerners, who find "homosex" disgusting. Why this disparity? The most obvious explanation is that human sexuality is not overly constrained by physiological exigencies; rather, it is extraordinarily plastic and therefore capable of fitting many disparate cultural molds. Although the basic physiological apparatus is universal, sexuality is necessarily filtered through a cultural lens.

The concept of gender provides a particularly striking example. In contemporary Western culture there are two choices: male and female. At one level, this two-category gender system makes perfect sense, corresponding as it does to normative assumptions about both genetic differences (XX vs. XY chromosomes) and genital differences (vagina vs. penis). Nevertheless, this sensible, and seemingly obvious, two-gender system is far from universally endorsed. In the Dominican Republic, for example, an unusual genetically transmitted hormonal abnormality, 5-alpha-reductase deficiency, causes genetically male boys to be born with ambiguous or partially feminized external genitalia. Supposedly, these "pseudohermaphrodites" are mistakenly assigned to the female gender at birth and thereafter raised as girls.[55]

However, a surprising change takes place at puberty: These "girls' " voices deepen, their penises grow, their testes descend, and so forth. (In 5-alpha-reductase deficiency, the fetus produces normal quantities of prenatal testosterone but is unable to convert this hormone into dihydrotestosterone, which prevents the appearance of external male genitalia. This deficiency is overcome at puberty when the genetically male body begins its preprogrammed increase in testosterone.) Moreover, these "girls" start acting like boys, and for the most part, begin to express interest in the opposite sex. Despite being raised as girls, most pseudohermaphrodites adopt a male gender role following their physiological transformation at puberty. Thus, it appears that in the Dominican Republic, girls can become boys. (A similar phenomenon is observed among the Sambia of Papua New Guinea, where 5-alpha reductase deficiency is also endemic.[56])

However, a closer look at the data suggests an alternative interpretation.[57] In both the Dominican Republic and Papua New Guinea, the cultural formulation of gender includes a third category, a generic "other," in addition to the biologically obvious categories of male and female.[58] Indeed, in the Dominican Republic, the local term for 5-alpha reductase deficiency is *guevedoche*, meaning "penis at twelve." In a similar fashion, the Sambia of New Guinea refer to *kwolu-aatmwol*, "male-thing-transforming-into-female-thing." Since this condition is widely recognized, guevedoche infants are actually (as opposed to "medically") assigned to the third category of gender, where they remain until puberty unfolds, at which time most assume the male cultural role. Because gender categories are not rigidly maintained, the culture can flexibly accommodate the initial ambiguity and the subsequent gender switching necessitated by the presence of 5-alpha reductase deficiency. Gilbert Herdt, an anthropologist specializing in gender issues, explains:

In a three-sex system, with its fuzzier boundaries, the person's sex and identity are reckoned in relation to a more complex sexual code and social field having three alternate socialization regimes and outcomes, each of which is known to be historically coherent: male, female, and hermaphroditic. In this sense, these persons are not mistaken females, but, rather, *guevedoche* and *kwolu-aatmwol*; that is, third genders.[59]

In cultures where the prevalence of pseudohermaphroditism is high, the three-gender system makes perfect sense. In other cultures, such as our own, genital ambiguities are either ignored, or resolved by assigning children with ambiguous genitals to either the male or female category (often with accompanying surgery). Such a choice is mandated by cultural assumptions that conceptualize gender as a strict dichotomy. This isn't the case in the Dominican Republic and Papua New Guinea, where questions of gender are resolved according to different cultural belief systems.

The Dominican Republic and Papua New Guinea are not the only places where three-gender systems are embraced. In India, *hijras*—males who have had their penises and testicles surgically removed—constitute a third distinct gender category.[610] Psychologically, hijras are neither predominantly male nor predominantly female, at least not in the way that most Westerners conceptualize these categories. Instead, they are psychologically, as well as physically, androgynous. The social position of the hijra is also marked by profound ambiguity. Hijras, it is believed, bestow good fortune and fertility when they dance at weddings and bless newborn infants, but they are also accused of maliciously inducing impotence in men by pulling up their saris to reveal their post-operative scars.[61]

Other examples of three-gender systems include the Native American *berdache* introduced in the preceding chapter. Berdache are men—often thought to have vast spiritual powers—who have been transformed into women by virtue of their dress and behavior; that is, they are culturally constituted females (although in some cases the transformation is from female to male).[62] In Tahiti, members of the third gender are called *mah'u*, and in Omani they are called *xanith*.[63] The Burmese equivalent, the *acault*, are considered to be neither male nor female (despite biologic maleness), with the social consequence that a man can have sex with an acault without violating the cultural prohibition on homosexual behavior.[64]

Another exception to the strict male-female dichotomy, and one that is a bit closer to home, are the transgendered individuals known as *she-males*.[65] She-males, like other transsexuals, typically adopt stereotypically female attire (dresses, skirts, and so on) and undergo extensive feminization procedures, including breast implants, female hormone therapy, and electrolysis to remove masculine body hair. However, unlike other transsexuals, they elect to keep their masculine genitals. Although sexually active primarily with men, some she-males engage in sex with both men and women. But society remains confused: Are they men with breasts, or women with penises?*[66] In truth, it seems, they are neither.

We introduce these examples to make a simple point. If something so obvious—and apparently biological—as gender can be culturally constructed, what does this say about the rest of human sexuality? Furthermore, if sex is so important to reproduction, how can such wide intercultural variability be tolerated? Shouldn't there be a single, universal set of rules of sexual conduct? The resolution to these issues, we believe, once again hinges on how extremely pleasurable sex is, and how little it takes to ensure the survival of the human genome, hence the species.

In particular, there is plenty of room for alternative, culturally determined expressions of sexuality precisely *because* sex is so pleasurable. The search for pleasure engenders experimentation, hence the extraordinary malleability of human sexuality. On the other hand, because penile-vaginal intercourse is extremely pleasurable, it is largely inevitable. The reproductive (or evolutionary) imperative to be fruitful and multiply is easily satisfied due to the year-round fertility enjoyed by men and women. Combined, these observations suggest that regardless of what humans *choose* to believe (or do), the sexual system is largely self-corrective, because sex is so pleasurable.

But if all culturally constructed systems of sexuality are equally valid, why do some cultural beliefs dominate over others? If the previous argument is correct, then there is little reason to favor one sexual belief system over another. By now, of course, completely maladaptive belief systems should have been weeded-out from the cultural landscape. Hence, the systems that survive today should express at least marginally reasonable interpretations of sex, which, although not necessarily accurate or veridical, incorporate some plausible chain of logic, gaping holes notwithstanding. To repeat, one set of beliefs is not necessarily better, or more adaptive than another, even if it is more prevalent. The beliefs that have survived and predominated (such as those that pathologize homosexuality and canonize heterosexuality) are merely those that happen to have been adopted by cultures that grew rapidly. When the demographics change, so will the dominance of cultural beliefs about sexuality. However, *sex*, at some level, will remain the same: plastic and pleasurable.

The main contribution of culture to the sexual psychology of the individual is to establish a fundamental outlook, or a framework, for conceptualizing sexual behavior. A culture's sexual norms delimit socially acceptable behavior, and thereby provide a guide to be followed with impunity, or ignored under threat of censure. Depending on whether or not these norms are internalized by the individual, cultural influences may appear to arise wholly from within, or to be imposed from without. To the deeply acculturated, normatively proscribed behaviors are inviolable; even the mere thought of transgression may be enough to precipitate an emotional response, ranging from a vague disquietude to outright disgust.

The Church's stance on contraception provides a case in point. Most truly devout Catholics would experience feelings of betrayal and intense guilt, were they to utilize contraception. Many less devout Catholics, in contrast, *do* use contraceptives. But, although they may consciously acknowledge and feel guilty over their contravention of Church teachings, the sense of culpability is largely externalized because their behavior does not constitute a violation of individual conscience. Finally, there are those who simply reject the prevailing norms (or Church dogma in this particular example) and determine for themselves, to a greater or lesser degree, the limits of acceptable behavior. This is especially likely to occur when cultural norms are widely divergent from mainstream practice, as in the United States, where only a minority obey the Judeo-Christian proscription on nonprocreative sex, and even fewer comply with Catholic teachings on contraceptive use.

Nowhere is the contrast of normative sexual belief systems greater than between the Mangaians of Polynesia and the rural Irish community of Innis Beag. Sex is an important component of Mangaian life. Both boys and girls first experiment with intercourse between the ages of twelve and fourteen, and begin having sex on a nightly basis soon thereafter.[67] A minimum of two or three orgasms per night is expected of young Mangaian males, and a "good" man is able to bring his partner to climax two or three times for every one of his. Parents encourage their daughters to have sex with a number of different men before marriage because sexual compatibility is considered the primary determinant of a successful marriage. Indeed, Marshall notes that "personal affection may or may not result from acts of sexual intimacy, but the latter are requisite to the former—exactly the reverse of the ideals of Western society."[68]

In marked contrast, in Innis Beag all sexual expression is severely repressed, and is undertaken solely for reproductive purposes.[*69] The Catholic population of this small island community is notable both for its aversion to sex, as well as for its overwhelming ignorance in sexual matters. Whereas Mangaian youth are carefully instructed by their elders in sexual behavior and technique (young men are physically instructed by older village women), the sexual education received by children and adolescents in Innis Beag is minimal, if not entirely nonexistent. Experimentation with the opposite sex is strongly discouraged, with the result that masturbation, which is rare in Mangaia, is quite prevalent in Innis Beag. Finally, whereas the primary objective of Mangaian sexual intercourse is "to continue the in-and-out action of coitus over long periods of time,"[70] in Innis Beag intercourse is invariably completed quickly, with the man falling asleep shortly after achieving orgasm. It is perhaps not surprising, therefore, that female orgasm is essentially unknown in this exceedingly repressed culture.[71]

The matter of sexual fidelity is also culture dependent. Consider, for example, the Mehinaku Indians, who live in Brazil's Xingu National Park, a tropical rainforest. The Mehinaku are most notable for their amazing lack of marital fidelity. When Thomas Gregor, who has studied the Mehinaku culture extensively, inquired into their sexual habits, he found that the average married adult was involved in more than four extramarital affairs![72] These affairs add intrigue to sexual life, as might be expected, but also provide sustenance; for the Mehinaku, gifts from lovers are an important food source. Of course, the Mehinaku are not unique in their acceptance of extramarital affairs, although they would appear to represent an extreme end of the continuum. The Puritans of seventeenth century New England epitomize the other extreme. In this culture (which is not so far removed from our own), adultery was a capital offense, punishable by death.[*73]

Attitudes toward adolescent sexuality also vary by culture. In most Western cultures, children and adolescents are usually assumed to be sexually naïve, but this is hardly a universal belief. Some cultures, in fact, ritualize adolescent sexuality. As mentioned earlier, fellatio is required of young Sambia males and coitus is promoted among Mangaian youths of both sexes. Likewise, the Muria of central India create adolescent dormitories (called *ghotuls*), in which boys and girls freely cohabitate, pairing-off nightly for sexual intercourse, or just to sleep.[*74]

The belief systems of the Mehinaku, Sambia, Mangaia, and Muria are obviously very different from our own. Because a culture's beliefs are usually adopted and assimilated by its members, it would therefore not be surprising to find fundamental differences in how Americans and

Mehinaku Indians, for example, view marriage, sex, and kinship. On the individual level, cultural beliefs about sex undoubtedly influence sexual guilt, erotophobia, and a host of other personality traits—so much so that anthropologists often speak of "sex-positive" and "sex-negative" cultures, as exemplified by Mangaia and Innis Beag, respectively. The same is true of the microcosmic societies known as families. Some are sex-positive and some are sex-negative.

Family Affairs

Ultimately, families, and parents especially, are the principal instruments through which children learn about sex.*[75] Almost all cultural learning in Western societies, including incest and other taboos, arrives at the child only after passing through a parental filter, although this is less true today than it was in the past. (Peer group influences are instrumental as well, but during the formative years of early childhood, parental influences are primary.) The traditional (or in some cases, mythical) "birds and the bees" talk is a familiar example of familial learning. Children also learn indirectly, by observing their parents' behavior and sensing their attitudes. If parents whisper about sex, it sends a message; if they shut their doors during sex, that too sends a message. In fact, everything that parents and families (including siblings) do with regard to sex is instructional, even if some of the messages are quite subtle. The taboo on discussing sex in public, for example, clearly distinguishes sex from all other human activities in the mind of the child. Even in "sex-positive" families, in which sex is discussed openly within the privacy of the home, parents may inadvertently send bewildering or conflicting messages about sex to their children.

The immense pleasurability of sex is especially hard to convey to the sexually uninitiated. People simply don't have the vocabulary necessary to communicate the feelings, both physical and emotional, that accompany sex. Pleasure, it would seem, must be experienced to be appreciated. Perhaps this is why, in part, the "birds and the bees" isn't the "women and the men." The mechanics of sex, though confusing, are simpler to communicate to children than is the visceral experience of sexual pleasure.

Of course, children's familiarity with sexual pleasure usually begins long before their parents design to explain it to them. The functional capacity for sexual pleasure, it appears, exists at birth. In the infant, this capacity is evoked in a variety of random and spontaneous movements toward contact with the genitals, nipples, or other body parts. It is these movements that are eventually rectified and channeled into the purposive action that facilitates the evocation and subjective recognition of sexual pleasure. Once recognized, these behaviors get repeated—which is not surprising, since positive sensations usually elicit repetition. However, if repeated often enough, they also eventually get noticed by caretakers, such as parents, nannies, and so on, who serve as the initial purveyors of cultural beliefs about sexual pleasure (usually that such experiences are "bad").

Parental intrusions notwithstanding, sexual pleasure is an essential part of childhood. Historically, childhood has been a protected harbor from adult concerns and responsibilities (e.g., hunting, gathering, etc.), and therefore the time best devoted to intrinsic pleasures, sexual and otherwise. Furthermore, because procreation is impossible in childhood, sexual pleasure can be enjoyed multidimensionally—orally, anally, genitally, and so forth—without reproductive consequences. Self-stimulation in early childhood becomes the precursor to sexual pleasure, and the agent through which it unfolds in later childhood and young adulthood. That is, sexual self-stimulation and the pleasure that results provide the awareness, knowledge, and incentive for the desire to share sexual pleasure with others.

The magnitude of parental influences should not be minimized, however. By and large, parents convey most of their training about sex through their reactions to genital stimulation, childhood sexual play, privacy, nudity, and so on. These lessons can be helpful, benign, or destructive. In any case, it is these early lessons that provide the foundation for subsequent learning and socialization regarding sexual functioning, as well as its pleasurability.

Perhaps a blatant example of how cultural and familial influences help to shape sexual attitudes and behavior would help clarify the issues involved. In our culture, young children are sometimes slapped and scolded by their parents for touching their genitals, especially in front of company. In other cultures this same behavior might be tolerated, or, in special circumstances, even encouraged. Cultural change is also manifest in sexual attitudes. Far fewer parents would react to a display of self-stimulation with violence and approbation today than would have 50 or 100 years ago. On the other hand, whereas in Victorian England it was considered quite acceptable for a nurse or nanny to quiet a male infant by taking his penis into her mouth, such behavior would today be considered a form of child abuse.[*76]

Suppose, for the sake of argument, that childhood sexual displays are taboo in a particular society. Classical (Pavlovian) conditioning predicts that a young boy who is physically punished or otherwise admonished each time he fondles his genitals would subsequently learn to associate touching himself with the pain and scorn heaped upon him by his parents or other authority figures. As a result, self-stimulation might cease, for a time. But sexual pleasure is a powerful motivator, much too powerful to be completely deterred by any but the strongest negative associations. Hence, for most children, observance of the prohibition on masturbation will be short-lived. Nevertheless, parental admonitions are not without consequences. Depending on the extent to which parental standards have been internalized, the boy can be expected to experience guilt whenever he masturbates (in addition, perhaps, to a fear of getting caught). In some cases this fear will generalize to other sexual activities, so that sexual pleasure cannot be enjoyed without residual guilt even in adulthood. Likewise, the fear of discovery and possible physical punishment may be carried over into adulthood, creating a need for dangerous and illicit activities to achieve sexual gratification.

Thus, sex-negative training in childhood and adolescence may have far-reaching effects, such as increased erotophobia and sexual guilt in later life. Of course, people aren't rats or salivating dogs, and direct causal links between specific behaviors and particular past experiences don't usually exist. Instead, sexual behavior is determined by the interacting influences of context, emotional factors, and the totality of the individual's past sexual experiences, as well the logical (and sometimes illogical) consequences derived from these experiences.

The Brain: The Ultimate Fetish

One area of sexual behavior in which simple learning mechanisms such as imprinting or conditioning might play a significant role is in the establishment of fetishistic interests. The two main types of fetishes are: (1) preferential sexual attraction to an inanimate object, and (2) obsession with a particular body part. For unknown reasons, it is primarily men who are vulnerable to fetishistic impulses.

Fetishes are thought by many experts to represent a learned preference.[77] Krafft-Ebing, for example, suggested that fetishes arise as a symbolic representation of attraction toward another person:

> Erotic fetishism makes an idol of physical or mental qualities of a person or even merely of objects used by that person, etc., because they awaken mighty associations with the beloved person, thus originating strong emotions of sexual pleasure.[78]

Apparently, when the object of the fetish includes the entire person, it is instead called "love," the establishment of which, according to Darwin, "depends on pleasure from close contact with a beloved person."[79]

It is also possible to establish an "artificial fetish" in men through classical conditioning, by pairing slides of a normally neutral stimulus, such as a pair of black leather boots, with slides of an attractive naked woman.[*80]

In a similar vein, Freud interpreted fetishes within the context of his somewhat overworked "castration complex," which holds that little boys believe girls and women to be the unfortunate victims of castration. According to Freud, fetishistic attachment arises from a form of imprinting:

> The last impression received before the uncanny traumatic one [the boy's first realization that women, especially his mother, have no penis] is preserved as a fetish. Thus the foot or shoe owes its attraction as a fetish, or part of it, to the circumstance that the inquisitive boy used to peer up the woman's leg towards her genitals.[*81]

The fetish thereafter symbolizes the mother's supposedly missing penis.

Thus, in this view, a single traumatic event may be sufficient to establish a life-long fetish. In support of this hypothesis is the claim that many transvestites (men who gain erotic pleasure by dressing up in women's clothing) have childhood memories of being dressed-up in little girl's clothes by adult family members, either for entertainment, or as a form of punishment.[82] The reaction of the adults in attendance (amusement, for example) supposedly provides positive reinforcement for the fetishistic cross-dressing behavior; either that or the humiliation he experiences does permanent injury to the young boy's masculine self-image. Robert Stoller suggests that for a young boy, being dressed in girl's clothes (usually by a female relative) constitutes a symbolic act of castration.[83] For the adult transvestite (typically heterosexual and in other ways unremarkable), dressing as a woman reaffirms his maleness by juxtaposing the threat of castration symbolized by his feminine attire with the ultimate marker of masculinity, his intact penis. A similar dynamic may underlie deviant behaviors such as exhibitionism and voyeurism. In the former, for example, the male seeks confirmation of his masculine power through the embarrassment his victims display at the sight of his penis.

The association of the fetish object with the attainment of orgasm may also serve to reinforce such behaviors through conditioning. In one retrospective report, a male cross-dresser recalled numerous instances in which the pantyhose and underwear of female family members were present while he masturbated to orgasm, often touching or gazing intently at these objects.[84] Orgasm, as we have repeatedly suggested, is a powerful reinforcer, and although the usual object of the transference of positive emotions is one's (human) partner, it is certainly possible that transference to an inanimate object could occur.[*85]

A similar dynamic has been adduced to explain the English flagellation craze of the nineteenth century. As Reay Tannahill explains:

> The English happily concluded that it was the public school that was largely to blame for turning gentlemen into deviants. Trained from infancy by nannies and schoolmasters who believed that to spare the rod was to spoil the child, upper-class boys (they argued) found it habit-forming and continued in their adult years to need a good beating to set the blood coursing through their veins.[86]

However, as Tannahill also notes, "if being regularly whipped in childhood was all that was needed to make a flagellant, the practice would have been less an upper-class sport than an international pandemic."[87] In a similar vein, Steven Marcus, in his history of Victorian sexuality, *The Other Victorians*, relates that in 1828 a flogging machine was developed for a prostitute, Mrs. Theresa Berkeley, who was known for her expertise with the whip. This machine represents, in Marcus' words, "perversity's contribution to the Industrial Revolution."[88]

More generally, it has been argued that the cultural repression of sexuality precipitates widespread fetishism and sexual "perversion." In what is perhaps a slight exaggeration, Judd Marmor suggests that:

> When the sexual taboos of the Medieval Church began to be widely enforced by cruel sanctions, a veritable epidemic of sexual pathology ensued—sodomy, flagellation, hysterical "possession" by witches and devils, incubi, succubi, phantom pregnancies, stigmata, and the like. In contrast, it is worth noting that in societies in which access to sexuality was open and guilt-free—the early Greeks, Europe prior to the Middle Ages and most "primitive" societies—the so-called sexual perversions tended not to be present.[89]

In the nineteenth century, the fetishism of the sexually repressed Victorian age escaped its usual confines, infecting women as well as men. As noted earlier, fetishism is rare in women, and in the exceptional case in which it does exist, it usually takes the form of an inordinate attraction to a particular tactile or kinesthetic sensation, such as the feel of fur or a certain texture.[*90] Thus, according to Australian commentator

Beatrice Faust, "the coincidence of unique sexual repression among women [in Victorian England] and unique devotion to the corset was probably not accidental."[91] Instead, erotic pleasures derived from the tight lacing of the corset provided a much-needed alternative outlet for an otherwise frustrated sexuality. Similarly, the high heels and tight girdles in vogue in the 1950s and early 1960s may have offered the wearer certain kinesthetic delights.[92] More recently, young people of both sexes have begun to explore the erotic potential of genital and other body piercings.

These obvious cultural and temporal fluctuations in the prevalence and particular manifestations of fetishistic behaviors suggest that complex psychocultural dynamics are at work; much more complex than can be accounted for by simple learning theories. What, for example, determines the fetishistic potential of a particular object or body part? In Western societies, men may construct elaborate fantasies featuring female breasts, buttocks, or feet, but seldom is an obviously erotic zone, the mouth, the focus of fetishistic obsessions.[93] Not so for Sambia men, who "go on and on about the shapes and aesthetics of mouths."[94] Furthermore, the dynamic proposed by simple learning theories, in which an originally neutral object is paired with an erotic sensation by chance, and then reinforced by subsequent orgasmic episodes with the fetishistic object, leaves much unanswered. The most glaring omission again concerns the choice of the object. Why panties, stockings, a shoe, or a foot, rather than any of a multitude of other objects that might have been seized upon? Clearly, the fetish must have some pre-existing meaning that predisposes the fetishist to endow it with excess erotic significance.[95] Remember also that the vast majority of men are exposed to potentially fetishistic objects and images throughout their lifetimes, yet never develop a fixation.

The orgasmic-reinforcement dynamic has also been suggested as an explanation for the development of same-sex erotic preferences.[96] In this view, an adolescent or young adult's first sexual experience (defined how?) is of critical importance in the development of either a fetish or an attraction to members of his or her own sex.[97] Supposedly, even a single episode of homosexual activity or attraction, if reinforced by masturbatory fantasy, could be sufficient to permanently determine adult sexual orientation. However, it is exceedingly difficult to reconcile this hypothesis with the Sambia data. Conditions could not be more favorable for the development of a homosexual orientation, according to this theory, than they are for the Sambia. The young boys' first sexual experiences are with older, respected boys and men, while all contacts with women and girls are forbidden. Later, when the boys switch from the receptive to the insertive role in fellatio, these same-sex behaviors are "reinforced" by frequent orgasm. Yet the normative developmental outcome for these boys is strict heterosexuality, not homosexuality, as learning theory would predict.[98]

This is not to deny the existence of possibly momentous events, particularly in childhood, that shape adult sexuality, but to caution against the adoption of simplistic formulations that minimize the complexity of human sexual responses, especially the integrative and elaborative role of the human brain. In most cases, the developmental determinants of a person's sexual proclivities will forever remain a mystery. The defining events—if indeed any truly exist—are rarely available for conscious introspection. Instead, at least according to Freud and his multitudinous followers, when such memories exist they tend to be deeply repressed, awaiting rediscovery only after years of extensive (and expensive) psychoanalysis.

Given the importance of the concept of repression to Freud's famous "ego/id" theory of the structure of personality, it is rather surprising that so few attempts have been made to provide it with a firm biological basis. In the following section we make just such an attempt. Our theory provides a novel interpretation of the Freudian concepts of ego and id, extrapolated from observations of the evolution and development of the brain. Of course, it may turn out that the ego and the id exist only in the fertile imagination of Sigmund Freud, or, if they do exist objectively, that their physiological basis is very different than the one we suggest.

The Primordial Onion

There are very few evolutionary imperatives: to find food, to find a mate, and for humans, perhaps, to find shelter. The genes of individuals that are successful at these tasks tend to be passed down to succeeding generations, while those of failures disappear from the gene pool. In his seminal book, *The Selfish Gene*, English biologist Richard Dawkins proposes that evolution can best be understood by treating humans (and their bodies) as "gene machines" whose function is to ensure that the DNA they contain gets propagated further. That is, the functional unit of evolution is the gene, not the species as a whole, or even the individual. Despite this caveat, it is often convenient to speak as though the survival of the individual were important, with the understanding that, from a strict evolutionary standpoint, the individual matters only in his or her capacity as a container/propagator for human genes.

The human capacity to make tools and communicate (abilities we share with other primates) increases the survivability of the genes responsible for these complex abilities. At a macroscopic level of analysis, we observe that tools help people conserve energy, and the capacity for interpersonal communication allows them to aggregate into much more effective social (and hunting, gathering, and protective) units. Sometime in the distant evolutionary past, toolmakers and communicators had an advantage—but not just a survival advantage, a *reproductive* advantage. In the end, if people are but gene machines, what's important is not the survival of the machine, but the propagation, hence eternal survival, of the genes themselves. And for humans, mammals, and most other members of the higher phyla of the animal kingdom, gene propagation requires sexual intercourse.

Evolutionary theory, therefore, is ultimately a theory of sex. No matter how awesome a hunter, provider, or builder of huts a man might be, if he isn't also a good fornicator, his genes won't survive. We should therefore expect the pursuit of sex to be a primary determinant of brain anatomy and physiology. And while the human cerebral cortex offers innumerable advantages over more primitive brain designs, even rats and cats need elaborate neural mechanisms to control their reproductive organs and sexually antecedent behaviors, such as courtship. It is therefore not surprising that the portions of the brain that directly regulate sexual activity, such as the hypothalamus and the limbic system, are some of the oldest neural structures, evolutionarily speaking. In contrast, the cerebral neocortex—where people's higher thought processes reside—is evolutionarily rather recent.

The cerebral cortex plays a pivotal role in the sexual life of humans and other highly evolved mammals. The ability to become aroused by a fantasy, for example, bespeaks of direct cortical involvement. Greater cortical control may also be responsible for the relative emancipation of the human female from the tyranny of hormonally induced estrus. Furthermore, many researchers and philosophers believe that consciousness resides in the cortex, so that the conscious experience of sexual pleasure may itself be a cortical artifact. In the advanced primates, the lower, more primitive neural systems (e.g., the limbic cortex) remain critical to sexual functioning, but are subject to increased cortical supervision and subjugation.

The notion that the human brain is composed of multiple centers, or "mini-brains," was popularized by Paul MacLean in his "triune" model of the brain.[99] According to MacLean, the human brain is not the monolithic whole it sometimes appears; rather, it is a composite of three distinct mini-brains: one dating from humankind's ancient reptilian past, a second (limbic) brain that is shared by all mammals, and an evolutionarily recent neomammalian brain evident in only the most advanced species of *mammalia*.

According to MacLean, the reptilian brain concerns itself with instinctual behaviors, such as selecting and defending a home territory, hunting, forming social hierarchies, mating, and breeding. These behaviors are largely stereotypical, and are often enacted at inappropriate times and with insufficient regard for conditions prevailing in the external world, as when, for example, a bull mounts a wooden dummy, grossly mistaking it for a heifer (and thereby supplying the semen that is later used to artificially impregnate a sexually inexperienced cow).

The second neural center, the limbic brain, integrates perceptions of the outside world with internal sensations. Such integration allows for much greater behavioral flexibility and environmental congruity than does the simple reptilian brain. The limbic brain's primary function in mammalian species lacking a well-developed cerebral cortex is to process olfactory data within the context of the animal's current goals; in more advanced species it serves a similar integrative role, combining perception and thought in a goal-directed fashion. The limbic brain also oversees the expression of complex emotions, and partially regulates the evolutionarily critical functions of self-preservation and reproduction.

However, the greatest behavioral flexibility originates in the late-evolving neomammalian brain, which consists primarily of the enlarged cerebral cortex observed in the higher mammals, such as dogs, cats, monkeys, and apes. This is the brain of reading, writing, and 'rithmetic, and the seat of complex human sexual behaviors, over-and-above their animalistic components. As the pinnacle of the hierarchical triune brain, the cortex also exerts controlling influences over the more primitive limbic and reptilian brains.

MacLean did not develop his theory of the triune brain in an intellectual vacuum, of course. The intellectual history of the idea that the brain is composed of multiple centers—sometimes competing, other times cooperating—is quite extensive. One of the most famous early proponents of this notion was the nineteenth-century neurologist, John Hughlings Jackson, who suggested that critical functions are multiply represented in the brain, with phylogenically more recent areas actively inhibiting older, more primitive areas that subserve the same function. He also proposed that cerebral trauma could cause behavioral deficits indirectly, by releasing the lower centers from supervisory inhibition. In the rhesus monkey, for example, it has long been known that bilateral

ablation (removal) of the anterior temporal lobe of the cerebral cortex—
which makes extensive connections with the sexual behavior modulat-
ing limbic system—causes a condition marked by hypersexuality and
inappropriate behaviors.[*100] A similar effect is observed in humans: Anterior temporal lobectomy increases sexuality.[*101] The mechanisms underlying this hypersexual behavior are presently unknown. Is it possible that
removal of this section of the brain releases older areas from inhibition,
thereby allowing them to express their phylogenically old sexual control
functions? Hughlings Jackson suggested that a related mechanism might
be responsible for the licentiousness of dreams: "People are said to be
more immoral in their dreams; strictly their immorality is not kept
under; they are reduced to automaticity; only their lower processes are
active."[102]

Although MacLean argues for the existence of three distinct component brains, evolution is a largely continuous process; hence, we prefer
to think of the brain as a layered structure, with multiple processing
centers lying side by side, or layered one on top of the other, melding
together with often indistinguishable demarcations. One way to visual-
ize this arrangement is to imagine the brain as an onion, with the older
sexual centers at the core, surrounded by layer after layer of higher,
more recent structures, such as the cerebral cortex. The core corre-
sponds to a raw, bestial sexuality that knows little or no restraint. In
humans, at least, this core is overlaid with newer self-repressive layers
that provide greater direction and selectivity to the primordial sexual
urges in an attempt to integrate them into a unified, complex personality. (This repression is fortunate because the unbridled pursuit of sexual
pleasure would interfere with other important survival functions, inadvertently decreasing fitness; humans do not live by sex alone—although
they do reproduce thereby.)

This view of "brain as onion" bears certain striking similarities to
the ego/id theory of personality structure proposed by Freud. Many
neuroscientists believe that the deeper layers of the onion/brain are im-
penetrable to consciousness, which is thought to reside primarily in the
cerebral cortex. Furthermore, the higher, conscious levels are presumed
to actively inhibit or repress the lower levels. The obvious identification
of the primordial, sex-seeking, unconscious limbic brain with the Freudian id, and the more recently evolved, conscious, repressive functions of
the cortex with the ego, provides an intriguing anatomical basis for
Freud's structural theory of personality organization.

Recall that the id is the portion of the psyche governed by the
pleasure principle, which seeks immediate gratification in the form of

tension reduction. The ego, on the other hand, is dominated by the *reality principle*, which ensures that the discharge of tension sought by the id is appropriate to the situation at hand, and fulfills other goals of the individual. The ego is thus the mediator between the id and the outside world, with the power to repress the id when necessary. Of course, as pointed out in Chapter 3, according to Freud, successful repression is accompanied in many cases by deleterious psychological side-effects such as the development of neuroses. Indeed, the observation that neuroses often take the form of sexual obsessions may be adduced as additional evidence of the primacy of sex in the organization of the brain and personality. As Freud's contemporary and one-time mentor, the famous French neurologist Jean Charcot observed, "sex is always at the bottom of the trouble."[103]

One further implication of this view of brain as onion is that the ability of people to conceptualize, organize, and communicate their sexual feelings can be expected to be woefully inadequate because the neural structures that mediate primal sexuality predate the development of the specialized cortical centers that subserve language and complex thought. Literature, art, and even movies have attempted to describe the orgasmic experience; nevertheless, the orgasm of each gender remains basically inscrutable to the other. Thus, we are left to wonder, can orgasm *really* be described in words? Or, as intimated in the film *When Harry Met Sally*, do animalistic moans and groans convey a better sense of climactic experience than language ever could?

The conceptual gulf that separates the experience of sexual pleasure from the cognitive structures that mediate verbal expression has very real implications for the study of human sexuality in general, and for memory research in particular. Among the surprising findings in this area is the discovery that people are inordinately poor at remembering past sexual episodes, even very recent ones.

Waking Up in a Strange Bed

Few sexuality researchers entirely accept the psychoanalytic notion that memories, particularly emotionally or erotically charged ones, are actively repressed by the conscious mind. Despite such disagreements, however, one thing is clear: most people's memory for past sexual episodes is extremely poor.

The porousness of sexual memory is demonstrated, for example, by a study of 100 male and female college students who were asked to keep a daily diary of their sexual activities over a two-week "target" period.[104]

Two weeks later (i.e., a total of four weeks after the start of the target period), the students were asked to fill out a sexual behavior questionnaire describing their activities during the target period. At issue was the question of whether the students could accurately recall their sexual activities after a brief (two week) delay. In particular, would the answers provided on the questionnaire reproduce the behaviors reported in the diaries?

Because it was so short, most of the students had only one or no sexual partners during the target recall period. Not surprisingly, therefore, most were able to accurately recall the number of partners with whom they had had sex. Memory for specific sexual activities (such as penile-vaginal intercourse, cunnilingus, or fellatio) was much less accurate, however. For example, many more acts of penile-vaginal intercourse were reported on the questionnaire than in the diaries, even though the absolute number of occurrences was relatively small (a reported mean of 2.5 for the diaries and 3.3 for the questionnaire). In agreement with the stereotype of the sexually boastful male, the discrepancy in reported instances of intercourse was much greater for men than for women.

Memory for oral-genital sexual activities was even more suspect. Again, students apparently overreported the number of occurrences on the questionnaire, but with women rather than men being the worse offenders. Furthermore, an interesting asymmetry was detected: women were substantially more likely to report both "giving" and "getting" oral sex (50 percent "giving," 40 percent "getting") than were men (25 percent "giving," 20 percent "getting"). It is difficult to see how such an imbalance could arise unless there were systematic differences between the men in the study and the male partners of the women in the study—an unlikely possibility. Instead, perhaps women evaluate, store, and recall these experiences differently than men. For example, oral sex might be more salient for women because they achieve orgasm relatively more often during oral sex than during intercourse, whereas men orgasm readily in both situations (only oral-genital activities that led to orgasm were included in the study). Thus, men may be less likely than women to encode cunnilingus and fellatio as "sex," causing them to underreport the occurrence of these activities.

Although memory for sexual episodes is generally poor, there are four circumstances in which recall should improve dramatically—namely, when the sexual experience was either: unique, the first or last occurrence of its particular category (e.g., the first "blow job"), or especially pleasurable. Memory failure, on the other hand, can arise from a number of causes, including incomplete initial encoding, decay, and retrospective distortion (where the acquisition of new information precipitates a reevaluation or reinterpretation of existing memories). However, the single most important cause of forgetting is likely to be interference among similar memories.[105] Because of this, memories for infrequent or rare occurrences are much more robust than those for commonplace events, which tend to be easily confused (interfere) with one another. Thus, one is liable to better remember a sexual activity enjoyed only once or twice than a more frequent sexual activity.[106] (From an adaptive standpoint, infrequent events are more salient because such events often signal changes in the physical or behavioral environment.) The first occurrence of a particular event is also significant, hence better remembered than subsequent occurrences (a phenomenon known as the "primacy effect"). One's first love and one's first lover are seldom forgotten, despite their possible irrelevance to current life situations. What is relevant, in most cases, is one's current lover. In addition, the most recent occurrence of an event (e.g., sexual intercourse) is usually especially salient, and therefore recalled more easily (the "recency effect"). Finally, we would like to suggest that, perhaps where sex is concerned, the more exquisitely pleasurable the experience, the more likely it is to be accurately remembered, due to the increased salience engendered by the heightened pleasurability of the experience. (This last hypothesis has yet to be tested.)

Surprisingly, the available evidence indicates that men and women are exceedingly poor at recalling past sexual episodes, even when the recall period is short (e.g., two weeks), and the delay until recall is similarly brief. The implications of these findings for human sexuality research are obvious. Sex is an intensely personal and private behavior, which makes it exceedingly difficult to study with traditional scientific techniques, such as direct observation and measurement. Hence, the process of obtaining data on sexual behaviors often requires a public or overt disclosure of private or covert behaviors. Unfortunately, the translation of private behaviors into public disclosures invariably diminishes the accuracy of recall, especially when sensitive and often culturally taboo practices are involved.[*107] Self-reports of sexual behavior are subject to a wide range of influences, most notably the pull of social desirability (i.e., the tendency to tell the researcher exactly what he or she wants to hear, or what is socially acceptable).

One might even question the *ability* of people to accurately report their sexual activities and feelings, given the conceptual gulf that separates the experience of sexual pleasure and the cognitive structures employed to relate those experiences. Many linguists, cognitive psychologists, and others who study humankind's expressive capacity believe that the key to our language abilities is representation.[*108] According to the prevailing theory, innate mechanisms in the human brain support the acquisition of language skills by providing a "universal grammar" in which various linguistic constructs can be represented.[109] It is probably not an exaggeration to suggest that most cognitive scientists consider representation to be the cornerstone of cognition.[*110]

How, then, is sex represented in the human brain? At one level, it has been suggested that sexual knowledge and beliefs are organized in the form of "scripts," which are situationally specific sets of coordinated behavioral responses based on principles of sexuality that the individual has internalized, or learned, from a variety of external sources, including parents, peers, television, movies, books, and society in general.[111] Other sexual principles are derived internally through sometimes logical, but often illogical, thought processes. These principles, together with those arising from exogenous sources, form the core of the individual's sexual belief system, and elaborated as scripts, guide his or her sexual behavior.

Memory for particular sexual experiences, on the other hand, is maintained by the episodic memory system,[*112] utilizing representations shaped by the sexual scripts the person has internalized. In other words, a person's sexual belief system affects *how* sexual information is encoded in memory. Thus, as noted earlier, erotophobic or sexually guilty people have difficulty absorbing information on contraception and other sex-related topics (erotophobia, for example, is negatively correlated with success in college-level human sexuality classes[113]). Furthermore, as the experimental data clearly indicate, the sexual memory system is subject to numerous additional distorting influences beyond erotophobia and sexual guilt.

However bad our memory for sexual *episodes* may be, our memory for sexual *pleasure* is infinitely worse. Stated flatly, provocatively, and somewhat provisionally: We have *no* memory for sexual pleasure (or any other sort of pleasure, for that matter). Pleasure—the sensation of pleasure—is simply not represented in the human brain. By way of proof we can offer little more than introspection. Think back to the last time you enjoyed a pleasurable experience and try to describe how it felt, not in words, but by reinstating the feeling. As you'll see, the beauty of a sunset is easily recalled, yet the pleasures of an erotic touch are not.

Although research on memory for pleasure is sadly lacking, memory for pain has been examined in some detail. The main finding is that duration is relatively unimportant to the retrospective evaluation of how painful an experience (typically a surgical procedure) was. Instead, people tend to remember the peak discomfort they felt, and the intensity of feeling at the end of the painful event.[114] These observations provide important clues to how the brain evaluates and categorizes painful experiences, but they offer little in the way of evidence that the feeling associated with the pain—the qualia of the pain—is itself remembered. In a brief note published in the *International Journal of Psychoanalysis* in 1957, Sigmund Freud's biographer, Ernest Jones, observed that:

> It is very hard to imagine severe pain or to recall in one's imagination the memory of it. One knows about it intellectually but one cannot reproduce it.[115]

Jones attributed this inability to recall the sensation of pain to "a simple act of intense repression."

With regard to sexual memory, there is little doubt that certain pleasurable aspects of the sexual encounter will be remembered (though perhaps not very well). Given the duality that exists between pleasure and pain, it would not be surprising to find that what people remember is how good the sex felt at its peak (usually orgasm) rather than the duration of the experience.*[116] Once again, however, only summary information is retained. Although people are clearly capable of extracting and remembering the salient features of a pleasurable experience, it would seem that they are incapable of remembering the pleasure itself. The visual analogy would be to someone who can remember that a banana is yellow, smooth-skinned, and rather crescent-shaped, but cannot form a mental image of it. That, apparently, is how our memory for pleasure operates: We can remember the labels but not the sensations.

It is clear that our memory for the qualia of pleasure is severely impoverished, as is evident in our inability to mentally reinstate or replay a pleasurable sensation as we might the image of a lover's face or a favorite Beatles tune. But does this necessarily mean that the qualia themselves are not represented in the brain? Perhaps people can *recognize* the pleasures they have experienced previously even if they cannot *recall* them. This would certainly appear to be the case. An example from the realm of pain may help clarify this point. Most everyone knows what a headache feels like—the throbbing, the pounding, etc.—and can recognize the onset of such a pain when it arises. For the frequent sufferer, a headache is instantly recognizable; there is no question that the pain might be something else. Similarly, the pleasure of an orgasm is instantly recognized as such; it may feel better or worse than "usual," but it is decidedly an orgasm. It would appear, then, that people can instantly recognize the pleasure of orgasm or the pain of a headache as one that has been experienced before. Such an act of recognition requires, of course, that the qualia be represented in some fashion in the brain, although not necessarily in a form that permits their recall.

Compelling though this argument may at first appear, it is not decisive (this, of course, is the problem with conclusions derived solely from intuition). Perhaps all that a person needs to know about a pleasure or a pain to properly identify it is its physical location, or some other secondary, nonqualitative aspect. An ache in the head is a headache; an intensely pleasurable sensation with associated muscular contractions, altered blood flow patterns, and so on, is an orgasm. Expectations also play an important role in shaping the quality of subjective experience. Intuition supports this observation, too. Who hasn't touched a supposedly hot object on the stove, flinched in "pain," and then realized that the object was, in fact, not hot at all? In summary, it is not at all clear what aspects of an experience mediate its recognition. More to the point, the role played by the subjective qualities of an experience—its associated qualia—is still uncertain.

The preceding is largely speculation. Scientific research into the role of cognitive factors (memory, perception, and so on) in the experience of sexual pleasure is still very much in its infancy. Unfortunately, there are very few researchers investigating this fascinating area of human psychology. In general, sex has remained an essentially taboo subject in academic circles, with few scholars willing to risk their personal and professional reputations for the limited acclaim that comes from pioneering advancements in this field.[117] However, the AIDS epidemic has forced a reevaluation of academic squeamishness about sex, as researchers discover just how little is known about sexual behaviors in general, and practices implicated in the transmission of HIV (the virus that ultimately causes AIDS) in particular.

Too Much of a Good Thing?

Because of the threat of AIDS, sexual restraint has suddenly become a hot topic among clinicians and academicians. Even now, psychiatrists are busily identifying new pathologies of sexual "compulsion" and "impulse control." Twelve step programs for the "sex addict," modeled after Alcoholics Anonymous, are sprouting up across the country to serve the growing ranks of self-diagnosed sexual impulse control sufferers.*[118]

But is sex really addictive? Many psychiatrists and therapists believe so.[119] Sex, according to them, provides the "sex addict" with the temporary "fix" or "high" necessary to overcome feelings of loneliness, emptiness, and low self-esteem. In men, sexual addiction is thought to cause uncontrolled promiscuity and masturbation, transvestism, homosexuality, exhibitionism, voyeurism, fetishism, incest, child molestation, and rape.[120]

Technically, however, addiction requires the interaction of an exogenous substance with the brain. Sex, being an experience rather than a substance, cannot, therefore, be addictive in this strict sense.[121] Furthermore, unlike the treatment for other addictions, abstinence is not required of the recovering sex addict, only moderation and self-control.*[122]

Others suggest that "sexual addiction" is no more than a social construction of the conservative 1980s.[123] In this view, the construction of sexual addiction as an ontological category is symptomatic of a greater and more general backlash against the sexual revolution of the previous two decades. In essence, the creation of this new behavioral disorder (sexual addiction) legitimized conservative—and especially fundamentalist Christian—attempts to repathologize nonrelational sex.

The truth no doubt lies somewhere betwixt and between. People who perceive themselves as having a problem with sexual compulsivity should certainly seek treatment. On the other hand, the conservative trend of the 1980s was very real, and repression of sexual freedoms was a centerpiece of the conservative agenda. And then, of course, there was, and still is, AIDS.

According to the prevailing wisdom, if ever sexual self-restraint were needed, it is now, in the time of AIDS. To some, AIDS is a gloomy harbinger of the end of sexual freedom. But does the current AIDS epidemic really signal the end of sex, or at least nonrelational sex? Or can the pleasures and variety of sex still be enjoyed? The answer, as discussed in the next chapter, is clearly *yes*, especially if the pleasures of nonprocreative sexuality are embraced.

6.

AIDS: The End of Pleasure?

In 1999, 2.8 million people died of AIDS (Acquired Immune Deficiency Syndrome), and another 5.4 million people were newly infected with the human immunodeficiency virus (HIV), which causes AIDS. Disheartening, yes, but these numbers pale in comparison with the cumulative totals. By the start of the twenty-first century, nearly 19 million people had died of AIDS since the epidemic began in the 1980s, and more than 53 million had contracted HIV.[1] Thus far, Africa has been the hardest-hit region of the world: In many sub-Saharan countries, one out of every ten adults is infected with HIV.

In the United States, over one million people have been infected with HIV, and nearly a half million people have died of AIDS.[2] The epidemic has slowed among its earliest targets, gay men and other men who have sex with men, and is now considered by many to be mainly a disease of the poor and disenfranchised. More than half of all new AIDS cases now occur among African Americans and Hispanics; women make up about a quarter of all new diagnoses. Most of these infections were sexually transmitted.

In the present era of AIDS, sex—the ultimate giver of life—is sometimes also the merciless destroyer of life. Indeed, in many quarters it seems as though AIDS has become the new primary meaning of sex. The Catholic church, for one, opposes safer sex and instead promotes abstinence and monogamy as the only acceptable solutions to the problem of AIDS. (In a survey of Catholic priests conducted by the *Los Angeles Times,* 46 percent responded that it was "always a sin to use condoms as a protection against AIDS."[3]) Many politicians view AIDS as an opportunity to turn back the clock on the sexual revolution to a time when repression and secrecy were commonplace. To Christian fundamentalists, AIDS represents "God's punishment" for our collective sexual sins, particularly homosexuality and the sexual liberalism of the 1960s and 1970s.

Even condom manufacturers seem to view sex in terms of AIDS. Condom ads in the 1970s emphasized pleasure and intimacy, albeit in a rather overstated manner (for example, "Rough Rider . . . the only condom with 468 orgasmic studs that send sensory signals that make me tingle with ecstasy for you"). Today, in contrast, many condom ads stress disease prevention (for example, "Trojan condoms . . . because the heat of the moment can burn you for a lifetime").[4] The element of fear also is prominent in these ads, such as one for LifeStyles condoms that features an attractive woman and the tag line "I'll do a lot for love, but I'm not ready to die for it."[5]

To some, the condom is itself a symbol of death and disease. As one gay man relates:

> [When I pulled out a condom] I saw his eyes get filled with fear. Suddenly I realized that death was in the room with us. . . . The condom reminded us of the disease.[6]

The threat of AIDS has caused a reduction in the quality as well as the quantity of sex in some people's lives. For many people, gay and straight alike, sex without fear is a thing of the past.

But are sex and AIDS really inseparable? Or can fear of AIDS be overcome by a combination of safer sex techniques and positive attitudes toward sex? Obviously, condoms need not be a symbol of death. They can instead be a symbol of love for one's partner and concern for his or her health.[7] Condoms can also be erotically integrated into foreplay, becoming a part of sex rather than a hindrance to it. Furthermore, positive attitudes toward safe sex can be inculcated at an early age. As a twenty-one-year-old, condom-using gay man explains:

> I know I'm probably unusual. . . . For me, condoms have been the thing since the beginning. I don't find it difficult and it doesn't affect sex. I don't mind condoms at all.[8]

Unfortunately, this young man *is* unusual—only a scant minority of men regularly use condoms (although a far greater percentage of gay men than straight men use them on a consistent basis).

One reason why calls for safer sex have met with less than rousing success, we believe, is that the discourse on AIDS centers on disease rather than pleasure. In the current climate surrounding AIDS, pleasure is taboo.

A sex education pamphlet called "The A to Z of Love and Sex" was banned from use in British schools because a vocal group of conservatives complained about its content.[9] In the United States, Surgeon General Joycelyn Elders was fired for suggesting (at an international AIDS conference) that children be taught how to masturbate as an integral component of safer sex education.

A new dialogue on AIDS is clearly needed, one that acknowledges the importance of sex and the willingness of people to engage in risky behaviors if the perceived benefits are great enough. A much broader definition of "sex" also is needed. Nonpenetrative activities, such as cuddling, oral explorations, and mutual masturbation, need to be accepted as valid alternatives to vaginal and anal intercourse. Above all, there needs to be more open discussion of sexuality in general and pleasure in particular.

Although some form of sex education is a standard component of the curriculum in most American schools, too little is taught about the *meaning* of human sexuality. Gaining a rudimentary understanding of sexual physiology and the role of condoms in contraception and disease control is simply not enough. Children need to be taught that sex is a natural and pleasurable way to express love and affection for another person and that heterosexual and homosexual forms of expression are equally valid. Specific practices should also be discussed, both as possible sources of pleasure and to ensure an adequate fund of knowledge to combat the spread of sexually transmitted diseases, such as HIV/AIDS.

Unfortunately, many sex education programs now emphasize strict sexual abstinence before marriage as the *only* way to prevent the potentially adverse effects of adolescent sexuality. In 1996, the U.S. Congress passed a bill providing $50 million of annual federal support to the states for the implementation of sexuality education programs whose "exclusive purpose" was to teach the "social, psychological and health gains" of sexual abstinence (the bill required each state to match the federal contribution with $3 of its own funds for every $4 received from Washington). This action was taken despite the lack of conclusive evidence that abstinence-only programs prevent adolescents from becoming pregnant or acquiring sexually transmitted diseases. According to researchers at the Center for AIDS Prevention Studies at the University of California, San Francisco, "No abstinence-only curricula have offered scientific proof of their effectiveness. On the other hand, sex education programs that stress both abstinence and protected sex have been shown to be effective in delaying the initiation of sex, reducing the number of partners, and increasing condom use among the sexually active."[10]

The battle against AIDS also would be helped by (re-)eroticizing condoms. In particular, condom advertising should once again emphasize erotic pleasure and intimacy. In India, for example, the government has dominated the multimillion-dollar condom market for years, accounting for over 90 percent of all sales. In 1992 the first real challenge to the government's stronghold on the market appeared: Kama Sutra condoms, whose advertising campaign was launched with a twenty-three-page supplement to *Debonnaire* magazine (the Bombay-based equivalent of *Playboy*), which featured Hindi film actress Pooja Bedi and model Mark Robinson in a steamy pictorial.[11] Several fifteen- and sixty-second cable television commercials have also been developed for Kama Sutra. In one sexy spot (deemed too risque for the government-controlled broadcast network), the couple is shown sitting on a bed playing chess. She sweeps the pieces off the board and mouths the word "check," while he mouths the word "mate."[12] The tag line then appears: "Kama Sutra, for the pleasure of making love."

Finally, condoms should be improved to increase sensitivity and pleasure for both the wearer and his partner. Condoms could be made thinner, for example. Comfort could be further enhanced by making available a variety of shapes and sizes to ensure proper fit. (At least two specially sized condoms, Huggers and Magnums, have been marketed in the United States. Perhaps, as suggested by a participant at a 1987 AIDS conference, condoms should "be marketed in sizes like olives: super, colossal, jumbo."[13]) The market could also be expanded by producing a wider variety of specialty condoms, including "French ticklers" and ribbed condoms, which supposedly heighten the receptive partner's pleasure, flavored condoms for oral enjoyment, and brightly colored sheaths, all of which reemphasize the fun and pleasure in sex.[14]

Despite naive calls for sexual abstinence and monogamy, the simple fact remains that the consistent use of condoms provides the most effective means *for most people* of decreasing their vulnerability to becoming infected with HIV. Condoms are so effective that the simple expedient of always wearing a condom provides greater protection under most circumstances than does the elimination of all nonmonogamous sexual contacts. For example, in many situations, engaging in a hundred condom-protected one-night stands is actually safer than having a hundred unprotected sexual contacts with a single partner of unknown HIV status.[15] (The model from which these conclusions are derived is described in detail in Appendix B.)

The use of condoms also confers ancillary benefits on both the wearer and his partner. Most important, perhaps, is the ability of condoms to prevent the spread of *other* sexually transmitted diseases (STDs). This is particularly relevant because STDs (besides being potentially dangerous and unpleasant in themselves), facilitate the transmission of HIV and hasten progression to AIDS in those who are already infected. Condoms also prevent conception and thereby help decrease the incidence of unwanted pregnancies.[16]

In the United States and other Western nations, condoms are readily available and fairly inexpensive. So much so that buying condoms is a rite of passage for many American boys. Nevertheless, very few men (and, therefore, their partners) in Western countries consistently use condoms. In a national survey of heterosexual Americans conducted in the early 1990s, only 12.6 percent of those with risky sexual partners reported using condoms all the time.[17] Similarly, only 40 percent of unmarried adults questioned in a 1996 survey of sexual risk behaviors reported using a condom the last time they had intercourse.[18] The question is, given the severity of AIDS and the recognized efficacy of condoms in preventing the transmission of HIV, why do so few men wear them consistently, and why don't their partners insist?[19]

Is Risky Sex Rational?

One way to conceptualize the complex issues of safer sex and the threat of AIDS is to consider the choices confronting the individual sexual decision maker. HIV disease is a lifelong, severely debilitating, potentially fatal illness that—even with effective medical treatment—can significantly reduce the quality, if not the length, of an infected person's life.[20] Given the potential for such dire consequences, engaging in risky sexual activities may seem completely irrational, foolhardy, or even suicidal. Nevertheless, millions of Americans continue to endanger themselves by participating in high-risk sexual activities, despite being bombarded by educational messages ranging from "Just say no to sex!" to "No glove, no love!" The problem is clearly not ignorance. Is it stupidity? Or could there be *valid* reasons for continuing to engage in risky sexual practices?

Our 1992 article, "Is Risky Sex Rational?" provides a rudimentary answer to this complex question.[21] In a nutshell, we argue that in some cases risky sexual behavior could be considered *rational* in the sense that the perceived physical, emotional, and psychological benefits accruing from sex outweigh the threat of AIDS, as internalized by the decision maker.

What are the factors that need to be considered in making such a decision? On the positive side of the equation, sexual expression is an important aspect of human existence and, as we've discussed throughout this book, fulfills a number of important functions beyond mere physical satisfaction and reproduction. Sexuality plays an important role in shaping self-image and enhancing self-esteem and provides a mechanism to express feelings of intimacy for another person. Among gay men "sexual acts compose a language of love and affection."[22] Furthermore, the raw experience of pleasure is itself an immensely powerful attractor. If rats will starve themselves or cross electrified grids for sex, what will people do?

On the negative side are two main factors. The first is the perceived threat of AIDS, as mediated by one's subjective assessment of personal risk. Clearly, if one believes oneself immune to HIV infection, then it doesn't matter how horrible AIDS is. Many adolescents don't perceive themselves to be at risk, regardless of their sexual behaviors. Studies have also found that "high-risk" gay men often believe that they are no more likely than the "average" gay man to become infected with HIV.[23] One explanation for the tendency of "swinging singles" of all persuasions to underestimate their own risk is that no one sees themselves as the "type of person" who gets AIDS.[24] Furthermore, the "I'm not the type" fallacy is easily extended to potential partners, with whom one need not take precautions because they also "aren't the type" to be infected with HIV.

The second factor that must be considered in evaluating decision making with respect to HIV/AIDS is the perceived severity of the disease. Although most people are aware that AIDS is often fatal, the impact of this knowledge is diluted in several ways. First, death—whether by AIDS or otherwise—is often discounted because it is intangible, unimaginable, and distant. Many people would gladly face death prematurely in order to lead a more fulfilling life. Others approach death with a fatalistic attitude and the knowledge that death comes to us all eventually.[25] Perhaps, then, death is simply too ethereal and too distant to have a direct impact on people's behavior. Pain and suffering, on the other hand, are not. Consistent with this suggestion are studies that show that gay men who can remember the visual image of someone in the advanced stages of AIDS are more likely to reduce their number of sexual partners than those who do not have such an image, even if they are otherwise acquainted with someone with AIDS.[26] Moreover, the development of effective antiretroviral therapies, which have the potential to transform HIV into a lifelong, chronic disease for some patients, may further dilute the perceived severity of HIV/AIDS, as discussed below.[27]

The preceding observations may be formalized in a simple decision-making model. Let V_u and V_p denote the value or "utility" of engaging in either unprotected or protected intercourse, respectively. The utility measures V_u and V_p are meant to encode the myriad pleasures—physical, emotional, and intellectual—of sexual intercourse. The difference, $V_u - V_p$, is of primary interest, because it is this quantity that measures the expected gain from forgoing protection, which is usually perceived as increased pleasure, spontaneity, and intimacy. It is only when this gain is sufficiently great, say $V_u - V_p > T$, that the "rational" individual forgoes condoms and engages in unprotected sex. But what determines the threshold T? As suggested earlier, T is a highly complex, aggregate quantity that measures the individual's subjective fear of AIDS and perceived personal risk. The greater the perceived danger, or the more adverse the consequences of infection are believed to be, the greater the threshold T. For young adults who think themselves invincible, T is essentially nil.[28]

In this formulation, risky (that is, unprotected) sex is rational provided that $V_u - V_p > T$; in other words, as long as the benefits derived from unprotected sex are worth the risk. It is important to emphasize that in this model rationality is derived from inherently subjective estimates of perceived risk, fear of AIDS, and expected gain. A sexual decision maker is rational only to the extent that he or she behaves in accordance with his or her perceptions of the situation.[29]

Rationality aside, Americans are in many ways an exceedingly risk-averse group. Thus, if there is even a minute risk that a condom might permit HIV to pass, then condoms cannot be trusted. So suggested a particularly vocal anti–safe sex group called the Catholic League for Religious and Civil Rights. This group plastered the walls of New York City subways with posters bearing the misleading message "Want to know a dirty little secret? Condoms don't save lives. But restraint does. Only fools think that condoms are foolproof."[30] Although it is true that condoms provide less than perfect protection, the same holds for seat belts, yet no sensible person would ever proclaim that "seat belts don't save lives" and therefore that people should abstain from driving. This sentiment is echoed throughout the United States, in PTA and school board meetings, and in sex education classes that stress abstinence and eschew any mention of condoms, except to note that they do not always work. (Actually, the main cause of condom failure is human error. Teaching people how to use condoms correctly is very possibly the single most efficient way to improve condom effectiveness.)

But, while American institutions and groups tend to be highly risk-averse (especially when it suits their political agendas), individual Americans are much more willing to take risks. People enjoy sex and the myriad benefits it provides, including both pleasure and intimacy. Therefore, it is no surprise that many people are willing to risk their future health in order to enjoy the immediate and intense pleasures of sex.

A similar tension is evident in the contrast between "official" and individual attitudes toward oral-genital sex. The risk of HIV transmission during oral sex is very small—much smaller than the risk associated with vaginal or anal intercourse—but it is not zero. In the official discourse, unprotected oral sex is often grouped together with much riskier activities under the broad rubric of "risky" sex acts.[31] The attitude toward oral sex among many epidemiologists and other AIDS experts appears to be "better safe than sorry," which roughly translates to "let them find something else to do." In their view, all unprotected sex is taboo, whether high risk (e.g., taking the receptive role in anal intercourse) or low risk (e.g., receiving oral sex). But all risks are not created equal. Oral sex is very low risk: There are no more than a dozen suspected cases of HIV transmission resulting from cunnilingus or from receiving fellatio (and many of these cases are disputable). Giving fellatio is a bit higher risk, but it is much less risky than unprotected vaginal or anal intercourse and might even be safer than condom-protected intercourse, although there are little reliable data with which to test this hypothesis.

For many people oral sex serves as a substitute for riskier activities, such as unprotected vaginal or anal intercourse.[32] Oral sex is highly valued by both men and women as a means of giving and receiving pleasure. It is also the most widely practiced sexual activity among gay men and lesbians.[33] One indication of the popularity of oral sex is that prostitutes are called upon to perform this service more than any other activity (the ease with which fellatio can be performed—in a moving car, for example—may also influence its popularity). To the extent that oral sex provides an alternative to riskier activities, it should be encouraged. People, after all, are going to have sex. As one young gay man complained in reference to oral sex, "First you told me I couldn't fuck and now you're telling me I can't do the other thing I like."[34]

The trick is to make oral sex, or any sexual activity, as safe as possible within the individual's limits of acceptability. Different people are willing to accept different sexual risks, and they need accurate information about the risks associated with different activities in order to make intelligent choices. Labeling all unprotected sex as "risky" is neither helpful nor accurate. Condoms should (ideally) be used for all penetrative sexual activities, but if someone is going to have unprotected sex, it is safer for him or her to have oral sex than to engage in vaginal or anal intercourse.

Showers in Raincoats

Probably the most influential reason that many people choose to forgo safe sex is that they believe it to be less pleasurable than the riskier alternatives. This is particularly true of condoms,[35] the use of which has been unflatteringly compared to taking a shower in a raincoat.[36] The primary

complaint of men is that condoms decrease penile sensitivity, hence pleasure;[37] some women also complain of a loss of sensation.[38] (As one
eighteenth-century rake brags, "I picked up a fresh agreeable girl called
Alice Gibbs. We went down a lane to a snug place, and I took out my
armor, but she begged that I might not put it on, as the sport was much
pleasanter without it."[39]) Both men and women further dislike condoms for
the related reason that they form an artificial barrier against intimate contact. Many people also believe that condoms decrease sexual spontaneity
and therefore romance.

These are, for the most part, valid complaints. Condoms could certainly be made thinner to increase sensitivity and enjoyment. In 1995 a
British company began marketing a thinner plastic condom, which it
claimed is more comfortable and pleasurable than comparable latex condoms. And, as noted previously, the receptive partner's pleasure could
further be enhanced by thoughtfully designed condoms.

However, even if condoms were vastly improved, there would probably still be people who would refuse to use them. Some men claim to be
unable to perform while wearing a condom. Others simply dislike them
because they decrease sensitivity and pleasure; so much so that some men
are willing to pay male or female prostitutes extra for unprotected sex.[40]
Although this practice increases the prostitute's risk of becoming infected
with HIV or some other STD, a skillful prostitute can slip a condom onto a
customer without him ever knowing it (or so we've been told).[41] This trick
requires the prostitute to hide a rolled-up condom in his or her cheek and
then nimbly slip it onto the customer during oral sex, just prior to vaginal
insertion. The fact that some men are unable to discern that they've been
protected against their will suggests that whatever loss of sensitivity condom
use entails cannot be that great. A slight loss of sensitivity might even be
desirable in some instances because it helps stave off ejaculation, prolonging
the pleasures of intercourse (some prostitutes dislike condoms for exactly
this reason).

Inventing novel ways to put on condoms could also be a playful way
for couples to eroticize condom usage. More generally, simply incorporating condoms into erotic foreplay can have measurably positive effects on
how condom use is perceived and even on how much pleasure is experienced during protected intercourse.[42] Furthermore, the power of sexual
reward suggests that positive experiences with condoms should be self-
reinforcing. Perhaps, with enough practice, even couples that initially de-
tested condoms could grow to love (or at least tolerate) them.[43]

The adoption of behaviors, such as always using condoms, that reduce

HIV risks is liable to be gradual at best. People must decide on a situation-by-situation basis whether or not to take risks. Positive experiences with safer sex practices tend to reinforce protective behaviors, whereas negative experiences reduce the likelihood of these behaviors being repeated. But individuals do not make sexual decisions in a vacuum—it takes two to tango. Ideally, HIV-prevention decisions should be made jointly by the partners involved. In practice, however, the male half of a heterosexual couple often has the final say in whether or not condoms are used. (Not surprisingly, condoms are more likely to be utilized by couples who communicate freely about sexual issues.) This is especially true in traditional cultures. In parts of Africa, for example, some married women are at high risk of becoming infected with HIV as a result of having sex with their husbands, many of whom frequent prostitutes. Knowledge about HIV/AIDS and specifically about the effectiveness of condoms in preventing HIV transmission is generally poor in Africa. Moreover, when women do attempt to protect themselves by suggesting that their husbands wear condoms, their suggestions are viewed with distrust, or worse, as a sign that the wife has been unfaithful.[44] As a result, condoms are seldom used in marital relations, and millions of African women have become infected with a catastrophic, yet preventable, disease.

Social influences play an important role in shaping how safer sex practices are viewed. For example, some men refuse to wear condoms because they believe condoms are for boys, not for men.[45] Others insist that "real men don't wear condoms." Furthermore, as a consequence of past "social hygiene" campaigns, condoms are inextricably linked with prostitution in many people's minds.

However, the remarkable success of safer sex campaigns in the gay communities of large urban areas throughout the United States and Europe suggests that the social norms that regulate sexual behavior are at least somewhat malleable. By the early to mid-1990s the use of condoms had already been incorporated into socially accepted sexual scripts in many gay communities.[46] Of course, gay sexual practice has always embraced a wide range of activities, many of which are completely safe. According to Donald Crimp, "We [gay men] were able to invent safe sex because we have always known that sex is not, in an epidemic or not, limited to penetrative sex."[47] Indeed, many gay men do not participate in anal intercourse at all, while others prefer only the relatively safer insertive role.

Despite the widespread (though sometimes grudging) acceptance of safer sex by many gay men, as therapies for treating HIV improved in the late 1990s, disturbing signs of complacency began to appear. As the twentieth century came to a close, incidence rates for many sexually transmitted diseases began to climb among some groups of men who have sex with men, and several studies of the behavior of these men documented increases in sexual risk taking, such as having unprotected anal sex.[48] This apparent trend toward unsafe behaviors by some gay men reflects many factors, including "condom burn out" (dissatisfaction with the continued need for condoms more than a decade after the start of the epidemic) and a persistent desire for the pleasures of unprotected intercourse. It may also be related to the availability of effective therapies, which slow the progression of HIV disease in infected persons. These "combination therapies" consist of multiple antiretroviral drugs, which, when taken in large doses, can help keep the virus from proliferating, resulting in improved health and greater longevity for HIV patients. (These drugs do not work for everyone, however, and they are very toxic, causing myriad side effects that range from nausea to the development of anomalous fatty deposits, including so-called buffalo humps.) In short, the outlook for many—but not all—people living with HIV is much brighter than ever before.

In the language of the risky sex framework introduced above, combination therapies have markedly diminished the perceived severity of HIV/AIDS. According to the model, as perceived severity decreases, condom use should too. The model also predicts that condom use should decrease with reductions in the perceived risk of HIV transmission. The limited data available suggest that combination antiretroviral therapies can, *in some cases,* reduce the probability of HIV transmission during sex by limiting the amount of virus in the semen of infected men.[49] Whether this is true or not, many people *believe* that antiretroviral therapy reduces the probability of HIV transmission. As a result, having sex with a potentially infected partner is now perceived as being less risky than it was ten years ago, provided that the sex partner is receiving combination antiretroviral therapy.

Thus, the availability of effective HIV treatment options has affected two critical determinants of AIDS fear. Many people believe that these therapies reduce the likelihood that they will become infected, even if they engage in unprotected sex, and they also believe that combination therapies have made HIV a more manageable disease, and therefore that it would not be as terrible to be infected as it once was.[50] Together, these perceptions may have led to the increase in sexual risk taking observed in the late 1990s and early in the twenty-first century.[51]

A number of other factors can also influence whether or not people decide to engage in particular sex acts and whether condoms are used in these activities. Adolescents, in particular, may have different reasons for having unprotected sex.

Ignorance and Death

Growing up in the age of AIDS is a frightening and difficult process. Nevertheless, even with the specter of AIDS hanging overhead, adolescents are beginning to have sex at younger and younger ages. Are these "children" equipped to handle the difficult decisions and complex negotiations demanded by today's sexual society? The answer, we believe, is an incontrovertible *no*.

Most kids know what "safer sex" is. That is, they know they are supposed to use condoms when having sex. But most kids, gay or straight, don't practice safer sex, citing many of the same reasons as adults. However, for adolescents the issues are even more complicated because ignorance, immaturity, inexperience, and the imbalance of sexual power in relationships with older partners must be added to the mix. The following quotes are drawn from a *Los Angeles Times* article that discusses the reasons young gay men give for practicing unsafe sex:

> I figured that this guy was older and he knew what was right. He never mentioned safe sex.

> I knew about AIDS of course, but at that time I couldn't conceive of worrying about something that would kill me in ten years. I mean, ten years seemed like forever.

> For me, AIDS wasn't an issue because I thought it was something that happened to older guys.

> Sometimes I think that if I hadn't been so alone when I was fifteen and sixteen, none of this [becoming infected with HIV] would have happened. I was so scared of letting anyone know I was gay that I didn't have anyone to talk to and tell me I was doing everything wrong. At the time I felt like I was the only kid in the world like me.[52]

One commonality that emerges from studies of sexual risk taking in both adolescent and adult gay men is the theme of loneliness and isolation. And when sex becomes a tool to gain emotional closeness, precautions fly out the window:

> If life is bad enough, AIDS isn't seen as being very important. If you are freezing, you tend to accept any warmth you can get. For gay men without any close ties to other people, an active sex life can be the only tie to community.[53]

For young gay men and lesbian women the problem of isolation is especially acute. Afraid they will lose their parents' love if their sexual preference is uncovered, afraid they will be ostracized by their peers, and afraid of a world that discriminates against homosexuals, gay and lesbian teenagers can feel very alone. This type of psychological deprivation makes them vulnerable to expedient relief in the form of (often unprotected) sex. One additional indication of this isolation is the alarmingly high suicide rate among gay and lesbian teenagers.

For adolescents as well as adults, sex in the twenty-first century can be dangerous. However, in response to the question posed by the title of this chapter, AIDS certainly does *not* represent the end of pleasure. Not all sexual activities are risky: Cuddling, kissing, erotic massage, role playing, and mutual masturbation can all be quite satisfying. Oral sex also appears to be reasonably safe (but use a condom just in case!). Indeed, provided that latex barriers are used, most sex acts are relatively safe.

Of course, irresponsible sex has always been dangerous, especially when back-alley abortions are included in the equation. Sex in the new millennium is no different. Hence, before discussing further the prospects for a safer sexual future, it might be helpful to take a historical excursion back to a time when syphilis likewise threatened to put an end to pleasure.

Scourge of Syphilis

The history of syphilis presents an extraordinary lesson about the power of sex and the ravages of sexually transmitted diseases. As long ago as 1713, syphilis was recognized as "the true scourge of that vile carnality, and one should induce serious reflection amongst those rash young folk who give themselves over so easily, even wildly to a pleasure which is so ephemeral and whose consequences are so regrettable."[54] Yet, despite causing pain, death, disfigurement, and debility; despite countless educational campaigns warning people of its dangers; and despite the availability of preventive measures and, more recently, an antibiotic cure, syphilis has endured and even flourished. The history of syphilis thus provides a valuable and instructive analogy to the current HIV/AIDS epidemic.[55]

Syphilis first made its presence known in Europe shortly after the return of Columbus and his men from their explorations in the New World at the end of the fifteenth century. Although it is not certain that Columbus and his sailors transported the disease from the Americas to Europe, many scholars believe this to be the case.[56] (Columbus, incidentally, appears to have died of syphilis, in 1508.) A second school of thought contends that syphilis is an ancient disease found in Europe and elsewhere, citing biblical references as evidence, including Psalms 38:5, 7, "my wounds stink and are corrupt because of my foolishness . . . for my loins are filled with a loathsome disease; and there is no soundness in my flesh," and Deuteronomy 28:27–29:

> The Lord will smite thee with the botch of Egypt, and with the emerods, and with the scab, and the itch, whereof thou canst not be healed. The Lord shall smite thee with madness, and blindness, and astonishment of heart.[57]

Regardless of its origin, syphilis had spread throughout Europe by 1500 A.D. The international flavor of the epidemic is reflected in the various names by which this dreaded disease was called:

> The Italians called it the Spanish or French disease; the French called it the Italian or Neapolitan disease; the English called it the French disease; the Russians called it the Polish disease; the Turks called it the French disease.[58]

The ravages of syphilis apparently provided little deterrent to the practice of unsafe sex. Describing the syphilis epidemic in France in the first quarter of the twentieth century, one commentator concludes, "We are obliged to admit that, whatever the actual figures involved, syphilis was certainly not in decline, despite the intense prophylactic campaign which had been under way since the beginning of the century."[59]

Syphilis is now endemic throughout the world. But today's syphilis is different from the epidemic syphilis of the 1500s; the spirochete itself appears to have evolved during the interim. From the first hundred years of its reign of terror, syphilis was an unusually virulent disease, sweeping through towns and cities, leaving decimation in its wake.[60] The primary manifestation of syphilis, then as today, was the presence of a chancre or ulcer at the point of infection; secondary manifestations often included systemic debilitation and death. In contrast, syphilis in its modern form is comparatively mild and is readily cured if treated with antibiotics in the early stages. However, if left untreated, syphilis can still cause blindness, insanity, and even death.

Syphilis has become a ubiquitous hazard of modern sexual life. Despite its prevalence, it remains a badge of immorality and shame and has not been normalized as a routine medical complaint. Unfortunately, shame breeds silence (hence, further infections). Of course, as with any rule, there are exceptions. For example, the fabled eighteenth-century Italian playboy, Casanova, regarded the permanent scarring and disfigurement caused by "the tax on pleasure" (as syphilis was then known) as a mark of distinction:

The sickness we describe as [syphilis] does not curtail life, for those who know how to cure themselves of it; all it does is leave scars; but we can easily console ourselves with the thought that we have won them in pleasure, like soldiers who are delighted at the sight of their wounds, the signs of their virtue and the sources of their glory.[61]

Even with modern antibiotic treatments, the global prevalence of syphilis has not abated. Worldwide, an estimated 3.5 million new cases occur each year.[62] This continued high incidence is really not surprising given that antibiotics are merely curative, not preventive. Just because a sexually transmitted disease can be cured doesn't mean it will go away. Sexual pleasure, as we have repeatedly emphasized, is a powerful motivator. If the fatal form of syphilis did not change sexual lifestyles, it should not surprise us to find that treatable syphilis presents but a small deterrent to unsafe sex.

Unlike syphilis, the prospects for discovering a cure for AIDS are slim, although billions of research dollars have already been devoted to this cause.[63] One reason for pessimism is that it may be impossible to completely eliminate HIV from the body once infection is established because HIV is unusually adept at evading detection by the weakened immune system.[64] About the best we can hope for in the near future is to change HIV/AIDS from an often fatal disease to a chronic but manageable disease, through the continued development of newer and more effective antiretroviral therapies to control viral replication.

Developing a vaccine against HIV infection is a similarly daunting challenge. Most experts believe it will take many years to achieve this goal, if indeed inoculation against HIV is possible (there is still no vaccine against syphilis or gonorrhea). Even if the search for an effective vaccine proves successful, it is likely to be exceedingly difficult to ensure that those most in need of protection receive it.[65] Economics, logistics, and prejudice could prevent the vaccine from securing either the widespread global distribution (e.g., in sub-Saharan Africa, India, and Southeast Asia) or the targeted domestic utilization necessary to significantly affect HIV infection rates.[66] Furthermore, mathematical models suggest that unless substantial vaccine coverage can be achieved, the consistent use of condoms and the adoption of safer sexual practices will remain the most effective means of preventing the further spread of AIDS.[67]

Learn the Message Now

As should be clear from the preceding discussion, the time to learn the message of safer sex and condom use is *now*. AIDS is just the latest in a long line of sexually transmitted disease epidemics. Before that, it was "incurable" genital herpes. Even before that, it was syphilis. One wonders how far back the trail leads. Philippe Ricord, the famous nineteenth-century syphilographer, once remarked, "In the beginning, God created the heavens, the earth, man and venereal diseases."[68] What this suggests, using history as a barometer, is that STDs only get worse. So let's learn the message now!

At present, experts in the United States, Europe, and elsewhere are busily engaged in the search for a biomedical "magic bullet" that will do for HIV/AIDS what antibiotics did for syphilis and gonorrhea.[69] Or, if a cure cannot be found, perhaps some biomedical means of preventing HIV infection or arresting progression of HIV disease before it reaches full-blown AIDS can be discovered (the long-term effectiveness of current antiretroviral therapies is not known). This strategy is problematic, however, both because magic bullets are elusive and because such bullets, when obtained, are disease-limited. Thus, even if an HIV/AIDS vaccine were successfully developed *and* deployed—a monumental achievement that would save millions of lives worldwide—it would remain limited to preventing a single STD, namely HIV/AIDS.[70]

It hardly seems cost-effective to fight each new pathogen as it arises. The development of an HIV/AIDS vaccine will cost billions of dollars. The number of known infectious agents, meanwhile, grows each year at an exponential rate.[71] Twenty-five years ago, no one had heard of HIV, Legionnaire's disease, Ebola River virus, or the hantaviruses. Humanity's continued encroachment into the natural world ensures ever-increasing contact with hitherto unknown pathogens. Can society afford the massive expenditures necessary to wage biological warfare on each newly recognized infectious disease that threatens the public health? Of course, only a small proportion of these pathogens will be sexually transmitted. But despite its size, this small proportion is significant. The list of STDs already includes such nasty viruses as cytomegalovirus, hepatitis B, HIV, herpes, and syphilis, in addition to gonorrhea, genital ulcers, and chlamydia. And newly discovered (or evolved) pathogens tend to be relentlessly virulent, as the syphilis epidemics of centuries past amply demonstrate.

Taking a long-range perspective, we believe that a cheaper and more effective solution to the STD problem already exists, namely, the ignoble condom. When used properly, condoms prevent the transmission of most STDs and have the greatest potential for preventing future ones as well. Yes, they could be more comfortable and sensitive. And yes, they may be a drag to use. But what's the alternative? Like budget deficits and rock 'n' roll, STDs are here to stay. Must we spend hundreds of millions of dollars—

and lose countless lives—fighting recurring sexually transmitted disease epidemics? The pharmaceutical companies would profit from such a strategy, but are they appropriate beneficiaries?

For condom-based campaigns against STDs—both current and future varieties—to succeed requires the cooperation not only of individuals, but of governments and societies as well. As a society, we must first acknowledge that the primary motivational characteristic of sex is pleasure and then acknowledge that the pursuit of pleasure is a universal of human nature. Hence, if sex is pleasure, and if humans inevitably pursue pleasure, it stands to reason that sex will be repeatedly pursued. Rail against it, repress it, and moralize it ad infinitum; sex will find a way. Consequently, given the ineluctable risks (STDs, unwanted pregnancies, and so on) that sexual behavior entails, sex and condoms would appear to be a marriage made in heaven. And, as in all marriages, acceptance and compromise are essential. Humans need to learn to play safely, societies need to acknowledge the fundamental role of sex and pleasure, and governments need to encourage condom manufacturers to make products that are inexpensive, comfortable, and pleasurable.

Can We Talk?

Unfortunately, sex remains a taboo subject with a highly restricted discourse.[72] Pleasure is seldom mentioned in the mainstream HIV/AIDS prevention literature, much less popular press accounts of HIV/AIDS prevention strategies. Honest discourse about sex is shunned, it appears, because honesty requires explicit acknowledgment of the prevalence and joys of nonprocreative sexuality.

Young men and women are dying from ignorance (for example, not knowing the proper way to use a condom) while self-imposed censorship remains in effect as we try not to offend the morally hypersensitive. As Randy Shilts observes in *And The Band Played On,* as of November 6, 1984, nearly four years after the first clinical cases of AIDS had been reported:

> President Reagan had never publicly spoken the word AIDS or ever alluded to the fact that he was aware that an epidemic existed. . . . By the time President Reagan had delivered his first speech on the epidemic of Acquired Immune Deficiency Syndrome [in mid-1987], 36,058 Americans had been diagnosed with the disease; 20,849 had died.[73]

The censorship regarding AIDS also extends to advertising, if only implicitly. Thus, *explicit* descriptions of condoms and their usage are considered obscene and, until recently, were effectively banned from appearing on television or in widely disseminated publications. For example, the Fox television network finally agreed in 1991 to air condom ads provided that they focused only on disease prevention and did not mention specifics about a particular brand (for example, what distinguishes one brand from another, such as how they *feel*). Two months later, however, the network had broadcast only a single fifteen-second ad.[74] The public service messages released in the mid-1990s by the Centers for Disease Control (CDC) promoting condom use have suffered a similar fate. Of the three largest networks, only ABC showed any of these spots within the first two months of their release and then only during late-night programming, to avoid "exposing youngsters to the ads."[75] Earlier the CDC was forced to kill a series of radio ads that, among other proposals, would have featured Whoopi Goldberg proclaiming, "Ain't making no Whoopi without a condom," and George Burns confessing, "I first started using condoms when I was a young man. I think I was seventy-two," because they were deemed "too explicit" for the American public.[76]

Condom ads do occasionally appear on cable television stations, such as MTV and other youth-oriented channels. And, in the twenty-first century, they finally found their way to network TV. In December 2000, the venerable late-night comedy show "Saturday Night Live" aired a fifteen-second advertisement for Trojan condoms. The commercial opens with a scene of a young man wearing a silly party hat, sitting on his couch, rocking out to bad techno music. The voice-over intones, "This New Year's Eve you can wear one of these, and look stupid" [*cut to a table with a blue condom on it*] "Or you can wear one of these and look smart. Trojan latex condoms—the most trusted. Have a happy and healthy New Year!"[77] The makers of Trojans are to be commended (as is NBC) for breaking through the barrier against condom advertising on network television. In light of the current AIDS epidemic and the proliferation of other sexually transmitted diseases (including chlamydia and herpes), America's reluctance to promote condoms through every available avenue is sad at best and criminal at worst.

Of course, reticence regarding the frank discussion of sex is hardly new. In the United States, restrictions on the advertisement and distribution of condoms and other contraceptive devices can be traced to the passage by Congress, in 1873, of the grandiosely titled "Act for the Suppression of Trade in, and Circulation of Obscene Literature and Articles of Immoral Use," more popularly known as the Comstock Act.[78] This act stated, in part:

> [No] article or thing intended for the prevention of conception or procuring of abortion . . . shall be carried through the mail, and any

person who shall knowingly deposit, or cause to be deposited, for mailing or delivery, any of the hereinbefore-mentioned articles or things, or any notice, or paper containing any advertisement relating to the aforesaid articles or things . . . shall be deemed guilty of a misdemeanor.[79]

(As will be discussed in Chapter 7, the Comstock Act also prohibited the distribution of obscene literature.)

In the late nineteenth-century United States, contraceptives were inherently obscene. In one case, brought to trial in 1893, a schoolteacher was fired for allegedly mailing a letter advertising "certain appliances for females," that is, contraceptives.[80] Upon learning the rudimentary facts of the case, the court concluded, "Without further description, it is sufficient . . . to say that it was grossly obscene and indecent."[81] The identification of contraception with obscenity extended well into the twentieth century. Many states continued to forbid the sale of condoms and other contraceptives through general obscenity statutes that prohibited the sale of any article for "immoral or indecent purposes" until as recently as 1960.[82]

Although only one state (Connecticut) specifically outlawed the *use* of condoms, the manufacture, advertisement, and distribution of such devices was forbidden throughout the United States. The first relaxation of anti-contraceptive laws came in 1918, when birth control advocate Margaret Sanger challenged the New York state prohibition on contraceptive devices, arguing that the ban was unconstitutional because it prohibited doctors from prescribing to married women items of proven medical value.[83] In ruling that the ban on contraceptives did not apply to doctors, the judge in this case set a long-enduring precedent in which the medical aspects of contraceptives were emphasized, rather than their (non)reproductive consequences. The Massachusetts Supreme Court, for example, held that "where an appliance, in this case a condom, had the dual capacity of being a contraceptive and at the same time preventing venereal disease, the prosecution must show that the seller is aware that the buyer intends to use the device for contraceptive purposes."[84]

The emphasis on married couples in the Sanger case also is significant. The need for effective contraception was clearly much greater for unmarried sexual partners than it was for married couples. However, to acknowledge this and extend contraceptive protection to all couples would have been to recognize explicitly the legitimacy (or, at least, the existence) of nonmarital sexuality.

Similarly, when the Connecticut ban on the private use of contraceptives was finally removed in 1965, the stated beneficiaries were once again *married* couples.[85] Married people, it was ruled, should be free to make contraceptive decisions in private, unencumbered by governmental interference. Some seven years later this right was finally extended to all individuals, married or single.[86]

In its 1977 decision lifting the remaining restrictions on condom advertising (the anticontraceptive provisions of the Comstock Act having been overturned in the 1936 decision *United States v. One Package*[87]) the U.S. Supreme Court rejected the argument that "advertisements of contraceptive products would offend and embarrass those exposed to them" or would "legitimize sexual activity of young people."[88] Nevertheless, condom advertising remained the province of men's magazines until the middle of the 1980s, when mainstream magazines, including *Time, Newsweek,* and *People,* and some cable television networks (such as MTV) began accepting ads in response to the AIDS crisis.[89] However, the condom has been desexualized to make it more palatable to the masses. It is no longer a device of shared intimacy and pleasure; instead, it now merely "helps reduce the risk."[90] Fear-based ad campaigns are less likely to be effective at motivating behavioral change than those based on pleasure, but fear is the driving force behind such campaigns—not just fear of disease but fear of offending the delicate sensibilities of the self-righteous few.

The history of antiobscenity crusades in both England and the United States suggests that the denial of truth that currently threatens to engulf the discourse on AIDS is unlikely to abate. Deep-seated, irrational fears underlie the prohibition of sexually explicit books, movies, magazines, and advertisements. In the following chapter we suggest that a profound aversion to masturbation and nonprocreative sex in general animates much of the past and present antipornography fervor. Unfortunately, this history suggests that because safer sex is necessarily nonprocreative, any attempt at an honest, sensible discourse on AIDS will be accorded the same censorial treatment as more traditionally "obscene" materials have received in the past.

7.

Porn: Tempest on a Soapbox

Imagine this movie: A helpless and troubled, though attractive woman is married off to an ineffectual man. Later, a second man coerces her into selling herself sexually, and somehow, she falls in love with her coercer. When her husband learns of the affair he attempts to rape her, and then, when she continues the affair, he mutilates her.

Despicable? Yes. Horrific? Definitely so. Obscene? Perhaps, but probably not. Certainly the vast majority of critics who saw the film *The Piano,* whose plot is summarized here, deemed it Art—a feminist achievement, in fact. They thought it was so good, so original, that they even honored it with three Academy Awards (best actress, best original screenplay, and best supporting actress).

To some of us, however, *The Piano* was merely despicable, and even more so because the woman's daughter in the film was a witness to both the rape and the mutilation. This film and the critical acclaim it has garnered aptly demonstrate the hypocrisy surrounding the issue of pornography. An X-rated movie that suggested that victims of rape and attempted rape sometimes fall in love with their victimizers would be vigorously condemned and possibly even successfully prosecuted as obscene. Yet, it now appears that if the actors' genitals are not depicted and the production values are first-rate, then a movie such as this can become a cultural ideal. More so if it is written and directed by a woman and rendered more believable by a competent actress (Jane Campion and Holly Hunter, respectively, in *The Piano*).

Although we are certainly not arguing that *The Piano* was obscene, the preceding discussion does suggest that obscenity is often a question of

168

packaging, of style over substance. Is this what the framers of the U.S. Constitution intended? As currently interpreted, the First Amendment to the Constitution is held to protect ideas, even sexually provocative ideas.[1] It should not matter whether the ideas are articulate or inarticulate, fancy or drab. Freedom of speech should extend to all speakers—those who wax poetic and those who do not. Merely making speech more attractive, as in *The Piano,* should not confer upon it greater protection than would be afforded the same idea when rendered less ornamentally. That this is not presently the case, nor has it ever been, suggests a profound misunderstanding of the meaning and relevance of pornography, both in theory and in practice.

Pornography as Pleasure

The significance of pornography is fairly obvious: Pornography is a powerful and effective vehicle for graphically portraying the idea that sex is pleasurable and for extolling sexual diversity. Maybe it isn't realistic, but the message—that sex is fun, malleable, and pleasurable—is one with which we are all quite familiar. As we have demonstrated throughout this book, in many ways sex *is* pleasure.

If pornography is largely the conveyance of the idea that sex is pleasurable, why is it so threatening? It is threatening because it challenges conventional morality in a particularly provocative way. It describes or portrays people enjoying sex—usually nonprocreative sex—void of guilt and shame. The effect is especially dramatic when the moral constraints of genital modesty and heterosexual monogamy are challenged. Multiple-partnered sex, homosexual sex, anal sex, interracial sex, and so forth are graphically conveyed in a palatable and pleasing manner. This, in and of itself, constitutes blasphemy in some quarters. Furthermore, the more graphic and real it appears and the more the participants seem to enjoy themselves, the more challenging it is to conventional morality.

Even the term *pornography,* drawn from the Greek word referring to representations of harlots and prostitutes, conveys the notion of indulging in alternative forms of erotic pleasure.[2] The historical conception underlying pornography is the doubtful premise that sex with a prostitute is more pleasing, or in some other way superior, to more conventional sexual liaisons. In this regard, pornography is, by definition, unconventional. It is unconventional in format, ideation, and configuration—necessarily so—because it challenges the orthodox perspective. Thus, anything that is unconventional or a bit unsavory, as judged by the prevailing morality, may be called pornographic.[3]

Because it challenges the prevailing morality, pornography has been attacked as "sick," perverted," and even "demonic." Among other things, it has been accused of causing young men and women to masturbate (thereby depleting their strength and perverting the natural function of sex), as well as converting heterosexual innocents into vile homosexuals. More recently, pornography has been blamed by radical feminists for the appallingly high incidence of sexual violence against women. But, if true evil—in the Nazi sense—is ultimately banal, as argued by Hannah Arendt,[4] then depictions of the pleasures of sex (in the absence of guilt and shame) are at worst commonplace. To categorize pornography as inherently demonic fails to appreciate the social and political nuances involved. Thus, the English historian Lawrence Stone advises us not to underestimate the political significance of obscene verse in destroying the charisma of the monarchy in seventeenth-century England.[5] Aubrey Beardsley's graphics, meanwhile, clearly challenged the prevailing Victorian morality.[6] Along another dimension, the poems of Sappho are a sensual celebration, whereas darker motives pervade the ancient Indian *Jaiminiya Brahama*.[7] The transgression of taboos incites eroticism,[8] and eroticism often contains elements of hostility, fetishization, and dehumanization.[9] As these examples attest, pornography, like sexuality itself, defies any attempt at naive categorization.

Furthermore, the power of a demon is measured by the extent to which it can fight back. Several thousand years of pornography—from cave drawings to X-rated movies—provide ample evidence of its strength and, therefore, perhaps, its worth. Pornography is not easily suppressed nor discarded because it is a singular voice of sexual dissent. In it the nonnormative finds expression. It is homosexual. It mixes races. It employs inanimate objects. It is a celebration of sexual liberation that is enjoyed by millions of Americans. Pornography is a powerful voice against conventional morality in general and powerful moralizers in particular. As such, we'll argue later in this chapter, it is protected by the First Amendment to the U.S. Constitution.

Pornography elicits widespread disapproval precisely because it is unconventional in how it depicts pleasure. Consider for a moment the pornographic imagery of the ancient Greeks, such as the artwork on an Attic vase. These paintings depict the sexual lives of satyrs and are replete with enormous penises, phallic birds, fetishes, bestial sex, and so on. They are licentious in sexual detail, as well as comical and absurd.[10] The pleasures of heterosexual anal intercourse and male homosexuality are also clearly evident in these and similar Greek paintings.[11] The depictions explore and extol alternative forms of sexual expression and reinforce sexual hedonism. And this is precisely their value: They provide a welcome alternative to conventional morality.[12]

Sinning against Oneself

There is an even more powerful rationale for society's extreme animosity toward pornography. Pornography is much maligned, and even feared, because it is a highly visible correlate of masturbation, principally male masturbation.[13] Because masturbation is perceived (by some) as a pernicious evil, pornography is indicted as an accessory to the crime.

While most experts today believe that masturbation and other forms of self-pleasuring are important and healthy (or at least benign) expressions of human sexuality, this view is by no means universally endorsed, culturally or historically. The opposite belief—that masturbation is debilitating and debasing—has historically held sway, especially in the Judeo-Christian world, where the expenditure of semen outside of procreative marital intercourse has been vigorously condemned (see Chapter 2).[14] For example, the Jewish Zohar identifies masturbation as the most abhorrent of the sins recorded in the Scriptures.[15] In a similar vein, St. Thomas Aquinas suggested, "After the sin of homicide whereby a human nature already in existence is destroyed, this type of sin appears to take next place, for by it the generation of human nature is precluded."[16] Since fornication is strictly forbidden as well, the prohibition on autoeroticism effectively denies sexual expression to all but the married. One can scarcely doubt the importance of this policy to the preservation of the Church's authoritative position in past centuries, but G. Rattray Taylor surely overstates the case in his monumental review, *Sex in History:*

> This is particularly significant, for we now know that the belief that sexual pleasure is wicked springs primarily from parental taboos on infantile masturbation; the fact that the punishment is given when the child is too young to understand its significance, and when masturbation is the only means by which he can afford himself pleasure by his own unaided efforts, results in a fear of pleasure becoming embedded in the unconscious, and being generalized until it becomes a fear of pleasure in all its forms. No doubt the Church realized, even if unconsciously, that the maintenance of its system of repression was ultimately founded on the willingness of parents to frown on infantile masturbation, and, therefore, concentrated a great deal of attention on the matter.[17]

The psychoanalytic tone evident in this passage is not surprising. Freud himself suggested that the sexual guilt exhibited by neurotics is "regularly attached to the memory of some masturbatory activity, usually at puberty," because "masturbation represents the executive agency of the whole of infantile sexuality and is, therefore, able to take over the sense of guilt attaching to it."[18] Although the specific consequences of parental inculcation of negative attitudes toward masturbation have not, to our knowledge, been studied, there is ample evidence linking masturbatory guilt with other manifestations of sexual repression.[19]

And All Its Frightful Consequences

Early in the eighteenth century, age-old religious preoccupations with masturbation were transformed into secular medical concerns with the publication in England (by an anonymous author) of *Onania; or, The Heinous Sin of Self-Pollution, and All Its Frightful Consequences, in Both Sexes Consider'd, &c.*[20] This book, which had gone through nineteen editions by 1750,[21] condemned in heavily moralistic tones the "sin" of masturbation but was notable chiefly for its insistence that masturbation caused grievous injuries to the health of its practitioners, not the least of which were "stanguries, priapisms and gonorrheas, thin and waterish seed, fainting fits and epilepsies, consumptions, loss of erection and premature ejaculation, and infertility."[22]

The level of scholarly achievement in *Onania* was relatively low. Not so for *Onania*'s ideological successor, a book by Swiss physician Samuel Tissot titled *L'Onanisme; ou, Dissertation physique sur les maladies produites par la masturbation*. First published (in French) in 1758, Tissot's work was soon translated into English (*Onanism; or, A Treatise upon the Disorders Produced by Masturbation; or, The Dangerous Effects of Secret and Excessive Venery*), German, and Italian, and it remained popular (and in print) through the end of the nineteenth century.[23] Like the author of *Onania*, Tissot soundly condemned the practice of masturbation, citing various ill effects to both physical and mental health. But rather than justifying this condemnation on moral or religious grounds, Tissot offered a scientific explanation for the causative evils of masturbation. To Tissot, the root of the problem was the "excessive and unnatural" expenditure of semen, and the concomitant energy depletion.[24] For, as Tissot argued, "The seminal liquor has so great an influence on the corporeal powers . . . that physicians of all ages have been unanimously of the opinion that the loss of an ounce of this humour would weaken more than that of forty ounces of blood."[25]

Following Tissot, the antimasturbation literature grew "awfully damn quickly" in the ensuing years of the late eighteenth and early nineteenth centuries,[26] culminating in the 1857 publication of William Acton's *The Functions and Disorders of the Reproductive Organs*, which will be discussed shortly. The antimasturbation fervor was so widespread and captivating that, in 1775, the ever-so-ingenious French even created a wax museum with exhibits depicting the horrendous medical consequences of masturbation. As suggested by *Onania* and Tissot, these putative consequences were by no means trivial, encompassing as they did multifarious threats to virility, sanity, and moral well-being. The alleged physical sequelae ranged from acne to epilepsy and even death.[27] But the principal concerns were the twin threats of permanent impotence and mental illness. Freud, for example, held masturbation to be among the leading causes of the nervous disorder known as "neurasthenia."[28]

Masturbation, it was feared, might also interfere with the economic basis of society by sapping the strength of its young men. As Virgil remarked, "Men are a hard, laborious species,"[29] unless, according to nineteenth-century medical authorities, they masturbate. Masturbators, in contrast, are weak and withdrawn, the typical sufferer being distinguished by "the haggard expression, the sunken eye, the long cadaverous-looking countenance,"[30] and a notable lack of initiative and drive. Masturbation is bad for a free market economy, it was argued, because "the masturbator risks losing the personal qualities needed to dominate wife and children and to compete successfully in the capitalist economy."[31] Furthermore, it was believed that the depletion of energy caused by the unnecessary expenditure of sperm enfeebled men and made them incapable of fully productive labor.

Female masturbation, in contrast, challenged prevailing beliefs in the asexuality of women, and allegedly incited lusts that could only be satisfied by the wanton expenditure of the male essence; female masturbation was thus as much a threat to masculinity as to femininity.[32] Chief among concerns over female masturbation was the stimulatory potential of bicycles, treadle sewing machines, and, in at least one case, a foot-driven milling machine.[33] Other temptations included music, horseback riding, certain foods and drinks, wearing heavy hair pieces and wigs, and lacing oneself too tightly into a girdle or corset.[34] Regarding the last of these, Beatrice Faust suggests that the visceral pleasures of wearing corsets and high heels should not be overlooked: "The Victorian corset was probably as much a tactile fetish among women as it was a visual fetish among men."[35]

Because of the threat to society posed by masturbation, unmarried men and women were advised to sublimate their sexual drives into scholarly, socially, or economically profitable pursuits. For those who were unable to control their lusts—children included—a number of novel and exceptionally revolting methods of forced compliance were devised. Various restraints were employed to prevent young boys from genitally stimulating themselves. Masturbation prevention methods ranged from simply pinning the child's bedclothes to his sheets, thereby restricting all bodily movement, to the use of large penis rings with needles, spikes, or saw teeth attached to the interior of the ring. Fitted around the penis, the ring caused only minor discomfort to the boy as long as he did not rub his hand against his penis, roll over on his stomach or side while in bed, or (worst of all) get an erection.[36]

Even more extreme measures were undertaken to keep adult men and women from masturbating, including the application of electrical shocks to the urethra and anus, surgery to close the foreskin over the penis, clitoridectomy to reduce sexual responsiveness in women, and infibulation of the labia to restrict access to the vagina.[37]

In the nineteenth century, dietary protocols for the prevention of masturbation were also popular, including one that might sarcastically be called "corn flakes therapy." Toward the end of the century, John H. Kellogg served inmates at his Battle Creek Sanitarium his namesake cereals as an integral part of a strict dietary and behavioral regimen meant to quell masturbatory desires.[38] Cold cereals were also advised for children, reflecting the naive belief that hot cereals, porridges, and the like induced lascivious thoughts in young, impressionable minds.[39] In the 1830s, Sylvester Graham, an American health reformer better known today for the crackers that still bear his name, counseled abstinence from all lustful activities, especially masturbation, and recommended bland foods, cold baths, and fresh air.[40]

Tellingly, Graham, the author of *Lecture to Young Men on Chastity,* considered marital intercourse to be nearly as unhealthful as masturbation, advising young men to abstain if possible, and if not, to engage in intercourse with their wives not more than once a month.[41] According to Graham, the key to abstinence was not will power, but diet: "A proper system of diet and general regimen [would] so subdue their sexual propensity, as to be able to abstain from connubial commerce, and preserve entire chastity of body, for several months in succession, without the least inconvenience."[42] And how effective were such regimens at preventing masturbation? As Jack Weatherford, the author of *Porn Row,* concludes, "Despite the changes in diet, however, youngsters continued to masturbate and still managed to grow into the tallest generations in recorded history, proving that masturbation does not stunt growth."[43]

The most prominent and influential mid–nineteenth-century dissertation on the subject of masturbation was contained in William Acton's treatise, *The Functions and Disorders of the Reproductive Organs,* which was first published in England in 1857 and provided inspiration to millions in the following decades. Acton describes the habitual masturbator as follows:

The frame is stunted and weak, the muscles undeveloped, the eye is sunken and heavy, the complexion is sallow, pasty, or covered with spots of acne, the hands are damp and cold, and the skin moist. The boy shuns the society of others, creeps about alone, joins with repugnance in the amusements of his schoolfellows. He cannot look any one in the face, and becomes careless in dress and uncleanly in person. His intellect has become sluggish and enfeebled, and if his evil habits are persisted in, he may end in becoming a drivelling idiot or a peevish valetudinarian.[44]

Like his predecessors, Acton attributed a plethora of afflictions to the evils of masturbation, including impotence, consumption, curvature of the spine, and insanity.[45] With regard to the last of these, Acton noted that cases of derangement "chiefly occur in members of families of strict religious education. . . . those who from this cause have become insane have generally . . . been of strictly moral life, and recognized as persons who paid much attention to the forms of religion."[46] Many of the people diagnosed as suffering from masturbation-induced insanity probably were quite sane, the misdiagnosis stemming from the fact that masturbation was treated as both a cause and a symptom, so that the mental stability of anyone who masturbated was immediately suspect.[47] No doubt there were also cases of genuine insanity, but in light of Taylor's thesis, presented earlier, one cannot help wonder if masturbation guilt rather than masturbation itself might not have been the cause of insanity in the cases Acton observed. That is, perhaps the dangers of self-pleasuring reside in society's moral and religious condemnation, not in the act itself.[48]

Acton, echoing the conventional wisdom of the era, suggested that the ill effects of masturbation were due to "the large expenditure of semen . . . [which] exhausted the vital force."[49] "Self-abuse" was viewed as both a threat to health and an impediment to proper masculine development. The healthy boy is one who has "not expended that vital fluid, semen, or exhausted his nervous energy, and his youthful vigor has been employed for its legitimate purpose, namely, in building up his growing frame."[50] Thus, the proper function of semen in the mature male is procreation, whereas in the adolescent it is the attainment of maturity. This attitude is made explicit by Robert Baden-Powell, who founded the Boy Scouts in Britain in 1907. In an early scout manual, Baden-Powell cautioned his young charges that masturbation prevented semen from

making you the strong manly man you would otherwise be. You are throwing away the seed that has been handed down to you as a trust instead of keeping it and ripening it for bringing a son to you later on.[51]

(Notice the hypermasculinity expected of the young scouts: Not only should they grow up to reproduce, they should produce sons in obvious preference to daughters!)

In many ways the attitudes just described are reminiscent of the Sambia, who believe that semen, rather than being produced by men and older boys, must be acquired from other males via fellatio (in other cultures with similar beliefs, anal intercourse is instrumental in the transfer of semen).[52] As the essence of male masculinity, semen is a vital resource and is not to be squandered. Fears of semen depletion present an obvious obstacle to successful heterosexual intercourse for Sambia men, who believe intercourse to be exceptionally draining. What is needed, therefore, is a means of replenishing the depleted life force; ingestion of tree sap serves this important function for the Sambia. (Not surprisingly, masturbation is strictly forbidden, and apparently is not practiced by the Sambia.[53]) Similarly, the Etoro of New Guinea believe that the masculine life force, or *hame,* is concentrated in semen, and that heterosexual intercourse robs a man of his vitality.[54]

Although couched in the language of science and reason, theories of semen depletion were common in nineteenth-century America as well. As noted earlier, Sylvester Graham thought it wise for men, whether married or single, to avoid intercourse altogether (except, one supposes, when required for procreation)[55] because intercourse drained men of the masculine essence.[56] According to an anonymous author in the *Boston Medical and Surgical Journal* of 1835, the preservation of semen was critical, because "sturdy manhood . . . loses its energy and bends under too frequent expenditure of this important secretion; and no age or condition will protect a man from the danger of unlimited indulgence, [even] legally and naturally exercised."[57]

In retrospect, it appears that, at least in the United States, anxiety over semen depletion was largely symptomatic of a more pervasive fear—that of nonprocreative sexuality, as epitomized by masturbation. Thus, Graham's exhortation to "recollect that the final cause of your organs of reproduction—the propagation of your species—requires but seldom the exercise of their function!"[58] may be understood quite simply as a pseudoscientific rationalization of millennia-old biblical teachings. The theological argument against pornography can be summarized as follows:

> [Catholic] teaching holds, as a basic and cardinal fact, that complete sexual activity and pleasure is licit and moral only in a naturally completed act in valid marriage. All acts which, of their psychological and physical nature, are designed to be preparatory to the complete act, take

their licitness and their morality from the complete act. If, therefore, they are completely divorced from the complete act, they are distorted, warped, meaningless, and hence immoral. It follows, therefore, that any deliberate indulgence in thoughts, words, or acts which, of their own intrinsic nature, are slanted toward, destined for, preparation for the complete act, and yet performed in circumstances in which the complete act is impossible, have ceased to be a means toward an end and have become an end in themselves.[59]

The expenditure of semen is sanctioned only in procreative marital intercourse, and even then is fraught with potential dangers, and so "should be made but sparingly."[60] Any other use of this procreative power is "unclean, polluting, an abomination, in short, obscene."[61]

Masturbation, or "self-pollution" as it was also known, is obscene precisely because it violates taboos regarding the natural function of the reproductive organs. And pornography, because it aids and abets this perversion, is likewise obscene. The war against pornography is thus, in effect, a war against masturbation.

Porn Battles

The significance of the timing of the massive antimasturbation campaign in the United States and England warrants special notice. It hardly seems coincidental that in 1873, at the height of Acton's antimasturbatory influence in both countries, the foes of pornography were effectively marshalled to action in America. In that year, the New York Society for the Suppression of Vice was chartered, and Anthony Comstock, its founder, was made a special agent of the U.S. Post Office. This society, and Comstock in particular, were America's foremost antiporn zealots. Comstock's position as special agent permitted him access to every post office in the United States. Comstock's self-imposed mandate was to eradicate the postal distribution of "obscene" material, and his power was such that he could open *any* piece of mail that he suspected was obscene.

The year 1873 also witnessed the passage of the so-called Comstock Act, which made it a federal crime to knowingly send "obscene, lewd, or lascivious" publications through the mail. According to Comstock, in the first six months after passage of the act, 194,000 obscene pictures and photographs, and 134,000 pounds of books were seized.[62] The human toll was significant: Between 1873 and 1882, more than 700 people were arrested by Comstock and his allies.[63] Several of those arrested committed suicide rather than face Comstock's humiliating accusations.[64]

Comstock himself often conflated the alleged effects of obscenity and masturbation, arguing that pornography's "most deadly effects are felt by the victims in the habit of secret vices."[65] Thus, the problem with obscenity is masturbation, and the problem with masturbation is that it corrupts and debilitates youth, and perhaps most important, causes an unnatural spilling of seed.

The ultimate goal of antiobscenity campaigns can thus be viewed as the prevention of masturbation. However, masturbation is extraordinarily difficult to detect, and hence to control, because it is an extremely clandestine activity. A direct attack against the evils of masturbation is therefore unfeasible. This being the case, Comstock and like-minded antiobscenity crusaders instead attacked the "scourge" that provokes, accompanies, and reinforces the sin of masturbation, namely, pornography.

Of course, if one is going to expend enormous amounts of energy destroying pornography, one might as well also destroy *all* material that facilitates nonreproductive sex. As discussed in Chapter 6, the Comstock Act permitted this very thing, making it a crime to mail advertisements or other information about abortion, condoms, and other contemporary methods of contraception. Also covered was "any article or thing intended or adapted for any indecent or immoral use or nature,"[66] which included rubber goods and putatively aphrodisiac pills and powders. Through the broad powers encompassed by the Comstock Act, American antivice campaigners were able to legally interfere both with self-pleasuring specifically, and with nonprocreative sex generally: "Comstock and his allies attacked not only sexual literature sold for profit but also any dissenting medical or philosophical opinion that supported the belief that sexuality had other than procreative purposes."[67]

The Comstock Act was not the first law to regulate the distribution of obscene materials in the United States. Indeed, laws regulating and prohibiting pornography had already been adopted at the state level (in Connecticut) in 1821 and at the federal level in 1842 (a customs statute).[68] All indications suggest, however, that the American pornography industry flourished in the absence of vigorous prosecution prior to the publication of Acton's antimasturbation diatribe in 1857. Similarly, in England, little attention was paid to obscenity in pre-Victorian times, although in 1729 it was ruled that obscene *libel* constituted a common law offense.[69]

John Cleland's *Memoirs of a Woman of Pleasure* (more popularly known as *Fanny Hill*), which was first published in 1748, is a case in point. Described as a "lively piece of cheerful and literate hardcore pornography which was the first of its kind to be written by an Englishman,"[70] this book created quite a stir when released in the mid-eighteenth century, and resulted in the prosecution of its author, publisher, and printer for violating existing English obscenity codes, but "nothing serious in fact happened to them, and . . . the book was defended as 'not offensive to decency' by the *Monthly Review*."[71] Naturally, this lack of effective enforcement of obscenity laws did little to contain the growth of the budding English cottage industry in pornographic materials.

Pornographic magazines (for example, *Amorous Repository*) as well as books were produced and distributed during the 1700s. English magazines featured provocative stories interspersed with advertisements for prostitutes and brothels (five shillings "for a temporary favor" and half a guinea for a night's lodging).[72] Though generally pornographic, these magazines could also be quite prosaic. The 1786 *Harris List of Garden Ladies* promoted the physical attributes of one particular prostitute as follows:

> Despite seven years in the trade, the coral-tipped clitoris still forms the powerful erection . . . nor has the sphincter vaginae been robbed of any of its contractive powers; the propelling labia still make the close fissure.[73]

Just one year after this issue of the *Harris List* appeared, the Constitution of the United States of America was drafted, and two years later, in 1789, the First Amendment was submitted to Congress by James Madison. This amendment, which forbade Congress from passing any law abridging the freedom of speech, press, or religion, was ratified in 1791. Over 150 years later, this subtle yet powerful addition to the Constitution would become the centerpiece of courtroom defenses of the right to produce, distribute, and consume pornographic materials not that different in content from *Amorous Repository*. In contrast, no such formal protection exists in Great Britain.

Books and magazines were not the only form of pornography produced in England during this time. There was also a brisk trade in sexually explicit prints. As Lawrence Stone describes it:

> An early but abortive attempt to supply the market was made by some young dons at All Souls College in 1675. They were caught in the act of using the Oxford University presses after closing hours to print off copies of Guilio Romano's engravings from Aretino's Postures—the most famous, indeed almost the only, illustrated how-to-do-it sex manual of the day.[74]

Pornographic prints soon became so popular that they had even found their way into fashionable drawing rooms by the mid-eighteenth century and into the hands of such notables as the prince regent.[75]

Pornography produced in England and the rest of Europe eventually made its way to the United States. Prior to the 1840s, in fact, the pornography found in America was almost exclusively of European origin. (Only recently has the United States become a bigger exporter than importer of pornography.) From the 1840s to the 1870s, however, American pornography flourished. The first productions were sexually explicit novels, the most prominent being *Maria Monk,* which was published in 1836. The furor caused by *Maria Monk* was due both to its sexual explicitness and to its blasphemous allegations of sexual dalliances between priests and nuns. More explicit, and perhaps more blasphemous, books followed. By the time of the American Civil War, cheap erotic novels known as "barracks favorites" were widely available in the United States, as were erotic prints and photographs, which were widely collected by soldiers.[76]

What use did Civil War soldiers have for erotica? For entertainment purposes? Perhaps. But much more likely, the material was fantasy-complementing grist for the masturbatory mill. Pornography, then as now, probably contributed the fantasy element many men require for masturbatory motivation, thereby providing Civil War soldiers a safe, nonviolent means for sexual expression while they were separated from wives and other lovers. It is probably no coincidence, therefore, that the antimasturbation and antipornography movements merged shortly after the conclusion of the Civil War, led by Anthony Comstock and the New York Society for the Suppression of Vice. Prior to that time, as suggested earlier, the production, distribution, and consumption of pornography was essentially unencumbered by existing statutes because of the lack of vigorous enforcement. However, subsequent to the publication of Acton's book, the combined forces of Catholicism (historically opposed to masturbation and other forms of nonprocreative sex) and the "medical" moralists were effectively exploited by Comstock and his antivice society.

New Comstockery

To Comstock and his crusaders, masturbation was the vice, and pornography the villain. But masturbation is only one of several ills traditionally blamed on pornography and opposed through the institution of vague obscenity laws. According to Ellen Willis, a feminist writer, "The basic purpose of obscenity laws is and always has been to reinforce cultural taboos on sexuality and suppress feminism, homosexuality, and other forms of sexual dissidence."[77] In so doing, obscenity laws suppress the *idea* of nonprocreative sex and reinforce the sexual status quo.

Although technically not an obscenity law, the Helms Amendment

passed by Congress in 1989 is nevertheless a good example of such legislation. This bill sought to prevent the federally funded National Endowment
for the Arts from providing grants to support works that the agency "may
consider obscene," especially "depictions of sadomasochism, homoeroticism, the sexual exploitation of children, or individuals engaged in sex acts
and which, taken as a whole, do not have serious literary, artistic, political
or scientific value."[78] Though clearly intended to stifle all sexually adventurous artistic expression, the amendment is particularly noteworthy because it
singles out *homoeroticism* for special consideration. What is it about the
depiction of homoeroticism (such as Robert Mapplethorpe's photographs)
that invites excessive scrutiny?

One possibility is the fear that homosexuality, like HIV, is contagious,
with pornography as the carrier. In other words, exposure to gay or lesbian
pornography might cause one to "become" homosexual. In this view,
homosexuality is a disease to be avoided. Of course, homosexuality is
neither a disease nor contagious. As to the link with gay and lesbian pornography, a year-long study in Britain concluded that "the evidence does not
point to pornography as a cause of deviant sexual orientation in offenders.
Rather it seems to be used as part of that deviant sexual orientation."[79] The
arrow of causality is thus reversed: Pornography exists because there is a
market for it; its existence does not create the market.

Nevertheless, gay and lesbian pornography continues to be specially
targeted for legislative restrictions. In Britain, postal and customs regulations
are commonly used to enforce obscenity and indecency laws (roughly,
"obscenity" is that which corrupts, whereas "indecency" is that which
merely offends). The prejudicial use of such laws to eradicate gay pornography is clearly in evidence in the following anecdote from British sociologist
Simon Watney:

> A hapless tourist returning to the UK had a copy of the national
> American gay newspaper *The Advocate* seized at London's Gatwick
> airport, together with a video tape, a *Colt* calendar, and some twenty
> sex magazines. This, in spite of a directive issued to customs officers in
> June 1978, which clearly states that, with the significant exception of
> child pornography, they are not permitted to detain small quantities of
> obscene or indecent books or magazines when they are intended
> solely for the personal use of an incoming traveller.[80]

As was the case with nineteenth-century American Comstockery, postal
regulations have played an important role in limiting the distribution of
allegedly indecent or obscene materials in Britain. Thus, in 1985 Britain's
only nationally distributed gay newspaper, *Gay Times,* was fined more than

£5,000 for sending "indecent materials" through the mails.[81] Another attempt in this same direction was Britain's failed Churchill Amendment, which would have "effectively criminalized all images of homosexuality within Britain."[82]

British antiobscenity laws have also been harnessed to silence scientific debate. Havelock Eliss's monumental work *Sexual Inversion* (volume 1 in his *Studies in the Psychology of Sex*) was banned immediately upon publication because authorities feared it would encourage homosexuality. In 1897 the publisher of the book was tried and convicted in London on an obscenity charge, and all known copies were destroyed.[83]

Selective enforcement of existing obscenity and indecency laws lays bare the true agenda of the antipornographers: the restriction of sexual freedom in accordance with the Judeo-Christian ideal of heterosexual monogamy. Sexual freedom and diversity have no place in this ideal, which condemns homosexuality as "a crime against nature," and implicitly denies the existence of female sexuality.

In light of this, and given the considerable affinity of modern feminism with the gay and lesbian rights movement, it is therefore rather surprising to find a small group of otherwise radical feminists arm in arm with the religious right at the forefront of recent antipornography campaigns.

Sisters against Porn

A new twist has been added to the antipornography rhetoric. It comes in the guise of radical feminism and is fueled primarily by the writings of Andrea Dworkin and Catharine MacKinnon, although the ideas they expound are largely incipient in the theoretical framework advanced by Susan Brownmiller and others.[84] The central thesis in these writings is the same: Pornography degrades women and incites men to violence against them. In other words, "pornography is the theory and rape the practice."[85]

In her influential book *Against Our Will,* Brownmiller argues that "rape is not a crime of irrational, impulsive, uncontrollable lust, but is a deliberate, hostile, violent act of degradation and possession on the part of the would-be conqueror, designed to intimidate and inspire fear."[86] Brownmiller places the blame for the attitudes that encourage "young men, who form the potential raping population,"[87] to commit these acts of aggression squarely on the twin evils of prostitution and pornography. "Pornography," she writes, "like rape, is a male invention, designed to dehumanize women, to reduce the female to an object of sexual access."[88] (Brownmiller neglects to mention, however, that the typical consumer of pornography is a middle-aged man rather than a member of her hypothetical "potential raping population" of young men.)

Similar sentiments—and confusions—are echoed in the more volatile writings of Dworkin and MacKinnon, who have become the de facto spokespersons of the feminist antipornography crusade.[89] According to the feminist perspective advanced by these authors, pornography engenders sexual violence, as well as discrimination against women through as yet unspecified psychological and sociological pathways. MacKinnon makes this conflation of social inequality, violence, and male sexuality explicit: "If there is no inequality, no violation, no dominance, no force, there is no sexual arousal."[90] At the very least, claims such as these reflect an ignorance of both the content of mainstream pornography and the complexities of the male (and female) sexual psyche; nevertheless, they abound in the writings of both MacKinnon and Dworkin.

In 1983, MacKinnon and Dworkin authored a civil ordinance that decreed pornography to be a form of sexual discrimination against women.[91] Versions of this ordinance were introduced at various times in Minneapolis, Indianapolis, Suffolk County (New York), Madison (Wisconsin), and Los Angeles County. It has since been ruled that the ordinance violates the freedom of speech guarantee of the First Amendment. Many commentators have also remarked on the ordinance's antisexual premise. As Donna Turley observes, "It is incomprehensible that sexually explicit images would be given special treatment unless the feminist proponents of the law believe, as do many people on the right, that there is something wrong with most sex."[92]

Dworkin's incendiary book *Intercourse* is a case in point. Make no mistake, *Intercourse* is not about dialogue nor a town in Pennsylvania. It is, instead, about sex, and about heterosexual intercourse in particular. Dworkin does not mince words. She believes that heterosexual intercourse enslaves, degrades, defiles, and subordinates women. To extend her point, Dworkin declares, "If the goal of mankind is universal peace then the end of intercourse would be an essential utterly logical part."[93]

Absurdities aside, the theoretical direction of this work is particularly relevant to the present discussion. *Intercourse* is clearly antiheterosexual—anti-*male* heterosexual. It is also antisexual. Dworkin herself admits as much, "I just refuse to say that I'm not anti-sex."[94] As we demonstrate in the following pages, this antisexualism is the leitmotif that drives the shared perspective of MacKinnon and Dworkin. Like the antimasturbation crusaders, the antisex feminists have targeted pornography as their demon. Both groups make use of legal convolutions and political cachet to disguise the

underlying object of their expressed vehemence and to make their plat-
forms more palatable. Protecting morals—or women—is a stronger rally-
ing point than attacking the vicissitudes of masturbation or the power
differentials that maintain the sexual status quo in a world controlled predominantly by male heterosexuals.

For Dworkin and the antiporn feminists it is simply easier, and quite a
bit less messy, to blame pornography for the social ills of sexism and violence against women than to face the underlying causes.[95] Despite their
claims to the contrary, pornography doesn't cause rape. Instead, as Willis
suggests, "It is men's hostility toward women—combined with their power
to express that hostility and for the most part get away with it—that causes
sexual violence."[96] Of course, sexual desire might also play a role.

Dworkin insists that the problem with pornography is that it is a system
of exploitation that injures all women by creating inequality and abuse.[97]
That is, pornography sexualizes inequality and, as such, is a central practice
in the subordination of women. From this rather overstated supposition,
Dworkin then concludes that all pornography must be eliminated.

However, Dworkin's assumptions reveal a fundamental naivete regarding the *content* of pornography. Most obviously, she presumes that pornography invariably includes or depicts women. This, of course, is nonsense.
Although, as noted in Chapter 3, pornography is produced primarily for
consumption by men, the objects of pornographic lust are quite varied.
Male homosexual pornography, for example, represents a sizable market,
including videos, magazines, dial-a-porn, and so on. To rail against pornography as the subordination of women fails to appreciate, at the very least,
the variability extant in the pornographic marketplace.

Perhaps Dworkin's comments were directed solely against pornography that *does* contain depictions of women. This leaves at least three possibilities: (1) heterosexual pornography depicting both men and women, (2)
feigned lesbian pornography produced for consumption by heterosexual
men, or (3) true lesbian pornography, intended for a lesbian audience. This
last category, incidentally, is by no means tame. True lesbian pornography
often contains depictions of sadomasochism, anal sex, genital piercing, violence, and so forth, along with some of the wildest sexual slang imaginable.

Although produced for and marketed to a lesbian (and often self-
identified feminist) audience, lesbian pornography has also endured the scorn
of antipornography feminists. Lillian Faderman notes that many feminists

> simply could not take seriously the assertion that more and better sex
> would help in the fight for liberation. They saw the (lesbian) sexual
> radicals as provocateurs who threw out the red herring of wild sexual-

ity during a conservative, repressive era—or worse, as idiots who were removing their attention from truly pressing issues that affected women in general and lesbians in particular, in order to waste their energies on the trivialization of sex.[98]

Perhaps Dworkin is of a similar mind. That is, maybe she abhors all sexually explicit material, whether targeted to heterosexuals, gay men, or lesbians. We doubt this, however. Her novel *Ice and Fire* contains the following graphic description:

> N is easy to love, devotedly. She is very beautiful, not like a girl. She is lean and tough. She fucks like a gang of boys. She is smart and quiet. She doesn't waste words. She grins from ear to ear. She is never afraid. . . . Women pursue her. She is aloof, amused. She fucks everyone, eventually, with perfect simplicity and grace. She is a rough fuck. She grinds her hips in. She pushes her fingers in. She tears around inside. She is all muscle and jagged bones. She thrusts her hips so hard you can't remember who she is or how many of her there are. The first time she tore me apart. I bled and bled.[99]

Clearly, Dworkin, by her own hand, has produced what some would consider violent lesbian pornography. It is certainly substantially more violent and sexually explicit than Radclyffe Hall's *The Well of Loneliness*. Published in 1928, *The Well* was seized and declared obscene in both the United States and England, merely for *hinting* at the pleasures and value of lesbian relationships. Dworkin does more than hint, however, and her graphic descriptions of violent, even sadistic, lovemaking raise a troubling question. If, as argued by Dworkin and others, heterosexual pornography degrades women and incites men to violence against them, then one cannot help but wonder whether violent lesbian pornography of the type penned by Dworkin wouldn't do the same, only with women the oppressors as well as the victims.

By process of elimination, it appears that Dworkin's diatribe is specific to *heterosexual* pornography, meaning *male* heterosexual pornography, especially visual pornography. As we argued in Chapter 3, heterosexual pornography is invariably male because most heterosexual women are not aroused by emotionally detached pictorial representations of naked men. As Beatrice Faust summarizes:

> Kinsey, *The Hite Report,* and the *Viva* experiment all suggest that women's indifference to visual pornography derives from something more intractable than negative messages about sex. Women have accepted new freedoms in abortion, birth control, living together,

masturbation, and loving other women. Some women have even risked losing their friends, their jobs and their sanity to fight for these freedoms. If women reject the freedom to enjoy pornography and even male cheesecake, it must be because—no matter what permissions society gives us—women do not want it.[100]

Although the specific target of the antiporn feminist platform is supposedly male heterosexual pornography, the effect is ultimately to reinforce the censorship of pornography in general. In practice, this means pornography outside of the mainstream: gay male pornography, true lesbian pornography, transsexual pornography, depictions of interracial sex, and so forth. In practice, then, the antiporn feminist rhetoric is but another means of suppressing the expression of sexual minorities. Presumably, this was *not* what was intended. It is, however, a substantial gain for the supporters of the religious right who, though the strangest of bedfellows, find themselves in league with the antiporn feminists.

Dworkin argues that heterosexual pornography is despicable (and warrants elimination) not because it challenges conventional morality, as the religious right would have it, but because it depicts the pleasures of an activity (heterosexual intercourse) that is presumed to enslave and degrade women by virtue of the power differential that exists between men and women in our society. According to this view, "In a patriarchy, all sex with men is pornographic."[101] However, as Willis noted back in 1983, "To attack pornography, and at the same time equate it with heterosexual sex, is implicitly to condemn not only women who like pornography, but women who sleep with men."[102]

The generality of Dworkin's perspective also is problematic. Although it is true that some people (both men and women) enjoy heterosexual intercourse more than others, the mere existence of such differences does not in itself sanction legislation forbidding access to heterosexual intercourse, regardless of how abhorrent some people might find it. The same is true of the differences concerning heterosexual pornography. Some appreciate it, others don't. The big question, again, is whether the conservative tastes of a vocal minority should be allowed to dictate social policy.[103] Does the fact that some people find heterosexual pornography revolting justify its abolition? The First Amendment would suggest not. Just because heterosexual pornography depicts an activity that is despised by some is no reason to eliminate it.

On the other hand, it is easier to suppress heterosexual pornography than heterosexual intercourse. Intercourse, not surprisingly, has many more vocal advocates. In contrast, heterosexual pornography lacks public appeal and is therefore a convenient target. Pornography is neither politically nor socially privileged. In fact, it is just the opposite: It is scorned and denigrated. Furthermore, pornography is closeted so effectively that its champions often claim to despise it; supposedly, it is only in service of the First Amendment that they have thrown down the gauntlet in defense of pornography.

The reasons for this reticence to publicly advocate pornography are obvious. Pornography flouts conventional morality and is intimately associated with masturbation, a most secretive activity in its own right. Advocating pornography is tantamount to admitting masturbation, thereby assuming a considerable social liability. Unlike homosexuality, masturbation has yet to parade out of the closet. Influential X-rated pornography consumers do not actively challenge antipornography rhetoric, no matter how specious. Politicians do not exclaim their support for pornography nor has the media made it a cause célèbre. In fact, the high visibility of feminist antiporn groups such as Women against Pornography has provided the procensorship forces with a newfound air of liberal legitimacy. As noted earlier, the antisex religious right is no longer alone in its fight against pornography; instead it has been joined by progressive feminists in an unprecedented—and, some would argue, unholy—alliance. Despite fundamental differences on such crucial issues as the role of women in the workplace, abortion, and subsidized childcare, the antiporn right and the antiporn left have managed to establish a minuscule plot of common ground, namely, a shared opposition to certain forms of sexuality. For both groups, sex is laden with political overtones, whether the ostensible focus is the preservation of the "family" or the protection of personal autonomy.

Not all feminists share this pessimistic view of sex, of course. An important tenet of the unreconstituted feminist movement is an insistence that women be free to define for themselves a personal, feminist sexuality, rather than having a male fantasy of female sexuality forced upon them.[104] Unfortunately, the antiporn feminists seemingly wish to co-opt sexual choice,[105] replacing the freedom of the individual woman to self-define herself with an idealized version of female sexuality that is insistently romantic. According to Willis, adherents of this view believe:

> Lovemaking should be beautiful, romantic, soft, nice, and devoid of messiness, vulgarity, impulses to power, or indeed aggression of any sort. Above all, the emphasis should be on *relationships,* not (yuck) *organs.*[106]

This ideal of feminine sexual purity is, of course, every bit as fantastic as the always-available, always-ready fantasy woman portrayed in heterosexual pornography.[107] True sexual freedom should entail liberation from all externally imposed ideals, whether from the right or the left. In *Women against Censorship,* Ann Snitow argues:

> Present antipornography theory, rather than advancing feminist think-ing about sexuality, continues sexist traditions of displacement or dis-tortion of sexual questions. Instead of enlarging the definition of sexual pleasure to include a formerly invisible female subjectivity, antipornography thinking perpetuates an all too familiar intellectual legacy, one that defines male arousal as intrinsically threatening to female autonomy. Once again, women's experience fades into the background while men fill the foreground. Antipornography theory limits this focus further by collapsing a wide range of sexually explicit images into only one thing: violence against women.[108]

The "unorthodox feminists" provide a further contrast to the antiporn feminists and the feminine ideal of demure sexual behavior they seemingly endorse. Echoing the observations of Willis and Snitow, Turley suggests:

> Implicit in the arguments of the antipornography campaign is the assumption that there is a female sexuality that is excluded from most pornography and sex. It can be described as romantic, egalitarian, natural, gentle, free of power dynamics, monogamous, emotional, nurturing and spontaneous. This feminist prescription reflects and re-produces dominant cultural assumptions about women. Thus women's sexual freedom means freedom from male-centered images of women rather than the freedom to engage in a variety of sexual behaviors. . . . Unorthodox feminists believe that since pleasure is cre-ated consciously and historically, women have the power to change it. Instead of starting with an analysis of our society as patriarchal and oppressive, and then fitting sex into a slot, unorthodox feminists start with the idea that sexual pleasure simply is. . . . Instead of asking what a particular practice means or reflects about politics, the only question is how, so as to learn from others about the possibilities for pleasure.[109]

Obviously, not all feminists subscribe to the sexually liberated perspec-tive of the unorthodox feminists. We've already heard from Brownmiller and Dworkin, two of the most vocal opponents of heterosexual pornogra-phy. It is now time to consider a third, Catharine MacKinnon.

Pornographic Rape

The antisexual and anti-male heterosexual vehemence apparent in Dworkin's work finds further expression in the antipornography rhetoric of

Catharine MacKinnon,[110] who has been described in the press as "the Anthony Comstock of our time."[111] An ardent feminist and colleague of Dworkin, MacKinnon argues that heterosexual pornography is not merely the depiction of a despised activity, nor simply a popular adjunct to masturbation. It is, instead, the depiction of actual *rape*. That is, what seems to the viewer as pleasurable or consensual sex is in fact the rape of an actress (if it is even appropriate still to speak of "actresses"). Note carefully the double standard at work here. Actresses must be physically coerced into participation, but actors, it appears, perform willingly. Indeed, if MacKinnon is correct, the actors must themselves be rapists. Thus, pornography is the ultimate form of female enslavement because it depicts actual instances of rape, thereby perpetuating male abuse and domination of women.[112]

To support this tenuous contention, MacKinnon relates anecdotal evidence of women who were allegedly coerced into appearing in pornographic films (most notably, Linda Lovelace of *Deep Throat* fame[113]), or who allegedly were raped during the course of such filming. MacKinnon also makes frequent allusions to the undeniable horrors of incest, implying a causal connection, and rails against the evils of the ever-elusive snuff film. (Snuff films belong to a seemingly chimeric pornographic genre that allegedly depicts the *actual* torture and murder of women. If such films exist, they are clearly illegal and abhorrent. However, to MacKinnon, all pornographic films are essentially snuff.) The purpose of the rhetorical devices MacKinnon employs is obvious: They are contrived to provoke outrage against pornography and elicit sympathy for its "victims."

Her evidential methods are quite problematic, however, as are the extrapolations derived from them.[114] MacKinnon's sleight of hand is designed to create the appearance that *all* pornographic actresses are coerced into, and raped during, the filming of X-rated videos and movies. But her small sample of testimonials is neither random nor unbiased, the participants having been selected chiefly for emotional impact. The charge that pornography depicts actual rape is, on the face of it, patently absurd.[115] But what of the claim that women are forced to participate in pornographic videos and movies? Again, the evidence is scant, and where available, it is highly questionable.[116]

Moreover, MacKinnon's biased sample ignores the many testimonials from pornographic actresses, such as Kay Parker, who have publicly extolled the virtues of their work. Parker was one of the most prolific and popular actresses of her time and was featured in more than fifty X-rated films and videos, most notably the extraordinarily popular and controversial film *Taboo*. In her lectures at college campuses around the country, Parker describes her experiences in X-rated movies as both enjoyable and empowering.[117]

Nina Hartley is another example of a woman who, like Parker, enjoyed her participation in X-rated filmmaking and considered it instructive, for both her own sexuality and for the messages that it conveyed.[118] Finally, in regard to former porn actress Linda Lovelace's claim that she was forced at gunpoint to participate in *Deep Throat,* at least one pornography industry insider insists that "the only gun put to her head was the gun of poverty, and she turned it on this industry and began firing hypocritical bullets at it. The woman lied."[119] There is obviously a credibility gap that cannot be bridged by yet more rhetoric. MacKinnon's cherished testimonials are, after all, "only words."

MacKinnon also fails to note the prominence of women in the *business* of pornography. Two of the largest adult entertainment corporations in the country feature women executives. Mary Gates is the CEO of Adam and Eve, and Cathy Green is head of postproduction at Leisuretime Entertainment. Of the alleged ubiquity of rape in heterosexual pornography, Green observes:

> The majority of women working in adult movies do so voluntarily. At worst, some are seduced—in the metaphoric sense. Rarely is someone coerced. The only example that I am aware of is the case of an actress who had done a number of sexual scenes with several men, but balked at sex with a particular man. She felt pressured into having sex with that particular man. She also described it as a no big deal thing. . . . With the companies that I am familiar with, if you don't want to do it, you don't do it. That is their policy. Violations of this policy would put the company at risk and create adverse publicity. As such, this policy is strictly enforced. In fact, there is probably much more rape and coercion in Hollywood—on the proverbial casting couch. It's just more sublimated.[120]

Not surprisingly, testimonials such as these are given short shrift in the antipornography feminist literature. Because they are a threat to the prevailing gospel, they are either labeled as falsehoods or are discarded out of hand as being naive and patriarchally inspired. Objectively, however, they seem no less veracious than those upon which MacKinnon relies. Of course, this tactic of pitting testimonial against testimonial is thoroughly unproductive. Simple generalizations are just that: simple.

We raise these issues because the power and fury of MacKinnon's rhetoric derives from the characterization of heterosexual pornography as rape and sexual slavery.[121] But, if heterosexual pornography is *not* rape nor traffic in sexual slavery, then the substance of MacKinnon's position is rendered specious. For instance, the claim that pornography depicts women unequally, or subordinates women unduly, lacks specificity. The same is true of the Bible, television commercials, opportunities for scientists, and so on.

Similarly, the claim that pornography precipitates rape is not supported by the scientific literature. There is absolutely no evidence that pornography causes rape.[122] In fact, much of the available evidence points to the opposite conclusion: By providing an alternative outlet, pornography may actually *prevent* some cases of rape and sexual abuse. In Japan, where violent pornography (often incorporating depictions of rape) is the norm, the incidence of rape is only one-sixteenth of that in the United States,[123] and in both Denmark and West Germany sex crimes were *reduced* when the availability of pornography was increased.[124] Furthermore, according to the eminent sexologist John Money, "Patients who request treatment in a sex offender clinic commonly disclose that pornography helps them contain their abnormal sexuality within imagination only, as a fantasy, instead of having to act it out in real life with an unconsenting, resentful partner, or by force."[125] However, for sheer incendiary power, and to legitimize their claims that pornography is an abhorrent form of discrimination, the antiporn feminists *need* X-rated pornography to be rape and sexual slavery.

Fortunately, for everyone's sake, it isn't. However, to claim it as such allows MacKinnon and those of like perspective to position themselves as contemporary abolitionists, battling the sexual slavery of women in pornography. The first several pages of Dworkin's *Pornography: Men Possessing Women,* for example, concern the life of former slave and abolitionist Frederick Douglass. Positioned as modern abolitionists, those who wage war against pornography are clearly "fighting the good fight." However, the battle is premised on a falsehood. Heterosexual pornography is *not* sexual slavery.

The ridiculousness of the "sex is slavery" hypothesis is abundantly evident in the following passage from Linda Grant's book *Sexing the Millennium:*

> In November 1992, [Dworkin] told the London *Evening Standard,*
> "The fact is women do not like intercourse very much. Our lack of
> orgasms is proof enough; we think we like sex as some slaves may have
> thought they liked picking cotton."[126]

Besides the obvious absurdity that equates a lack of orgasms with a complete absence of pleasure, this passage is noteworthy for the flaming arrogance it evinces,[127] as well as the manner in which it trivializes slavery and those subjected to its inhumanities. By and large, women, unlike slaves, participate in pornography (and intercourse) voluntarily. Thus, they do not need emancipation and liberty in the sense remedied by the Thirteenth, Fourteenth, and Fifteenth amendments.

Although analogies to the enslavement of black Americans may have symbolic value, they ultimately diminish the true meaning of slavery and emancipation. Not all forms of discrimination are alike. Some are more symbolic than others, hence require different forms of redress. Therefore, while many women may be appalled by heterosexual pornography, this does not entitle them to eliminate the First Amendment protection of such by claiming an analogy to the enslavement of blacks. Equal protection under the law was designed to protect the liberties of all Americans from state-implemented discrimination. The liberty of women—and their protection from rape—does *not* necessitate abolishing pornography. On the contrary, in her aptly titled book *Defending Pornography,* Nadine Strossen (former president of the American Civil Liberties Union) argues that pornography should be *defended* in the service of maintaining women's equality, status, dignity, and autonomy. Perhaps it is no coincidence that Denmark and The Netherlands—two countries with considerable gender equality—have extraordinarily liberal policies toward pornography and sexual commerce in general.

Finally, we wish to take strong exception to another of MacKinnon's claims, namely, her insistence that because heterosexual pornography precipitates physiological reactions (e.g., erection) and behavior (e.g., masturbation), it is properly considered conduct, not speech, and therefore falls outside the protection of the First Amendment:

> Pornography is masturbation material. It is used as sex. It therefore is sex. . . . The women are in two dimensions, but the men have sex with them in their own three-dimensional bodies, not in their minds alone. Men come doing this. This, too, is a behavior, not a thought or an argument.[128]

The vacuity of this reasoning is easily discerned. Pornography's expressive capacity is clearly independent of its ability to provoke physiological reactions, and thereby, perhaps, to influence conduct.[129] Few jurists would classify mystery novels and horror movies as conduct, even though they are expressly formulated to precipitate physiological reactions (e.g., palm sweating, increased heart rate) and behaviors (e.g., looking over one's shoulder, locking doors). Obviously, the more powerful the idea, the more powerful the impact, behavioral and otherwise. Such consequences, however, do *not* invalidate pornography's claim to First Amendment protection as speech.

Porn and the Law

Foremost among the amendments to the U.S. Constitution, in both position and breadth, is the First Amendment; it is often described as having a "preferred position," entitling it to greater judicial protection. The First Amendment states: "Congress shall make no law respecting an establishment of religion, or prohibiting the free exercise thereof; or abridging the freedom of speech, or of the press; or the right of the people peaceably to assemble, and petition the Government for a redress of grievances."[130]

Concerns over the freedoms of speech and press are further addressed by the Fourteenth Amendment, which protects the liberties of speech and press against state deprivation without "due process of law."[131] The constitutional guarantees of the First and Fourteenth amendments are vitally important to the conduct of democracy, as they ensure a free and open exchange of ideas. For democracy to flourish, dissent must be heard, *especially* if it challenges widely held political or moral beliefs. As Steven Shiffrin notes, the First Amendment may even be said to *promote* dissent:

> A major purpose of the First Amendment, I will claim, is to protect the romantics—those who would break out of classical forms: the dissenters, the unorthodox, the outcasts. The First Amendment's purpose and function in the American polity is not merely to protect negative liberty, but also affirmatively to sponsor the individualism, the rebelliousness, the antiauthoritarianism, the spirit of nonconformity within all of us.[132]

The First and Fourteenth amendments thus ensure and protect diversity of opinion, as both an individual liberty and a political corrective that gives citizens control over the government through challenge and dissent.[133]

The voice of dissent is particularly important in maintaining a separation between church and state. The ancient belief that the earth is the center of the universe is a case in point. In the seventeenth century, Galileo proposed the then-heretical theory that the Earth revolves around the sun, rather than vice versa.[134] His planetary theory, though subsequently shown to be essentially accurate, was deemed blasphemous by the Catholic church, and Galileo was forced to publicly recant his "heresy." Galileo, unfortunately, did not benefit from First Amendment protection.

Other examples of blasphemous threats to conventional moral teachings include Charles Darwin's theory of evolution via natural selection and, of course, pornography. The vehement reaction both have received is due, we believe, to the persuasiveness of the ideas they express. Pornography is seen as a powerful attack on conventional morality in much the same way as

Darwin's theory of evolution attacked a cherished religious precept. Though vastly different in content, pornography and evolutionary theory are similarly dangerous to the extent that they are provocative and powerful, and therefore a threat to the existing moral order. Pornography extols the pleasures of sex and implicitly condones masturbation and nonreproductive sexuality. Evolution challenged creationism, as told in the story of Genesis, as well as calling into doubt humankind's privileged position in the natural order.

Although it is probably easier to sympathize with the image of an unjustly persecuted scientist, such as Galileo or Darwin, than it is with an X-rated video producer, we remind the reader that many sympathetic literary figures have also been branded pornographers. The list of celebrated "pornographers" includes such literary luminaries as James Joyce, Radclyffe Hall, D. H. Lawrence, Theodore Drieser, Edmund Wilson, and Chaucer, all of whom have had works ruled obscene in the United States. Translations of Aristophanes, Ovid, and Apuleius have likewise been declared obscene.[135]

Sexually explicit subject matter is abundantly represented in other art forms as well, and has been produced by some of the world's most prominent artists. Hieronymus Bosch is famous for his explicit paintings, as is Pablo Picasso. Others in the fold include Rembrandt, Edvard Munch, Marc Chagall, Claes Oldenburg, Salvador Dali, and Man Ray. The roster of contemporary artists dabbling in mature themes includes Robert Mapplethorpe, Holly Hughes, Jeffrey Koons, Steve Rogers, Larry Rivers, Charles Gatewood, Karen Finley, and Eric Fischl. Their works, incidentally, are by no means restricted to classical nude forms. Instead, they may depict a man masturbating in a bathtub (Rogers), a bullwhip inserted into an anus (Mapplethorpe), the "smell of ass in open air" (in a monologue by Finley), and genital piercing (Gatewood). None of these images would appear out of place in the work of Bosch, the late fifteenth–early sixteenth-century Dutch painter best known for his depictions of hell and its grotesque inhabitants.

History is filled with unpopular and nonnormative ideas that, like pornography, challenge the existing moral order. Such ideas are as evident in the arts and sciences as they are in political and religious discourse, and all are protected as speech under the First Amendment.[136] This protection is conferred independently of the content of the speech itself and of the identity of the speaker. The First Amendment protects foolish speech, sublime speech, rigorous speech, and nonsensical speech, as well as political, provocative, and religious speech. In the words of Supreme Court Justice William J. Brennan, writing for the majority in *Roth v. United States,* "all ideas having even the slightest redeeming social importance—unorthodox ideas, controversial ideas, even ideas hateful to the prevailing climate of opinion" warrant full protection under the First Amendment.

The United States versus the World of Pleasure

Not all pornography is protected by the First Amendment, however. According to the Supreme Court decision in *Roth,* "obscene" materials (including books, films, works of art, and so on) do not fall within the area of constitutionally protected speech or press because they are "utterly without redeeming social importance." *Roth* is particularly important because, despite isolated prosecutions for the production or distribution of obscene materials dating back to before the Comstock Act, the Supreme Court had not previously been called upon to address the constitutionality of existing obscenity statutes.[137]

It is perhaps fitting that the constitutional examination of obscenity began with the subject of pleasure, in the form of a publication entitled *Good Times: A Review of the World of Pleasure.* This pamphlet was distributed by Samuel Roth, along with publications entitled *Nus* and *American Aphrodite* (which included erotic graphics by Aubrey Beardsley). The distribution of these publications landed Roth in jail, and a drawn-out legal skirmish ensued, eventually reaching the Supreme Court in 1957. At that time, Roth's attorneys argued that because the publications in question could not be shown to pose a "clear and present danger" to society, there was no constitutional justification for permitting their suppression. The government, in opposition, argued that speech can be categorized hierarchically in terms of the protection it warrants under the Constitution. Obscenity, the government contended, was at the bottom of the heap (along with libel, profanity, and so on). Unfortunately for Roth, the high court sided with the government and upheld his conviction for distributing obscene materials.[138]

In this landmark decision, Justice Brennan was at pains to make it clear that discussions of sex, as opposed to obscenity, *are* protected speech. Brennan stated:

> Sex and obscenity are not synonymous. Obscene material is material that deals with sex in a manner appealing to the prurient interest. The portrayal of sex in art, literature and scientific works is not itself sufficient reason to deny material the constitutional protection of speech and press. . . . Sex, a great and mysterious motive force in human life . . . is one of the vital problems of human interest and public concern. As to all such problems, this Court said in *Thornhill v.*

> *Alabama* . . . "The freedom of speech and of the press guaranteed by
> the Constitution embraces at the least the liberty to discuss publicly
> and truthfully all matters of public concern without previous restraint
> or fear of subsequent punishment."[139]

Once again, art and literature were rescued from blasphemous condemnation. Subsequent to *Roth,* so long as expression contained socially redeeming importance, it was entitled to full protection under the First Amendment. However, problems with this definition continued to arise, including variability in perceptions of "socially redeeming importance." With regard to the distinction between protected and unprotected materials, Harry Kalven Jr. opines that "the touchstone is more likely to be the social status of the publisher than the content of the item."[140]

Kalven tried to resolve this dilemma, in part, by emphasizing the value or worth of expression, for "if the obscene is constitutionally subject to ban because it is worthless, it must follow that the obscene can only include that which is worthless."[141] This strategy was meant to distinguish art and ideas from hardcore pornography. Ultimately, however, it too was patently flawed, at least as articulated. There was—and continues to be—substantial objective evidence of the value and worth of hardcore pornography. One billion dollars in annual sales and rentals provide prima facie evidence of pornography's value and worth to consumers. In the Smithian economic sense, certainly, the *value* of pornography is resoundingly exclaimed.

The Court's insistent focus on the restraint of ostensibly *immoral* speech also reflects a persistent failure to acknowledge the protected status of *moral* speech:

> Freedom of speech covers much more than political ideas. It embraces
> all discussion which enriches human life and helps it to be more wisely
> led. Thus in our first national statement of the subject by the Continental Congress in 1774, this freedom was declared to include "the advancement of truth, science, *morality* and arts in general."[142]

Justice Brennan, as other jurists before him, selectively addressed his attention to literature and art, and to the protection afforded them by the First Amendment. Morality, per se, was conspicuously avoided, presumably because it was thought that the only way to advance morality is through restraint. But this need not be the case. As suggested by Shiffrin, the First Amendment is an innately *progressive* document. Thus, not only is sexual speech (which often communicates controversial ideas about morality) protected, it should also be encouraged to the degree that it "enriches human life." In considering this point, it is important to acknowledge that sexually liberalizing speech is not necessarily inconsistent with religious proclamations. Many of the great religions of the world incorporate, and advance, sexuality within the ream of righteous behavior. Hindu artists have infused spirituality and sexual explicitness into the temple structures of Khajuraho and Konarak. The *Kama Sutra* provides another graphic example, as do sexually forthright fertility symbols in Africa and Japan. To many people the world over, sexual restraint is neither moral nor righteous. Although some Americans may find the notion that sexuality should be celebrated as a human birthright "unorthodox, controversial, and hateful to the prevailing climate of opinion," sexual speech is nonetheless protected because it represents morality dialogue and dissent. Furthermore, because explicit pornography—from temple sculptures to X-rated videos—is an effective vehicle for emphasizing sexual ideas, this expression is also protected.

This view of pornography is eloquently summarized by David Richards, a noted constitutional scholar:

> Pornography can be seen as the unique medium of a vision of sexuality . . . a view of sensual delight in the erotic celebration of the body, a concept of easy freedom without consequences, a fantasy of timelessly repetitive indulgence. In opposition to the Victorian view that narrowly defines proper sexual function in a rigid way . . . pornography builds a model of plastic variety and joyful excess in sexuality. In opposition to the sorrowing Catholic dismissal of sexuality as an unfortunate and spiritually superficial concomitant of propagation, pornography affords the alternative idea of the independent status of sexuality as a profound and shattering ecstasy.[143]

While these ideas complement the arguments advanced in this chapter, they have yet to be incorporated in Supreme Court decisions, even though Justice Brennan himself, after struggling many years with the complex issue of obscenity law, concluded that *all* such laws (applicable to consenting adults) should be repealed.[144]

He Said, She Said

Of course, many people, including the antiporn feminists, have argued that pornography (or its legal embodiment, obscenity) were never *intended* to be protected as speech. We find this conclusion curious for two reasons. First, the original intent of the free speech and press clauses is vague at best.[145] That is, it is difficult to discern with any confidence exactly what the framers of the Constitution intended the First Amendment to include or exclude. This being the case, it is perhaps more parsimonious, and certainly less dangerous, to take the First Amendment at face value and to make *no* law abridging the freedoms of speech and press.

Second, pornographic publications were widely available at the time the First Amendment was ratified. They were part of the grist of expression. This expression, as we have already demonstrated, challenges conventional morality by extolling the pleasures of sex. If such challenges were readily available, yet not explicitly excluded from the First Amendment, it seems reasonable to conclude that they warrant the same protection as other types of expression.

Furthermore, our constitutional forebears were not all prudes, nor necessarily adverse to challenging conventional morality. Benjamin Franklin, an active debater at the Constitutional Convention, was also the author of *Advice to a Young Man on the Choice of a Mistress*. Though he begins with a comment that marriage is best, he continues, "But if you will not take this counsel and persist in thinking a commerce with sex inevitable, then I repeat my former advice, that in all your amours, you should *prefer old women to young ones*." Franklin listed eight reasons for preferring older mistresses:

1. Older women have greater knowledge of the world;
2. "When women cease to be handsome, they study to be good. To maintain their influence over men, they supply the diminution of beauty by an augmentation of utility";
3. There is no hazard of children [thus, by "older" Franklin apparently meant postmenopausal];
4. They are more discreet in conducting an affair;
5. Although an older woman could be distinguished from a younger one by her face, "regarding only what is below the girdle, it is impossible of two women to know an old from a young one";
6. Because "the sin is less. The debauching of a virgin may be her ruin, and make her for life unhappy";
7. Likewise, "the compunction is less. The having made a young girl *miserable* may give you frequent bitter reflections; none of which can attend the making an old woman *happy*";
8. Finally, older women are to be preferred because "they are *so grateful!*"[146]

It is interesting that although Benjamin Franklin could indulge in and even publish such ruminations in the 1700s, 250 years later the state of New York refused to issue a license for the motion picture *Lady Chatterley's Lover* because it "portrays adultery as proper behavior." However, the Supreme Court ultimately ruled that the license refusal represented a violation of the

First Amendment,[147] and in so doing reaffirmed that films were within the scope of the First Amendment. Movies were thus guaranteed the freedom to advocate ideas, even if the ideas in question provide a justification for adultery.

This example is by no means the only instance of hypocrisy and misunderstanding meeting at the crossroads of sexuality and the law. The history of the concept of "obscenity" is filled with well-documented instances of similar foolishness.

Obscenity: To Be or Not To Be

What do Emile Zola's *Nana,* James Joyce's *Ulysses,* D. H. Lawrence's *The Rainbow,* Henry Miller's *Tropic of Cancer,* Theodore Dreiser's *An American Tragedy,* Erskine Caldwell's *God's Little Acre,* Kurt Vonnegut's *Breakfast of Champions,* Lillian Smith's *Strange Fruit,* and Edmund Wilson's *Memoirs of Hecate County* have in common? First, they are often assigned as reading in college-level English courses. Second, they are frequently circulated at public libraries. And third, they have all been destroyed or prosecuted for being obscene.

This final characteristic is important to emphasize. At the very least, it underscores Cervantes' warning, "He that falls today, may rise tomorrow." This is certainly true where art, literature, and science are concerned: Materials and ideas historically condemned as blasphemous and obscene often reemerge to critical acclaim. The works of Leonardo da Vinci, Galileo, and Darwin fit in this category, as do those of Margaret Sanger, Anaïs Nin, and Henry Miller. The line that separates the obscene from the acceptable often vacillates in unpredictable ways.

Prior to the 1930s, the demarcation adopted by the U.S. courts followed the English Victorian standard established in *Queen v. Hicklin,* which identified obscenity by its "tendency . . . to deprave and corrupt those whose minds are open to such immoral influence."[148] Obscenity was thus defined by its effect on the most vulnerable members of society (typically children and innocent young women).

In the United States, the *Hicklin* guidelines were abandoned with the *United States v. "Ulysses"* cases of the mid-1930s, which came to define obscenity by the dominant effect of a work, taken in artistic and thematic context, on the "average" reader or viewer.[149] This shift in test audiences— from the most vulnerable to the median—was further strengthened in *Butler v. Michigan* and later codified in *Roth.* The test of obscenity adopted in *Roth* was "whether to the average person, applying contemporary community standards, the dominant theme of the material taken as a whole

appeals to prurient interest."[150] The most serious problem with this definition is its circularity. As Kalven observes:

> The key word "prurient" is defined by one dictionary in terms of
> "lascivious longings" and "lewd." The obscene, then, is that which
> appeals to an interest in the obscene.[151]

Presently, the 1973 *Miller v. California* definition of obscenity, which
incorporates the *Roth* definition, is the law of the land. According to *Miller,*
a work is obscene if (1) the "average" person applying "contemporary
community standards" would find that the work, taken as a whole, appeals
to prurient interest, (2) the work depicts or describes, in a patently offensive
way, sexual conduct specifically defined by the applicable state law, and (3)
the work, taken as a whole, lacks serious literary, artistic, political, or
scientific value. All three prongs of the Miller definition must be satisfied
for a work to be constitutionally obscene.

This new definition has had a number of interesting consequences.
Most significantly, it has enervated the national standard of obscenity by
transferring regulatory power to the individual states and the vagaries of
"contemporary community standards." Consequently, if interracial sex is
objectionable in one state, the probability of obtaining an obscenity conviction there is likely to be higher than it is in other states. The same is true for
homosexuality, transvestism, and so on.[152] Thus, the community standard
provision clearly enforces the tyranny of the majority, in violation, we
believe, of the original intent of the framers of the Constitution.

Whether hardcore pornography is protected under *Miller* depends on
the answers to the three-pronged test. Child pornography, for example,
fails on two counts. First, and foremost, children cannot give informed
consent. In the absence of informed consent, children are not participating
voluntarily or with foreknowledge of the consequences of their actions.
Second, sex with a minor is a criminal act, being classed as either assault or
statutory rape. In either case, it translates child pornography into the actual
depiction of a felony offense and transforms it from speech to admissible
evidence in criminal proceedings. (Similarly, adult pornography that depicts
actual rape would provide documentary evidence of sexual abuse.)

However, the generic pornographic film that features voluntarily participating adult actors and is intended exclusively for private consumption by
consenting adults generally does fit within the *Miller* guidelines, or at least
case law would suggest as much. The value of such pornography is threefold
(see also Chapter 3). First, sexuality—in this culture especially—is a privatized behavior. It is generally not expressed in public, nor do people usually
learn about it through the direct observation of others. Pornography is thus

one of the many secondary sources through which people learn about various facets of human sexuality, including the seemingly endless possibilities for sexual pleasure, the range and variability inherent in genital anatomy and physiology, and the heterogeneity evident in sexual expression.

Second, pornography serves a didactic purpose when it increases sexual knowledge, reduces unwanted sexual inhibitions, or enhances a sexual relationship. Many behavioral specialists, including Christian marital counselors, recommend the introduction of pornography into the sexual repertoires of couples whose sex lives have become routine. The therapeutic use of pornography can lower inhibitions, provide new sexual inspiration, offer instruction on technique, and increase communication between partners. It also can be fun, provided both partners participate willingly. Pornography can teach tolerance for alternative sexualities and can serve as a documentary record of the variety and underlying themes inherent in sexual relationships and fantasies.

Moreover, viewing, reading, or listening to pornography, whether accompanied by masturbation or not, is clearly safe sex, that is, sex without the threat of sexually transmitted diseases, including AIDS. From an epidemiologic standpoint, it therefore has substantial societal value. As we argued in the previous chapter, sexually transmitted diseases, like rock 'n' roll, are here to stay. One way in which society can keep them under control is to enhance nonpenetrative sexual options. Masturbating to pornography—or merely enjoying the fantasies it provokes—is one important option. These seldom-mentioned epidemiological and personal health benefits deserve serious consideration in the debate over pornography.

The Pornographic Future

Pornography and its accompaniment, masturbation, are still taboo. It has been said of masturbation that "everyone does it, but nobody talks about it." The courts, for example, have expended copious amounts of energy in the pursuit of an adequate definition of "obscenity," yet have left largely unspecified the harm allegedly caused by obscene materials. As Kalven suggests:

> It is one of the ironies of discussion of obscenity that it has been too polite to put the point that must be invoked. The talk is of "arousing sexual thoughts." Presumably what is meant is a physiological (sexual) response to a picture or the written word. And one suspects that the real fear is one that everyone, except Anthony Comstock, has been too reticent to mention, the fear of masturbation.[153]

Furthermore, despite the prevalence of masturbation (according to one poll, 94 percent of all men and 63 percent of all women have masturbated at one time or another[154]), and despite more than thirty years of attempts by counseling psychologists to extol its many joys and to increase its satisfactory practice (for example, by learning orgasmic responsiveness), the normalization of masturbation is far from complete. But perhaps the "evil" dyad of pornography and masturbation can still redeem itself, as more and more people begin to acknowledge that autoeroticism is a completely safe form of sex, and that pornography is an integral accompaniment to masturbation for many men (and some women). Perhaps. But given the past history of antipornography and antimasturbation crusades, this seems an unlikely possibility at best.

Of course, the nature of pornography is continually changing. With the recruitment of novel computer and telecommunications technologies, pornography is becoming more and more high tech. Men now masturbate while listening to disembodied voices describe erotic activities over the phone. CD-ROMs permit users to interact with animated characters in the computerized equivalent of a pornographic video. Internet bulletin board services with names like KinkNet, ThrobNet, and SwingNet let men and women exchange pornographic images, text, and thoughts,[155] while thousands upon thousands of sexually oriented websites offer images, videos, and all manner of porno pleasures. All of this is *presently* available to anyone with a computer, phone, modem, and CD-ROM. The even wilder future of computerized pornography approaches the limits of science fiction, as epitomized by the promise of "virtual reality." Virtual reality, its proponents claim, may soon make full-body sexual simulations (and stimulations) possible. Just "jack" (plug) yourself in and have sex with the move star of your choice. Although the full implications of virtual sex are as yet unclear, new technologies are rapidly blurring the boundaries among masturbatory pornography, prostitution, and conventional one-on-one-sex.

8.

Epilogue: The Future of Sex

Throughout this book we have argued that sex for pleasure and sex for reproduction are conceptually distinct entities. With modern forms of birth control, wider acceptance of homosexual behavior, and advances in non-sexual reproductive techniques (e.g., artificial insemination), the perpetuation of this distinction seems assured. But does this mean that we are headed inexorably toward Aldous Huxley's prophetic *Brave New World,* with its appropriately named Malthusian belts (containing an unspecified contraceptive) and its sex hormone chewing gum?[1] That is, will the current trend continue unabated, the two functions of sexuality ultimately becoming completely divorced from one another? Or, as the conservative fundamentalist movement would have it, is the sexual liberation of the previous decades simply a fad, ready for reversal?[2] What, in other words, *is* the future of sex?

As is often the case, the best way to predict the future is to scrutinize the past. Despite occasional objections by the Church, the pleasurability of sex was widely acknowledged by both physicians and the lay populace in pre-eighteenth-century Europe. And, of course, its reproductive potential was obvious. We can symbolize the prevailing belief system via the two equations *Sex = Reproduction* and *Sex = Pleasure*. However, these equations omit an important relation. In the sixteenth to eighteenth centuries, the reproductive and pleasurable aspects of sex were not only *appreciated,* they were *equated,* so that *Pleasure = Reproduction.*[3]

More precisely, prevailing medical and lay wisdom held that both men's and women's enjoyment of sexual intercourse was *necessary* for the sexual act to be a fruitful one, for "apart from pleasure nothing of mortal kind comes into existence."[4] Conception, it was believed, could not take place without orgasm by both men *and* women. This belief provided a partial counterpoint to prevailing theological opinion, which held that the enjoyment of sex was at best unseemly, and at worst a sin. In contrast, under the revised belief system, pleasureless sex is "unnatural" because the raison d'être for sex is procreation, and procreation, according to this view, *demands* enjoyment on the part of the participants.

But why did our forebears believe it necessary for people to enjoy intercourse to ensure procreation? In particular, why the insistence that women orgasm? The answer lies in the observation that men enjoy sex, and the conflation of the psychological experience of male orgasm with the physiological experience of ejaculation. The difference between these two events is critical: Orgasm often occurs without procreation, but seldom without pleasure, whereas ejaculation is necessary for procreation, but not for pleasure. This subtle difference is seldom appreciated, even today. However, prior to the eighteenth century and the rise of scientific conceptualizations of reproduction, male orgasm and ejaculation were considered to be synonymous, as were, by analogy, female orgasm and "ejaculation." This prescientific notion followed naturally from the widely accepted "single-sex" model of human anatomy and physiology.[5] According to this model, the difference between men and women was one of degree only, not of kind. Women were simply men with their genitals turned inside out, the vagina corresponding to the penis, the ovaries to the testes, and so on. Given this correspondence, it was thought, ejaculation/orgasm in the male must necessarily have an analogue in the female.

Thus, the "father of medicine," Hippocrates (and later Galen) proposed that women must also have a "seed," which they emit upon successful (that is, pleasurable or orgasmic) intercourse. It was thought that the female seed then mixed with the male seed (sperm) to produce a child. Aristotle argued against this theory, with pleasure, or a lack thereof, once again adduced as evidence: "A sign that the female does not emit the kind of seed that the male emits, and that generation is not due to the mixing of both as some hold, is that often the female conceives without experiencing the pleasure that occurs in intercourse."[6] Nevertheless, Galen's pronouncements to the contrary held the day, and pleasure was henceforth considered a prerequisite for procreation "for without the enjoyment of pleasure in the venereal act no conception can possibly take place."[7] (Although this theory of conception had a liberating effect on female sexuality overall, one unfortunate consequence was that women who were raped, and subsequently conceived, were branded as liars and harlots because it was believed that impregnation could only result from pleasurable, hence consensual, intercourse.)

Scientific advancements in the late eighteenth and nineteenth centuries led to improved understanding of reproductive sexuality and the different roles assumed by men and women. This increased knowledge, in turn, undercut the egalitarian assumption that both sexes must necessarily enjoy intercourse for conception to take place.[8] Coupled with the introduction of relatively effective methods of contraception, such as the condom or penile sheath, the dissolution of the tripartite equation

$$\text{Sex}$$
$$\diagup \quad \diagdown$$
$$\text{Pleasure} = \text{Reproduction}$$

into the separate relations *Sex* = *Reproduction* and *Sex* = *Pleasure* was complete. As historian Thomas Laqueur observes:

> Previously a sign of the generative process, deeply embedded in the bodies of women and men, a feeling whose existence was no more open to debate than the warm, pleasurable glow that usually accompanies a good meal, orgasm was relegated to the realm of mere sensation, to the periphery of human physiology—accidental, expendable, a contingent bonus of the reproductive act.[9]

In modern American society, the equality symbol in *Sex* = *Pleasure* is seldom allowed to function independently of recognized social bonds. That is, sex equals pleasure only for socially sanctioned unions such as marriages and, increasingly, premarital cohabitants (especially betrothed couples) and others in committed relationships. In other words, sex is okay only for people in love. This attitude toward sex both reflects and partially contradicts the ideals of the sexual revolution of the 1960s and 1970s; on the one hand it extends the umbrella of social acceptability to unmarried couples, but on the other it requires a lasting bond. In the current climate of fear engendered by AIDS, more and more people are looking for longer-term relationships incorporating sexual monogamy. Pleasure is still "in," but so is safety.

The dizzying array of modern contraceptive methods further separates sex from its reproductive function. In addition to that old standby the (male) condom, today's roster of contraceptive options includes female condoms, hormonal regulation via "the pill," diaphragms, cervical caps, spermicidal jellies and foams, contraceptive implants, and so on. The advent of the birth control pill, in particular, had a major impact on sexual mores and behaviors in America and Europe, contributing significantly to the sexual revolution of the past decades. The pill freed men and women—especially women—to explore their sexual natures as no other contraceptive method could: without the messiness of diaphragms or foams, without the medical foresight of the IUD (intrauterine device), without the fear of pregnancy that accompanied the rhythm method, and without the sensation-dampening effects of condoms. Without the pill, some say, there could never have been a sexual revolution.[10] It is therefore not surprising that the next important advancement is expected to be the development of a male pill.

Kurt Vonnegut's short story "Welcome to the Monkey House" describes a future society in which such a pill exists, and indeed is mandatory for men as well as women. In a world overflowing with 17 billion people, "[Those] who understood science said people had to quit reproducing so much, and [those] who understood morals said society would collapse if people used sex for nothing but pleasure."[11] The solution was the development of an "ethical" birth control pill that made people numb from the waist down:

> The pills were ethical because they didn't interfere with a person's ability to reproduce, which would have been unnatural and immoral. All the pills did was take every bit of pleasure out of sex. . . . Thus did science and morals go hand in hand.[12]

Ultimately, however, there arose a movement of "nothingheads" who refused to swallow their ethical birth control pills or the moralistic justification for their necessity. One of the leaders of the movement, a nothinghead known as Billy the Poet, rebuked the moralists' claim that the world cannot afford sex anymore: "Of course it can afford sex. All it can't afford anymore is reproduction."[13] So it goes.

Whereas contraception makes sex without procreation possible, modern artificial reproductive techniques make procreation without sex a reality. It is perhaps no coincidence, therefore, that the first artificial insemination procedure was performed in 1776, at about the same time that essentially modern theories of conception first began to proliferate.[14] Today there are a number of options for sexless reproduction in addition to artificial insemination, including in vitro fertilization ("test tube" babies) and surrogate parenthood.

Thus, reproductive and contraceptive technologies march on. Newer forms of birth control will inevitably mean increased sexual freedom, while advances in artificial reproductive techniques will provide otherwise infertile individuals the offspring they desire. Although history teaches us that there are no absolutes, few forces are as irresistible as technological progress. And as technology progresses, society adapts, slowly but inevitably (Rosseau notwithstanding). There can be no turning back to an age in which reproduction demanded sex, or in which pregnancy was an overriding fear. Modern technology has seen to that. Thus, it appears that the distinction between reproduction and pleasure is here to stay.

A Brave New World?

Nowhere are the consequences of the separation of pleasure and reproduction explicated as entertainingly as in Huxley's Brave New World, first published in 1932. In this prophetic masterpiece, Huxley describes a world some 500 years hence in which all of society is planned, monitored, and controlled, from "birth" to death. Properly speaking, babies are not born, but "decanted"; their lives begin in a test tube somewhere down the production line. Reproductive sex has been eliminated, and with it the archaic notion of "birth parents." Indeed, the majority of the populace is sterile, since fertile men and women are needed only as obsolete backups to the ever-fecund decanting system. In the Brave New World, reproduction is much too important to be left to amateurs.

Freed of the shackles of reproduction, alternative meanings of sex flourish in the "year of our ford A.F. 600." Erotic play is encouraged among young children, and required of adults. Sex is freely given, and promiscuity is the governmentally sanctioned norm. Monogamy, in contrast, is sternly frowned upon:

> Lenina shook her head. "Somehow," she mused, "I haven't been feeling very keen on promiscuity lately. There are times when one doesn't. Haven't you found that too, Fanny?"
>
> Fanny nodded her sympathy and understanding. "But one's got to make the effort," she said, sententiously, "one's got to play the game. After all, every one belongs to every one else."[15]

In this far-off future, the government views sex as just another diversion, like taking a holiday from reality courtesy of the wonder drug Soma, or playing an invigorating round of Obstacle Golf. Sex, drugs, and sports keep the citizenry happy and the workforce productive. Meanwhile, interpersonal relationships, sexual or otherwise, are actively discouraged because "every one belongs to every one else."

Similarly, interpersonal sex is a mere relic of the past in Woody Allen's futuristic comedy Sleeper. Thus, although Diane Keaton's character has an "advanced degree in oral sex," her training is for naught. In the future envisioned by Allen, all sexual needs are serviced by the ubiquitous Orgasmatron, which appears to function as a sophisticated mechanical masturbator. With the Orgasmatron always at the ready, sexual gratification is instantly available, with or without a partner.

The Orgasmatron is fiction, of course. But recent technological advances, including the promise of virtual reality programming, suggest that, in the future, sex will become an increasingly solitary activity for many people. This trend is already evident in currently available high- and not-so-high-tech sexual options, including phone sex, X-rated videos, CD-ROMs, DVDs, and the numerous sexual possibilities to be found on the Internet, especially the World Wide Web.[16]

Higher-Tech Sex

The VCR (video cassette recorder) is a ubiquitous feature of the modern American living room or den. VCRs free people to tape and watch their favorite television programs whenever it is convenient, in the privacy of their own homes. This privacy extends to purchased and rented videos as well, and is especially important for people who want to watch X-rated videos without risking their social reputations. Gone are the days when porn films were confined to 8-millimeter reels at "stag" parties, seedy downtown theaters (such as the famous Pussycat chain), or sticky backroom booths of adult bookstores. Now, adult videos can be viewed in private by anyone with a TV and a VCR at home, and a few dollars in his or her pockets.

Those few dollars add up quickly. Each year, Americans spend nearly $5 billion on adult videos and nearly twice that on adult images in general.[17] Approximately one of every five households with a VCR or cable access at least occasionally watches adult videos. Adult video rentals and sales make up nearly a third of the total revenue of video rental shops that stock these titles. Variety, it appears, truly is the spice of life: More than 10,000 new adult video titles are produced each year, mostly in southern California.

Pornographic videos are also carried by cable and beamed by satellite into homes throughout the world. Most mid- to upscale hotel rooms permit guests to tune in a selection of adult videos, for an exorbitant fee, of course. According to hotel industry estimates, at least half of all guests take advantage of these pay-per-view services, generating nearly $200 million a year in revenue. Pay-per-view is also big business in the home. The satellite entertainment provider DirectTV bills its customers approximately $200 million annually for pay-for-view adult programming, and another large satellite provider, EchoStar Communications Corporation, makes more money selling adult entertainment than Playboy does with its magazine, videos, and cable enterprises combined.[18]

However, video is quickly becoming passé, as more and more people discover the joys of clean, crisp digital detail. Fortunately for them, these folks need not do without pornography, thanks to the burgeoning market in adult-oriented CD-ROMs (compact disk–read only memory) and DVDs (digital video disk). These disks can store massive amounts of information, including digitized images and sounds, full-length adult videos, text, and software programs.

Adult-oriented CD-ROMS, which are meant for computer usage, typically contain photographic images and short video clips, and some embed these elements in fantasy scripts, but their storage capacity is insufficient for full-length videos. DVDs, on the other hand, have immense capacities and thus can be used as an alternative to video cassettes, as well as permitting pornophiles to view adult videos on their computers, once they're purchased a DVD drive. Some stand-alone DVD players have an additional interesting feature, which allows users to select any one of several camera angles from which to view the action. The potential of user-selectable perspectives has not been lost on adult video producers, such as Vivid Video's cofounder, David James, who calls the multiple-angle button "a perfect tool for your cultivated voyeur."[19] With the multiple-angle button, viewers can tailor the action to their own personal tastes, becoming, in essence, the director of their own private porn shoot.

CD-ROM–based software packages also allow users greater flexibility to tailor their fantasies. For example, a user could select an ideal partner by specifying such attributes as appearance (blonde or brunette? slim or athletic?), personality (shy or seductive? reserved or loquacious?), and attire (miniskirt or lingerie? jeans or a suit?).[20] A particular script or situation can be chosen, for example, "nanny catches young boy masturbating and 'punishes' him," "pool man services more than just pools," and so on. Once the scenario and actors have been tailored to the user's tastes, the program begins—animated or video images, sounds, and all. As the program unfolds, the user is drawn into the story line, becoming a character in what amounts to an interactive X-rated video. Animated or photographic characters await his or her command to disrobe, to pose, and to engage in various simulated sex acts. This simulated reality is made possible by the enormous storage capacity of CD-ROM and DVD disks, the high speed of modern computers, and the detailed resolution of today's televisions and video monitors.

Before continuing further, we should note that the sexism evident in the preceding paragraph is not accidental. "Cybersex" software is primarily produced for and purchased by men (as is all pornography). According to one software executive:

> Regardless of the content, it's men who buy it. Men are more voyeuristic. Some women do enjoy this kind of software, but mostly it is men. Generally, nothing is being done by or for women.[21]

Although many of the products might be considered appealing by women, such as the photographic collection of nude and near-nude men on *Heavenly Hunks* and similar CD-ROMs (which borrow liberally from gay fantasy scripts[22]), several adult entertainment companies have begun crafting "couples-friendly" products, which interject a bit of romance into the still-raunchy proceedings.

In short, video-based products offer considerable flexibility to satisfy the user's particular tastes and to involve him or her in the selected fantasy. But ultimately the interaction is between man (or woman) and machine. This is all well and good, but some people prefer to interact with other people.

Phone Sex and Online Sex

Talking dirty on the phone is nothing new: Men and women have been doing it, no doubt, since just after Alexander Graham Bell first summoned his assistant over a telephone line. But it seems reasonable to assume that, through the years, the vast majority of illicit phone conversations have involved lovers, friends, or at the very least, proper acquaintances. The advent of the "900 number" in the 1980s changed all that. Now people (primarily men) can have intimate, erotic conversations with strangers—for a fee, of course. For $4.95 a minute (plus toll charges), men can enjoy a live, sex-filled conversation with a "hot, horny woman," who is there, the caller is told, "to make your every fantasy come true." Simulated oral sex (complete with sucking sounds), faked orgasms, and lots of "ooh, baby, oohs" are the standard fare, but specialized numbers are also available for those with more esoteric preferences, such as simulated lesbian sex or bondage and discipline.

Depending on your point of view, phone sex is either harmless entertainment, a mild form of prostitution, or yet another indication of the moral quagmire into which society has fallen. In our opinion, phone sex is simply an innocuous, if inane, form of aural pornography, which exists, like the printed variety, to serve primarily as a masturbatory aid for men (and, to a lesser degree, women). What distinguishes it from more traditional forms of pornography is the active, interpersonal nature of the sexual transaction.

Phone sex straddles the line between pornography and prostitution, combing the fantasy and masturbatory elements of the former with the interactive intimacy of the latter.

Beginning in the 1980s, the digital equivalent of phone sex became available to computer users hooked up the Internet. In the earliest years of the Internet revolution, online communication was mainly confined to text-based messages. Users could post information to electronic bulletin boards, read messages on sex-themed newsgroups, such as alt.sex.spanking, email each other, and engage in real-time conversations in designated chat rooms (chat rooms permit multiple users to post and receive messages, almost simultaneously, in real time). Of course, the majority of Internet communications concern mundane nonsexual topics, such as computers, baseball, and politics, but the Internet also provides an ideal forum for those who desire more explicit exchanges. Private encounters range from coquettish flirting via email to torrid, X-rated banter in any one of thousands of chat rooms devoted to sex. In some chat rooms, users can even observe—or participate in—the electronic equivalent of an orgy.[23] There is something for everyone on the Internet, as the following newsgroup posting makes clear:

> Hi, I am a 29 yo bi male xdresser that is looking for m/f/cpls that own dogs/horses/donkeys/etc for animal action. I have had a cpl exp with dogs and am dying to try more with them and other animals. I am open to many scenarios and am willing to be photographed or videotaped in action. If you can help me and are serious about it e-mail me.[24]

Internet sex between consenting adults offers a number of advantages over the more traditional variety. Provided that the sexual encounter remains virtual, there is no danger of disease transmission (below we discuss some of the harmful consequences that can result when the sexual encounter extends beyond the electronic confines of the Internet). Women and men can play out sexual fantasies online that they would never, or could never, act out in real life. Or they can use the Internet to explore alternative sexual possibilities, to "try them on" so to speak, and to see whether they enjoy them and how their partners react. Like other forms of fantasy role playing, online sex can be used to open new, freer communication channels, which can help couples share their feelings, desires, and erotic fantasies.[25] Single people too can expand their sexual horizons in directions that they would be too shy, inhibited, or scared to explore otherwise. Moreover, Internet fantasies are not limited by the physical reality of the partner or situation. People can imagine their partners—as well as themselves—to be anything they want them to be.[26] This deemphasis of the primacy of physical qualities may foster greater emotional closeness between partners, based on common interests and personal compatibility, as opposed to just physical attractiveness.

Privacy is another important benefit of the Internet. Because electronic communications are protected (to a greater or lesser degree) by the privacy guarantees of the Bill of Rights, most Internet service providers are forbidden from intercepting messages and censoring their contents (this is *not* true for employers however). This privacy also means that individuals can hide their true identities and pretend to be whoever they want to be. A graying middle-aged man with an ever-expanding beer belly can portray himself as an eighteen-year-old stud with endless stamina, rippling muscles, and a restored Mustang fastback. He could even pretend to be a woman, or a gay man, and communicate with other men under his assumed identity. The Internet thus provides opportunities for self-explorations that are not possible in "real" encounters.

The disembodiment that characterizes interpersonal relationships in cyberspace actually facilitates online sex by emphasizing the mental, imaginative side of sex. Cybersexual encounters are freed from the physical constraints of space and time. In cyberspace, distance is immaterial. The Internet spans the globe, bringing people together without regard to international boundaries. It makes little difference whether one's partner lives in another country, another state, or just down the street. All that matters is that he or she has a computer (or personal digital assistant) with Internet access. Although time zones can affect real-time cybersexual rendezvous, such as those that occur in chat rooms or using instant messaging technologies, e-mail opens up the possibility of truly asynchronous—although somewhat less interactive—sex. Sexual encounters can be drawn out over hours, days, or weeks, with messages passing back and forth at convenient times.

One unfortunate consequence of the Internet's sometimes empowering freedom to explore alternate identities is the ability to wrongfully deceive others, and perhaps to hurt them by doing so. In some cases, the Internet has been abused by sexual predators to meet children or adolescents, often by men posing as children or adolescents themselves. These men first establish a friendship with their victim and then use this relationship as a pretext to meet them and, ultimately, to sexually abuse them. In other cases, men have used more traditional methods to entice children into risky situations. As the following news story makes clear, children should never take cybercandy from strangers:

WANTAGH, N.Y. (APBnews.com)—A Queens man has been indicted on charges of sexually abusing two preteen boys he allegedly lured into a park with promises of toys and a ride on his motorcycle, authorities said today. James Cleary, 36, of Howard Beach, apparently met the boys, ages 10 and 12, in an Internet chat room. Authorities allege he had told them he would buy them toys if they would meet him on Nov. 11 in Wantagh Park, a New York City suburb on the south shore of Long Island, Nassau County district attorney spokesman Ed Grilli said. He also tempted the boys with promises of rides on his motorcycle, Grilli told APB News. When the boys arrived at the park, he gave them gifts and lured them into a secluded section of the playground where he sexually abused them, authorities said.[27]

Another disturbing example of Internet abuse is the so-called Orchid Club case in which two men (one of whom was a correctional officer) raped a ten-year-old girl and broadcast their crimes live on the Internet.[28] Men who belonged to the club could watch the rape from the comfort of their homes and could e-mail requests for specific acts, which the perpetrators would then force upon the girl. Cases like this are truly sickening, but fortunately also are exceedingly rare.[29]

More typical is the following story of a police sting operation. Arthur Garrod, a sixty-six-year-old Bible teacher in Florida, posted an image of his penis on the Internet, stating that he was looking for a fifteen-year-old white girl. The police responded to his posting, with a young female officer posing as the requested fifteen-year-old. After an exchange of emails, the officer told Garrod that they could meet in private because her mother was away, if he would just come over. When he showed up at the address she had given him, he was arrested for "cruising the Internet for illicit purposes by soliciting a teenager for oral sex."[30] Many law enforcement agencies (such as the FBI) make use of the deceptive potential of the Internet to ensnare potential child molesters by posing as underage boys and girls and arranging meetings with suspected pedophiles.

The Internet can also be used as a forum for arranging "live" sexual affairs (including the extramarital kind) between consenting adults. Unfortunately, anything that facilitates sex between relative strangers is likely to promote the transmission of sexually transmitted diseases.[31] For example, a 1999 outbreak of syphilis in San Francisco was traced to a handful of men who met new sexual partners in the America Online chat room SFM4M (San Francisco Men for Men), for whom the Internet provided an efficient, cost-effective alternative to the gay bar scene.[32] At the same time, the Internet constitutes an intriguing avenue for *preventing* such outbreaks. When the San Francisco Department of Public Health made the link between the syphilis cases they were seeing and the Internet, they enlisted the aid of PlanetOut, an online service for gays, lesbians, and bisexuals, to help disseminate STD prevention messages to other patrons of SFM4M. Still, preliminary evidence suggests that people who use the Internet to find partners for casual sex may be at elevated risk for acquiring HIV and other STDs.[33] (This is not surprising, given that sex with anonymous partners can be dangerous, regardless of where the partners are met.)

Another danger posed by Internet sex is the potential for overindulgence. A 1999 study on Internet use conducted by Alvin Cooper and his associates at the San Jose Marital and Sexuality Centre[34] garnered substantial attention in the media for its conclusion that "heavy users [of online sex resources] . . . reported significant problems associated with compulsive disorders."[35] The online survey of approximately 10,000 visitors to the MSNBC news website,[36] the overwhelming majority of whom were men, found that about 8 percent spent eleven or more hours a week online pursuing sexual entertainment. This group was more likely than less-frequent visitors to online sex sites to report negative effects as a result of the time they spent online, for example, more of them said that it interfered with other areas of their lives. But this finding is not surprising. Couldn't we have predicted that spending substantial amounts of time online would interfere with other aspects of living? Wouldn't the same be true of any other pursuit that monopolizes over 10 percent of a person's waking hours? Moreover, given the correlational nature of this study, it is impossible to determine whether spending excessive amounts of time online *caused* the respondents' distress, or whether it is simply a symptom of that distress. Nevertheless, in reporting this story, the BBC News headline trumpeted, "Online Sex Carries Health Risk," while Reuters focused on the sheer number of "sex addicts" prowling the Internet. "Compared with a few years ago," it quoted Dr. Cooper as saying, "that would mean 120,000 new [sex] addicts. It's an epidemic that nobody's talking about." Notably, the published report of this research provides no direct evidence that frequent online-sex seekers suffer from any form of addiction, sexual or otherwise (see Chapter 5 for a fuller discussion of sexual addiction).

Naughty.com

In the 1990s, the text-based Internet exploded in colors and images, and was transformed, like a caterpillar morphing into a butterfly, into the World Wide Web. Although early bulletin board systems allowed users to transfer erotic images—dirty pictures, if you will—the images themselves were not displayed on the Internet and were transferred sight unseen. The graphics-based Web is light years ahead of its predecessors. Millions of nude and pornographic photos are available in every category of desire—from blonde babes to gay hunks to forced infancy fantasies.[37] Reduced-size "thumbnails" make it easy to peruse hundreds of photographs at a sitting, and select favorites for individual downloading. Because the resolution of today's computer monitors often approaches photographic standards, digitized images (which often are copies of pictures that have been scanned into a computer) can provide nearly the same level of detail as glossy porn magazines.

There are literally thousands of websites devoted to sex. Try typing the URL (universal resource locator) http://www.whitehouse.com into your browser. Did you get the president of the United States or his administrative assistant? No, you got a porn site! (The president's web address is http://www.whitehouse.gov.) And, apparently, you're not the only person visiting sexually oriented websites. According to one estimate, the top five porn sites collected 9 million visitors in a single month in 1998.[38] Moreover, one out of every four Internet users visits porn sites at least once a month.[39]

Internet sex is a big business, a very big, $1 billion-a-year business.[40] Some Internet porn sites produce millions of dollars of annual revenue for their owners.[41] Free sites make their money by selling advertising space (so-called banner ads), usually to other websites. But the most profitable porn sites charge a membership fee (usually around $20). In exchange, the patron receives access to thousands of X-rated photographs and movies and, on some websites, to special areas where he or she can engage in sexually explicit chat with other members or with paid models, and possibly even view a striptease or live sex show through the magic of "streaming video" (which looks like a movie would, if you deleted four out of every five frames). There are sites for every taste, from vanilla sex to bestiality. At least one site features a "voyeur cam" that purports to spy on people as they perform their bathroom duties.

At the present time, the sexual potential of the Internet is limited by the slow-data transfer rates of typical phone lines. Although 56K may seem extremely fast to Internet old-timers, who remember going out for a burger while their 1200-baud modem downloaded a large file (a photo of Teri Hatcher, perhaps?), it is still much too slow to make real-time video a possibility. Instead, the options are to put up with the jerky picture offered by streaming video, or to grab a burger while downloading the entire video for later viewing. Greater bandwidth (transfer speeds) is needed, and fortunately, it's on its way (indeed, it's already available in some places). Within a decade, some 50 million Americans will have broadband access to the Internet thanks to satellite and rewired cable Internet connections. The goal is nothing short of real-time video transmission, which would permit users to dial up an adult video and watch it on their TV or computer, watch a truly "live" and interactive sex show with the clarity of a DVD, or hook up with a friend for some Internet sex, complete with live video feeds generated by digital cameras and some dirty talk courtesy of computer microphones and speakers.

Virtual Virtue

The various forms of computer sex described thus far provide the user with a realistic and detailed simulation of the "real thing." Ultimately, however, cybersex is little more than glorified pornography—the orgasm (if any) comes courtesy of the user's own hands. But what if, instead of sitting upright in front of a computer display, typing and mouse-clicking away, you could put on a full-body suit and visor, and actively explore your sexual fantasy world? Perhaps you have the software set to a Grecian orgy, or a wild fling with this year's most popular virtual sex star. Imagine that what you see through your goggles changes as you turn your head, just as if the fantasy world created by the computer were real. And suppose you could feel—thanks to the body suit—every touch and caress of your fantasy partner, your senses fooled completely. Imagine, in other words, a world in which "virtual reality" *is* a reality.[42]

At present, the promise of virtual reality is just that—a promise. Some computer games provide a hint of the potential of this melding of computers, animation, and video technology, as do the still-crude virtual reality simulators found in upscale video arcades. One company claims to have developed a prototype bodysuit that

> will one day let the user reach out over the Internet and touch some-one in a very special way. . . . By clicking on the appropriate parts of an onscreen body image . . . a remote partner will be able to send stimulating sensations—heat, feather touch, vibration—direct to the suit wearer's wired erogenous zones.[43]

Despite these advances, a virtual reality worthy of the name is decades away at best. This leaves us a bit of time to consider the consequences of a world in which full sexual (though not necessarily emotional) gratification is available at the flip of a switch.[44] In contrast to the currently available options for self-gratification, which ultimately require self-stimulation of one form or another, virtual sex could be varied, unpredictable, and interactive—in short, just like the real thing, but without the hassles of interpersonal relations. True (safe) sex on demand, twenty-four hours a day.[45]

But would this, could this, be a good thing? We have argued at length that *all* consensual adult sexuality should be accepted and even embraced, because no matter how pleasurable the alternatives, there will always be enough people who find the pleasures of reproductive sex sufficiently enticing to ensure the continuation of the human species. But what if all that pleasure could be obtained without the costs associated with interpersonal sex?[46] Is it possible that sex would become an entirely solitary affair? And if so, what would become of the reproductive functions of intercourse? Would they be subsumed by artificial reproductive technologies, or would couples meet for the sole purpose of conceiving a child and then return to their "virtual" sex lives?

Only time can provide definitive answers to these questions. Nevertheless, it seems clear to us that as long as there are people, there will be interpersonal sex and the pleasures it provides. As a highly evolved species of social animals, humans require diverse avenues through which to express feelings of intimacy and closeness to one another. Interpersonal sexuality fulfills this purpose and much, much more. Sex, as we have argued at length, is a many-splendored thing, be it of the procreative or the nonprocreative variety. And, fortunately for us, both are escorted with pleasure.

Appendix A

A Contextual Glossary for Chapter 4

Some definitions for the terms used in Chapter 4 follow. The information-processing cells of the brain are called *neurons*. There are on the order of 10^{11} neurons in the human brain, interconnected with one another in an intricate network. (Each neuron is connected to as many as 10,000 other neurons.) The connecting elements are called *synapses*. Synapses relay signals from one neuron to the next by exuding a chemical message, called a *neurotransmitter*, that is captured by the receiving neuron, which then processes the received information.

A *nucleus* (plural: *nuclei*) is an organized collection of neurons in the brain. The function of the *sexually dimorphic nucleus (SDN)* in rats is unknown, but it is believed to be involved in the regulation of sexual behavior (it is considered sexually dimorphic because it differs in size in males and females). The SDN is located in *hypothalamus*; this brain structure is implicated in a number of functions, including the control of sexual behaviors in humans and other animals. Anatomically, the hypothalamus is divided into several ill-defined regions, including the *preoptic area*, so named because it lies anterior to the optic chiasm (the point at which the visual signals from the two eyes meet and crossover). In rats, the SDN lies in the preoptic area. Four small bodies in the human hypothalamus, the interstitial nuclei of the anterior hypothalamus (*INAH1* through *INAH4*), have been suggested as functional homologues of the SDN.

The hypothalamus has extensive connections with the *limbic system*, an evolutionarily ancient part of the brain considered by many to be the seat of the emotions. Principal subdivisions of the limbic system include the *amygdala*, the *hippocampus*, and the *fornix*. The *septal region* links the hypo-thalamus to the limbic system, and is therefore implicated in sexual behav-ior as well.

The *spinothalamic* tract is a bundle of nerve fibers that carries sensory information from the body to the brain, and back again. This fiber bundle terminates in the *thalamus*, where incoming sensory signals are integrated with other afferent sources prior to being relayed to the *cerebral cortex* (the most highly evolved and advanced region of the human brain) and other brain structures. The *intralaminar nucleus* is one of more than a dozen nuclei that make up the thalamus; it is thought to be important in the control of movements.

Unlike the vast majority of the neurons in the body, *motor neurons* do not reside in the brain, but are instead distributed throughout the body. These neurons represent the endpoints of behavioral control paths initiated in the brain. Their function is to cause individual muscles to contract or relax, depending on the signals they receive from the brain.

Appendix B

A Mathematical Model
of HIV Transmission

One of the main messages that public health educators have stressed is that "anyone can get AIDS." But how accurate is this claim? Although it is certainly true, at least in theory, that anyone *could* get AIDS (e.g., as a result of receiving tainted blood in a much-needed transfusion), the message is meant to convey more than this simple truism. It is meant to suggest that any sexually active person could become infected with HIV through sex. Although this, too, may be true, the facile claim that nearly everybody has a nonzero risk of infection is essentially meaningless. There is also a nonzero probability that the Earth will be destroyed sometime soon by a collision with a massive meteor, but this doesn't mean it's time to pack it up and move to Mars. The question people want answered is not "Can I get AIDS?" but "How *likely* is it that I will get AIDS?" The trouble is that uncertainty in critical parameter values precludes an easy answer to this all-important question.

One promising approach to this complex issue is provided by the Bernoulli process model of the sexual transmission of HIV, which can be used to estimate the probability of infection under particular circumstances (see, for example, our 1993 paper, "Evaluating the Risks: A Bernoulli Process Model of HIV Infection and Risk Reduction").[1] In the Bernoulli model, each sexual contact (meaning an activity capable of transmitting the virus, such as penile-vaginal or penile-anal intercourse) is treated as an independent probabilistic event, rather like the flip of a coin. However, unlike the flip of a coin, the two possible outcomes—Transmission and No Transmission—are not equally likely. Instead, the probability of HIV being transmitted from an infected person to his or her partner as the result of a single sexual contact is very small. This probability, which is called the *infectivity* of HIV, is commonly estimated to be between 0.001 and 0.01, depending, as we shall see, on the particular sexual activity and on a host of other factors.[2] In other words, the risk of becoming infected after having sex just once *with an infected partner* is between 1 in 1,000 to 1 in 100. This does not mean that 1,000 (or 100) sexual encounters are *required* for transmission to occur, any more than two flips of a fair coin are *required* to get heads to come up. You could flip a coin all day long and never have heads come up, or you could get heads on the first flip. But, on average, if you flip a coin long enough, half the time (1 in 2) it will come up heads.

In the case of a fair coin the probability of heads and tails both equal one half. For HIV infection, in contrast, the probabilities are highly asymmetric. Let α denote the infectivity of HIV, that is, the probability of Transmission during a single sexual contact. The probability of No Transmission is then $1 - \alpha$, because the two probabilities must sum to one (either HIV is transmitted or it is not—there is no third alternative). Thus, in the Bernoulli model, having sex with an infected partner is analogous to flipping a badly weighted coin that comes up heads $100 * \alpha$ percent of the time and tails $100 * (1 - \alpha)$ percent of the time.

Although for this badly weighted coin the probability of heads coming up on any one flip is very small (1 in 1,000 or 1 in 100), the effect is cumulative, so that after a hundred or a thousand flips the overall probability of heads coming up *at least once* is much larger. The exact probability of at least one heads in n flips of a badly weighted coin is easily quantified:

$$P(\text{one or more heads}) = 1 - (1 - \alpha)^n. \qquad \text{(Eq. 1)}$$

This equation can be understood as follows. First notice that the sum, $P(\text{one or more heads}) + P(\text{not one or more heads})$, must equal one because one of the two possibilities must occur (either one or more heads comes up, or not). Of course, "not one or more heads" is the same as "all tails," so the equation

$$P(\text{one or more heads}) + P(\text{not one or more heads}) = 1$$

can be rewritten

$$P(\text{one or more heads}) + P(\text{all tails}) = 1.$$

Simple arithmetic then produces the equivalent equation

$$P(\text{one or more heads}) = 1 - P(\text{all tails}).$$

To complete the derivation of Eq. 1, it is necessary only to show that P(all tails) $= (1 - \alpha)^n$. That is, we must show that the probability of getting tails on every one of the n flips of the coin is $(1 - \alpha)^n$, but this follows immediately from the fact that the probability of tails on any one flip is $1 - \alpha$.

In the case of HIV transmission, the equivalent equation is

$$P(\text{HIV transmitted}) = 1 - (1 - \alpha)^n, \qquad \text{(Eq. 2)}$$

where the probability, P(HIV transmitted), really means P(HIV transmitted at least once). To reiterate, Eq. 2 gives the probability that an infected person would transmit the virus to his or her partner during one (or more) of their n sexual contacts.[3]

To estimate P requires approximations of both the infectivity, α, and the number of contacts, n. As noted previously, most estimates of the per-contact probability of transmission (i.e., the infectivity) for unprotected intercourse suggest a value in the 0.001 to 0.01 range, with anal intercourse tending toward the higher bound and vaginal intercourse toward the lower; however, there is a great deal of uncertainty in these estimates.

In general, the probability of transmission also depends on the sexual role. It is easier for the insertive partner to infect the receptive partner than vice versa, although in Africa the male-to-female and female-to-male transmission rates are nearly equal due to the widespread prevalence of genital ulcers and other STDs, which can facilitate the transmission of HIV, as well as other factors that can assist female-to-male transmission.[4]

Fortunately, the infectivity of HIV can be severely curtailed by the proper use of latex condoms. Precise estimates of the effectiveness of condoms in preventing the transmission of HIV are difficult to obtain, but current estimates suggest that condoms are 90–95% percent effective against HIV.[5] A 10 percent failure rate (or alternatively, 90 percent effectiveness) is equivalent to reducing the per-contact infectivity of HIV by a factor of ten, for example, from 1 in 1,000 to 1 in 10,000. So, although condoms aren't perfect, they can significantly reduce the infectivity of HIV.

The other parameter needed to estimate the probability of infection is the number of contacts, n. In the case of a single sexual contact with an infected partner the probability of transmission equals the infectivity, α. But the risk gets much greater as n grows larger, as illustrated in Figure 1. Three values of the infectivity parameter are shown in this figure: $\alpha = 0.01, 0.001$, and 0.0001. If, as suggested earlier, the per-contact infectivity for unprotected intercourse is between 0.01 and 0.001, then the infectivity for protected intercourse should be an order of magnitude smaller—that is, between 0.001 and 0.0001. Thus, the largest value, $\alpha = 0.01$, pertains only to

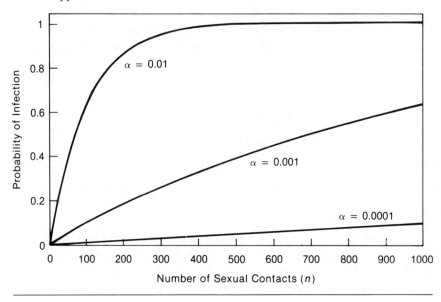

Figure 1. Probability of HIV transmission from an infected individual to an uninfected partner as the result of n sexual contacts, for several infectivity values, α.

unprotected intercourse; the smallest estimate, $\alpha = 0.0001$, pertains only to protected intercourse; and the intermediate value, $\alpha = 0.001$, may apply to either protected or unprotected sex.

As shown in Figure 1, if the infectivity is high ($\alpha = 0.01$), then the risk of transmission is very large: it exceeds one-half after only 100 sexual contacts, and is nearly one after 500 contacts. However, if condoms are used, so that the infectivity is reduced to 0.001 or less, then the risk is greatly diminished. For example, when $\alpha = 0.001$ the probability of infection after 100 contacts is about 10% and remains less than one-half even after 500 contacts. Finally, in the low infectivity condition ($\alpha = 0.0001$)—which requires condom use to achieve—the probability of infection is only 1% after 100 contacts and never exceeds 10%. Of course, many relationships between single, unattached people never reach 100 sexual encounters. Therefore, the 1 to 100 contact portion of Figure 1 is shown magnified in Figure 2 (notice that the ordinate is a logarithmic scale). From this figure it is clear that the use of condoms has a marked effect on the probability of transmission, reducing it by approximately an order of magnitude (i.e., 90%).

Remember that the estimates provided in Figs. 1 and 2 refer to sexual contacts with an *infected* partner. If the partner is not infected, then, of course, the risk is zero. If the partner's HIV status is unknown there is still a

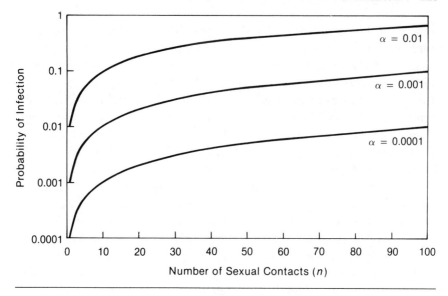

Figure 2 (Detail of Fig. 1). Probability of HIV transmission from an infected individual to an uninfected partner as the result of n sexual contacts, for several infectivity values, α.

risk, but in most cases it is substantially less than indicated in these figures. For example, in a population in which the prevalence of HIV is 0.01 (meaning that, on average, one person in 100 is infected), the probability that a randomly selected partner is infected is about 1 in 100. So the overall probability of becoming infected as the result of n sexual encounters with a partner selected at random from a population with HIV prevalence 0.01 is about 100 times less than shown in Figs 1 and 2.

More generally, let π denote the prevalence of HIV in the population from which partners are selected. We can then answer the question: What is the probability of becoming infected from n sexual encounters with a randomly selected partner of unknown HIV status? For HIV transmission to occur requires that two conditions be met: First, the selected partner must be infected (probability $= \pi$), and second, the virus must be transmitted (probability $= 1 - (1 - \alpha)^n$, according to Eq. 2). Thus, for n contacts with a randomly chosen partner,

$$P(\text{HIV transmitted}) = \pi\,[1 - (1 - \alpha)^n]. \qquad \text{(Eq. 3)}$$

The prevalence of HIV in the "general public" is probably much less than one in 200 ($\pi = 0.005$), so that the risk entailed by a (monogamous) sexual relationship with a partner of unknown HIV status is approximately as shown in Figure 3 (notice that these data differ from Figure 2 only by a multiplicative factor equal to the HIV prevalence). Importantly, the prevalence of HIV among heterosexual college students and other "low-risk" individuals is certainly much less than 1 in 200. Conversely, the prevalence of infection among highly sexually active individuals could be substantially higher than 1 in 200. Indeed, one-fourth or more of the gay men in large urban areas such as San Francisco and New York may be infected. Caution is thus warranted in any case. In particular, condoms should be used for all sexual encounters with a partner of unknown HIV status.

Figure 3 also illustrates the effectiveness of condoms in reducing infection risks. By decreasing the effective infectivity by an order of magnitude, for example from $\alpha = 0.01$ to $\alpha = 0.001$, the use of condoms decreases the risk by a similar amount. Because of this, the risk resulting from 100 *protected* contacts is about the same as that arising from only 10 *unprotected* contacts.

For sexually active individuals with more than one partner the situation is slightly more complicated. Although the probability of becoming infected as a result of sexual contact with any one of these partners can be calculated using Eq. 3, the rules of the probability calculus prevent us from simply adding them together to arrive at the overall risk of infection.

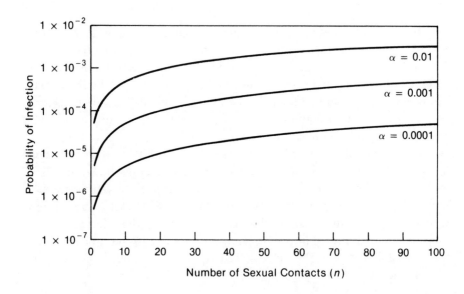

Figure 3. Risk of HIV infection from n sexual contacts with a partner selected at random from the "general public" (HIV prevalence = 0.5%), for several infectivity values, α.

Consider the special case of an individual who has sex only once with each partner (a "one–night stand"), so that the number of partners equals the total number of sexual contacts, n. In this case, the correct formula for the overall risk of infection is

$$P(\text{HIV transmitted}) = 1 - (1 - \pi\alpha)^n \qquad \text{(Eq. 4)}$$

where, as before, α is the per–contact infectivity and π is the HIV prevalence in the population from which partners are selected.[6]

As might be expected, the probability of infection arising from n one–night stands is greater than the risk from n contacts with a single partner (monogamy); however, the difference is not nearly as great as one might suppose. Figure 4 illustrates the relative difference in risk, $(P_o - P_m)/P_o$, where P_o and P_m are the probabilities of infection resulting from n one–night stands or n contacts with a single partner, respectively. (In Figure 4 a prevalence of 0.005 is assumed. Similar results obtain for other values of this parameter.) As shown in this figure, the *relative risk reduction* achieved by engaging in n sexual contacts with a single partner rather than n one–night stands is greater in the high infectivity condition ($\alpha = 0.01$) and increases as the number of one–night stands gets large, but is less than 40 percent in any case. In contrast, the relative risk reduction due to the consistent use of

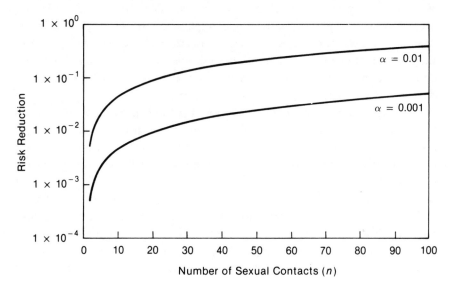

Fig. 4. Relative reduction in HIV risk achieved by engaging in n sexual contacts with a single partner rather than n one–night stands, where partners are selected at random from the "general public" (HIV prevalence = 0.5%).

condoms (not shown) is about 90 percent regardless of the infectivity or the number of partners. In other words, in this situation even the most dramatic change in the number of sexual partners—from 100 to 1—provides less protection against HIV infection than does the simple expedient of always wearing a condom![7]

These results highlight the inadequacy of educational programs that focus on getting people to limit the number of sexual partners as a means of reducing HIV risk. Although there are conditions for which this is sound advice (such as in populations with a high prevalence of HIV or other STDs), the simple strategy of always using condoms is usually a superior means of reducing risk. Of course, the best advice is to do both—use condoms *and* decrease the number of sexual partners. However, many people are unwilling to limit themselves in more than one way. Getting someone to adopt even one risk-reduction practice is difficult enough, and having modified his or her sexual lifestyle, it may be difficult to convince him or her that additional sacrifices are needed. After all, additional precautions are required only if the already adopted precaution provides insufficient protection. If someone believes in the effectiveness of a particular method of reducing risk, as they must to have adopted it in the first place, then the need for additional precautions is unlikely to be acknowledged. Thus, the authors of one study of risk taking by gay men conclude that "gay men may believe that limiting themselves to a single partner or restricting contact to a few regular partners can minimize the dangers of risky sexual practices."[8] The preceding analysis suggests that any message that interferes with people's desire or ability to use condoms in risky sexual encounters could be epidemiologically counterproductive. As grandma says, "Always wear your rubbers!"

Finally, to return to the question posed at the beginning of this discussion: is everyone at risk? Obviously, that depends on her sexual behavior, including who she has sex with, what kind of sex, and whether or not her partners wear condoms for penetrative activities. For the sake of argument, suppose the infectivity is 1 in 1000 and she selects 10 male partners at random from a population in which 1 out of every 200 men is infected with HIV. If she has intercourse 100 times with each of these men and never uses condoms, then she faces an infection risk of 0.0047 (in other words, out of 211 such women, we would expect one to become infected with HIV as a consequence of her sexual behavior). If, instead, she and her partners used condoms for every act of intercourse, her risk would be reduced by about 90%, to 0.0005 (1 out of 2010). Are these risks large or small? Each person must judge for him or herself. To some people, the horrible consequences of HIV infection are sufficiently frightening that any risk is too great. While for others, the pleasures of sex far outweigh any small risk of getting HIV.

Notes

Chapter 1. Introduction

1. This quote is from Oscar Wilde's *A Woman of No Importance* (1894/1990).

2. Ellman (1988).

3. Eribon (1991), p. 315 (emphasis in original).

4. Sedgwick (1993), pp. 204–05 (emphasis in original).

5. Donald Symons (1995) defines *evolutionary psychology* as "psychological research that is explicitly informed by the knowledge that human psychological adaptations were shaped over vast periods of time to solve the recurrent behavioral problems that our ancestors faced." (See also Tooby, 1985; Cosmides & Tooby, 1987; Daly & Wilson, 1988; Symons, 1992). Evolutionary psychology differs from more traditional evolutionary theories (including the closely related field of *sociobiology*—see Barkow, 1980, and Wilson, 1975) in its explicit focus on the innate psychological mechanisms through which particular adaptations are expressed.

6. Buss (1994).

7. Quoted in Laqueur (1990), p. 3; see also McLaren (1984).

8. Quoted in Laqueur (1990), p. 192.

9. See, for example, Masters & Johnson (1966).

10. Katchadourian & Lunde (1982).

11. Kushner (1978).

12. Freedman (1982), p. 203.

13. Freedman (1982), p. 210.

14. "Adaptive" is used here in its traditional sense to describe a beneficial adjustment, and not in the neo-Darwinian sense of describing an evolutionary adaptation. Population limitation is seldom adaptive in the evolutionary sense because genes that might cause one to exercise excessive reproductive restraint

eventually disappear from the gene pool as more fecund genes increase in prevalence (see, for example, Dawkins, 1976).

15. Davenport (1977), p. 123.

16. Kennedy & Davis (1993), p. 191.

17. Kennedy & Davis (1993), p. 205. For further discussions on the butch/femme lesbian culture of the 1950s and its revival in the 1980s and 1990s, see Faderman (1991), Morgan (1993), and Nestle (1992). For a report of fantasy-induced orgasm in presumably heterosexual women, see Whipple, Ogden, & Komisaruk (1992).

18. Written and directed by Neil Jordan.

19. Ellis (1903).

20. For example, Mead (1928); see also Freeman (1983).

21. For example, Malinowski (1927, 1929, 1962).

22. Tiger (1992).

23. See Robinson (1976) and Bullough (1994).

24. Kinsey, Pomeroy, & Martin (1948); Kinsey, Pomeroy, Martin, & Gebhard (1953).

25. Masters & Johnson (1966).

26. See Grube (1935) for an explication of Plato's views on pleasure and eros.

27. Aristotle (1962), book vii, p. 204.

28. Aristotle (1962), book vii, p. 210.

29. Freud (1938).

30. See Fenichel (1945).

31. Psychoanalytic theory has elaborated Freud's notion of the pleasure principle to extend beyond instinctual gratification. Pleasure and pain are no longer polarized, and the emotional component of pleasure is now more pronounced. See Glick & Bone (1990).

32. Freud (1935), p. 64.

33. Freud (1920), p. 273.

34. Robinson (1976), p. 5.

35. Krafft-Ebing (1965), p. 56.

36. Foucault (1985, 1986, 1990).

37. Foucault (1990), p. 36.

38. Edward Abbey, in Trimble (1988), pp. 56–57.

39. See, for example, Abramson & Pinkerton (1995) and Tuzin (1995).

40. Herdt (1981, 1987).

41. Herdt (1984). See also Carrier (1980).

42. Stoller & Herdt (1985), p. 404 (emphasis in original).

43. Halperin (1989).

44. Foucault (1985).

45. Bullough & Bullough (1964); Sanger (1897).

46. Tannahill (1980).

47. Antipater, in Pope (1962), p. 3.

48. Asclepiades, in Pope (1962), p. 4; cf. Fitts (1938), p. 16.

49. Plutarch, *Life of Lycurgus, 18*, quoted in Tannahill (1980), p. 99.
50. Tannahill (1980).
51. Sanger (1897), p. 63. According to Bullough and Bullough (1964), Phryne was the most famous, beautiful, and dangerous of the Athenian *hetairai*:

> Phryne was once on trial before an Athenian court, so the story goes, when her defender, Hyperides, saw that her case was lost; in desperation he suddenly tore off her clothes to disclose the beauty of her breasts. The judges were so taken with awe at her beauty that they did not venture to find her guilty (*Athenaeus*, XIII, 590, quoted in Bullough & Bullough, 1964, p. 41).

52. Orsy (1986).
53. Bullough (1982), p. 11. Compare with the biblical quotation, "I was shapen in iniquity; and in sin did my mother conceive me" (Psalms 51:5).
54. Flandrin (1985), p. 115.
55. Robertson (1962), p. 429.
56. Flandrin (1985).
57. Canon 1013, in Bouscaren & Ellis (1951), p. 455.
58. Flandrin (1985). One cannot help but wonder if the prevalence of adultery among males of the chivalrous class wasn't due, at least in part, to St. Jerome's injunction against a husband fully appreciating his wife's sexual virtues.
59. 1 Corinthians 6:9.

Chapter 2. Sex as Procreation: Is That All There Is?
1. Boswell (1980), p. 313.
2. Bullough (1982).
3. Boswell (1980).
4. Bullough (1982).
5. In violation of Mae West's contention that "sex is an emotion in motion."
6. 1 Corinthians 7:1–9.
7. Flandrin (1985).
8. Nor was the emphasis on procreation restricted to Western cultures. In early Japanese agrarian society fertility was sacred, extending to gods, crops, and family (Sansom, 1974).
9. Greenberg (1988). The Platonic ideal of man-boy love entailed an aim-inhibited homosexuality that was rarely, if ever, consummated (Richards, 1979).
10. Boswell (1980); Foucault (1985); Greenberg (1988); Halperin, Winkler, & Zeitlin (1990).
11. Hanson (1990).
12. Dover (1978).
13. Keuls (1985).
14. Martial (1987, pp. 332–33), quoted in Greenberg (1995).
15. Nagel (1974).

16. Female cats probably don't enjoy sex. The male cat's penis is studded with small sharp spikes, angled with their tips pointing toward the base of the organ, so that while insertion is relatively painless, removal is—judging by the female's howls—excruciatingly painful (Morris, 1986).

17. See, for example, Dagg (1984).

18. Boswell (1980).

19. McBride & Hebb (1967); Wells (1984).

20. Wundram (1979). See also Dagg (1984), Denniston (1980), and Ford & Beach (1951).

21. de Waal (1989).

22. de Waal (1989); Sibley & Ahlquist (1984).

23. de Waal (1989), p. 177. Photographs of these wonderful animals may be found in de Waal (1989, 1995).

24. de Waal (1995). See also de Waal (1987, 1989).

25. de Waal (1989, 1995); Kuroda (1980). The vulva of the female bonobo is positioned more ventrally than it is in other nonhuman primates, which facilitates G-G rubbing.

26. de Waal (1995).

27. de Waal (1989, 1995).

28. *Webster's II.*

29. Bullough (1976).

30. See, for example, Abramson, Perry, Rothblatt, Seeley, & Seeley (1981), and Taylor (1953).

31. As Woody Allen protests in the film *Annie Hall* (1977): "Hey, don't knock masturbation. It's sex with someone I love."

32. Benedicti (1601).

33. Comfort (1967), p. 71.

34. Anonymous (1835), quoted in Barker-Benfield (1976), p. 179.

35. Kern (1981).

36. Hippocrates (1952).

37. Davenport (1977).

38. Tannahill (1980).

39. See Taylor (1953).

40. The bonobo is actually a strikingly intelligent animal capable of intricate forms of communication. The epithet "dumb animal" is employed here only for the sake of emphasis.

41. Quoted in Taylor (1953), pp. 300–301.

42. Wundram (1979), p. 100.

43. LeVay (1993).

44. Malthus (1985).

45. Darwin (1905), pp. 361–62.

46. Wallace, quoted in Darwin (1892), pp. 200–201.

47. These suggestions are largely in keeping with Malthus' original thesis.

Malthus, for instance, included "vice" (which referred to marital intercourse without the intention to reproduce) as a natural check on population growth.

48. Ehrlich & Ehrlich (1990), p. 14 (emphasis added).

49. Ehrlich & Ehrlich (1990).

50. Bongaarts (1994).

51. As one reproductively conscientious spermatozoa reminds his comrades in Woody Allen's *Everything You Always Wanted to Know about Sex (But Were Afraid to Ask)*, "This is no time to doubt our mission. You took an oath when you entered sperm training school to fertilize an ovum, or die trying!"

52. As the great English poet, Alfred Tennyson (1987), observes of Nature in his poem, *In Memoriam A.H.H.*:

> *That I, considering everywhere*
> > *Her secret meaning in her deeds,*
> > *And finding that of fifty seeds*
> *She often brings but one to bear (p. 372).*

53. Not all experts agree that the current rate of population growth is necessarily catastrophic. Some economists and agricultural scientists assert that the earth can readily produce more than enough food to sustain the 10 million inhabitants expected by the year 2050 (Bongaarts, 1994). "In reality, the future of global food production is neither as grim as the pessimists believe nor as rosy as the optimists claim" (Bongaarts, 1994, p. 42). However, food production is only one aspect of the problem posed by the burgeoning population. Significant technological advancements will also be required to reverse, or at the very least contain, the environmental damage caused by overpopulation.

54. This interpretation is due to Dover (1978), among others. One translation of the passage in question (Aristotle's *Politics*, 1272b, 20–26) is: "The lawgiver [in Crete] conceived many devices aimed at beneficial frugality in the use of food; and to keep husbands apart from their wives, thus preventing them from having too many children, he sanctioned homosexual relation among men" (Apostle & Gerson, 1986).

55. We should also mention the population control theory of V. C. Wynne-Edwards. According to Wynne-Edwards (1978), animals regulate their birthrates in order to keep the population down, and the food supply adequate, *for the good of the species*. In contrast, most adherents to the widely accepted "selfish gene" theory of evolution interpret the evidence of self-regulation of birthrates as indicative of evolved mechanisms to ensure that each *individual* produces an optimal number of offspring. (See Dawkins, 1976, for more on this controversy.) Likewise, it is important to emphasize that although population control via nonreproductive sexuality is beneficial for the human race as a whole, it is not an evolutionarily advantageous strategy for the individual, and his or her "selfish genes."

56. The term *sexual intercourse* is used here, and elsewhere, to denote penile-vaginal intercourse.

57. Freud (1905/1962), p. 27 (emphasis in original).

58. Actually, this no longer need strictly hold true. Thanks to the wonders of modern artificial reproductive technologies, women can become pregnant without ever having had sex, and intimacy with a plastic cup is all that's required for men to become fathers. We return to this topic in the epilogue.

59. Ridley (1985).

60. Although we are thinking primarily of violence pitting male against female (procurement) and male against male (retainment), other combinations are certainly possible.

61. Davenport (1977); Herdt (1981); Paige & Paige (1981).

62. Smith–Rosenberg (1974).

63. Herdt (1981, 1990a).

64. Herdt (1990a), p. 391 (emphasis in original).

65. Freud (1908/1963), p. 35.

66. Technically, of course, all "dogs" are male; canine females are properly called "bitches."

67. This is another reason why it is so important to spay and neuter pets—they live longer. Two of the main causes of death in unneutered outdoor cats are cars and cat fights.

68. For an extensive analysis of sex and rationality, see Posner (1992).

69. Pinkerton & Abramson (1992). See also Gilbert, Bauman, & Udry (1986).

70. The evolution of rational thought might even be intrinsically tied to the evolution of pleasure and pain. That is, decisions regarding pleasure and pain might be, evolutionarily, the oldest decisions. As such, the capacity to experience pleasure and pain may be an integral component of general intelligence.

71. In the modern language of cultural relativism, morality systems are said to be *culturally constructed*.

72. Also, in the case of heterosexual intercourse, male orgasm may be delayed as a means of heightening the woman's pleasure and increasing her opportunities to orgasm. We should also remind the reader that the duration of intercourse is jointly determined by the man and woman, and is influenced by psychological, physiological, and behavioral factors.

73. See Weatherford (1986).

74. "Many men associate masturbation with sexual deprivation, rejection by women, dirtiness, shame, secrecy, etc." (Kennedy, 1993, p. 197). On the other hand, 94 percent of the men and 63 percent of the women sampled by Hunt (1974) reported that had they masturbated at least once.

75. Morris (1967), p. 65 (emphasis added).

76. For example, see Buss (1994).

77. Kinsey, Pomeroy, Martin, & Gebhard (1953), p. 313 (emphasis added).

78. de Waal (1989, 1995); see also Mori (1984), and Savage–Rumbaugh & Wilkerson (1978).

79. de Waal (1989).

80. de Waal (1989).

81. de Waal (1987, 1995).

82. de Waal (1989).

83. Norris & Dohl (1980).

84. Ostman (1991).

85. Wells & Norris (1994), p. 199.

86. Donald Tuzin (personal communication).

87. This viewpoint ignores the possibility that there might also be sexual competition among females. This certainly is the case among bonobos.

88. Eve Sedgwick (1990) suggests that the "homo/heterosexual definition has been a presiding master term of the past quarter century, one that has the same, primary importance for all modern Western identity and social organization" (p. 11).

89. It does not seem too far a stretch to suppose that what we experience as consciousness is essentially an elaboration of the pleasure and pain common to many of the higher species. Pleasure and pain, in other words, are a primitive form of consciousness.

90. Griffin (1976); Lorenz (1971).

91. Darwin (1872/1979), p. 215.

92. de Waal (1995); Pavelka (1995).

93. Lewis (1966), p. 17.

94. Kenny (1970), p. 135.

95. See, for example, Bechtel (1988), Churchland (1990), Lewis (1966), and Smart (1962).

96. The question of whether or not it is *possible* for two people (or robots) to have functionally identical mental states, but for one to experience qualia while the other is "qualialess" is known as the "Absent Qualia Problem." See, for example, Block (1980), Block & Fodor (1972), and Shoemaker (1981).

97. Dennett (1991); Jaynes (1976); Ornstein (1991).

98. See also Popper & Eccles (1977).

99. Frank Jackson (1982) dismisses similar arguments (e.g., see Popper & Eccles, 1977) with the observation that:

> All we can extract from Darwin's theory is that we should expect any evolved characteristic to be *either* conducive to survival *or* a by-product of one that is so conducive. The epiphenomenalist holds that qualia fall in the latter category. They are a by-product of certain brain processes that are highly conducive to survival. (p. 134; emphasis in original)

However, it is hard to see how qualia (and consciousness in general) could have arisen as a "by-product" of anything. Qualia are clearly of a very different sort than the physical processes of which they supposedly are a by-product. They also possess properties, such as subjectivity, that are absent elsewhere in the physical world. Their singular nature suggests that intense (and unusual) selection pressures would have been required for their evolution, if they evolved at all.

100. Nagel (1974), p. 160.

101. The difficult conceptual nature of qualia is illustrated by the fact that although a robot with feelings is easily imagined, the manner in which such a robot could be constructed is not. Robots, computers, and other machines simply do not have feelings (although they can be programmed to act as though they did), and it is nearly impossible to conceive of what technological or intellectual advancement might permit the construction of such machines. Furthermore, if the capacity to experience qualia is an integral component of general intelligence and decision-making abilities, then the future of truly intelligent computers is bleak.

102. Nagel (1974).

103. Freud (1905/1962).

104. Davenport (1977), p. 119.

105. Foucault (1985); Greenberg (1995); Winkler (1990).

106. Veblen (1899).

107. Veblen (1899).

108. Ancient Greek constraints on sexual behavior are discussed in Foucault (1985, 1986), Greenberg (1995), and Winkler (1990).

Chapter 3. The Regulation and Marketing of Sexual Pleasure

1. Blake (1988), p. 67.

2. Not everyone panders, of course. In *Braided Lives*, Marge Piercy warns, "if sex is a war, I am a conscientious objector: I will not play."

3. Taylor (1953), p. 50.

4. Taylor (1953), p. 19.

5. Posner (1992), p. 204.

6. Freud (1908/1963).

7. Krafft-Ebing (1978).

8. Krafft-Ebing (1978), p. 1.

9. Connelly (1980), p. 8.

10. Freud (1908/1963), pp. 24–25.

11. Freud (1943), pp. 376–77.

12. See, for example, Freud (1905/1962).

13. Freud (1905/1962).

14. Encyclical *Casti Connubii*, December 31, 1930, quoted in Flandrin (1985), p. 116 (emphasis added).

15. Kern (1981).

16. Kern (1981), p. 115.

17. Quoted in D'Emilio & Freedman (1988), p. 245.

18. Artful packaging and aggressive advertising are not invariably successful at enticing people to use condoms, however. A case in point is the extraordinary poster art campaigns aimed at syphilis during the first and second World Wars. Grave images of the Grim Reaper and "Fallen Angels" had little impact on the proliferation of syphilis, presumably underscoring the limits of fear-based campaigns (Brandt, 1987; Quetel, 1990). See Chapter 6 for more on the history of

19. See Feldblum & Rosenberg (1989), Himes (1963), McLaren (1990), Riddle (1992), and Riddle & Estes (1992).

20. McLaren (1990); Reed (1978).

21. de Waal (1989).

22. One notable exception being Rubin (1975).

23. Early suffrage leaders Susan B. Anthony and Elizabeth Cady argued that women exchanged sex for economic support in both prostitution and marriage.

24. Fox (1967).

25. The applicable statues of the Canon Law specify that marriage is intended to unite one man and one woman. Both polygyny (one man, several wives) and polyandry (one woman, several husbands) are forbidden. Concern over paternity is reflected, however, in the determination that polyandry is directly opposed to a primary goal of the marital union, whereas polygyny injures but a secondary aim. According to St. Thomas, this difference—based on the doubtful paternity that ensues from polyandry—provides the missing justification for the apparent tolerance of polygyny but not polyandry in Old Testament accounts (Bouscaren & Ellis, 1951).

26. Dante (1321/1981).

27. Davenport (1977), p. 141.

28. Davenport (1977); Paige & Paige (1981). See also Deuteronomy 22: 13–21.

29. Tannahill (1982). A similar dynamic operates in present-day Africa, where young girls are especially sought after as sexual partners because it is believed that they are less likely to be infected with HIV. Similar attitudes have also fueled the market for underage prostitutes (to serve a primarily American and European clientele) in Thailand, India, the Philippines, and elsewhere in Asia.

30. Schlegel (1991, 1995).

31. Schlegel (1995).

32. Engels (1942).

33. See Gray (1946).

34. Engels (1942), p. 147.

35. Torgovnick (1990). According to Torgovnick, evolutionary theory provides part of the rationale for primitive discourse. Primitive peoples are presumed to be less "evolved" than their "modern" counterparts, thereby making primitive societies an ample testing ground for universal truths about human nature. This perspective, of course, fails to consider the similarities between all people, of all time (and all primates, for that matter; Clark, 1965). If universal similarities exist (see Brown, 1991), and if primitive people are not "simpler," but merely different, these facts would obviously undermine primitive discourse and the myths that surround primitive peoples. This is particularly true of sexuality and gender. Torgovnick argues that there is a very strong connection between Western conceptions of the primitive and our notions of gender and sexuality. Freud's theories about sexuality (e.g., Freud, 1918) and Malinowski's observations of male and female rules (e.g., Malinowski, 1929, 1967) are deeply imbedded in primitive myths, yet are also crucial

36. Wilson & Daly (1992).
37. Paige & Paige (1981).
38. de Waal (1989).
39. Heilbroner (1986a,b).
40. Heilbroner (1986b), p. 65.
41. Veblen (1899).
42. See also Posner's (1992) economic analysis of sexual behavior, which interprets variations in sexual expression according to substitutability, costs, externality, fraud, and theft.
43. Gardner & Maier (1984); Sandars (1972); Tigay (1982).
44. Tablet 1, column 4—see Gardner & Maier (1984), p. 77.
45. Bullough (1976), p. 27.
46. Gardner & Maier (1984).
47. The nature of the friendship between Gilgamesh and Enkidu, whether sexual or simply companionable, is not specified. However, it is noted in the text that Gilgamesh embraced Enkindu "like a wife" (Bullough, 1976).
48. Davenport (1977).
49. Summarizing the available evidence, Bullough (1976) concludes, "it seems certain that the ancient Mesopotamians [including the Sumerians] had fewer prohibitions against sex than our own civilization, and regarded as acceptable many practices which later societies condemned" (pp. 33–34).
50. Kramer (1963), p. 250.
51. Kramer (1963), p. 254.
52. de Waal (1982, 1989, 1995).
53. The contemporary ramifications of male force are elucidated by Kennedy (1993) as follows:

> That most women *could* be raped or beaten by most men is an important physical datum. Its actual effect on the balance of power between men and women depends on how often rape and battery actually occur, and on the way men and women see society as viewing it when it occurs. That effect is modified by the legal remedies available to women in these cases, to the extent that legal remedies deter men from raping and battering through punishment and convey a social message of disapproval. (p. 103)

We should add, however, that the *threat* of force, per se, is itself instrumental in maintaining existing gender-based power differentials. Therefore, it is not strictly true that the "effect on the balance of power between men and women depends on how often rape and battery *actually* occur" (emphasis added).

54. See Veblen (1899).
55. Pavelka (1995).
56. The complicated issue of marital rape is discussed in detail by Posner (1992).
57. Paige & Paige (1981); Posner (1992).
58. See Note 75.

60. Winkler (1990).

61. Greenberg (1995).

62. Notably, Stoller (1985, 1991).

63. Davenport (1977), p. 116.

64. Engels (1942).

65. *Viva*, the sister publication to *Penthouse*, ceased publishing male nudes in 1976, just three years after being launched, due to readers' avowed distaste for the pictures (Faust, 1980).

66. Snitow (1983), p. 257. Referring to the popular romance novels of the nineteenth century, Duffey (1876) wrote, "the ideas are presented in a voluptuous guise, purposely shaped to inflame the blood and make sin attractive and excusable" (quoted in Lewis, 1980, p. 26)

67. Faderman (1991).

68. Faderman (1991), p. 258.

69. Faderman (1991), p. 270.

70. A possible resurgence in lesbian pornography is evident in the current proliferation of S/M-influenced publications, such as *Bad Attitude*, and the enduring popularity of *On Our Backs* (which is perhaps meant more as an antidote to political correctness than as true pornography).

71. This is not to deny the very real enjoyment that some women derive from pornography, nor for that matter, to suggest that all men are consumers of pornography. For example, Sally Tisdale, author of *Talk Dirty to Me* (1994), unabashedly advocates "hardcore" pornography for women as well as men, citing its liberating effects on sexuality.

72. See Symons (1979) for a comprehensive overview of this issue.

73. See, for example, feminist Catherine MacKinnon's (1993) diatribe, or the first-hand testimony of Linda Lovelace (1980). This topic is discussed further in Chapter 7.

74. Abramson & Mosher (1979).

75. See, for example, Buss (1994) and Symons (1979). The most famous (probably apocryphal) anecdote regarding men's desire for sexual variety is related by Bermant (1976) as follows:

One day the President and Mrs. Coolidge were visiting a government farm. Soon after their arrival they were taken off on separate tours. When Mrs. Coolidge passed the chicken pens she paused to ask the man in charge if the rooster copulates more than once each day. "Dozens of times" was the reply. "Please tell that to the President," Mrs. Coolidge requested. When the President passed the pens and was told about the rooster, he asked, "Same hen every time?" "Oh no, Mr. President, a different one each time." The President nodded slowly, then said "Tell that to Mrs. Coolidge." (pp. 76–77)

76. Although complete nudity was the norm among Australian Aborigines until well into the twentieth century, anatomical secrecy was nevertheless ensured

seated, are expected to maintain a modest posture so as to hide the vaginal open-
ing" (Davenport, 1977, p. 128).

77. People may also learn a bit of technique. In *Coming Attractions: The Making
of an X-rated Video* (Stoller & Levine, 1993), video sex star Nina Hartley offers the
following review of the work of another leading actress:

> She was giving good head. The way she was touching it, you can tell. She
> really likes cocks. I would show this to people on how to give good
> head . . . You know how many paragraphs it would take to describe that
> motion of pulling the hand up and twisting it over the ridge of the corona
> as you . . . This picture is worth a thousand words. (p. 146)

78. As male fantasy, pornography also portrays female sexuality in an un-
realistic fashion. In pornography, women are always accessible and always willing.
Although most young men will be quickly disabused of this naïve notion of female
sexuality, it won't be by pornography. This crucial aspect of a young man's sexual
education must be obtained elsewhere.

79. Paglia (1990), pp. 34–35.

80. The dangers of prostitution also include exposure to myriad sexually
transmitted diseases, for both the prostitute and his or her clients. The advice of Dr.
Maurice Bernays, a French physician of the 1920s is instructive in this regard.
When considering sex with a prostitute, "it remains necessary to assure oneself with
one's own eyes that at the gateway there lurk neither tigers nor snakes (ulcerations,
mucous plaques, purulent secretions) which might bite one as one passes" (quoted
in Quetel, 1990, p. 182).

81. Attributed to Demonsthenes, quoted in Tannahill (1982), p. 100. Taylor
(1953) offers the alternative translation, "we have wives for childbearing, hetairae
for companionship and slaves for lust" (p. 238).

82. Fitts (1938), p. 8.

83. Brandt (1985); Cominos (1963); Connelly (1980).

84. Taylor (1953), p. 238.

85. Quoted in Richards (1979), p. 1211.

86. Quoted in Richards (1979), p. 1244.

87. D'Emilio & Freedman (1988).

88. D'Emilio & Freedman (1988), p. 181.

89. Connelly (1980).

90. Kern (1981).

91. Walkowitz (1980).

92. Quoted in Kushner (1978), p. 40.

93. Connelly (1980); Freedman (1982); Kushner (1978).

94. Brandt (1985); Burnham (1973). An elaborate history has been crudely
summarized here. See the excellent exposition by Brandt (1985) for details.

95. Kushner (1978).

96. Burnham (1973), p. 901.

97. Walkowitz (1980), p. 130.

98. Walkowitz (1980).

99. Adler (1953).

100. Posner (1992) suggests that, "it remains difficult to resist the conclusion that the United States criminalizes more sexual conduct than other developed counties do and punishes the sexual conduct that it criminalizes more severely" (p. 78). A similar conclusion was reached by Green (1992), "prostitution exemplifies not the misapplication of sexual science to law . . . but its total circumvention" (p. 203).

101. Richards (1979).

102. Richards (1979), pp. 1229–30.

103. This ignores, of course, the many equally valid reasons why someone might choose to become a prostitute. In his 1858 survey of New York City prostitutes, William Sanger unearthed a surprising (and widely discounted) statistic: over one-fourth of those interviewed said they had voluntarily become prostitutes, "in order to gratify the sexual passions" (see Kushner, 1978, and Sanger, 1897).

104. Richards' "maximin" principle may be contrasted with the position that what is rational (in an economic sense) is not the maximization of the *minimum* condition, but the maximization of the *average* condition. Decriminalization of prostitution would be justified under such an analysis only if, in the balance, it improved the condition of the average member of society, and not necessarily that of the prostitute him or herself. The question of balancing the rather nebulous social benefits of prostitution versus its more visible harms is obviously well beyond the scope of the present work; we note however, that intellectual luminaries ranging from Homer to St. Augustine have previously advanced arguments purporting to find social good in prostitution, as summarized in the text.

105. Rubin (1990), p. 36.

106. Paglia (1990), p. 26.

Chapter 4. The Biology of Sexual Pleasure

1. If phantom orgasm is merely a remembrance of things past, then Marcel Proust's (1926) observation that, "the true paradises are paradises we have lost" (p. 216) would seem especially apropos.

2. Kinsey, Pomeroy, & Martin (1948); Kinsey, Pomeroy, Martin & Gebhard (1953); Richardson & Hart (1981); Troiden (1980).

The intransigence of sexual preference is reflected in the following Greek epigram:

My boyish loves no longer form the base
Of their low jokes, when my companions jest:
For I have changed, and it's a woman's face,
Well rouged and powdered, I now view with zest.
(Pope, 1962, p. 57)

3. Perhaps, as Woody Allen suggests, bisexuality is preferable because it "doubles your chances for a date on Saturday night." (This quote appeared in the *New York Times*, December 1, 1975.)

4. Population Information Program (1983).

5. *Androgens* are masculinizing sex hormones found primarily in men, but also in women. The principal and most potent androgen is *testosterone*.

6. Burnham (1973).

7. Parringer (1980).

8. Katchadourian & Lunde (1982), p. 45.

9. Krafft-Ebing (1978), p. 26.

10. Freud (1905/1962), p. 76.

11. Freud (1905/1962), p. 76.

12. Masters & Johnson (1966), p. 216. In women, "there is a direct correlation between the number and intensity of contractions [of the so-called orgasmic platform] and the perceived intensity of orgasm" (Morokoff, 1978, p. 148). Moreover, "the contractions of the female's orgasmic platform involve the same muscles that produce ejaculation and orgasm in males" (Morokoff, 1978, p. 148).

13. Freud (1920).

14. Freud (1905/1962), p. 87.

15. Kinsey, Pomeroy, Martin, & Gebhard (1953).

16. Masters & Johnson (1966).

17. Konner (1988). Singer and Singer (1972) postulate the existence of three distinct types of orgasm: vulval, uterine, and mixed, none of which appear to correspond to the G-spot orgasm. See also Morokoff (1978).

18. Marshall (1971a,b).

19. The classic American symbol of repressed female sexuality is the character Hester Prynne in Nathaniel Hawthorne's *The Scarlet Letter*. Kathy Acker (1978) brings the interrogation of Hester up to date with the following contemporary translation:

> The cops are screaming at Hester: "You hideous woman." "Look at the hideous woman." "Who did the hideous woman fuck?" "You're such a nice hideous woman, we know you didn't mean to do the tremendously horrible thing you did, just pretty please tell us who you fucked. We know what'll make you feel better" (p. 68).

20. Hamburg (1978), p. 76. Similar views are expressed by Beach (1974), Eibl-Eibesfeldt (1975), Fisher (1982), Lovejoy (1981), and Morris (1967). For a critical review of the pair-bond hypothesis, see Symons (1979).

21. Hrdy (1988).

22. Konner (1988).

23. Gould (1987); Symons (1979). See also Hrdy (1988) and Konner (1988).

24. Symons (1979), p. 93.

25. Alexander, Sipski, & Findley (1993).

26. See, e.g., Lindsley & Holmes (1984).

27. O divine power, if you lend yourself to me
So that the ghost of the blessed kingdom
Traced in my brain, is made manifest.

28. Harvey & Krebs (1990).

29. Olds (1956); Olds & Milner (1954).

30. Olds (1956), p. 116.

31. Herberg (1963a,b); Miller (1957).

32. Herberg (1963a,b).

33. Specifically, the medial preoptic–anterior region of the hypothalamus.

34. Hart (1986).

35. Herberg (1963a,b); Miller (1957); MacLean (1976).

36. Hart (1986).

37. MacLean, Dua, & Denniston (1963). The thalamic structures referred to are the intralaminar nucleus and the spinothalamic tract.

38. Robinson & Mishkin (1966). In this experiment, the preoptic region of the hypothalamus was stimulated.

39. Heath (1972).

40. LeVay (1991, 1993).

41. However, the different studies disagree as to which nuclei are sexually dimorphic. Swaab & Fliers (1985) investigated only INAH1 and found it to be dimorphic. According to Allen, Hines, Shryne, & Gorski (1989), both INAH2 and INAH3 are dimorphic, but not INAH1. In contrast, LeVay (1991) reports that only INAH3 is dimorphic, the sizes of the other three nuclei being essentially the same in women and men.

42. LeVay (1991), p. 1034.

43. For example, see Byne & Parsons (1993).

44. Byne (1994).

45. AIDS is known to decrease testosterone production, hence the smaller INAH sizes could be due to lower testosterone levels. Suggestive evidence in gerbils linking testosterone levels to the size of a brain region thought to be functionally homologous to the SDN has also been reported (Commins & Yahr, 1984). See also Byne & Parsons (1993).

46. Bailey & Greenberg (1993).

47. LeVay (1993), p. xii (emphasis in original).

48. Abramson & Pinkerton (1995); Tuzin (1995).

49. LeVay (1993), p. 105.

50. See also De Cecco (1990), Richardson (1984), and Weinberg (1978).

51. For whatever it's worth, we prefer *Samuel Adam's Boston Lager* (S.P.) and *Mackeson's Stout* (P.A.).

52. The basis of the Judeo-Christian condemnation of (male) homosexual behaviors is God's commandment to Moses, "thou shalt not lie with mankind, as with womankind: It is abomination" (Leviticus 18:22).

53. Boswell (1980).

54. See Foucault (1990); Weeks (1977).

55. De Cecco (1990).

56. Halperin (1989); Herzer (1985).

57. Quoted in Bullough (1967), p. 637.

59. Marshall (1981), p. 139.

60. Whisman (1993), p. 54.

61. Herdt (1981, 1987).

62. The Sambia belief that masculinity can be passed from man to boy through the former's semen bears certain similarities to the Greek pederastic tradition in which sex was "supposed to transmit manly virtues of mind and body from nobleman to young lover" (Karlen, 1980, p. 79).

63. Stoller and Herdt (1985) describe one instance of a "rubbish man." See also Herdt (1987).

64. Carrier (1980); Herdt (1984); Evans-Pritchard (1971); Murphy & Murphy (1974).

65. Callendar & Kochems (1983); Devereaux (1937); Meikle (1982); Roscoe (1994).

66. Blackwood (1984).

67. Devereaux (1937).

68. See Carrier (1980); Ford & Beach (1951).

69. Herdt (1987).

70. Cohen (1995); Herdt (1990b, 1994).

71. Carrier (1980).

72. Blackwood (1984), p. 35.

73. Blackwood (1984), p. 35.

74. Carrier (1980).

75. Meikle (1982); Winkler (1990).

76. A good example of the numerous complexly nuanced meanings of homosexuality comes from John Rechy's (1977) book, *The Sexual Outlaw*. He describes the homosexual "outlaw" as the:

> Archetypal outsider, he is a symbol of survival, living fully at the very edge, triumphant over the threats, repression, persecution, prosecution, attacks, denunciations, hatred that have tried powerfully to crush him from the beginning of "civilization": each night after the hunt, the outlaw knows he's won an ancestral battle—just because he's still alive and free. (p. 299)

77. Symons (1992).

78. Old (1993).

79. Herdt (1990c); Meikle (1982).

80. Hutchinson (1959). See also Kirsch & Rodman (1982).

81. Hamilton (1964). See also Dawkins (1976).

82. Dawkins (1976); Williams (1966).

83. See Kirsch & Rodman (1982).

84. Bailey & Pillard (1991); Bailey, Pillard, Neale, & Agyei (1993); Kallmann (1952a,b); King & MacDonald (1992); Whitam, Diamond, & Martin (1993). See also Pillard, Poumadere, & Carretta (1981).

85. Bailey & Benishay (1993); Pillard & Weinrich (1986); Pillard (1980).

86. See also Buhrich, Bailey, & Martin (1991), and Pillard & Weinrich (1986).

87. Reviewed in Pattatucci & Hamer (1995).

88. Hall (1978); Pattatucci & Hamer (1995).

89. Hamer, Hu, Magnuson, Hu, & Pattatucci (1993). See Pattatucci & Hamer (1995) for a less technical account of this work.

90. Technically, of course, we should be talking about alleles, not genes.

91. Crews (1994).

92. Crews (1994).

93. Abramson & Pinkerton (1995).

94. Gould (1977).

95. Byne & Parsons (1993); LeVay & Hamer (1994).

96. Genetic sex is determined by the sex chromosomes inherited from the parents. A genetic female has two X chromosomes, whereas a genetic male has both an X (inherited from his mother) and a Y (inherited from his father).

97. LeVay (1993).

98. Wilson (1995).

99. Exceptions to this generalization include the many morphological activational effects of androgens in the spinal nucleus of the bulbocavernosus system of castrated adult male rats (Tanaka & Arnold, 1993).

100. One mechanism by which the developmental influences of testosterone might be blocked in females is through the selective cell death of neurons having testosterone receptors, due to insufficient levels of this hormone. See LeVay (1993), and Nordeen, Nordeen, & Sengelaub (1985).

101. See, for example, Dörner & Hinz (1968), Gladue, Green, & Hellman (1984), and Glass, Denel, & Wright (1940). Relevant reviews may be found in Gartrell (1982), Meyer-Bahlburg (1977, 1979, 1995), and Richardson (1981).

102. Beach (1976).

103. Green (1987).

104. Richardson (1981).

105. Meyer-Bahlburg (1984). There is, however, evidence that hormones may play a role in determining the sexual orientation of so-called intersex individuals suffering from disorders of chromosomal, gonadal, or phenotypic sexual development (Meyer-Bahlburg, 1995; see also Wilson, 1995).

106. Downey, Erhardt, Schiffman, Dyrenfurth, & Becker (1987).

107. Burr (1993). See also Heim & Hursch (1979), and Murphy (1992).

108. Other forms of "treatment" for homosexuality have included electroshock therapy, lobotomy, and, of course, psychotherapy (including analysis, aversion therapy, systematic desensitization, etc.). See Coleman (1982) for an instructive review of the psychotherapeutic approach.

109. See, for example, LeVay & Hamer (1994).

110. Beach (1974), p. 354.

111. Wallen (1989, 1990, 1995).

112. Hrdy (1988).

113. Fisher (1992); Fox (1975); Lancaster (1975); Pavelka (1995).

114. Wallen (1990), p. 236.

115. Then, as now, in the immortal words of Mae West, "a man in the house is worth two in the streets" (from *Belle of the Nineties*).

116. Beach (1947); Wilson (1995). There is strong anecdotal evidence for a hormonal influence in female sexual desire:

> Many women experience periods in which sexual arousal is enhanced and overall sexual desire more profound. During these periods, women report increased fantasizing, accompanied by frequent masturbation. Curiously, the period most commonly cited is five to ten days prior to menstruation—a time when intercourse is most likely to result in conception. (Angela Pattatucci, personal communication)

Nevertheless, if hormones exert a reliable influence on sexual interest in women, this effect has thus far escaped conclusive scientific documentation (Wilson, 1995; see, however, Wallen, 1995).

117. Wilson (1995).

118. In contemporary Western societies, children and young adults are subjected to severe heterosexual socialization. This suggests an alternative possibility for the scenario described in the text. Perhaps the woman in question is homosexually inclined "by nature" and has only "learned" to be heterosexual. Same-sex experiences, in this case, would help to reinstate her "true" self.

Chapter 5. The Psychology of Sexual Pleasure

1. Davenport (1977).

2. For more on the Bala, see Merriam (1971); Mangaia is described by Marshall (1971). There is also a third scenario in which women usually go topless *and* men view breasts with excitement and appreciation; such appears to be the case in parts of New Guinea (Donald Tuzin, personal communication).

3. Symons (1995). Similarly, men who are attracted to other men also highly value youth and health in potential sexual partners (Symons, 1979).

4. See, for example, Peplau, Rubin, & Hill (1977), and Sherwin & Corbett (1985).

5. Aron & Aron (1991); Gregor (1985, 1995).

6. Gregor (1995); Marshall (1971a); Schlegel (1995).

7. Freud (1965).

8. There are, of course, many theories of love (see Fisher, 1992; Hendrick & Hendrick, 1992; Sternberg & Barnes, 1988). For example, the psychoanalytic perspective, via Ovid, Freud, and Kristeva (1987), implicates narcissism as a critical factor; love of another is thus rooted in the love of oneself.

9. Krafft-Ebing (1978), p. 8. For a somewhat better balanced overview of the relationship between sex and love, see Aron & Aron (1991) or Tzeng (1992).

10. See, for example, Endleman (1989), Gregor (1995), or Singer (1984).

11. Messenger (1971), p. 8.

12. In his infamous five volume autobiography, *My Life and Loves*, Frank Harris (1925), offers the following on the relationship of pleasure and marriage:

Grace was already a wonderful lover. From the beginning she set herself to give one all the pleasure possible . . . Accordingly her progress in the art was outstandingly rapid . . . I know that whoever she marries later would esteem himself fortunate, and the more experienced he was, the higher he would prize her (p. 620).

13. In Kentucky, a young woman can get married at age 13 (with parental consent), and thereafter, presumably, can engage in unbounded marital sex, but cannot consent to *nonmarital* sex until age 16.

14. Flandrin (1985).

15. Quoted in Robertson (1962), p. 429.

16. See, for example, Person (1989).

17. See, for example, Mosher (1966), and Byrne & Schulte (1990).

18. Gerrard & Reis (1989); Goldfarb, Gerrard, Gibbons, & Plante (1988); Schwartz (1973).

19. Abramson & Handschumacher (1978); Galbraith, Hahn, & Lieberman (1968); Galbraith & Mosher (1968).

20. Byrne & Schulte (1990); Mosher & Abramson (1977); Mosher & Cross (1971); Schill & Chapin (1972); Schwartz (1973).

21. Byrne & Schulte (1990); Fisher & Byrne (1978); Mosher (1973).

22. One of the classic depictions of the differences between men and women is the following:

Women's faults are many
  Men have only two;
Everything they say
  And everything they do.

For more on the "battle of the sexes," the interested reader is advised to peruse the works of the great American humorist, James Thurber, especially, *The Thurber Carnival* and *Men, Women and Dogs*.

23. Kinsey, Pomeroy, & Martin (1948).

24. Abramson & Mosher (1979).

25. Symons (1979).

26. Kinsey, Pomeroy, Martin, & Gebhard (1953).

27. For example, Buss (1994); Symons (1979).

28. Angela Pattatucci (personal communication) expands upon this rationale for accentuating gender differences as follows:

A society with strict bipolar gender lines has a vested interest in maintaining the status quo. This is typically accomplished by maximizing differences (even though they may be few in number and relatively subtle) and minimizing similarities (even though they may be great in number and relatively pronounced). This has the effect of legitimizing the dominant group as "normal" (e.g., white, male, heterosexual, Republican, etc.) and pathologizing nondominant groups. The ultimate result is an intolerance of difference that causes the masses to strive for the dominant ideal, thereby further legitimizing the dominant group and pathologizing the rest. This is the essence of social construction.

See the forthcoming book, *A Matter of Will*, by Angela Pattatucci and Barbara Bond.

29. On the other hand, to invoke a famous Yiddish proverb, "If grandma had balls, she would be grandpa."

30. The statistical methods (e.g., "*t*-tests") that social scientists employ when comparing groups also bias the results obtained. It is much easier to show that two groups (such as men and women) are different with regard to some measure than it is to demonstrate that they are similar.

31. Acton (1857).

32. Shade (1978).

33. Gordon (1976).

34. Shade (1978), p. 17.

35. Freedman (1982).

36. Shade (1978).

37. Berk, Abramson, & Okami (1995).

38. Cochran & Mays (1990). Furthermore, as Adrienne Rich (1978) notes, "lying is done with words and also with silence."

39. Abramson, Perry, Rothblatt, Seeley, & Seeley (1981); Seeley, Abramson, Perry, Rothblatt, & Seeley (1980).

40. Pelvic blood flow can be monitored using an imaging technique known as *thermography*, which is a noninvasive means of measuring body temperatures. The resultant photograph, known as a thermogram, illustrates hot and cold areas of the body that might arise, for example, from increased or decreased blood flow. It is particularly suitable as a measure of sexual arousal because pelvic vasocongestion is reliably associated with both arousal (Masters & Johnson, 1966) and increased heat generation (Abramson, Perry, Seeley, Seeley, & Rothblatt, 1981; Seeley, Abramson, Perry, Rothblatt, & Seeley, 1980).

41. The belief that of men and women, "man has beyond a doubt the stronger sexual appetite of the two" (Krafft-Ebing, p. 9), has persisted for hundreds of years, and is not limited to Western cultures (see, for example, Davenport, 1977, and Marshall & Suggs, 1971). On the other hand, according to traditional Hindu beliefs, women derive greater pleasure from sex than do men (Bullough, 1967).

42. Hunt (1974); Kinsey, Pomeroy, & Martin (1948); Kinsey, Pomeroy, Martin, & Gebhard (1953); Laumann, Gagnon, Michael, & Michaels (1994).

43. Eysenck (1976).

44. Masters & Johnson (1966).

45. Hunt (1974); Kinsey, Pomeroy, Martin, & Gebhard (1953). Tavris & Sadd

(1977). The authors of the *Sex in America* survey report that 71 percent of women "always" or "usually" reach orgasm during sex with their primary partners (Michael, Gagnon, Laumann, & Kolata, 1994).

46. Fisher (1973); Morokoff (1978).

47. Fisher (1973); Hunt (1974); Kinsey, Pomeroy, Martin, & Gebhard, (1953).

48. See Hyde (1972).

49. For example, Heiman (1976).

50. Kinsey, Pomeroy, Martin, & Gebhard (1953); Michael, Gagnon, Laumann, & Kolata (1994).

51. Marshall (1971a,b).

52. Marshall (1971a), p. 123.

53. Marshall (1971a), pp. 161–62.

54. More generally, see Abramson & Pinkerton (editors), *Sexual Nature / Sexual Culture* (1995).

55. Imperato-McGinley, Guerrero, Gautier, & Peterson (1974); Imperato-McGinley, Peterson, Gautier, & Sturla (1979).

56. Herdt & Davidson (1988).

57. Herdt (1990b, 1994).

58. For a thorough exposition on third-gender systems, see Herdt (editor), *Third Sex, Third Gender* (1994).

59. Herdt (1990b), p. 442.

60. Cohen (1995); Nanda (1990, 1994).

61. Cohen (1995).

62. Blackwood (1984); Callendar & Kochems (1983); Devereaux (1937); Meikle (1982); Roscoe (1994).

63. Carrier (1980); Herdt (1994).

64. Coleman, Colgan, & Gooren (1992).

65. See Bolin (1994) for more on transgenderism.

66. Colloquially known as "chicks with dicks."

67. Marshall (1971a).

68. Marshall (1971a), p. 119.

69. Messenger (1971). The observations cited here are based on data collected prior to 1960, hence neglect the manifest changes wrought by the introduction of television and increasing contact with outsiders to Innis Beag.

70. Marshall (1971a), p. 120.

71. Messenger (1971).

72. Gregor (1995).

73. In practice, however, the ultimate punishment was seldom invoked (Oaks, 1980).

74. Elwin (1968); Schlegel (1995). In the ghotul, partners are changed routinely, because it is considered unhealthy to become too attached to a single lover. Ghotul partners, therefore, rarely become spouses (Schlegel, 1995). Similar rules regarding the rotation of sexual partners are observed by the Kikuyu of East Africa (Worthman, 1986). Attachment, as fostered by continued intimacy, is also discour-

aged in the *Brave New World* envisioned by Aldous Huxley, because "every one belongs to every one else."

75. Foucault (1990) suggests that the role of the family is "to anchor sexuality and provide it with permanent support . . . [the family] conveys the law and the juridicial dimension in the deployment of sexuality" (p. 108).

76. This practice still occurs elsewhere in the world—for example, in Mangaia (Davenport, 1971a).

77. McGuire, Carlisle, & Young (1965); Rachman (1966); Stoller (1985).

78. Krafft-Ebing (1978), p. 11.

79. Darwin (1872/1979), p. 216.

80. Rachman (1966); Rachman & Hodgson (1968). One might question whether these stimuli (black boots) are truly neutral. Would this experiment have been as successful if it had utilized brown boots? Or rubber boots? Or horseshoes?

81. Freud (1927/1963), p. 217. On the other hand, not all sexual behavior is learned in this way, if it is learned at all:

> The inclination to take a man's sexual organ into the mouth and suck at it, which in respectable society is considered a loathsome sexual perversion, is nevertheless found with great frequency among women of today—and of earlier times as well, as ancient sculptures show—, and in the state of being in love it appears completely to lose its repulsive character. Phantasies derived from this inclination are found by doctors even in women who have not become aware of the possibilities of obtaining sexual satisfaction in this way by reading Krafft-Ebing's *Psychopathia Sexualis*, or from other sources of information. Women, it seems, find no difficulty in producing this kind of wishful phantasy spontaneously. (Freud, 1910/1961, p. 38)

82. Walen & Roth (1987).

83. Stoller (1971, 1985).

84. Walen & Roth (1987).

85. Or to an animal, as exemplified by Gene Wilder's ongoing relationship with a ewe in Woody Allen's *Everything You Always Wanted to Know about Sex (But Were Afraid to Ask)*.

86. Tannahill (1980), p. 381.

87. Tannahill (1980), p. 382.

88. Marcus (1964), p. 67.

89. Marmor (1976), p. 238.

90. Kleptomania is viewed by some as a female fetish, as is pyromania in men (Socarides, 1960; Stoller, 1985).

91. Faust (1980), p. 53.

92. Faust (1980).

93. Stoller & Herdt (1985).

94. Stoller (1985), p. 123. See also Stoller & Herdt (1985).

95. Stoller (1985).

96. For example, McGuire, Carlisle, & Young (1965).

97. Grant (1954).

98. See Stoller & Herdt (1985) for further details.

99. MacLean (1973).

100. In many cases, ablation of the amygdala and hippocampus (components of the limbic system) is also required to precipitate the hypersexual condition referred to in the text, which is known as "Klüver-Bucy" syndrome, after the researchers who first characterized it (Klüver & Bucy, 1937).

101. Blumer & Walker (1975). Much of the sexual behavior displayed by such patients is unmistakably inappropriate, such as indiscriminate masturbation and making unsolicited sexual advances to hospital staff.

102. Hughlings Jackson, in Dewhurst (1982), p. 63.

103. Quoted in Brown (1961), p. 6.

104. Berk, Abramson, & Okami (1995). A similar methodology was employed by McLaws, Oldenberg, Ross, & Cooper (1990) in a study of the sexual practices of gay men.

105. Baddeley (1990).

106. McLaws, Oldenberg, Ross, & Cooper (1990).

107. In some sense we believe this to be a behavioral analogue of Heisenberg's Uncertainty Principle. The attempt at disclosure (measurement) necessarily disturbs the system being interrogated.

108. In the absence of a viable alternative to the representational assumption, Noam Chomsky (1980) states, "I will continue to assume that it is correct to analyze knowledge of language, and to offer explanations for particular instances, in terms of mental structures of rules and representations; to assume, in short, that our linguistic abilities are based on such mental structures" (p. 49).

109. Chomsky (1975).

110. Fodor (1981, 1983); Fodor & Pylyshyn (1988); Minsky (1981); Pylyshyn (1980). The importance of representations to mental functioning was, of course, also recognized by Descartes.

111. See, for example, Simon & Gagnon (1984).

112. Tulving (1972, 1983). Episodic memory is a hypothesized component of the long-term memory system that is responsible for the retention of information about personal experiences rather than general facts about the world.

113. Fisher (1980).

114. Moses-Zirkes (1993) reporting on the work of Daniel Kahneman.

115. Jones (1957), p. 255.

116. It could be, of course, that the factors responsible for forgetting pleasurable experiences differ radically from those that influence memory for pain. This would especially be true if Jones (1957) is correct in his suggestion that painful memories are actively repressed to protect the psyche. Clearly, there is no comparable rationale for people to forget pleasurable experiences.

117. Abramson (1990). See also Bullough (1994).

118. The progressive rock group Roxy Music's song, "Love Is the Drug,"

provides a fitting comment on the notion of sexual addiction. See also Robert Palmer's "Addicted to Love."

119. For example, Carnes (1983) and Schwartz & Brasted (1985).

120. Levine & Troiden (1988).

121. Coleman (1991).

122. Levine & Troiden (1988). A related conceptualization concerns the expression of "compulsive sexual behavior," which is defined as, "behavior that is driven by anxiety reduction mechanisms rather than by sexual desire" (Coleman, 1991, p. 37; see also Quadland, 1985).

123. Levine & Troiden (1988).

Chapter 6. AIDS: The End of Pleasure?

1. UNAIDS (2000).

2. Centers for Disease Control and Prevention (1999).

3. United States Catholic Conference (1987).

4. See, for example, Gamson (1990).

5. The advertising agency that developed the "I'll do a lot for love" campaign for Ansell-Americas (the makers of LifeStyles condoms) resigned the account in 1987 after an agency executive was quoted in *Time* as saying, "AIDS is a condom marketer's dream" (Sloan & Mandese, 1991).

6. Prieur (1990), p. 114.

7. Nearly three-quarters of the men surveyed by Grady, Klepinger, Billy, & Tanfer (1993) agreed that using a condom "shows that you are a concerned and caring person." In contrast, just under 18 percent supported the idea that condom use "shows you think your partner has AIDS."

8. Jones (1993), p. 35.

9. "Sex Education in Classroom Becomes Political in Britain," *Los Angeles Times,* April 16, 1994.

10. Center for AIDS Prevention Studies website (http://www.caps.ucsf.edu).

11. Suraiya (1992).

12. Alexander (1992).

13. Goldsmith (1987).

14. Who says condoms and humor don't mix? A small company in Texas has announced the development of a Stealth condom, which they plan to market with the tag line "They'll never see you coming."

15. Pinkerton & Abramson (1997a); see also Pinkerton & Abramson (1993a).

16. "Be good. And if you can't be good, be careful. And if you can't be careful, name it after me" (anonymous).

17. Catania, Coates, Stall, Turner, Peterson, Hearst, Dolcini, Hudes, Gagnon, & Groves (1992). Condom use rates for gay men are substantially higher (Binson, Michaels, Stall, Coates, Gagnon, & Catania, 1995).

18. Anderson, Wilson, Doll, Jones, & Barker (1999).

19. This question should not be limited to HIV. Condoms have been around for more than 400 years, at least 150 of them in their current form. Yet STDs

continue to wreak havoc, much of which could be avoided by the widespread adoption of the consistent use of condoms.

20. Holtgrave & Pinkerton (1997).

21. Pinkerton & Abramson (1992).

22. Prieuer (1990), p. 109.

23. McKusick, Horstman, & Coates (1985).

24. For example, see Maticka-Tyndale (1991). Some people not only *understimate* their own risk for HIV, they also badly *overestimate* other people's risks, even people who are similar to themselves (Pinkerton, Wagner-Raphael, Craun, & Abramson, 2000). That is, they may view themselves as being "uniquely invulnerable" to HIV (Cohen & Bruce, 1997).

25. "Sex and death. [Two] things which come once in a lifetime. At least after death, you're not nauseous" (Woody Allen, *Sleeper,* 1973).

26. McKusick, Horstman, & Coates (1985).

27. Gagnon & Godin (2000).

28. The decision-making model elaborated in Pinkerton & Abramson (1992) is slightly more complicated than the one presented here, but the conceptual framework is similar in both cases. See also Kaplan (1995).

29. In a follow-up to our paper (Pinkerton & Abramson, 1992), Don Symons (1993) argues that for many people (especially those drawing partners from a population in which the prevalence of HIV is low), unprotected intercourse may be less dangerous than, for example, driving a car.

30. *Newsweek,* September 26, 1994.

31. See, for example, Kingsley, Detels, Daslow, Polk, Rinaldo, Chmiel, Detre, Kelsey, Odaka, Ostrow, VanRaden, & Visscher (1987). In any case the risks associated with oral-genital sex are not well established (Rothenberg, Scarlett, del Rio, Reznik, & O'Daniels, 1998).

32. Empirical evidence suggests the possibility that fears over the riskiness of oral-genital sex might lead to an increase in unprotected anal intercourse or other "high-risk" behaviors (de Vroome, Sandfort, & Tielman, 1992). See also Spencer (1993).

33. See, for example, Connell & Kippax (1990) and Simon, Kraft, & Kaplan (1990). However, oral sex has not always been popular among all lesbians (see Kennedy & Davis, 1993).

34. Jones (1993), p. 13.

35. Catania, Coates, Stall, Turner, Peterson, Hearst, Dolcini, Hudes, Gagnon, & Groves (1991).

36. Chapman & Hodgson (1988).

37. Pool, Whitworth, Green, Mbonye, Harrison, Hart, & Wilkinson (2000).

38. See, for example, the condom buyers' survey conducted by Consumer Reports (1979).

39. James Boswell (1763), quoted in Parisot (1987), p. 14.

40. Cohen (1989); Sterk (1989).

41. Sterk (1989).

42. Tanner & Pollack (1988).

43. If positive condom attitudes and behaviors can indeed be learned, there is no reason why young men should not familiarize themselves with how condoms are used and how they feel *prior* to their first sexual encounter with a partner. The tripartite association of sex, condoms, and pleasure could be further reinforced by the incorporation of condoms into masturbatory activities.

44. Pool, Whitworth, Green, Mbonye, Harrison, Hart, & Wilkinson (2000).

45. Chapman & Hodgson (1988).

46. Watney (1990).

47. Crimp (1988), p. 253. See also Berkowitz & Callen (1983); Bolton (1992).

48. Suarez & Miller (2001).

49. Pinkerton & Holtgrave (1999).

50. Dilley, Wood, & McFarland (1997); Kalichman, Nachimson, Cherry, & Williams (1998); Kelly, Hoffman, Rompa, & Gray (1998); Suarez, Kelly, Pinkerton, Stevenson, Hayat, Smith, & Ertl (2001).

51. Suarez, Kelly, Pinkerton, Stevenson, Hayat, Smith, & Ertl (2001). There also is limited evidence that the availability of combination therapies may influence condom use by heterosexual college students (Gagnon & Godin, 2000).

52. Jones (1993).

53. Prieur (1990), p. 111.

54. Deidier (1713), quoted in Quetel (1990), p. 79.

55. Grmek (1990) lists the following parallels between

the expansion of syphilis at the beginning of the modern era and the present epidemic of AIDS: The sexual and maternal-child transmission, the moral and ethical implications, the impact on mores, the closing of public baths and so-called places of debauchery, the reactions of social alienation, and, to a certain extent, even the extreme danger. (p. 104)

For more on the political squabbles that resulted in the closing of gay bathhouses in the 1980s, see the excellent social history of the AIDS epidemic, *And the Band Played On* (1987) by Randy Shilts.

56. See Brown, Donohue, Axnick, Blount, Ewen, & Jones (1970); Fleming (1964); Llewellyn-Jones (1985).

57. See Brown, Donohue, Axnick, Blount, Ewen, & Jones (1970).

68. Pusey (1933), p. 8, quoted in Fleming (1964), pp. 592–593.

59. Quetel (1990), p. 199.

60. The severity of the disease can be adduced as evidence that syphilis was new to Europe in the sixteenth century (Fleming, 1964). See also Grmek (1990).

61. Quoted in Quetel (1990).

62. Mann, Tarantola, & Netter (1992). See also Aral & Holmes (1991).

63. By a "cure for AIDS" people usually mean a cure for HIV infection. As a complex syndrome of diseases, AIDS itself can be cured only to the extent that

cures can be found for the broad constellation of AIDS-defining maladies (Kaposi's sarcoma, *Pneumocystis carinii* pneumonia, cryptosporidiosis, and so on).

64. Aboulker & Swart (1993); Lagakos, Pettinelli, Stein, & Volberding (1993); Lundgren, Phillips, Pedersen, Clumeck, Gatell, Johnson, Ledergerber, Vella, & Nielsen (1994); Osmond, Charlebois, Lang, Shiboski, & Moss (1994).

65. Pinkerton & Abramson (1993b).

66. Pinkerton & Abramson (1993b).

67. Pinkerton & Abramson (1993b,c).

68. Quoted in Lasagna (1975), p. 17.

69 See Brandt (1985).

70. Pinkerton & Abramson (1995).

71. Garrett (1992).

72. See, for example, Patton (1985); Watney (1990).

73. Shilts (1987), pp. 495 and 596.

74. Bernstein (1992). There is also an industrywide insistence that condom commercials focus on disease prevention rather than contraception or pleasure. A 1991 *Advertising Age/Electronic Media* poll of television station managers revealed that although 85 percent thought the networks should accept disease prevention spots, only 18 percent believed they should air ads that focus on contraception (Mandese, 1991).

75. Hall (1994).

76. Gladwell (1992).

77. One minute after the Trojan ad aired, "SNL" viewers were treated to a commercial showing a male goat in a smoking jacket (a la Hugh Hefner), who was giving advice to a nicely dressed man on a date with a beautiful woman. "How's your love life?" asked the goat. "Stressed out? Too much pressure? Want to get back the fire you once had in the bedroom? The safe, pleasure-packed botanicals in Pinnacle Horny Goat Weed provide a potent solution for love in the fast lane." Sounds like good stuff! (Notice the use of key terms, such as "fire," "pleasure-packed," and "potent.") Oh, by the way, according to the goat, "[Horny Goat Weed] works for women too."

78. Sloan (1988).

79. Quoted in Sloan (1988), p. 27.

80. Hovey (1992), p. 31.

81. Hovey (1992), p. 31.

82. Hudson (1960), p. 257.

83. *People v. Sanger,* 222 N.Y. 193 (1918). See Hovey (1992).

84. Hudson (1960), p. 247.

85. *Griswold v. Connecticut,* 381 U.S. 479 (1965). See Gamson (1990); Sloan (1988).

86. *Eisenstadt v. Baird,* 405 U.S. 438 (1972). See Sloan (1988).

87. D'Emilio & Freedman (1988).

88. *Carey, Governor of New York, et al. v. Population Services International et al.,* 431 U.S. 678 (1977), quoted in Gamson (1990), p. 271.

89. Gamson (1990).

90. Taken from an ad for Trojan condoms that appeared in *People* magazine on July 11, 1994.

Chapter 7. Porn: Tempest on a Soapbox

1. The First Amendment to the Constitution states, in part, that, "Congress shall make no law . . . abridging the freedom of speech."

2. The original Greek term for prostitution was *porneia*. Aline Rousselle (1988) concludes, in reference to ancient Greek and Roman religious precepts: "For women as for men, any contact with another's body, whether pleasurable or not, became a sign of mortality and of loss; any manifestation of desire for another's body, called *porneia*, became a measure of human weakness in the service of God" (p. 4).

3. Sir Kenneth Dover (1978) suggests that the term "pornography" has evolved into the modern equivalent of "wanker" or "motherfucker," commonly used terms designating disapproval, sexual or otherwise.

4. Arendt (1963).

5. Stone (1979).

6. Aubrey Beardsley's illustrations, produced for a pornographer/publisher's version of *Lysistrata*, have been described as "strikingly scabrous" (Weintraub, 1976).

7. O'Flaherty (1985).

8. Bataille (1986).

9. Stoller (1985).

10. For details, see Lissarrague (1990).

11. Illustrations are provided in Dover (1978).

12. These depictions, incidentally, are by no means limited to Western cultures. Ancient Chinese scrolls, pre-Columbian Andean pottery, Indian paintings and carvings (including depictions of religious figures such as Krishna) all explore the pleasures of sex in graphic, and often quite comic, detail. Although many of these images are designed to convey a sexual idea, others are limited to fertility symbols. African carvings and Japanese *do so shin* are examples of the later.

13. Pornographic materials are sometimes called "stroke books," "cum magazines," "one-armed reading," "meat beaters," and "squirt books" (Weatherford, 1986).

14. The Catholic stand on wasted seminal emissions is parodied by the premiere British comedy group *Monty Python's Flying Circus* in the aptly titled song, "Every Sperm Is Sacred," from the 1983 film, *The Meaning of Life*.

15. Epstein (1948).

16. Aquinas, *On the Truth of the Catholic Faith: Summa Contra Gentiles*, quoted in Richards (1979), p. 1210, note 76.

17. Taylor (1953), p. 54.

18. Freud (1905/1962), p. 55, note 1.

19. Masturbation acts to facilitate the patterning of sexual arousal and orgasmic functioning, especially in regard to creating the capacity for pelvic engorgement.

Masturbation guilt is thereby capable of inhibiting the pattern of sexual arousal and creating orgasmic dysfunction, in addition to psychological turmoil that attends the recriminations often associated with masturbation (Abramson, Perry, Rothblatt, Seeley, & Seeley, 1981). Attitudes toward masturbation are also examined in Abramson (1973); Abramson & Mosher (1975, 1979); and Mosher & Abramson (1977). See also Phillip Roth's novel, *Portnoy's Complaint.*

20. See Boswell (1980). Boswell quotes from John the Faster (dated 595):

Likewise there are two types of masturbation: one wherein he is aroused by his own hand and another by someone else's hand, which is unfortunate, since what the parties begin by themselves ends up also harming others to whom they teach the sin. (pp. 363–64)

21. MacDonald (1967).
22. Neuman (1975).
23. Quoted in MacDonald (1967), p. 425.
24. MacDonald (1967).
25. Tissot (1772), quoted in Neuman (1975), p. 2.
26. Language "lifted" from Raymond Chandler's *The Big Sleep*, p. 154.
27. Neuman (1975).
28. Freud (1912/1958).
29. Virgil, Georgics, I.
30. Acton (1857), quoted in MacDonald (1967), p. 431.
31. For more on the vagaries of the antimasturbation literature, see Barker-Benfield (1973), Comfort (1967), Greenberg (1988), MacDonald (1967), and Walters (1974).
32. Barker-Benfield (1973).
33. Lewis (1980); Shade (1978).
34. Lewis (1980).
35. Faust (1980), p. 53.
36. Weatherford (1986), p. 50. See also Comfort (1967) and Tannahill (1980) for further information on, and illustrations of, some of the grotesque devices intended to prevent masturbation.
37. Weatherford (1986). The extremism evident in this quote was sometimes justified by the malevolent view of masturbators professed by some members of the medical establishment. Noted nineteenth century psychiatrist Henry Maudsley, for example, suggested that, "the sooner [the masturbator] sinks to his degraded rest the better for himself and the better for the world which is well rid of him" (quoted in Hare, 1963).

It should also be noted that, according to Barker-Benfield (1973), British gynecologists ceased performing clitoridectomies in 1866, but American surgeons continued this practice until at least 1904, and perhaps as recently as 1925. However, this and other forms of genital mutilation (predominantly, though not exclusively, of young girls) are routinely performed in many contemporary cultures

(Lightfoot-Klein, 1989; Alice Walker presents a compelling fictional account of the horrors of female "circumcision" in her novel, *Possessing the Secret of Joy*).

38. D'Emilio & Freedman (1988).

39. Weatherford (1986).

40. D'Emilio & Freedman (1988); Nissenbaum (1980); Weatherford (1986).

41. Nissenbaum (1980).

42. Graham (1834), quoted in Nissenbaum (1980), p. 32.

43. Weatherford (1986), p. 52.

44. Acton (1857), quoted in Marcus (1964), p. 19. Remarking on the similarity of the preceding description to the villainous clerk in Dickens's *David Copperfield*, Marcus suggests that, "masturbation was unquestionably at the bottom of all of Uriah Heep's troubles."

45. Marcus (1964).

46. Acton (1857), quoted in Marcus (1964), p. 21. See also Hare (1962).

47. See, for example, Neuman (1975).

48. See also Hare (1962) and Neuman (1975).

49. Acton (1857), quoted in Marcus (1964), p. 21.

50. Acton (1857), quoted in Marcus (1964), p. 21.

51. Baden-Powell, quoted in MacDonald (1967), p. 431, note 35.

52. Carrier (1980).

53. Herdt (1987).

54. Carrier (1980).

55. Anonymous (1835), quoted in Barker-Benfield (1976), p. 179.

56. Barker-Benfield (1973). In Stanley Kubrick's 1963 film, *Dr. Strangelove*, U.S. Army General Jack D. Ripper suggests that the prudent course for men wishing to avoid semen depletion is to deny women their "essence." Justifying his obsession with "purity of essence" and the threat of its loss to Royal Air Force Capt. Lionel Mandrake, Gen. Ripper explains:

> I first became aware of it [loss of essence], during the physical act of love . . . a profound sense of fatigue, a feeling of emptiness followed. Luckily I was able to interpret these feelings correctly—loss of essence. I can assure you it has not recurred, Mandrake. Women sense my power and they seek the life essence. I do not avoid women, Mandrake, but I do deny them my essence.

57. D'Emilio & Freedman (1988).

58. Graham, quoted in Walters (1974), p. 34.

59. Gardiner (1955), p. 564.

60. Anonymous (1835), quoted in Barker-Benfield (1976), p. 179.

61. Richards (1974), p. 52.

62. de Grazia (1992), p. 4.

63. Sloan (1988).

64. D'Emilio & Freedman (1988). See also Broun & Leech (1927).

65. Comstock, quoted in Richards (1974), p. 58.

66. Excerpted from the Comstock Act as quoted in Richards (1974), p. 50, note 31.

67. D'Emilio & Freedman (1988), p. 160.

68. Lockhart & McClure (1954); Richards (1974).

69. Taylor (1953).

70. Stone (1979), p. 539.

71. Stone (1979), p. 539.

72. Quoted in Stone (1979), p. 539.

73. Quoted in Stone (1979), p. 336.

74. Stone (1979), pp. 336–37.

75. Stone (1979).

76. D'Emilio & Freedman (1988).

77. Willis (1983), p. 466.

78. See Heins (1993).

79. Dworkin (1993), p. 38.

80. Watney (1987), p. 58.

81. Watney (1987).

82. Watney (1987), p. 59.

83. de Grazia (1992).

84. See, for example, the volume edited by Lederer (1980).

85. Robin Morgan, quoted in Press et al. (1985). That some pornography depicts overt violence is unquestionable. However, violence is neither a necessary, nor even a very frequent component of popular men's pornography.

86. Brownmiller (1975), p. 391.

87. Brownmiller (1975), p. 391.

88. Brownmiller (1975), p. 394.

89. See, for example, Dworkin (1985, 1989), and MacKinnon (1984, 1991, 1993).

90. MacKinnon (1984), p. 343.

91. See Turley (1986) for a comprehensive review of the Dworkin-MacKinnon ordinance.

92. Turley (1986), p. 89. See also Duggan, Hunter, & Vance (1985).

93. Dworkin (1987b), p. 12.

94. Quoted in Witomski (1985), p.26.

95. Turley (1986).

96. Willis (1983), p. 462.

97. Dworkin (1985).

98. Faderman (1991), p. 252.

99. Dworkin (1987a).

100. Faust (1980), p. 175. See also Symons (1979) for a detailed discussion of this issue.

101. Willis (1983), p. 465.

102. Willis (1983), p. 465.

103. A Gallup poll conducted in 1985 indicated that a majority of Americans

believe that the pornography statutes then in effect were sufficiently strict, and needed no additional strengthening (Press, Namuth, Agrest, Gander, Lubenow, Reese, Friendly, & McDaniel, 1985).

104. Turley (1986).

105. See Note 127.

106. Willis (1983), p. 464 (emphasis in original).

107. See also our remarks on romance novels in Chapter 3.

108. Snitow (1985), p. 114.

109. Turley (1986), pp. 62 and 89.

110. See, for example, MacKinnon's *Only Words*.

111. Cottingham (1984).

112. MacKinnon (1993).

113. The alleged evils of coercion do not end with the victim herself:

> If a woman had to be coerced to make *Deep Throat*, doesn't that suggest that *Deep Throat* is dangerous to all women anywhere near a man who wants to do what he saw in it? (MacKinnon, 1993, p. 21)

(See also Lovelace, 1980.) MacKinnon apparently believes that the sexual tastes of a single individual, in this case Linda Lovelace, necessarily represent the unitary preferences of others.

114. Similar methodological problems plagued 1986's Meese Commission on Pornography (Nobile & Nadler, 1986). The commission solicited testimony from numerous "victims" of pornography and various law enforcement officials (often armed with titillating slide shows), but paid little heed to experts in the field of sex research. Paul Abramson was one of the social scientists invited to provide expert testimony. However, because his testimony challenged the prevailing antiporn perspective of the commission, Abramson's testimony was not included in the commission's final report. Instead, he is merely described as "having testified." The treatment he was accorded, evidently, was not unusual:

> Witnesses appearing before the commission were treated in a highly uneven manner. Commissioners accepted virtually any claim made by antipornography witnesses as true, asking few questions and making only the most cursory requests for evidence or attempts to determine witness credibility. Those who did not support more restrictions of sexually explicit speech were often met with rudeness and hostility, and their motives for testifying were impugned. (Vance, 1986, p.77)

(See Baron, 1987, and Nobile & Nadler, 1986, for further details on the Meese Commission.)

115. Abuses undoubtedly do occur, in the pornography industry as elsewhere. The issue of redress appears quite simple. Rape is a felony crime. It should be treated as such, and prosecuted accordingly, despite the circumstances and participants involved—be they spouses, strangers, or actors and actresses. This is the most reasonable and just response to charges of rape within the pornography industry.

116. According to X-rated video performer Nina Hartley:

The horror stories are pretty much unfounded. I haven't heard any horror stories about women getting into the business by force. (quoted in Stoller, 1991, p. 147)

117. See Kay Parker's commentary in Stoller (1991).

118. Stoller (1991); Stoller & Levine (1993).

119. Quoted in Stoller (1991), p. 36.

120. Personal communications. Furthermore, Leisuretime Entertainment will not distribute an X-rated video that contains any of the following: (1) violence; (2) words that are demeaning to women; (3) depictions of coercive or forced sex; (4) sex acts that perpetuate rape myths, or that appear to involve unwilling participants, or that are performed as a result of blackmail or extortion; and so forth. Though some antiporn feminists (and others as well) may still find these films distasteful or demeaning to women, it is clear that the adult entertainment industry is not unresponsive to these issues.

121. MacKinnon (1991).

122. To date, the best source of research on the effects of pornography remains the final report of the Commission on Obscenity and Pornography (1970). After conducting an extensive series of investigations, this blue ribbon panel concluded that pornography is ultimately benign. The worst that could be said was that pornography might prompt the expression of antisocial behaviors already in the viewer's repertoire. More recent studies document contemporary attitudinal changes resulting from exposure to pornographic materials, but the link between attitudes and behaviors is weak at best. (See also R. Dworkin, 1993.)

The Meese Commission (see Note 114), in contrast, was not deterred in its quest to vilify pornography by the dearth of evidence that pornography causes violence against women. According to commission member Frederick Schauer, "the absence of evidence should by no means be taken to deny the existence of a causal link" (quoted in Baron, 1987, p. 9).

123. Abramson & Hayashi (1984).

124. For Denmark, see Kutchinsky (1985); for West Germany, see Green (1985). Similarly, the British Inquiry into Obscenity and Film Censorship (better known as the Williams Committee) observed a decrease in sexual violence when the availability and explicitness of pornography increased (Pally, 1994). Members of the Committee therefore, "unhesitatingly reject the suggestion that the available statistical evidence for England and Wales lends any support to the argument that pornography acts as a stimulus to the commission of sexual violence" (quoted in Pally, 1994, p. 58).

125. Money, quoted in Pally (1994), p. 51.

126. Grant (1993), p. 8.

127. Nina Hartley's responds as follows to the blatant paternalism exhibited by the antiporn feminists:

> Excuse me. I'm sorry you're troubled that I want something in there. It doesn't have to be a dick, but, actually, penises feel pretty good (quoted in Stoller & Levine, 1993, p. 162).

See also Joan Nestle's imaginatively titled essay, "My Mother Liked to Fuck."

128. MacKinnon (1993), p. 17. See R. Dworkin (1993) for a thorough critique of MacKinnon's *Only Words*.

129. Even if pornography were classified as conduct rather than speech, this would not necessarily invalidate an appeal to the First Amendment. The civil rights movement (which included sit-ins and freedom marches) clearly demonstrated that First Amendment protection can be extended to conduct (e.g., *NAACP v. Alabama*).

130. ". . . nor shall any State deprive any person of life, liberty, or property, without due process of law; nor deny to any person within its jurisdiction the equal protection of the laws . . ."

131. Of course, free speech has not always prevailed, even in the United States. A mere seven years after the First Amendment was ratified, Congress passed the Alien and Sedition Acts (1798). These acts were motivated in large part by the fearful prospects of war with France. Aliens, namely Frenchmen, and critics of the government (again, Frenchmen) were deemed threatening to the internal security of the United States. The Alien Enemies Act allowed the president to deport "dangerous" aliens. The Sedition Act, in turn, made it illegal to write, print, or publish "any false, scandalous and malicious writing . . . against the government of the United States, or either house of the Congress . . . or the President . . . with the intent to defame . . . or to bring them . . . into contempt or disrepute . . ." So much for free speech. In fact, shortly after its passage, Matthew Lyon, a congressman from Vermont, was convicted under the Sedition Act and imprisoned for four months for accusing President John Adams of "an unbounded thirst for ridiculous pomp, foolish adulation, and selfish avarice" (Zinn, 1990).

132. Shiffrin (1990), p. 5.

133. See Meiklejohn (1960).

134. See Cohen (1985).

135. See de Grazia (1992).

136. It is important to note that First Amendment protection extends to the listener (reader, etc.) no less than to the speaker (author, etc.). Ultimately, there can be no free speech without access and exposure to opinions, dissenting and otherwise. The unrestricted dissemination of ideas is required to bring home the "power for the people" that free speech represents.

137. Kalven (1960). According to de Grazia (1992):

> Through the first quarter of the twentieth century, neither Holmes, Brandeis, the Hands, nor Chafee had been able to see that prosecutions of publishers or distributors of allegedly obscene literature, or interference with the use of the mails to distribute such literature, implicated free speech values and conceivably violated constitutional law. (p. 216)

138. By today's standards, Roth's publications were unquestionably benign, and would certainly be constitutionally protected.

139. de Grazia (1992), pp. 322–23.

140. Kalven (1960), p. 43.

141. Kalven (1960), p. 13.

142. Chafee (1920), quoted in de Grazia (1992), p. 216 (emphasis added).

143. Richards (1974).

144. The same conclusion was reached by William Lockhart and Paul Bender (chair and general counsel, respectively, of 1970's National Commission on Obscenity and Pornography).

145. The judicial concept of "original intent" presumes that the Constitution should be interpreted according to the discernable intentions of its formulators (or adopters). Original intent, when discernable, is given Constitutional interpretive priority. The problem, of course, is discerning what the Constitutional formulators and adopters intended. As Leonard Levy (1988) notes:

> For several decades after the ratification of the Constitution the fading memories of those who had attended the Philadelphia Constitutional Convention supplied the main evidence of the Framers' intent. Even when those memories were fresh, the Framers disagreed vehemently about what the Convention had meant or intended. (p. ix)

146. Quoted in Clark (1983), p. 57.

147. *Kingsley International Pictures Corp. v. Regents,* 360 U.S. 684 (1959).

148. L.R. 3 Q.B. 360, p. 371 (1868).

149. Lockhart & McClure (1954).

150. Kalven (1960), p. 15.

151. Kalven (1960), p. 15.

152. The *persecution* value of the state standard is also high, in that it can force the distributors of pornography into continuous trials in "conservative" states, with the ultimate purpose of exhausting the legal resources of such distributors, and thereby forcing them out of business.

153. Kalven (1960), p. 4.

154. Hunt (1977). Laumann, Gagnon, Michael, & Michaels (1994) report that 37 percent of the men and 58 percent of the women that they surveyed had masturbated at least once during the past year. Nearly 27 percent of the men admitted masturbating weekly.

155. Elmer-Dewitt (1993).

8. Epilogue: The Future of Sex

1. Although sex hormone chewing gum remains a fiction, a Los Angeles company has announced the next best thing, LOVE gum, touted as "a full-potency gum to increase romantic power" (Harvey, 1994).

2. A return to conservative sexual morality is evident in the following rather surprising disavowal by guitarist Eric Clapton: "It sounds strange for me to be

saying this, but I've come around to the idea that sex really *is* just for procreation" (*Us*, May 1994, p. 96).

3. Laqueur (1990); McLaren (1984, 1985).

4. Philo (fifth century A.D.), quoted in Laqueur (1990), p. 3.

5. See Laqueur (1990) for an extensive analysis of the single-sex model.

6. Aristotle (1972), quoted in McLaren (1985), p. 326.

7. Samuel Farr (1815), quoted in McLaren (1985), p. 332.

8. Laqueur (1990); McLaren (1985).

9. Laqueur (1990), p. 3.

10. See, for example, Grant (1994).

11. Vonnegut, 1988, p. 36.

12. Vonnegut, 1988, p. 29.

13. Vonnegut, 1988, p. 45.

14. McLaren (1985).

15. Huxley, 1932, p. 43.

16. Interested readers might want to check out the (somewhat outdated) *Joy of Cybersex* (Robinson & Tamosaitis, 1993), the self-proclaimed "underground guide to electronic erotica."

17. Many of the numbers reported here are drawn from an excellent *New York Times* article, "Wall Street Meets Pornography" (Egan, 2000), which discusses the surprising infiltration of major U.S. corporations into the adult entertainment business.

18. Egan (2000).

19. Dibbell (1999).

20. One of the most popular CD-ROMS from the 1990s is *Virtual Valerie,* in which the user interacts with a more-than-willing animated image known as Valerie. Another well-known program follows the adventures of *Leisure Suit Larry,* a thirty-nine-year-old male virgin (really, a bit of a geek) in search of sex.

21. Robinson & Tamosaitis (1993), p. 31.

22. Robinson & Tamosaitis (1993).

23. Home is heaven and orgies are vile,
   But you need an orgy, once in a while.
   —Ogden Nash, *Primrose Path* (1935).

24. Kim & Bailey (1997).

25. Cooper & Sportolari (1997).

26. Referring to online chat exchanges between gay men, David Shaw (1997) suggests, "These fantasy texts thrive in the absence of the other user. The other is imagined and his text becomes a mere prop for the desires of the user" (p. 142).

27. Gotthelf (1999).

28. Cusack (1996).

29. Elmer-Dewitt & Dowell (1995); Kim & Bailey (1997).

30. Kim & Bailey (1997).

31. Toomey & Rothenberg (2000).

32. Klausner, Wolf, Fischer-Ponce, Zolt, & Katz (2000).

33. McFarlane, Bull, & Rietmeijer (2000).

34. Apparently, Dr. Cooper's center is in the British section of San Jose, hence the alternate spelling of "centre."

35. Cooper, Scherer, Boies, & Gordon (1999).

36. Obviously, there is enormous potential for self-selection bias in asking people whether they are interested in completing a survey on their online sexual habits. What type of people are likely to agree to do so?

37. Check out the "naughty linx" at www.naughty.com.

38. Goldberg (1998).

39. Egan (2000).

40. Dibbell (1999); Egan (2000).

41. One adult site, Danni's Hard Drive, grossed more than $3.5 million in 1998 (Dibbell, 1999).

42. Even more intricate scenarios can be concocted. Real people, for example, could have virtual sex in cyberspace. That is, users could interact with each other rather than with computer-simulated partners. The action would thus be real, but the appearances would be fantasy.

43. Dibbell (1999).

44. Of course, the separation of sex and emotion is nothing new. "There was Germain and there was that rosebush of hers. I liked them separately and I liked them together" (Miller, 1961, p. 44).

45. There is obviously a risk in encouraging a view of sex as a male entitlement. Some feminists argue that pornography fosters a sense of male dominance in sexual relationships (i.e., that men believe they have a right to orgasm whenever they want to, and that women must assent to their demands). Cybersex invites male control and, by providing a more realistic sexual environment, may lead to a blurring of the distinction between fantasy and reality.

46. Although this might seem to be a utopian fantasy to some men, as we discussed in great detail in the previous chapter, far fewer women than men are fans of visual pornography. (Online, women are more likely to spend their time in chat rooms, rather than perusing the thumbnail galleries.) Moreover, fewer women masturbate, and those who do tend to do so less frequently than men. All of this suggests that women might be less than enthusiastic about the future of virtual sex.

Appendix B: A Mathematical Model of HIV Transmission

1. Pinkerton & Abramson (1993a, 1998). See also Eisenberg (1989); Hearst & Hulley (1988); Reiss & Leik (1989).

2. Grant, Wiley, & Winkelstein (1987); Padian (1990); Mastro & de Vincenzi (1996); Royce, Sena, Cates, & Cohen (1997). Infectivity estimates as high as 0.1 have been reported for unprotected anal intercourse (Grant, Wiley, & Winkelstein, 1987), although most estimates suggest an infectivity one-tenth as large.

3. See Pinkerton & Abramson (1993a, 1994, 1998) for complete details on the Bernoulli process model of HIV transmission.

4. Laga, Nzila, & Goeman (1991); Wasserheit (1992). The epidemological impact of various transmission cofactors is examined in Abramson & Rothschild (1988).

5. Pinkerton and Abramson (1997b) conducted a metanalysis of studies of HIV transmission in couples where one partner is infected and the other is not, in order to determine the effectiveness of condoms in preventing the transmission of HIV. By comparing transmission rates among couples who consistently used condoms and those who used them inconsistently (if at all), this analysis indicated that condoms are 90–95 percent effective in preventing the transmission of HIV. However, these figures underestimate the true effectiveness of condoms because inconsistent condom users were classed together with non-users, despite evidence that even inconsistent condom use can have a protective effect (see Pinkerton and Abramson, 1996). Moreover, these estimates include user failures as well as so-called product failures. When condoms are used *consistently and correctly,* they are nearly 100 percent effective (Centers for Disease Control, 1993).

6. See Pinkerton & Abramson (1993a, 1998).

7. Pinkerton & Abramson (1993a, 1997a); Reiss & Leik (1989).

8. Bauman & Siegel (1987), p. 342.

References

Aboulker, J.-P. & Swart, A. M. (1993). Preliminary analysis of the Concorde trial. *Lancet, 341*, 889–890.

Abramson, P. R. (1973). The relationship of the frequency of masturbation to several aspects of personality and behavior. *The Journal of Sex Research, 9*, 132–142.

Abramson, P. R. (1990). Sexual science: Emerging discipline or oxymoron? *The Journal of Sex Research, 27*, 147–165.

Abramson, P. R. & Handschumacher, I. W. (1978). Experimenter effects on response to double-entendre words: Some additional implications for sex research. *Journal of Personality Assessment, 42*, 592–596.

Abramson, P. R. & Hayashi, H. (1984). Pornography in Japan. In N. M. Malamuth & E. Donnerstein (eds.), *Pornography and Sexual Aggression*. New York: Academic Press.

Abramson, P. R. & Mosher, D. L. (1975). The development of a measure of negative attitudes toward masturbation. *Journal of Consulting and Clinical Psychology, 43*, 485–490.

Abramson, P. R. & Mosher, D. L. (1979). An empirical investigation of experimentally induced masturbatory fantasies. *Archives of Sexual Behavior, 8*, 27–39.

Abramson, P. R., Perry, L. B., Rothblatt, A., Seeley, T. T., & Seeley, D. M. (1981). Negative attitudes toward masturbation and pelvic vasocongestion: A thermographic analysis. *Journal of Research in Personality, 15*, 497–509.

Abramson, P. R., Perry, L. B., Seeley, T. T., Seeley, D. M. & Rothblatt, A. (1981). Thermographic measurement of sexual arousal: A discriminant validity analysis. *Archives of Sexual Behavior, 10*, 171–176.

Abramson, P. R. & Pinkerton, S. D. (eds.) (1995). *Sexual Nature / Sexual Culture*. Chicago: University of Chicago Press.

Abramson, P. R. & Pinkerton, S. D. (1995). Nature, nurture, and in-between. In P. R. Abramson & S. D. Pinkerton (eds.), *Sexual Nature / Sexual Culture*. Chicago: University of Chicago Press.

Abramson, P. R. & Rothschild, B. (1988). Mathematical prediction of HIV infection. *The Journal of Sex Research*, *25*, 106–122.

Acker, K. (1978). *Blood and Guts in High School*. New York: Grove Weidenfeld.

Acton, W. (1857). *The Functions and Disorders of the Reproductive Organs*. London: Churchill.

Adler, P. (1953). *A House Is Not a Home*. New York: Rinehart.

Alexander, C. J., Sipski, M. L., & Findley, T. W. (1993). Sexual activities, desire, and satisfaction in males pre- and post-spinal cord injury. *Archives of Sexual Behavior*, *22*, 217–228.

Alexander, D. (1992). Condom controversy: Suggestive Kama Sutra ads arouse India. *Advertising Age*, *63*, 112.

Allen, L. S., Hines, M., Shryne, J. E., & Gorski, R. A. (1989). Two sexually dimorphic cell groups in the human brain. *Journal of Neuroscience*, *9*, 497–506.

Anderson, J. E., Wilson, R., Doll, L., Jones, T. S., & Barker, P. (1999). Condom use and HIV risk behaviors among U.S. adults: Data from a national survey. *Family Planning Perspectives, 31,* 24–28.

Apostle, H. G. & Gerson, L. P. (1986) (trans.). *Aristotle's Politics*. Grinnell, IA: The Peripatetic Press.

Aral, S. O. & Holmes, K. K. (1991). Sexually transmitted diseases in the AIDS era. *Scientific American*, *264*, 62–69.

Arendt, H. (1963). *Eichmann and Jerusalem: A Report on the Banality of Evil*. New York: Viking Press.

Aristophanes (1948). *Five Comedies*. Cleveland: World Publishing Co.

Aristotle (1962). *Nicomachean Ethics* (M. Ostwald, trans.). New York: Macmillan.

Aristotle (1972). *De Partibus Animalium I and De Generatione Animalium I* (D. M. Balme, trans.). Oxford: Clarendon.

Aron, A. & Aron, E. N. (1991). Love and sexuality. In K. McKinney & S. Sprecher (eds.), *Sexuality in Close Relationships*. Hillsdale, NJ: Lawrence Erlbaum.

Baddeley, A. (1990). *Human Memory: Theory and Practice*. Boston: Allyn and Bacon.

Bailey, A. S. & Greenberg, J. M. (1993). Do biological explanations of homosexuality have moral, legal, or policy implications? *The Journal of Sex Research*, *30*, 245–251.

Bailey, J. M. & Benishay, D. S. (1993). Familial aggregation of female sexual orientation. *American Journal of Psychiatry*, *150*, 272–277.

Bailey, J. M. & Pillard, R. C. (1991). A genetic study of male sexual orientation. *Archives of General Psychiatry*, *48*, 1089–1096.

Bailey, J. M., Pillard, R. C., Neale, M. C., & Agyei, Y. (1993). Heritable factors influence sexual orientation in women. *Archives of General Psychiatry*, *50*, 217–223.

Barker-Benfield, G. J. (1973). The spermatic economy: A nineteenth century view of sexuality. In M. Gordon (ed.), *The American Family in Social-Historical Perspective*. New York: St. Martin's Press.

Barker-Benfield, G. J. (1976). *Horrors of the Half-Known Life*. New York: Harper Colophon.

Barkow, J. H. (1980). Sociobiology: Is this the new theory of human nature? In A. Montagu (ed.), *Sociobiology Examined*. New York: Oxford University Press.

Baron, L. (1987). Immoral, inviolate or inconclusive? *Society, 24*, 6–12.

Bataille, G. (1986). *Eroticism: Death and Sensuality*. San Francisco: City Light Books.

Bauman, L. J. & Siegel, K. (1987). Misperception among gay men of the risk for AIDS associated with their sexual behavior. *Journal of Applied Social Psychology, 17*, 329–350.

Beach, F. A. (1947). Evolutionary changes in the physiological control of mating behavior in mammals. *Psychological Review, 54*, 297–315.

Beach, F. A. (1974). Human sexuality and evolution. In W. Montagna & W. A. Sader (eds.), *Reproductive Behavior*. New York: Plenum.

Beach, F. A. (1976). Cross-species comparisons and the human heritage. *Archives of Sexual Behavior, 5*, 469–485.

Bechtel, W. (1988). *Philosophy of Mind: An Overview for Cognitive Science*. Hillsdale, NJ: Lawrence Erlbaum.

Benedicti, J. (1601). *Somme des Peches*. Paris.

Berk, R., Abramson, P. R., & Okami, P. (1995). Sexual activity as told in surveys. In P. R. Abramson & S. D. Pinkerton (eds.), *Sexual Nature / Sexual Culture*. Chicago: University of Chicago Press.

Berkowitz, R. & Callen, M. (1983). *How To Have Sex in an Epidemic: One Approach*. New York: Tower Press.

Bermant, G. (1976). Sexual behavior: Hard times with the Coolidge effect. In M. H. Siegel & H. P. Zeigler (eds.), *Psychological Research: The Inside Story*. New York: Harper & Row.

Bernstein, S. (1992). Restrictions a barrier for condom ads. *Los Angeles Times*, January 25.

Binson, D., Michaels, S., Stall, R., Coates, T. J., Gagnon, J. H., & Catania, J. A. (1995). Prevalence and social distribution of men who have sex with men: United States and its urban centers. *Journal of Sex Research, 32*, 245–254.

Blackwood, E. (1984). Sexuality and gender in certain North American tribes: The case of cross-gender females. *Signs: Journal of Women in Culture and Society, 10*, 27–42.

Blake, W. (1988). *Selected Poetry*. London: Penguin.

Block, N. (1980). Are absent qualia impossible? *Philosophical Review, 89*, 257–274.

Block, N. & Fodor, J. (1972). What psychological states are not. *Philosophical Review, 81*, 159–181.

Blumer, D. & Walker, A. E. (1975). The neural basis of sexual behavior. In D. F. Benson & D. Blumer (eds.), *Psychiatric Aspects of Neurological Disease*. New York: Grune and Stratton.

Bogart, L. M., Cecil, H., Wagstaff, D. A., Pinkerton, S. D., & Abramson, P. R. (2000). Is it "sex"? *Journal of Sex Research, 37*, 108–116.

Bolin, A. (1994). Transcending and transgendering: Male-to-female transsexuals, dichotomy and diversity. In G. Herdt (ed.), *Third Sex, Third Gender*. New York: Zone Books.

Bolton, R. (1992). AIDS and promiscuity. *Medical Anthropology, 14*, 145–223.

Bongaarts, J. (1994). Can the growing human population feed itself? *Scientific American, 270*, 36–42.

Boswell, J. (1980). *Christianity, Social Tolerance, and Homosexuality*. Chicago: University of Chicago Press.

Bouscaren, T. L. & Ellis, A. C. (1951). *Canon Law: A Text and Commentary*. Milwaukee: Bruce Publishing.

Brandt, A. M. (1985). *No Magic Bullet: A Social History of Venereal Disease in the United States*. Oxford: Oxford University Press.

Broun, H. & Leech, M. (1927). *Anthony Comstock, Roundsman of the Lord*. New York: A. & C. Boni.

Brown, D. E. (1991). *Human Universals*. Philadelphia: Temple University Press.

Brown, J. A. C. (1961). *Freud and the Post-Freudians*. New York: Penguin Books.

Brown, W. J., Donohue, J. F., Axnick, N. W., Blount, J. H., Ewen, N. H., & Jones, O. G. (1970). *Syphilis and Other Venereal Diseases*. Cambridge, MA: Harvard University Press.

Brownmiller, S. (1975). *Against Our Will: Men, Women and Rape*. New York: Simon and Schuster.

Buhrich, N. J., Bailey, J. M., & Martin, N. G. (1991). Sexual orientation, sexual identity, and sex-dimorphic behavior in male twins. *Behavioral Genetics, 21*, 75–96.

Bull, S. S. & McFarlane, M. (2000). Soliciting sex on the internet: What are the risks for sexually transmitted diseases and HIV? *Sexually Transmitted Diseases, 27*, 545–550.

Bullough, V. L. (1967). *Sexual Variance in Society and History*. New York: Wiley.

Bullough, V. L. (1976). Attitudes toward deviant sex in ancient Mesopotamia. In V. L. Bullough, *Sex, Society, and History*. New York: Science History Publications.

Bullough, V. L. (1982). The sin against nature and homosexuality. In V. L. Bullough & J. Brundage (eds.), *Sexual Practices & the Medieval Church*. Buffalo, NY: Prometheus Books.

Bullough, V. L. (1994). *Science in the Bedroom: A History of Sex Research*. New York: Basic Books.

Bullough, V. L. & Bullough, B. L. (1964). *The History of Prostitution*. New Hyde Park, NY: University Books.

Burnham, J. C. (1973). The progressive era revolution in American attitudes toward sex. *The Journal of American History, 59*, 885–908.

Burr, C. (1993). Homosexuality and biology. *Atlantic Monthly, March*, 47–65.

Buss, D. M. (1994). *The Evolution of Desire*. New York: Basic Books.

Byne, W. (1994). The biological evidence challenged. *Scientific American*, *270*, 50–55.

Byrne, D. & Schulte, L. (1990). Personality dispositions as mediators of sexual responses. *Annual Review of Sex Research*, *1*, 93–117.

Callendar, C. & Kochems, L. M. (1983). The North American Indian berdache. *Current Anthropology*, *24*, 444–446.

Carnes, P. (1983). *Out of the Shadows: Understanding Sexual Addiction*. Minneapolis: CompCare Publications.

Carrier, J. M. (1980). Homosexual behavior in cross-cultural perspective. In J. Marmor (ed.), *Homosexual Behavior: A Modern Reappraisal*. New York: Basic Books.

Catania, J. A., Coates, T. J., Stall, R., Turner, H., Peterson, J., Hearst, N., Dolcini, M. M., Hudes, E., Gagnon, J., & Groves, R. (1992). Prevalence of AIDS-related risk factors and condom use in the United States. *Science*, *258*, 1101–1106.

Centers for Disease Control (1993). Update: Barrier protection against HIV infection and other sexually transmitted diseases. *Morbidity and Mortality Weekly Report*, *42*, 589–591.

Centers for Disease Control and Prevention (1999). *HIV/AIDS Surveillance Report*, *11*, 1–45.

Chafee, Z. Jr. (1920). *Freedom of Speech*. New York: Harcourt Brace and Howe.

Chandler, R. (1940/1964). *The Raymond Chandler Omnibus*. New York: Knopf.

Chapman, S. & Hodgson, J. (1988). Showers in raincoats: Attitudinal barriers to condom use in high-risk heterosexuals. *Community Health Studies*, *12*, 97–105.

Chomsky, N. (1975). *Reflections on Language*. New York: Pantheon.

Chomsky, N. (1980). *Rules and Representations*. New York: Columbia University Press.

Churchland, P. M. (1990). *Matter and Consciousness*. Cambridge, MA: MIT Press.

Clark, R. W. (1983). *Benjamin Franklin: A Biography*. New York: Random House.

Clark, W. E. L. (1965). *History of Primates*. Chicago: University of Chicago Press.

Cochran, S. D. & Mays, V. M. (1990). Sex, lies, and HIV. *New England Journal of Medicine*, *322*, 774–775.

Cohen, D. J. & Bruce, K. E. (1997). Sex and mortality: Real risk and perceived vulnerability. *Journal of Sex Research*, *34*, 279–291.

Cohen, I. B. (1985). *Revolution in Science*. Cambridge: Belknap Press.

Cohen, J. B. (1989). Condom promotion among prostitutes. *Condoms in the Prevention of STD*, December, 45–47.

Cohen, L. (1995). The pleasures of castration: The post-operative status of hijras, jankhas, and academics. In P. R. Abramson & S. D. Pinkerton (eds.), *Sexual Nature / Sexual Culture*. Chicago: University of Chicago Press.

Coleman, E. (1982). Changing approaches to the treatment of homosexuality: A review. In W. Paul, J. D. Weinrich, J. C. Gonsiorek, & M. E. Hotvedt (eds.), *Homosexuality: Social, Psychological, and Biological Issues*. Beverly Hills: Sage.

Coleman, E. (1991). Compulsive sexual behavior: New concepts and treatments. In E. Coleman (ed.), *John Money: A Tribute*. New York: Haworth Press.

Coleman, E., Colgan, P. & Gooren, L. (1992). Male cross-gender behavior in Myanmar (Burma): A description of the acault. *Archives of Sexual Behavior, 21*, 313–321.

Comfort, A. (1967). *The Anxiety Makers: Some Curious Preoccupations of the Medical Profession*. New York: Dell.

Cominos, P. T. (1963). Late Victorian sexual respectability and the social system. *International Review of Social History, 8*, 18–48 and 216–250.

Commins, D. & Yahr, P. (1984). Adult testosterone levels influence the morphology of a sexually dimorphic area in the Mongolian gerbil brain. *Journal of Comparative Neurology, 224*, 132–140.

Connell, R. W. & Kippax, S. (1990). Sexuality in the AIDS crisis: Patterns of sexual practice and pleasure in a sample of Australian gay and bisexual men. *The Journal of Sex Research, 27*, 167–198.

Connelly, M. T. (1980). *The Response to Prostitution in the Progressive Era*. Chapel Hill, NC: University of North Carolina Press.

Consumer Reports (1979). Condoms: A report based on laboratory tests and questionnaires filled out by nearly 1,900 readers. *Consumer Reports, 44*, 583–589.

Cooper, A., Scherer, C. R., Boies, S. C., & Gordon, B. L. (1999). Sexuality on the internet: From sexual exploration to pathological expression. *Professional Psychology: Research and Practice, 30*, 154–164.

Cooper, A. & Sportalari, L. (1997). Romance in cyberspace: Understanding online attraction. *Journal of Sex Education and Therapy, 22*, 7–14.

Cosmides, L. & Tooby, J. (1987). From evolution to behavior: Evolutionary psychology as the missing link. In J. Dupre (ed.), *The Latest on the Best: Essays on Evolution and Optimality*. Cambridge, MA: MIT Press.

Cottingham, L. (1984). Anti-porn and its discontents. *New York Native, December 3—16*, 24.

Crimp, D. (1988). How to have promiscuity in an epidemic. In D. Crimp (ed.), *AIDS: Cultural Analysis, Cultural Activism*. Cambridge, MA: MIT Press.

Crews, D. (1994). Animal sexuality. *Scientific American, 270*, 108–114.

Cusack, J. (1996). The murky world of internet porn: The "Orchid Club" shakes up the law. *World Press Review, 43*, 8–10.

Dagg, A. I. (1984). Homosexual behaviour and female-male mounting in mammals—a first survey. *Mammal Reviews, 14*, 155–185.

Daly, M. & Wilson, M. (1988). *Homicide*. New York: Aldine de Gruyter.

Dante Alighieri (1321/1981). *The Divine Comedy*. London: Pan Books.

Darwin, C. (1872/1979). *The Expression of Emotions in Man and Animals*. New York: Saint Martins / Friedmann.

Darwin, C. (1905). *My Life* (volume 1). London: Chapman & Hall.

Darwin, F. (1892). *The Autobiography of Charles Darwin and Selected Letters*. New York: D. Appleton & Co.

Davenport, W. H. (1977). Sex in cross-cultural perspective. In F. A. Beach (ed.), *Human Sexuality in Four Perspectives*. Baltimore: The Johns Hopkins University Press.

Dawkins, R. (1976). *The Selfish Gene*. Oxford: Oxford University Press.

De Cecco, J. P. (1990). Confusing the actor with the act: Muddled notions about homosexuality. *Archives of Sexual Behavior, 19*, 409–412.

de Grazia, E. (1992). *Girls Lean Back Everywhere: The Law of Obscenity and the Assault on Genius*. New York: Vintage.

D'Emilio, J. & Freedman, E. B. (1988). *Intimate Matters: A History of Sexuality in America*. New York: Harper & Row.

Dennett, D. C. (1991). *Consciousness Explained*. Boston: Little, Brown and Company.

Denniston, R. H. (1980). Ambisexuality in animals. In J. Marmor (ed.), *Homosexual Behavior: A Modern Reappraisal*. New York: Basic Books.

Descartes, R. (1969). *The Essential Descartes* (M. D. Wilson, ed.). New York: New American Library.

Devereaux, G. (1937). Institutionalized homosexuality of the Mohave indians. *Human Biology, 9*, 498–527.

de Vroome, E., Sandfort, T., & Tielman, R. (1992). Overestimating the risk of oral genital sex may increase unsafe anogenital sex. Presented at the *VII International Conference on AIDS*, Amsterdam, Netherlands, July 19–24. *Abstract PoD5125*.

Dewhurst, K. (1982). *Hughlings Jackson on Psychiatry*. Oxford: Sanford Publications.

Dibbell, J. (1999). The body electric. *Time Magazine Digital Supplement, April 12*, 25–28.

Dilley, J. W., Wood, W. J., & McFarland, W. (1997). Are advances in treatment changing views about high-risk sex? *New England Journal of Medicine, 337*, 501–502.

Dörner, G. & Hinz, G. (1968). Induction and prevention of male homosexuality by androgens. *Journal of Endocrinology, 40*, 387–388.

Dover, K. J. (1978). *Greek Homosexuality*. Cambridge, MA: Harvard University Press.

Downey, J., Erhardt, A. A., Schiffman, M., Dyrenfurth, I., & Becker, J. (1987). Sex hormones and lesbian and heterosexual women. *Hormones and Behavior, 21*, 347–357.

Duffey, E. B. (1876). *The Relation of the Sexes*. New York: Wood and Holbrook.

Duggan, L., Hunter, N., & Vance, C. S. (1985). False promises: Feminist antipornography legislation in the U.S. In V. Burstyn (ed.), *Women Against Censorship*. Vancouver, BC: Douglas & McIntyre.

Dworkin, A. (1985). Against the male flood: Censorship, pornography and equality. *Harvard Women's Journal, 8*, 1–23.

Dworkin, A. (1987a). *Ice and Fire*. New York: Grove Weidenfeld.

Dworkin, A. (1987b). *Intercourse*. New York: Free Press.

Dworkin, A. (1989). *Pornography: Men Possessing Women*. New York: Free Press.

Dworkin, R. (1993). Women and pornography. *New York Review of Books, October 21, 36–42.*

Egan, T. (2000). Wall street meets pornography. *New York Times, October 23.*

Ehrlich, P. R. & Ehrlich, A. H. (1990). *The Population Explosion.* New York: Simon & Schuster.

Eibl-Eibesfeldt, I. (1975). *Ethology: The Biology of Behavior.* New York: Holt, Rinehart and Winston.

Eisenberg, B. (1989). The number of partners and the probability of HIV infection. *Statistics in Medicine, 8, 83–92.*

Ellis, H. (1903). *Studies in the Psychology of Sex.* Philadelphia: Davis.

Ellman, R. (1988). *Oscar Wilde.* New York: Knopf.

Elmer-Dewitt, P. (1993). Orgies on-line. *Time, May 31, 61.*

Elmer-Dewitt, P. & Dowell, W. (1995). Fire storm on the computer nets: A new study of cyberporn, reported in a *Time* cover story, sparks controversy. *Time, July 24, 57–58.*

Elwin, V. (1968). *Kingdom of the Young.* Bombay: Oxford University Press.

Endleman, R. (1989). *Love and Sex in Twelve Cultures.* New York: Psyche Press.

Engels, F. (1942). *The Origin of the Family, Private Property, and the State.* New York: International Publishers.

Epstein, L. M. (1948). *Sex Laws and Customs in Judaism.* New York: Ktav Publishing.

Eribon, D. (1991). *Michel Foucault.* Cambridge, MA: Harvard University Press.

Evans-Pritchard, E. E. (1971). *The Azande.* Oxford: Claveudor.

Eysenck, H. J. (1976). *Sex and Personality.* Austin: University of Texas Press.

Faderman, L. (1991). *Odd Girls and Twilight Lovers.* New York: Penguin.

Farr, S. (1815). *Elements of Medical Jurisprudence.* London.

Faust, B. (1980). *Women, Sex, and Pornography: A Controversial and Unique Study.* New York: Macmillan.

Feldblum, P. J. & Rosenberg, M. J. (1989). A historical perspective on condoms. *Condoms in the Prevention of STD, December, 1–3.*

Fenichel, O. (1945). *The Psychoanalytic Theory of Neurosis.* New York: Norton.

Fisher, H. (1982). *The Sex Contract: The Evolution of Human Behavior.* New York: Quill Press.

Fisher, H. E. (1992). *Anatomy of Love: The Natural History of Monogamy, Adultery, and Divorce.* New York: Norton.

Fisher, S. (1973). *The Female Orgasm.* New York: Basic Books.

Fisher, W. A. (1980). *Erotophobia-erotophilia and Performance in a Human Sexuality Course.* Unpublished manuscript, University of Western Ontario.

Fisher, W. A. & Byrne, D. (1978). Individual differences in affective, evaluative, and behavioral responses to an erotic film. *Journal of Applied Social Psychology, 8,* 355–365.

Fitts, D. (1938) (trans.). *One Hundred Poems from the Palatine Anthology.* Norfolk, CT: New Directions.

Flandrin, J.-L. (1985). Sex in married life in the early Middle Ages: The church's teaching and behavioural reality. In P. Ariès & A. Béjin (eds.), *Western Sexuality: Practice and Precept in Past and Present Times*. Oxford: Blackwell.

Fleming, W. L. (1964). Syphilis through the ages. *Medical Clinics of North America, 48*, 587–612.

Fodor, J. A. (1981). *Representations: Philosophical Essays on the Foundations of Cognitive Science*. Cambridge, MA: MIT Press.

Fodor, J. A. (1983). *The Modularity of Mind*. Cambridge, MA: MIT Press.

Fodor, J. A. & Pylyshyn, Z. W. (1988). Connectionism and cognitive architecture: A critical analysis. In S. Pinker & J. Mehler (eds.), *Connections and Symbols*. Cambridge, MA: MIT Press.

Ford, C. S. & Beach, F. A. (1951). *Patterns of Sexual Behavior*. New York: Harper & Row.

Foucault, M. (1985). *The Use of Pleasure*. New York: Random House.

Foucault, M. (1986). *The Care of the Self*. New York: Vintage.

Foucault, M. (1990). *The History of Sexuality*. New York: Vintage.

Fox, R. (1967). *Kinship and Marriage*. Cambridge: Cambridge University Press.

Fox, R. (1975). Primate kin and human kinship. In R. Fox (ed.), *Biosocial Anthropology*. London: Malaby Press.

Freedman, E. B. (1982). Sexuality in nineteenth-century America: Behavior, ideology, and politics. *Reviews in American History, 10*, 196–215.

Freeman, D. (1983). *Margaret Mead and Samoa: The Making and Unmaking of an Anthropological Myth*. Cambridge, MA: Harvard University Press.

Freud, S. (1905/1962). *Three Essays on the Theory of Sexuality* (J. Strachey, ed. and trans.). New York: Basic Books.

Freud, S. (1908/1963). "Civilized" sexual morality and modern nervousness. In *Sexuality and the Psychology of Love* (P. Rieff, ed.). New York: Collier Books.

Freud, S. (1910/1961). *Leonardo da Vinci and a Memory of His Childhood* (A. Tyson, trans., and J. Strachey, ed.). New York: W. W. Norton.

Freud, S. (1912/1958). Contributions to a discussion on masturbation. In *The Standard Edition of the Complete Psychological Works of Sigmund Freud* (J. Strachey, ed. and trans.). London: The Hogarth Press.

Freud, S. (1918). *Totem and Taboo*. New York: Knopf.

Freud, S. (1920). *A General Introduction to Psychoanalysis*. New York: Boni and Liveright.

Freud, S. (1927/1963). Fetishism. In *Sexuality and the Psychology of Love* (P. Rieff, ed.). New York: Collier Books.

Freud, S. (1935). *An Autobiographical Study*. New York: W. W. Norton.

Freud, S. (1938). *The Basic Writings of Sigmund Freud*. New York: The Modern Library.

Freud, S. (1943). *A General Introduction to Psychoanalysis*. Garden City, NY: Garden City Publishing.

Freud, S. (1965). Being in love and hypnosis. In *Group Psychology and the Analysis of the Ego*. New York: Bantam Books.

Gagnon, M.-P. & Godin, G. (2000). The impact of new antiretroviral treatments on college students' intentions to use a condom with a new sexual partner. *AIDS Education and Prevention, 12,* 233–251.

Galbraith, G. G., Hahn, K., & Lieberman, H. (1968). Personality correlates of free-associative sex responses to double-entendre words. *Journal of Consulting and Clinical Psychology, 32,* 193–197.

Galbraith, G. G. & Mosher, D. L. (1968). Associative sexual responses in relation to sexual arousal, guilt and external approval contingencies. *Journal of Personality and Social Psychology, 10,* 142–147.

Gamson, J. (1990). Rubber wars: Struggles over the condom in the United States. *Journal of the History of Sexuality, 1,* 262–282.

Gardiner, H. C. (1955). Moral principles toward a definition of the obscene. *Law & Contemporary Problems, 20,* 560–571.

Gardner, J. & Maier, J. (1984). *Gilgamesh.* New York: Knopf.

Garrett, L. (1992). The next epidemic. In J. Mann, D. J. M. Tarantola, & T. W. Netter (eds.), *AIDS in the World.* Cambridge, MA: Harvard University Press.

Gartrell, N. K. (1982). Hormones and homosexuality. In W. Paul, J. D. Weinrich, J. C. Gonsiorek, & M. E. Hotvedt (eds.), *Homosexuality: Social, Psychological, and Biological Issues.* Beverly Hills: Sage.

Gerrard, M. & Reis, T. J. (1989). Retention of contraceptive and AIDS information in the classroom. *The Journal of Sex Research, 26,* 315–323.

Gilbert, M. A., Bauman, K. E., & Udry, J. R. (1986). A panel study of subjective expected utility for adolescent sexual behavior. *Journal of Applied Social Psychology, 16,* 745–756.

Gladue, B. A., Green, R., & Hellman, R. E. (1984). Neuroendocrine response to estrogen and sexual orientation. *Science, 115,* 1496–1499.

Gladwell, M. (1992). A matter of condom sense. *Washington Post,* April 9.

Glick, R. A. & Bone, S. (1990). *Pleasure beyond the Pleasure Principle.* New Haven: Yale University Press.

Glass, S. J., Denel, H. J., & Wright, C. A. (1940). Sex hormone studies in male homosexuality. *Endocrinology, 26,* 590–594.

Goethe, J. W. v. (1961). *Faust* (W. Kaufmann, trans.). New York: Doubleday.

Goldberg, A. (1998). *Monthly Users Report on Adult Sexually Oriented Sites for April 1998.* Washington, DC: Relevant Knowledge.

Goldfarb, L., Gerrard, M., Gibbons, F. X., & Plante, T. (1988). Attitudes toward sex, arousal, and the retention of contraceptive information. *Journal of Personality and Social Psychology, 55,* 634–641.

Goldsmith, M. F. (1987). Sex in the age of AIDS calls for common sense and 'condom sense.' *Journal of the American Medical Association, 257,* 2261–2266.

Gordon, L. (1976). *Woman's Body, Woman's Right: A Social History of Birth Control in America.* New York: Grossman.

Gotthelf, M. (1999). Man accused of using net to lure boys. APBNews.com, *February 2.*

Gould, S. J. (1977). *Ever Since Darwin.* New York: Norton.

Gould, S. J. (1987). Freudian slip. *Natural History,* April, 14–21.

Grady, W. R., Klepinger, D. H., Billy, J. O. G., & Tanfer, K. (1993). Condom characteristics: The perceptions and preferences of men in the United States. *Family Planning Perspectives, 25,* 67–73.

Graham, S. (1834). *Lecture to Young Men on Chastity.* Providence, RI.

Grant, L. (1993). *Sexing the Millennium.* London: HarperCollins.

Grant, R. M., Wiley, J. A., & Winkelstein, W. (1987). Infectivity of the human immunodeficiency virus: Estimates from a prospective study of homosexual men. *Journal of Infectious Diseases, 156,* 189–193.

Grant, V. W. (1954). A problem in sex pathology. *American Journal of Psychiatry, 11,* 589–593.

Gray, A. (1946). *The Socialist Tradition.* London: Longmans, Green.

Green, R. (1985). Exposure to explicit sexual materials and sexual assault: A review of behavioral and social science research. Presented at the U.S. Justice Department Hearings, Houston, TX.

Green, R. (1987). *The "Sissy Boy" Syndrome and the Development of Homosexuality.* New Haven: Yale University Press.

Green, R. (1992). *Sexual Science and the Law.* Cambridge, MA: Harvard University Press.

Greenberg, D. F. (1988). *The Construction of Homosexuality.* Chicago: University of Chicago Press.

Greenberg, D. F. (1995). The pleasures of homosexuality. In P. R. Abramson & S. D. Pinkerton (eds.), *Sexual Nature / Sexual Culture.* Chicago: University of Chicago Press.

Gregor, T. (1985). *Anxious Pleasures: The Sexual Lives of an Amazonian People.* Chicago: University of Chicago Press.

Gregor, T. (1995). Sexuality and the experience of love. In P. R. Abramson & S. D. Pinkerton (eds.), *Sexual Nature / Sexual Culture.* Chicago: University of Chicago Press.

Griffin, D. R. (1976). *The Question of Animal Awareness: Evolutionary Continuity of Mental Experience.* New York: Rockefeller University Press.

Grube, G. M. A. (1935). *Plato's Thought.* London: Methuen & Co.

Hall, J. (1994). Networks slow to air condom ads. *Los Angeles Times, January 27.*

Hall, J. C. (1978). Courtship among males due to a male-sterile mutation in *Drosophila melanogaster. Behavior Genetics, 8,* 125–141.

Halperin, D. M. (1989). *One Hundred Years of Homosexuality and Other Essays on Greek Love.* New York: Routledge.

Halperin, D. M., Winkler, J. J. & Zeitlin, F. I. (1990). *Before Sexuality: The Construction of Erotic Experience in the Ancient Greek World.* Princeton: Princeton University Press.

Hamburg, B. A. (1978). The biosocial basis of sex differences. In S. L. Washburn & E. R. McCowan (eds.), *Human Evolution: Biosocial Perspectives.* Menlo Park, CA: Benjamin/Cummings.

Hamer, D. H., Hu, S., Magnuson, V. L., Hu, N., & Pattatucci, A. M. L. (1993). A linkage between DNA markers on the X chromosome and male sexual orientation. *Science, 261,* 321–327.

Hamilton, W. D. (1964). The genetical evolution of social behaviour (I and II). *Journal of Theoretical Biology, 7,* 1–16 and 17–52.

Hanson, A. E. (1990). The medical writers' woman. In D. M. Halperin, J. J. Winkler, & F. I. Zeitlin (eds.), *Before Sexuality: The Construction of Erotic Experience in the Ancient Greek World.* Princeton: Princeton University Press.

Hare, E. H. (1962). Masturbatory insanity: The history of an idea. *Journal of Mental Science, 108,* 1–25.

Harris, F. (1925). *My Life and Loves.* New York: Grove Weidenfeld.

Hart, B. L. (1986). Medial preoptic-anterior hypothalamic lesions and sociosexual behavior of male goats. *Physiology and Behavior, 36,* 301–305.

Harvey, P. H. & Krebs, J. R. (1990). Comparing brains. *Science, 249,* 140–146.

Harvey, S. (1994). Only in L.A. *Los Angeles Times, July 14.*

Hearst, N. & Hulley, S. B. (1988). Preventing the heterosexual spread of AIDS. *Journal of the American Medical Association, 259,* 2428–2432.

Heath, R. (1972). Pleasure and brain activity in man. *Journal of Nervous and Mental Disease, 154,* 3–18.

Heilbroner, R. L. (1986a). *The Essential Adam Smith.* New York: Norton.

Heilbroner, R. L. (1986b). *The Worldly Philosophers.* New York: Simon & Schuster.

Heim, N. & Hursch, C. J. (1979). Castration of sex offenders: Treatment or punishment? A review and critique of recent European literature. *Archives of Sexual Behavior, 8,* 281–303.

Heiman, J. (1976). *Becoming Orgasmic: A Sexual Growth Program for Women.* Englewood Cliffs, NJ: Prentice-Hall.

Heins, M. (1993). *Sex, Sin, and Blasphemy.* New York: The New Press.

Hendrick, S. S. & Hendrick, C. (1992). *Romantic Love.* Newbury Park, CA: Sage.

Herberg, L. J. (1963a). A hypothalamic mechanism causing seminal ejaculation. *Nature, 198,* 219–220.

Herberg, L. J. (1963b). Seminal ejaculation following positively reinforcing electrical stimulation of the rat hypothalamus. *Journal of Comparative and Physiological Psychology, 56,* 679–685.

Herdt, G. H. (1981). *Guardians of the Flute.* New York: McGraw-Hill.

Herdt, G. H. (1984). *Ritualized Homosexuality in Melanesia.* Berkeley: University of California Press.

Herdt, G. H. (1987). *The Sambia: Ritual and Gender in New Guinea.* New York: Holt, Rinehart & Winston.

Herdt, G. H. (1990a). Sambia nosebleeding rites and male proximity to women. In J. W. Stigler, R. A. Schweder, & G. Herdt (eds.), *Cultural Psychology.* New York: Cambridge University Press.

Herdt, G. H. (1990b). Mistaken gender: 5-alpha reductase hermaphroditism and biological reductionism in sexual identity reconsidered. *American Anthropologist, 92,* 433–446.

Herdt, G. H. (1990c). Developmental discontinuities and sexual orientation across cultures. In D. P. McWhirter, S. A. Sanders, & J. M. Reinisch (eds.), *Hetero-sexuality / Homosexuality*. New York: Oxford University Press.

Herdt, G. (ed.) (1994). *Third Sex, Third Gender*. New York: Zone Books.

Herdt, G. (1994). Mistaken sex: Culture, biology and the third sex in New Guinea. In G. Herdt (ed.), *Third Sex, Third Gender*. New York: Zone Books.

Herdt, G. & Davidson, J. (1988). The Sambia "Turnim man": Sociocultural and clinical aspects of gender formation in male pseudohermaphrodites with 5-alpha reductase deficiency in Papua New Guinea. *Archives of Sexual Behavior, 17,* 33–56.

Herzer, M. (1985). Kertbeny and the nameless love. *Journal of Homosexuality, 12,* 1–26.

Himes, N. (1963). *Medical History of Contraception*. New York: Gamut Press.

Hippocrates (1952). *On Intercourse and Pregnancy*. New York: Henry Schuman.

Holtgrave, D. R. & Pinkerton, S. D. (1997). Updates of cost of illness and quality of life estimates for use in economic evaluations of HIV prevention programs. *Journal of Acquired Immune Deficiency Syndromes and Human Retrovirology, 16,* 54–62.

Hovey, E. (1992). Obscenity's meaning, smut-fighters, and contraception: 1872–1936. *San Diego Law Review, 29,* 13–38.

Hrdy, S. B. (1988). The primate origins of human sexuality. In R. Bellig & G. Stevens (eds.), *The Evolution of Sex*. San Francisco: Harper & Row.

Hudson, J. (1960). Birth control legislation. *Cleveland-Marshall Law Review, 9,* 245–257.

Hunt, M. (1974). *Sexual Behavior in the 1970s*. New York: The Playboy Press.

Hutchinson, G. E. (1959). A speculative consideration of certain possible forms of sexual selection in man. *American Naturalist, 93,* 81–91.

Huxley, A. (1932). *Brave New World*. New York: HarperCollins.

Hyde, J. S. (1972). *Understanding Human Sexuality*. New York: McGraw-Hill.

Imperato-McGinley, J., Guerrero, J., Gautier, T., & Peterson, R. E. (1974). Steroid 5-alpha reductase deficiency in man: An inherited form of male pseudo-hermaphroditism. *Science, 186,* 1213–1215.

Imperato-McGinley, J., Peterson, R. E., Gautier, T., & Sturla, E. (1979). Androgens and the evolution of male-gender identity among male pseudoherma-phrodites with 5-alpha reductase deficiency. *New England Journal of Medicine, 300,* 1235–1236.

Jackson, F. (1982). Epiphenomenal qualia. *Philosophical Quarterly, 32,* 127–136.

Jaynes, J. (1976). *The Origins of Consciousness in the Breakdown of the Bicameral Mind*. Boston: Houghton Mifflin.

Jones, E. (1957). Pain. *International Journal of Psychoanalysis, 38,* 255.

Jones, R. A. (1993). Dangerous liaisons. *Los Angeles Times Magazine, July 25.*

Kallmann, F. J. (1952a). Twin and sibship study of overt male homosexuality. *American Journal of Human Genetics, 4,* 136–146.

Kallmann, F. J. (1952b). Comparative twin study on the genetic aspects of male homosexuality. *Journal of Nervous and Mental Disease, 4,* 283–292.

Kalven, H. Jr. (1960). The metaphysics of the law of obscenity. *Supreme Court Review, 1,* 1–45.

Kaplan, E. H. (1995). Model-based representations of human sexual behavior. In P. R. Abramson & S. D. Pinkerton (eds.), *Sexual Nature / Sexual Culture.* Chicago: University of Chicago Press.

Karlen, A. (1980). Homosexuality in history. In J. Marmor (ed.), *Homosexual Behavior: A Modern Reappraisal.* New York: Basic Books.

Katchadourian, H. A. & Lunde, D. T. (1982). *Biological Aspects of Human Sexuality* (second edition). New York: Holt, Rinehart and Winston.

Kelly, J. A., Hoffman, R. G., Rompa, D., & Gray, M. (1998). Protease inhibitor combination therapies and perceptions of gay men regarding AIDS severity and the need to maintain safer sex. *AIDS, 12,* F91–F95.

Kennedy, D. (1993). *Sexy Dressing, Etc.* Cambridge, MA: Harvard University Press.

Kennedy, E. L. & Davis, M. D. (1993). *Boots of Leather, Slippers of Gold.* New York: Routledge.

Kenny, A. (1970). *Descartes' Philosophical Letters.* Oxford: Clarendon Press.

Kern, L. J. (1981). *An Ordered Love: Sex Roles and Sexuality in Victorian Utopias—the Shakers, the Mormons, and the Oneida Community.* Chapel Hill, NC: University of North Carolina Press.

Kim, P. Y. & Bailey, J. M. (1997). Sidestreets on the information superhighway: Paraphilias and sexual variations on the internet. *Journal of Sex Education and Therapy, 22,* 35–43.

King, M. & MacDonald, E. (1992). Homosexuals who are twins: A study of 46 probands. *British Journal of Psychiatry, 160,* 407–409.

Kingsley, L. A., Detels, R., Kaslow, R., Polk, B. F., Rinaldo, C. R. Jr., Chmiel, J., Detre, K., Kelsey, S. F., Odaka, N., Ostrow, D., VanRaden, M., & Visscher, B. (1987). Risk factors for seroconversion to human immunodeficiency virus among male homosexuals. *Lancet, 1,* 345–348.

Kinsey, A. C., Pomeroy, W. B., & Martin, C. E. (1948). *Sexual Behavior in the Human Male.* Philadelphia: W. B. Saunders.

Kinsey, A. C., Pomeroy, W. B., Martin, C. E. & Gebhard, P. H. (1953). *Sexual Behavior in the Human Female.* Philadelphia: W. B. Saunders.

Kirsch, J. A. W. & Rodman, J. E. (1982). Selection and sexuality: The Darwinian view of homosexuality. In W. Paul, J. D. Weinrich, J. C. Gonsiorek, & M. E. Hotvedt (eds.), *Homosexuality: Social, Psychological, and Biological Issues.* Beverly Hills: Sage.

Klausner, J. D., Wolf, W., Fischer-Ponce, L., Zolt, I., & Katz, M. H. (2000). Tracing a syphilis outbreak through cyberspace. *Journal of the American Medical Association, 284,* 447–450.

Klepinger, D. H., Billy, J. O. G., Tanfer, K., & Grady, W. R. (1993). Perceptions of AIDS risk and severity and their association with risk-related behavior among U.S. men. *Family Planning Perspectives, 25,* 74–82.

Klüver, H. & Bucy, P. C. (1937). "Psychic blindness" and other symptoms following bilateral temporal lobectomy in rhesus monkeys. *American Journal of Physiology*, *119*, 352–353.

Konner, M. (1988). Is orgasm essential? *The Sciences*, *28*, 4–7.

Krafft-Ebing, R. v. (1965). *Psychopathia Sexualis*. London.

Krafft-Ebing, R. v. (1978). *Psychopathia Sexualis with Especial Reference to the Antipathic Sexual Instinct* (F. S. Klaf, trans.). New York: Stein and Day.

Kramer, S. N. (1963). *The Sumerians*. Chicago: University of Chicago Press.

Kristeva, J. (1987). *Tales of Love*. New York: Columbia University Press.

Kuroda, S. (1980). Social behavior of the pygmy chimpanzees. *Primates*, *21*, 181–197.

Kushner, H. I. (1978). Nineteenth-century sexuality and the "sexual revolution" of the progressive era. *The Canadian Review of American Studies*, *9*, 34–49.

Kutchinsky, B. (1985). Pornography and its effects in Denmark and the United States. *Comparative Social Research*, *8*, 1–15.

Laga, M., Nzila, N., & Goeman, J. (1991). The interrelationship of sexually transmitted diseases and HIV infection: Implications for the control of both epidemics in Africa. *AIDS, 5 (suppl. 1),* S55–S63.

Lagakos, S., Pettinelli, C., Stein, D., & Volberding, P. A. (1993). The Concorde trial. *Lancet*, *341*, 1276.

Lancaster, J. B. (1975). *Primate Behavior and the Emergence of Human Culture*. New York: Holt, Rinehart, and Winston.

Laqueur, T. (1990). *Making Sex*. Cambridge, MA: Harvard University Press.

Lasagna, L. (1975). *The VD Epidemic*. Philadelphia: Temple University Press.

Laumann, E. O., Gagnon, J. H., Michael, R. T., & Michaels, S. (1994). *The Social Organization of Sexuality*. Chicago: University of Chicago Press.

Lederer, L. (1980). *Take Back the Night: Women on Pornography*. New York: William Morrow.

LeVay, S. (1991). A difference in hypothalamic structure between heterosexual and homosexual men. *Science*, *253*, 1034–1037.

LeVay, S. (1993). *The Sexual Brain*. Cambridge, MA: MIT Press.

LeVay, S. & Hamer, D. H. (1994). Evidence for a biological influence in male homosexuality. *Scientific American*, *270*, 44–49.

Levine, M. P. & Troiden, R. R. (1988). The myth of sexual compulsivity. *The Journal of Sex Research*, *25*, 347–363.

Levy, L. W. (1988). *Original Intent and the Framers' Constitution*. New York: Macmillan.

Lewis, D. K. (1966). An argument for the identity theory. *Journal of Philosophy*, *63*, 17–25.

Lewis, M. I. (1980). The history of female sexuality in the United States. In M. Kirkpatrick (ed.), *Women's Sexual Development: Explorations of Inner Space*. New York: Plenum Press.

Lightfoot-Klein, H. (1989). *Prisoners of Ritual: An Odyssey into Female Genital Circumcision*. Binghamton, NY: Harrington Park Press.

282 / References

Lindsley, D. F. & Holmes, J. E. (1984). *Basic Human Neurophysiology*. New York: Elsevier.

Lissarrague, F. (1990). The sexual life of satyrs. In D. M. Halperin, J. J. Winkler, & F. Zeitlin (eds.), *Before Sexuality: The Construction of Erotic Experience in the Ancient Greek World*. Princeton: Princeton University Press.

Llewellyn-Jones, D. (1985). *Herpes, AIDS, and Other Sexually Transmitted Diseases*. London: Faber and Faber.

Lockhart, W. B. & McClure, R. C. (1954). Literature, the law of obscenity, and the Constitution. *Minnesota Law Review, 38*, 295–395.

Lorenz, K. (1971). Do animals undergo subjective experience? In K. Lorenz, *Studies in Animal and Human Behavior VII*. Cambridge, MA: Harvard University Press.

Lovejoy, C. O. (1981). The origin of man. *Science, 211*, 341–350.

Lovelace, L. (1980). *Ordeal*. New York: Bell Publishing.

Lundgren, J. D., Phillips, A. N., Pedersen, C., Clumeck, N., Gatell, J. M., Johnson, A. M., Ledergerber, B., Vella, S., & Nielsen, J. O. (1994). Comparison of long-term prognosis of patients with AIDS treated and not treated with zidovudine. *Journal of the American Medical Association, 271*, 1088–1092.

MacDonald, R. H. (1967). The frightful consequences of Onanism: Notes on the history of a delusion. *Journal of the History of Ideas, 28*, 423–431.

MacKinnon, C. A. (1984). Not a moral issue. *Yale Law & Policy Review, 2*, 321–345.

MacKinnon, C. A. (1991). Pornography as defamation and discrimination. *Boston University Law Review, 71*, 793–808.

MacKinnon, C. A. (1993). *Only Words*. Cambridge, MA: Harvard University Press.

MacLean, P. D. (1973). *A Triune Concept of the Brain and Behavior*. Toronto: University of Toronto Press.

MacLean, P. D. (1976). Brain mechanisms of elemental sexual functions. In B. J. Sadock, H. I. Kaplan, & A. M. Freedman (eds.), *The Sexual Experience*. Baltimore: Williams & Wilkins.

MacLean, P. D., Dua, S., & Denniston, R. H. (1963). Cerebral localization for scratching and seminal discharge. *Archives of Neurology, 9*, 485–497.

Malinowski, B. (1927). *Sex and Repression in Savage Society*. London: Routledge & Kegan Paul.

Malinowski, B. (1929). *The Sexual Life of Savages*. New York: Harcourt, Brace & World.

Malinowski, B. (1962). *Sex, Culture, and Myth*. New York: Harcourt, Brace & World.

Malinowski, B. (1967). *A Diary in the Strict Sense of the Term*. London: Routledge.

Malthus, T. (1985). *An Essay on the Principle of Population*. London: Penguin Books.

Mann, J. M., Tarantola, D. J. M., & Netter, T. W. (eds.) (1992). *AIDS in the World*. Cambridge, MA: Harvard University Press.

Marcus, S. (1964). *The Other Victorians*. New York: Basic Books.

Marmor, J. (1976). "Normal" and "deviant" sexual behavior. In J. L. McCary & D. R. Copeland (eds.), *Modern Views of Sexual Behavior*. Chicago: Science Research Associates.

Marshall, D. S. (1971a). Sexual behavior on Mangaia. In D. S. Marshall & R. C. Suggs (eds.), *Human Sexual Behavior*. New York: Basic Books.

Marshall, D. S. (1971b). Too much on Mangaia. In C. Gordon & G. Johnson (eds.), *Readings in Human Sexuality: Contemporary Perspectives*. New York: Harper & Row.

Marshall, D. S. & Suggs, R. C. (eds.) (1971). *Human Sexual Behavior*. New York: Basic Books.

Marshall, J. (1981). Pansies, perverts and macho men: Changing conceptions of male homosexuality. In K. Plummer (ed.), *The Making of the Modern Homosexual*. Totowa, NJ: Barnes & Noble.

Martial (1987). *Epigrams of Martial Englished by Divers Hands* (J. P. Sullivan & P. Whigham, eds.). Berkeley: University of California Press.

Masters, W. H. & Johnson, V. E. (1966). *Human Sexual Response*. Boston: Little, Brown and Company.

Mastro, T. D., & de Vincenzi, I. (1996). Probabilities of sexual HIV-1 transmission. *AIDS, 10 (suppl. A)*, S75–S82.

Maticka-Tyndale, E. (1991). Sexual scripts and AIDS prevention: Variations in adherence to safer-sex guidelines by heterosexual adolescents. *The Journal of Sex Research, 28*, 45–66.

McBride, A. F. & Hebb, D. O. (1967). Modern dolphins. In E. Devine & M. Clark (eds.), *The Dolphin Smile: Twenty-Nine Centuries of Dolphin Lore*. New York: Macmillan.

McFarlane, M., Bull, S. S., & Rietmeijer, C. A. (2000). The internet as a newly emerging risk environment for sexually transmitted diseases. *Journal of the American Medical Association, 284*, 443–446.

McGuire, R. J., Carlisle, J. M., & Young, B. G. (1965). Sexual deviation as conditioned behavior: A hypothesis. *Behavioral Research and Therapy, 2*, 185–190.

McKusick, L., Horstman, W., & Coates, T. J. (1985). AIDS and sexual behavior reported by gay men in San Francisco. *American Journal of Public Health, 75*, 493–496.

McLaren, A. (1984). *Reproductive Rituals: The Perception of Fertility in England from the Sixteenth to the Nineteenth Century*. London: Methuen.

McLaren, A. (1985). The pleasures of procreation: Traditional and biomedical theories of conception. In W. F. Bynum & R. Porter (eds.), *William Hunter and the Eighteenth Century Medical World*. Cambridge: Cambridge University Press.

McLaren, A. (1990). *A History of Contraception: From Antiquity to the Present*. London: Basil Blackwell.

McLaws, M. L., Oldenburg, B., Ross, M. W., & Cooper, D. A. (1990). Sexual behaviour in AIDS-related research: Reliability and validity of recall and diary measures. *The Journal of Sex Research, 27*, 265–281.

Mead, M. (1928). *Coming of Age in Samoa*. New York: Morrow.

Meikle, S. (1982). Culture and sexual deviation. In I. Al-Issa (ed.), *Culture and Psychopathology*. Baltimore: University Park Press.

Meiklejohn, A. (1960). *Political Freedom: The Constitutional Powers of the People*. New York: Harper & Row.

Merriam, A. P. (1971). Aspects of sexual behavior among the Bala (Basongye). In D. S. Marshall & R. C. Suggs (eds.), *Human Sexual Behavior*. New York: Basic Books.

Messenger, J. C. (1971). Sex and repression in an Irish folk community. In D. S. Marshall & R. C. Suggs (eds.), *Human Sexual Behavior*. New York: Basic Books.

Meyer-Bahlburg, H. F. L. (1977). Sex hormones and male homosexuality in comparative perspective. *Archives of Sexual Behavior, 6*, 297–325.

Meyer-Bahlburg, H. F. L. (1979). Sex hormones and female homosexuality: A critical examination. *Archives of Sexual Behavior, 8*, 101–119.

Meyer-Bahlburg, H. F. L. (1984). Psychoendocrine research on sexual orientation: Current status and future options. *Progress in Brain Research, 61*, 375–398.

Meyer-Bahlburg, H. F. L. (1995). Psychoneuroendocrinology and sexual pleasure: The aspect of sexual orientation. In P. R. Abramson & S. D. Pinkerton (eds.), *Sexual Nature / Sexual Culture*. Chicago: University of Chicago Press.

Michael, R. T., Gagnon, J. H., Laumann, E. O., & Kolata, G. (1994). *Sex in America: A Definitive Survey*. Boston: Little, Brown and Company.

Miller, H. (1961). *Tropic of Cancer*. New York: Grove.

Miller, N. E. (1957). Experiments on motivation. *Science, 126*, 1271–1278.

Minsky, M. (1981). A framework for representing knowledge. In J. Haugeland (ed.), *Mind Design*. Cambridge, MA: MIT Press.

Morgan, T. (1993). Butch-femme and the politics of identity. In A. Stein (ed.), *Sisters, Sexperts, Queers: Beyond the Lesbian Nation*. New York: Penguin Books.

Mori, A. (1984). An ethological study of pygmy chimpanzees in Wamba, Zaire: A comparison with chimpanzees. *Primates, 25*, 255–278.

Morokoff, P. (1978). Determinants of female orgasm. In J. LoPiccolo & L. LoPiccolo (eds.), *Handbook of Sex Therapy*. New York: Plenum Press.

Morris, D. (1967). *The Naked Ape*. London: Jonathan Cape.

Morris, D. (1986). *Catwatching*. New York: Crown.

Moses-Zirkes, S. (1993). Pleasure, pain evaluation not always rooted in logic. *APS Monitor, 24*, 30–31.

Mosher, D. L. (1966). The development and multitrait-multimethod matrix analysis of three aspects of guilt. *Journal of Consulting Psychology, 30*, 25–29.

Mosher, D. L. (1973). Sex differences, sex experience, sex guilt, and explicitly sexual films. *Journal of Social Issues, 29*, 95–112.

Mosher, D. L. & Abramson, P. R. (1977). Subjective sexual arousal to films of masturbation. *Journal of Consulting and Clinical Psychology, 45*, 796–807.

Mosher, D. L. & Cross, H. (1971). Sex guilt and premarital sexual experiences of college students. *Journal of Consulting and Clinical Psychology, 36*, 27–32.

Murphy, T. F. (1992). Redirecting sexual orientation: Techniques and justifications. *The Journal of Sex Research, 29*, 501–524.

Murphy, Y. & Murphy, R. (1974). *Women of the Forest.* New York: Columbia University Press.

Nagel, T. (1974). What is it like to be a bat? *Philosophical Review, 83*, 435–450.

Nanda, S. (1990). *Neither Man nor Woman: The Hijras of India.* Belmont, CA: Wadsworth.

Nanda, S. (1994). Hijras: An alternative sex and gender role in India. In G. Herdt (ed.), *Third Sex, Third Gender.* New York: Zone Books.

Nissenbaum, S. (1980). *Sex, Diet, and Debility in Jacksonian America: Sylvester Graham and Health Reform.* Chicago: The Dorsey Press.

Nestle, J. (1983). My mother liked to fuck. In A. Snitow, C. Stansell, & S. Thompson (eds.), *Powers of Desire: The Politics of Sexuality.* New York: Monthly Review Press.

Nestle, J. (ed.) (1992). *The Persistent Desire: A Femme-Butch Reader.* Boston: Alyson.

Neuman, R. P. (1975). Masturbation, madness, and the modern concepts of childhood and adolescence. *Journal of Social History, 8*, 1–27.

Nobile, P. & Nadler, E. (1986). *United States of America vs. Sex: How the Meese Commission Lied about Pornography.* New York: Minotaur Press.

Nordeen, E. J., Nordeen, K. W., Sengelaub, D. R., & Arnold, A. P. (1985). Androgens prevent normally occurring cell death in a sexually dimorphic spinal nucleus. *Science, 229*, 671—673.

Norris, K. S. & Dohl, T. P. (1980). Behavior of the Hawaiian spinner dolphin, *Stenella longirostris. Fishery Bulletin, 77*, 821–849.

Oaks, R. (1980). "Things fearful to name": Sodomy and buggery in seventeenth century New England. In E. H. Pleck & J. H. Pleck (eds.), *The American Man.* Englewood Cliffs, NJ: Prentice-Hall.

O'Flaherty, W. D. (1985). *Tales of Sex and Violence.* Chicago: University of Chicago Press.

Old, R. (1993). Heterozygote advantage: Why are some deleterious genes so common? *Lancet, 341*, 214.

Olds, J. (1956). Pleasure centers in the brain. *Scientific American, 195*, 105–116.

Olds, J. & Milner, P. (1954). Positive reinforcement produced by electrical stimulation of the septal area and other regions of the rat brain. *Journal of Comparative and Physiological Psychology, 47*, 419–427.

Ornstein, R. (1991). *The Evolution of Consciousness.* New York: Prentice-Hall.

Orsy, L. (1986). *Marriage in Canon Law.* Wilmington, DE: Michael Glazier.

Osmond, D., Charlebois, E., Lang, W., Shiboski, S., & Moss, A. (1994). Changes in AIDS survival time in two San Francisco cohorts of homosexual men, 1983 to 1993. *Journal of the American Medical Association, 271*, 1083–1087.

Ostman, J. (1991). Changes in aggressive and sexual behavior between two male bottlenose dolphins (*Tursiops truncatus*) in a captive colony. In K. Pryor & K. S. Norris (eds.), *Dolphin Societies: Discoveries and Puzzles.* Berkeley: University of California Press.

Padian, N. (1990). Heterosexual transmission: Infectivity and risks. In N. J. Alexander, H. L. Gabelnick, & J. M. Spieler (eds.), *Heterosexual Transmission of AIDS*. New York: Alan R. Liss.

Paglia, C. (1990). *Sexual Personae*. New Haven: Yale University Press.

Paige, K. E. & Paige, J. M. (1981). *The Politics of Reproductive Ritual*. Berkeley: University of California Press.

Pally, M. (1994). *Sex & Sensibility: Reflections on Forbidden Mirrors and the Will to Censor*. Hopewell, NJ: Ecco Press.

Parisot, J. (1987). *Johnny Come Lately: A Short History of the Condom*. London: Journeyman Press.

Parringer, G. (1980). *Sex in the World's Religions*. New York: Oxford University Press.

Pattatucci, A. M. L. & Hamer, D. H. (1995). The genetics of sexual orientation: From fruit flies to humans. In P. R. Abramson & S. D. Pinkerton (eds.), *Sexual Nature / Sexual Culture*. Chicago: University of Chicago Press.

Patton, C. (1985). *Sex & Germs: The Politics of AIDS*. Boston: South End Press.

Pavelka, M. S. M. (1995). Sexual nature: What can we learn from a cross-species perspective? In P. R. Abramson & S. D. Pinkerton (eds.), *Sexual Nature / Sexual Culture*. Chicago: University of Chicago Press.

Peplau, L. A., Rubin, Z., & Hill, C. T. (1977). Sexual intimacy in dating relationships. *Journal of Social Issues, 33*, 86–109.

Person, E. S. (1989). *Dreams of Love and Fateful Encounters: The Power of Romantic Passion*. New York: Penguin Books.

Piercy, M. (1982). *Braided Lives*. New York: Summit Books.

Pillard, R. C. (1990). The Kinsey scale: Is it familial? In D. P. McWhirter, S. A. Sanders, & J. M. Reinisch (eds.), *Heterosexuality / Homosexuality*. New York: Oxford University Press.

Pillard, R. C., Poumadere, J., & Carretta, R. A. (1981). Is homosexuality familial? A review, some data, and a suggestion. *Archives of Sexual Behavior, 10*, 465–475.

Pillard, R. C. & Weinrich, J. D. (1986). Evidence of familial nature of homosexuality. *Archives of General Psychiatry, 43*, 808–812.

Pinkerton, S. D. & Abramson, P. R. (1992). Is risky sex rational? *The Journal of Sex Research, 29*, 561–568.

Pinkerton, S. D. & Abramson, P. R. (1993a). Evaluating the risks: A Bernoulli process model of HIV infection and risk reduction. *Evaluation Review, 17*, 504–528.

Pinkerton, S. D. & Abramson, P. R. (1993b). HIV vaccines: A magic bullet in the fight against AIDS? *Evaluation Review, 17*, 579–602.

Pinkerton, S. D. & Abramson, P. R. (1993c). A magic bullet against AIDS? *Science, 262*, 162–163.

Pinkerton, S. D. & Abramson, P. R. (1994). An alternative model of the reproductive rate of HIV infection: Formulation, evaluation, and implications for risk reduction interventions. *Evaluation Review, 18*, 371–388.

Pinkerton, S. D. & Abramson, P. R. (1995). The joys of diversification: Vaccines, condoms, and AIDS prevention. *AIDS & Public Policy Journal, 10,* 148–156.

Pinkerton, S. D. & Abramson, P. R. (1996). Occasional condom use and HIV risk reduction. *Journal of Acquired Immune Deficiency Syndromes and Human Retrovirology, 13,* 456–460.

Pinkerton, S. D. & Abramson, P. R. (1997a). Condoms and the prevention of AIDS. *American Scientist, 85,* 364–373.

Pinkerton, S. D. & Abramson, P. R. (1997b). Effectiveness of condoms in preventing HIV transmission. *Social Science & Medicine, 44,* 1303–1312.

Pinkerton, S. D. & Abramson, P. R. (1998). The Bernoulli process model of HIV transmission: Applications and implications. In D. R. Holtgrave (ed.), *Handbook of Economic Evaluation of HIV Prevention Programs,* 13–32. New York: Plenum.

Pinkerton, S. D. & Holtgrave, D. R. (1999). Combination antiretroviral therapies for HIV: Some economic considerations. In D. G. Ostrow & S. C. Kalichman (eds.), *Psychosocial and Public Health Impacts of New HIV Therapies.* New York: Kluwer Academic/Plenum.

Pinkerton, S. D., Wagner-Raphael, L. I., Craun, C. A., & Abramson, P. R. (2000). A quantitative study of the accuracy of college students' HIV risk estimates. *Journal of Applied Biobehavioral Research, 5,* 1–25.

Pool, R., Whitworth, J. A. G., Green, G., Mbonye, A. K., Harrison, S., Hart, G. J., & Wilkinson, J. (2000). Ambivalence, sexual pleasure and the acceptability of microbicidal products in south-west Uganda. *AIDS, 14,* 2058–2059.

Pope, P. M. (1962) (trans.). *Greek Love Poems.* Cape Town, South Africa: A. A. Balkema.

Popper, K. R. & Eccles, J. C. (1977). *The Self and its Brain.* New York: Springer-Verlag.

Population Information Program (1983). Vasectomy—safe and simple. *Population Reports, Series D,* no. 4, D61–D100.

Posner, R. A. (1992). *Sex and Reason.* Cambridge, MA: Harvard University Press.

Press, A., Namuth, T., Agrest, S., Gander, M., Lubenow, G. C., Reese, M., Friendly, D. T., & McDaniel, A. (1985). The war against pornography. *Newsweek, March 18,* 58–66.

Prieur, A. (1990). Norwegian gay men: Reasons for continued practice of unsafe sex. *AIDS Education and Prevention, 2,* 109–115.

Proust, M. (1926). *Time Regained.* London: Chatto & Windus.

Pusey, W. A. (1933). *The History and Epidemiology of Syphilis.* Springfield, IL: Charles C. Thomas.

Pylyshyn, Z. W. (1980). Cognitive representation and the process-architecture distinction. *Behavioral and Brain Sciences, 3,* 154–169.

Quadland, M. C. (1985). Compulsive sexual behavior: Definition of a problem and an approach to treatment. *Journal of Sex and Marital Therapy, 11,* 121–132.

Quetel, C. (1990). *History of Syphilis.* Baltimore: Johns Hopkins University Press.

Rachman, S. (1966). Sexual fetishism: An experimental analogue. *Psychological Record*, *16*, 293–296.

Rachman, S. & Hodgson, R. J. (1968). Experimentally induced "sexual fetishism": Replication and development. *Psychological Record*, *18*, 25–27.

Rechy, J. (1977). *The Sexual Outlaw*. New York: Grove Weidenfeld.

Reed, J. (1978). *From Private Vice to Public Virtue*. New York: Basic Books.

Reiss, I. L. & Leik, R. K. (1989). Evaluating strategies to avoid AIDS: Number of partners vs. use of condoms. *The Journal of Sex Research*, *26*, 411–433.

Rich, A. (1978). *On Lies, Secrets and Silence*. New York: Norton.

Richards, D. A. J. (1974). Free speech and obscenity law: Toward a moral theory of the First Amendment. *University of Pennsylvania Law Review*, *123*, 45–91.

Richards, D. A. J. (1979). Commercial sex and the rights of the person: A moral argument for the decriminalization of prostitution. *University of Pennsylvania Law Review*, *127*, 1195–1287.

Richardson, D. (1981). Theoretical perspectives on homosexuality. In J. Hart & D. Richardson, *Theory and Practice of Homosexuality*. London: Routledge & Kegan Paul.

Richardson, D. (1984). The dilemma of essentiality in homosexual theory. *Journal of Homosexuality*, *9*, 79–90.

Richardson, D. & Hart, J. (1981). The development and maintenance of a homosexual identity. In J. Hart & D. Richardson, *Theory and Practice of Homosexuality*. London: Routledge & Kegan Paul.

Riddle, J. M. (1992). *Contraception and Abortion from the Ancient World to the Renaissance*. Cambridge, MA: Harvard University Press.

Riddle, J. M. & Estes, J. W. (1992). Oral contraceptives in ancient and medieval times. *American Scientist*, *80*, 226–233.

Ridley, M. (1985). *The Problems of Evolution*. New York: Oxford University Press.

Robertson, D. W. Jr. (1962). *A Preface to Chaucer: Studies in Medieval Perspectives*. Princeton: Princeton University Press.

Robinson, B. W. & Mishkin, M. (1966). Ejaculation evoked by stimulation of the preoptic area in monkey. *Physiology and Behavior*, *1*, 269–272.

Robinson, P. & Tamosaitis, N. (1993). *The Joy of Cybersex*. New York: Brady.

Robinson, P. A. (1976). *The Modernization of Sex*. New York: Harper & Row.

Roscoe, W. (1994). How to become a berdache: Towards a unified analysis of gender diversity. In G. Herdt (ed.), *Third Sex, Third Gender*. Cambridge, MA: Zone Books.

Rothenberg, R. B., Scarlett, M., del Rio, C., Reznik, D., & O'Daniels, C. (1998). Oral transmission of HIV. *AIDS*, *12*, 2095–2105.

Royce, R. A., Sena, A., Cates, W. Jr., & Cohen, M. S. (1997). Sexual transmission of HIV. *New England Journal of Medicine*, *336*, 1072–1078.

Rubin, G. (1975). The traffic in women: Notes on the "political economy" of sex. In R. R. Reiter (ed.), *Toward an Anthropology of Women*. New York: Monthly Review Press.

Rubin, L. B. (1990). *Erotic Wars: What Happened to the Sexual Revolution?* New York: Farrar, Straus & Giroux.

Rousselle, A. (1988). *Porneia: On Desire and the Body in Antiquity*. Oxford: Basil Blackwell.

Sandars, N. K. (1972). *The Epic of Gilgamesh*. New York: Penguin.

Sanger, M. (1938). *Margaret Sanger: An Autobiography*. New York: Norton.

Sanger, W. W. (1897). *The History of Prostitution: Its Extent, Causes and Effects Throughout the World*. New York: Eugenics Publishing.

Sansom, G. (1974). *A History of Japan* (volume 1). Tokyo: Tuttle.

Savage-Rumbaugh, E. S. & Wilkerson, B. J. (1978). Socio-sexual behavior in *pan paniscus* and *pan troglodytes*: A comparative study. *Journal of Human Evolution, 7,* 327–344.

Schill, T. R. & Chapin, J. (1972). Sex guilt and males' preference for reading magazines. *Journal of Consulting and Clinical Psychology, 39,* 516.

Schlegel, A. (1991). Status, property, and the value on virginity. *American Ethnologist, 18,* 719–734.

Schlegel, A. (1995). The cultural management of adolescent sexuality. In P. R. Abramson & S. D. Pinkerton (eds.), *Sexual Nature / Sexual Culture*. Chicago: University of Chicago Press.

Schwartz, M. F. & Brasted, W. S. (1985). Sexual addiction. *Medical Aspects of Human Sexuality, 19,* 103–107.

Schwartz, S. (1973). Effects of sex guilt and sexual arousal on the retention of birth control information. *Journal of Consulting and Clinical Psychology, 41,* 61–64.

Sedgwick, E. K. (1990). *Epistemology of the Closet*. Berkeley: University of California Press.

Sedgwick, E. K. (1993). *Tendencies*. Durham, NC: Duke University Press.

Seeley, T. T., Abramson, P. R., Perry, L. B., Rothblatt, A. B., & Seeley, D. M. (1980). Thermographic measurement of sexual arousal: A methodological note. *Archives of Sexual Behavior, 9,* 77–85.

Shade, W. G. (1978). "A mental passion": Female sexuality in Victorian America. *International Journal of Women's Studies, 1,* 13–29.

Shaw, D. F. (1997). Gay men and computer communication: A discourse of sex and identity in cyberspace. In S. G. Jones (ed.), *Virtual Culture: Identity and Communication in Cyberspace*. London: Sage.

Sherwin, R. & Corbett, S. (1985). Campus sexual norms and dating relationships: A trend analysis. *The Journal of Sex Research, 21,* 258–274.

Shiffrin, S. H. (1990). *The First Amendment, Democracy, and Romance*. Cambridge, MA: Harvard University Press.

Shilts, R. (1987). *And the Band Played On*. New York: Penguin Books.

Shoemaker, S. (1981). Absent qualia are impossible—A reply to Block. *Philosophical Review, 90,* 581–599.

Sibley, C. G. & Ahlquist, J. E. (1984). The phylogeny of the hominid primates, as indicated by DNA-DNA hybridization. *Journal of Molecular Evolution, 20,* 2–15.

Simon, W. & Gagnon, J. H. (1984). Sexual scripts. *Society, 22,* 53–60.

Simon, W., Kraft, D. M., & Kaplan, H. B. (1990). Oral sex: A critical overview. In B. Voeller, J. M. Reinisch, & M. Gottleib (eds.), *AIDS and Sex*. New York: Oxford University Press.

Singer, I. (1984). *The Nature of Love*. Chicago: University of Chicago Press.

Singer, J. & Singer, I. (1972). Types of female orgasm. *The Journal of Sex Research, 8,* 255–267.

Sloan, I. J. (1988). *The Law Governing Abortion, Contraception & Sterilization*. New York: Oceana.

Sloan, P. & Mandese, J. (1991). TV nets warming to condom ads. *Advertising Age, 62,* 47.

Smart, J. J. C. (1962). Sensations and brain processes. *Philosophical Review, 68,* 141–156.

Smith-Rosenberg, C. (1974). Puberty to menopause: The cycle of femininity in nineteenth-century America. In M. S. Hartman & L. Banner (eds.), *Clio's Consciousness Raised: New Perspectives on the History of Women*. New York: Harper & Row.

Snitow, A. B. (1983). Mass market romance: Pornography for women is different. In A. Snitow, C. Stansell, & S. Thompson (eds.), *Powers of Desire: The Politics of Sexuality*. New York: Monthly Review Press.

Snitow, A. (1985). Retrenchment versus transformation: The politics of the anti-pornography movement. In V. Burstyn (ed.), *Women Against Censorship*. Vancouver, BC: Douglas & McIntyre.

Socarides, C. W. (1960). The development of a fetishistic perversion. *Journal of the American Psychoanalytic Association, 8,* 281–311.

Spencer, B. (1993). Oralgenital sex and risk of transmission of HIV. *Lancet, 341,* 441.

Stammer, L. B. (1994). Amid questions, priests, nuns back key doctrine. *Los Angeles Times*, February 20.

Sterk, C. E. (1989). *Living the Life: Prostitutes and Their Health*. Rotterdam: Erasmus University Press.

Sternberg, R. J. & Barnes, M. L. (eds.) (1988). *The Psychology of Love*. New Haven: Yale University Press.

Stoller, R. J. (1971). The term "transvestism." *Archives of General Psychiatry, 24,* 230–237.

Stoller, R. J. (1985). *Observing the Erotic Imagination*. New Haven: Yale University Press.

Stoller, R. J. (1991). *Porn: Myths for the Twentieth Century*. New Haven: Yale University Press.

Stoller, R. J. & Herdt, G. H. (1985). Theories of origins of male homosexuality. *Archives of General Psychiatry, 42,* 399–404.

Stoller, R. J. & Levine, I. S. (1993). *Coming Attractions: The Making of an X-rated Video*. New Haven: Yale University Press.

Stone, L. (1979). *The Family, Sex and Marriage in England, 1500–1800* (abridged edition). New York: Harper & Row.

Strossen, N. (1995). *Defending Pornography: Free Speech, Sex, and the Fight for Women's Rights*. New York: Scribner.

Suarez, T. P., Kelly, J. A., Pinkerton, S. D., Stevenson, Y. L., Hayat, M. J., Smith, M. D., & Ertl, T. (2001). The influence of a partner's HIV serostatus and viral load on perceptions of sexual risk behavior in a community sample of gay and bisexual men. *Journal of Acquired Immune Deficiency Syndromes*.

Suarez, T. P. & Miller, J. G. (2001). Negotiating risks in context: A perspective on unprotected anal intercourse and barebacking among men who have sex with men. *Archives of Sexual Behavior*.

Suraiya, J. (1992). The pleasure principle. *Far Eastern Economic Review, 155*, 25.

Swaab, D. F. & Fliers, E. (1985). A sexually dimorphic nucleus in the human brain. *Science, 228*, 1112–1114.

Symons, D. (1979). *The Evolution of Human Sexuality*. New York: Oxford University Press.

Symons, D. (1992). On the use and misuse of Darwinism. In J. H. Barkow, L. Cosmides, & J. Tooby (eds.), *The Adapted Mind*. New York: Oxford University Press.

Symons, D. (1993). How risky is risky sex ? *The Journal of Sex Research, 30*, 344–346.

Symons, D. (1995). Beauty is in the adaptation of the beholder: The evolutionary psychology of human female attractiveness. In P. R. Abramson & S. D. Pinkerton (eds.), *Sexual Nature / Sexual Culture*. Chicago: University of Chicago Press.

Tanaka, J. & Arnold, A. P. (1993). Androgenic modulation of the activity of lumbar neurons involved in the rat bulbocavernosus reflex. *Experimental Brain Research, 94*, 301–307.

Tannahill, R. (1980). *Sex in History*. New York: Stein and Day.

Tavris, C. & Sadd, S. (1977). *The Redbook Report on Female Sexuality*. New York: Delacorte Press.

Taylor, G. R. (1953). *Sex in History*. London: Thames and Hudson.

Tennyson, A. (1987). *The Poems of Tennyson* (C. Ricks, ed.). Berkeley: University of California Press.

Tigay, J. H. (1982). *The Evolution of the Gilgamesh Epic*. Philadelphia: University of Pennsylvania Press.

Tiger, L. (1992). *The Pursuit of Pleasure*. Boston: Little, Brown and Company.

Tisdale, S. (1994). *Talk Dirty to Me*. New York: Doubleday.

Tissot, S. A. D. (1772). *Onanism: or a Treatise upon the Disorders Produced by Masturbation: or The Dangerous Effects of Secret and Excessive Venery* (A. Hume, trans.). London.

Tooby, J. (1985). The emergence of evolutionary psychology. In D. Pine (ed.), *Emerging Syntheses in Science*. Sante Fe, NM: Sante Fe Institute.

Toomey, K. E. & Rothenberg, R. B. (2000). Sex and cyberspace—Virtual networks leading to high-risk sex. *Journal of the American Medical Association, 284,* 485–487.

Torgovnick, M. (1990). *Gone Primitive.* Chicago: University of Chicago Press.

Trimble, S. (ed.) (1988). *Words from the Land.* Salt Lake City: Gibbs M. Smith.

Troiden, R. R, (1980). Variables related to the acquisition of a gay identity. *Journal of Homosexuality, 4,* 383–392.

Tulving, E. (1972). Episodic and semantic memory. In E. Tulving & W. Donaldson (eds.), *Organization of Memory.* New York: Academic Press.

Tulving, E. (1983). *Elements of Episodic Memory.* New York: Oxford University Press.

Turley, D. (1986). The feminist debate on pornography: An unorthodox interpretation. *Socialist Review, no. 87/88,* 81–96.

Tuzin, D. (1995). Discourse, intercourse, and the excluded middle: Anthropology and the problem of sexual experience. In P. R. Abramson & S. D. Pinkerton (eds.), *Sexual Nature / Sexual Culture.* Chicago: University of Chicago Press.

Tzeng, O. C. S. (1992). *Measurement of Love and Intimate Relationships.* New York: Praeger.

UNAIDS (2000). *Report on the Global HIV/AIDS Pandemic.* Geneva: Joint United Nations Programme on HIV/AIDS.

United States Catholic Conference (1987). *The Many Faces of AIDS: A Gospel Response.* Washington, DC: United States Catholic Conference.

Vance, C. (1986). The Meese Commission on the road. *Nation, August 2–9.*

Veblen, T. (1899). *The Theory of the Leisure Class.* New York: Viking.

Vonnegut, K. (1988). *Welcome to the Monkey House.* New York: Dell.

de Waal, F. B. M. (1982). *Chimpanzee Politics.* London: Jonathan Cape.

de Waal, F. B. M. (1987). Tension regulation and nonreproductive functions of sex among captive bonobos (*Pan paniscus*). *National Geographic Research, 3,* 318–335.

de Waal, F. B. M. (1989). *Peacemaking among Primates.* Cambridge, MA: Harvard University Press.

de Waal, F. B. M. (1995). Sex as an alternative to aggression in the bonobo. In P. R. Abramson & S. D. Pinkerton (eds.), *Sexual Nature / Sexual Culture.* Chicago: University of Chicago Press.

Walen, S. R. & Roth, D. (1987). A cognitive approach. In J. H. Geer & W. T. O'Donohue (eds.), *Theories of Human Sexuality.* New York: Plenum Press.

Walkowitz, J. R. (1980). The politics of prostitution. *Signs: Journal of Women in Culture and Society, 6,* 123–135.

Wallen, K. (1989). Non-fertile mating in rhesus monkeys: Sexual aggression or miscommunication? *Primate Report, 23,* 23–34.

Wallen, K. (1990). Desire and ability: Hormones and the regulation of female sexual behavior. *Neuroscience and Biobehavioral Reviews, 14,* 233–241.

Wallen, K. (1995). The evolution of female sexual desire. In P. R. Abramson &

S. D. Pinkerton (eds.), *Sexual Nature / Sexual Culture*. Chicago: University of Chicago Press.

Walters, R. G. (1974). *Primers for Prudery*. Englewood Cliffs, NJ: Prentice-Hall.

Wasserheit, J. N. (1992). Epidemiological synergy: Interrelationships between human immunodeficiency virus infection and other sexually transmitted diseases. *Sexually Transmitted Diseases, 19,* 61–77.

Watney, S. (1987). *Policing Desire: Pornography, AIDS, and the Media*. Minneapolis: University of Minnesota Press.

Watney, S. (1990). Safer sex as community practice. In P. Aggleton, P. Davies, & G. Hart (eds.), *AIDS: Individual, Cultural and Policy Dimensions*. London: The Falmer Press.

Weatherford, J. M. (1986). *Porn Row*. New York: Arbor House.

Weeks, J. (1977). *Coming Out: Homosexual Politics in Britain from the Nineteenth Century to the Present*. London: Quartet Books.

Weinberg, T. S. (1978). On "doing" and "being" gay: Sexual behavior and homosexual male self-identity. *Journal of Homosexuality, 4,* 143–156.

Weintraub, S. (1976). *Aubrey Beardsley: Imp of the Perverse*. University Park, PA: Penn State University Press.

Wells, R. S. (1984). Reproductive behavior and hormonal correlates in Hawaiian spinner dolphins, *Stenella longirostris*. In W. F. Perrin, R. L. Brownell Jr., & D. P. DeMaster (eds.), *Reproduction in Whales, Dolphins, and Porpoises*. Cambridge: International Whaling Commission.

Whipple, B., Ogden, G., & Komisaruk, B. R. (1992). Physiological correlates of imagery-induced orgasm in women. *Archives of Sexual Behavior, 21,* 121–133.

Whisman, V. (1993). Identity crisis: Who is a lesbian anyway? In A. Stein (ed.), *Sisters, Sexperts, Queers*. New York: Penguin.

Whitam, F. L., Diamond, M., & Martin, J. (1993). Homosexual orientation in twins: A report on 61 pairs and three triplet sets. *Archives of Sexual Behavior, 22,* 187–206.

Wilde, O. (1891/1990). The picture of Dorian Gray. In *The Complete Works of Oscar Wilde*. Leicester: Blitz.

Williams, G. C. (1966). *Adaptation and Natural Selection*. Princeton: Princeton University Press.

Willis, E. (1983). Feminism, moralism, and pornography. In A. Snitow, C. Stansell, & S. Thompson (eds.), *Powers of Desire: The Politics of Sexuality*. New York: Monthly Review Press.

Wilson, E. O. (1975). *Sociobiology: The New Synthesis*. Cambridge, MA: Harvard University Press.

Wilson, J. D. (1995). Sex hormones and sexual behavior. In P. R. Abramson & S. D. Pinkerton (eds.), *Sexual Nature / Sexual Culture*. Chicago: University of Chicago Press.

Wilson, M. & Daly, M. (1992). The man who mistook his wife for a chattel. In J. H. Barkow, L. Cosmides, & J. Tooby (eds.), *The Adapted Mind*. New York: Oxford University Press.

Winkler, J. (1990). *The Constraints of Desire*. New York: Routledge.

Witomski, T. R. (1985). The "sickness" of pornography. *New York Native, July 29–August 11*, 26–27.

Worthman, C. M. (1986). Developmental dyssynchrony as normal experience: Kikuyu adolescents. In J. B. Lancaster & B. A. Hamburg (eds.), *School-Age Pregnancy and Parenthood: Biosocial Dimensions*. New York: Aldine De Gruyter.

Wundram, I. J. (1979). Nonreproductive sexual behavior: Ethological and cultural considerations. *American Anthropologist, 81*, 99–103.

Wynne-Edwards, V. C. (1978). Intrinsic population control: An introduction. In F. J. Ebling & D. M. Stoddart (eds.), *Population Control by Social Behaviour*. London: Institute of Biology.

Zinn, H. (1990). *Declarations of Independence*. New York: Harper & Row.

Index

on love, 116

on masturbation, 171, 173

on nonreproductive sex as perversion, 33–34

on pleasure, 11

pleasure principle, 11, 140–41

on psychosexual tension, 85

on repression, 55–57, 137, 141

restraint as central to, 53, 55–57

on sexual pleasure as incentive to endure childbirth, 36–37

on sublimation, 55–57, 63

Fruit flies (*Drosophila melanogoaster*), 103–4

Fruitless flies, 103–4

Functions and Disorders of the Reproductive Organs, The (Acton), 172, 174

Galen, 204

Galileo, 193, 194

Gates, Mary, 190

Gay men. *See* Homosexuality

Gay Times, 181

Gender

cultural construction of, 125–28

gender differences in sexual pleasure, 123

gender identity as resistant to change, 119

as simple dichotomy in Western science, 98, 125–26

third gender, 98, 126–28

Genes

environmental influence on, 105

46,XY-syndrome, 83

as functional unit of evolution, 137

genetic basis of homosexuality, 100–106

heritable traits, 35, 100, 102

heterozygotic advantage, 100, 101

for homosexual courtship behavior in fruit flies, 103–4

selfish-gene theory, 102, 137

Genital herpes, 163

Genital ulcers, 215

Genitals. *See* Clitoris; Penis; Vagina

Germany, 191

G-G rubbing, 25

Ghotuls, 130

Gilgamesh, 22, 66–67

Goats, pygmy, 90

Goethe, Johann Wolfgang von, 125

Goldberg, Whoopi, 165

Gonorrhea, 163

Good Times: A Review of the World of Pleasure, 195

Gould, Stephen Jay, 105

Graham, Sylvester, 174, 176

Grant, Linda, 191

Greece, ancient

anal intercourse in, 99

Aristotle, 11, 33

hetairai, 14, 76

Hippocrates, 27

lesbianism in, 15

male homosexuality in, 14

male prostitution in, 15, 51

Plato, 11, 22

pornography in, 170

propriety of sexual behavior determined by role not gender, 14

prostitution in, 14–15, 51, 76

sex scrutinized in, 12

sexual themes in art of, 22

sexual violence in, 70

Sparta, 15

virginity of lovers devalued in, 14–15

Green, Cathy, 190

Gregor, Thomas, 130

Group marriage, 71

G-spot, 86, 124

Guilt, sexual. *See* Sexual guilt

Gusii, 70

Hall, Radclyffe, 185

Hamburg, Beatrix, 87

Hamer, Dean, 103, 104

Harris List of Garden Ladies, 179

Hartley, Nina, 190

Hawaii, 51, 115

Hell's Angels, 44

Helms Amendment, 180–81

Herdt, Gilbert, 126

Heritable traits, 35, 100, 102

Herpes, genital, 163

Hetairai, 14, 76

Heterosexuality

bias toward learning in Western society, 113

as category of sexual orientation, 94

love and, 116–17
marital rape, 69
as marketing of sexual pleasure, 61–62
masturbation diminishing incentive for, 26, 63
men's gains from, 61
as men's ownership of women, 62, 66
monogamy, 62, 87
and property, 63–64, 65, 66
sexual force reduced by, 69
sexual pleasure in, 117
women's gains from, 61
Marriage of Heaven and Hell, The (Blake), 53
Marshall, Donald, 124, 129
Marshall, John, 96
Martial, 22–23
Marx, Karl, 66
Massachusetts, 166
Masters, William, 11, 85, 86
Masturbation (self-stimulation)
Acton on, 174–75
admonitions against, 26–27
in animals, 24
in bonobos, 25
brain stimulation and, 90
campaigns against in U.S. and England, 177–78
in children, 132–33
as debilitating, 171
as diminishing incentive to marry, 26, 63
female, 123, 173
female orgasm correlated with, 124
Freud on, 171, 173
"frightful consequences," 172–77
literature condemning, 172
male, 171
methods to prevent, 173–74, 178
as nonprocreative, 17
pornography and, 72, 74, 170, 171, 177, 178, 180, 187, 201–2
semen and, 172, 175
Thomas Aquinas on, 21, 171
Virgil on, 173
why it hasn't replaced intercourse, 41
widespread practice of, 6
Materialism, 47
Maternity, 62
Mead, Margaret, 11

Mehinaku Indians, 130, 131
Memoirs of a Woman of Pleasure (Cleland), 178–79
Memory, sexual. *See* Sexual memory
Men
admonished against masturbation, 26–27
admonished against spilling their seed, 25–26
anal intercourse, 4, 99
brain structure differing from women's, 92
as enjoying sex more than women, 83, 123
fetishes in, 133
frequency of intercourse in, 122
gains from marriage, 61
marriage as ownership of women by, 62, 66
masturbation in, 123, 171
orgasmic pleasure necessary in, 40–41
pornography as intended for, 72, 73, 120
pornography associated with masturbation, 72, 74
ruled by lust not hormones, 38, 111
sex drive of, 123
sexual addiction in, 147
sexual arousability in, 121–23
sexual fantasies of, 120
sexual force used by, 68–69
as sexually different from women, 120–25
sexual memory in, 142
sexual regulation as more advantageous for, 68
strategies for sexual gain, 68–71
variety as sexual imperative for, 74
why men seek prostitutes, 80
women as property of, 63–64, 65
See also Androgens; Castration; Male orgasm; Paternity; Penis
Menstruation, 36
Miller v. California, 200
Mind-body dualism, 46–47
Missionary position
as most intimate position, 41
as only position acceptable to Thomas Aquinas, 21
used by bonobos, 25